Athens at the Margins

Athens at the Margins

Pottery and People in the Early Mediterranean World

Nathan T. Arrington

PRINCETON UNIVERSITY PRESS

Princeton & Oxford

Published by Princeton University Press
41 William Street, Princeton, New Jersey 08540
6 Oxford Street, Woodstock, Oxfordshire OX20 1

press.princeton.edu

ISBN 978-0-691-175201
ISBN (e-book) 978-0-691-222660

British Library Cataloging-in-Publication Data is available

Editorial: Rob Tempio and Matt Rohal
Production Editorial: Brigitte Pelner
Jacket/Cover Design: Pamela L. Schnitter
Production: Erin Suydam
Publicity: Alyssa Sanford (US) and Charlotte Coyne (UK)
Copyeditor: Dawn Hall

Jacket Image: Late Protoattic louterion from Palaia Kokkinia (northern Piraeus) ca. 630–620 BC. Photo: Jeff Vanderpool

This publication is made possible in part by the Barr Ferree Foundation Fund for Publications, Department of Art and Archaeology, Princeton University

This book has been composed in Minion Pro

Printed on acid-free paper ∞

Printed in the United States of America

10 9 8 7 6 5 4 3 2 1

FOR CELESTE

Contents

Preface and Acknowledgments

After graduating from the university, I had the good fortune to work at the Princeton University Art Museum, and I vividly remember one day in the storage rooms holding a Near Eastern cylinder seal, turning it over and over again in my hand, wondering what Greeks might have thought of it. I pursued some form of this question in two master's theses on glyptics over the next few years at Cambridge and Berkeley, until an advisor warned (perhaps mistakenly) that there were no jobs in gems. But the bigger issue of the connections between Greece and the Near East continued to tug at me. As I started to work on the problem anew, I became increasingly frustrated with the elite-dominated narratives. Not only were these one-sided from a social point of view, but they also neglected the types of finds that I encountered on excavations, when I sorted through mundane albeit very old trash in the expectation that it could tell us something significant about the ancient world and the people who lived there. There was a tension between the types of objects that archaeologists thought could inform the writing of history and the types of objects that were used to understand "Orientalizing." So I set out to write a book about Greek–Near East relations and the role of the nonelite in cultural change— only to discover that it was not possible, or at least, not in the way I had first imagined it. Framing the question in terms of "Greek–Near East" relations entailed accepting a host of assumptions about geography, chronology, and cultures that proved problematic. The regional variation in the period was so pronounced that writing about "Greece" in the seventh century seemed as misleading as writing about an "Orient." I started to realize how limited, constrained, even chained I was by periodization and the acquiescence it demanded. It took me longer than I care to admit to recognize that I would need to narrow my focus—to ceramics and to Attica—in order to attempt to tackle the larger issues, and that I needed historiography to get out of the morass. Historiography took me to Phaleron and to the nomenclature Phaleron Ware, which once was used to describe seventh-century pottery but has been expunged from the scholarly vocabulary. As I was working on this book, excavations began anew in Phaleron, yielding sensational finds, including mass burials with bodies that seem to have suffered some form of capital punishment. Phaleron was suddenly back in the picture, but archaeologists and historians didn't seem to know where to place it. I hope this book can move that cemetery, the people buried in it, and others like them from the margins closer to the center of our attention.

In developing this project, I have benefited enormously from the generosity of the following colleagues who contributed their time and expertise to read parts of this manuscript: Anna Alexandropoulou, Seth Estrin, Nota Kourou, Jessica Lamont, Suzanne Marchand, J. Michael Padgett, Catherine Pratt, Avary Taylor, Marek Węcowski, and the Press's two anonymous readers. They have made this a better manuscript but are not to blame for my interpretations or my mistakes. I also would like to acknowledge the valuable input that I received from the following scholars: Marian Feldman, Tonio Hölscher, Carl Knappett, Antonis Kotsonas, Sarah Morris, Angelos Chaniotis, Stella Chryssoulaki, the members of Comparative Antiquity (organized at Princeton by Andrew Feldherr and Martin Kern), and the participants in New Antiquity (convened at Stanford by Jennifer Trimble and at King's College by Michael Squire). I appreciated the opportunity to talk about my work and to learn from audiences at Brown University, the Johns Hopkins University, the Institute of Fine Arts, the Institute for the Study of the Ancient World, the University of Oxford / Ashmolean Museum, and the University of Toronto / Royal Ontario Museum. Members of two graduate seminars on "The Orientalizing Phenomenon" offered trenchant readings of secondary scholarship and fresh, insightful ideas.

I owe the greatest debt of gratitude to my wife, Celeste, and to our two daughters. Even in the darkest moments of spring 2020, we found joy together.

Princeton, New Jersey
August 2020

Athens at the Margins

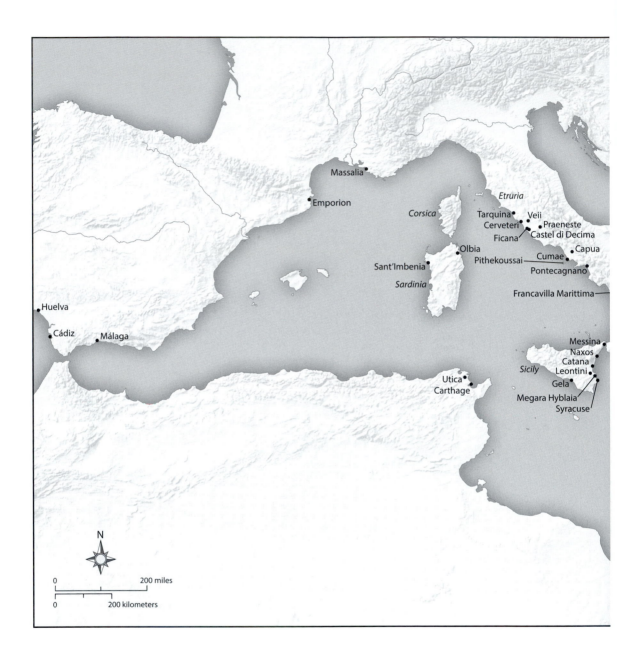

Massalia

Emporion

Etruria

Corsica

Tarquina Veii
Cerveteri   Praeneste
Ficana   Castel di Decima

Olbia   Capua
Sant'Imbenia   Cumae
Pithekoussai
Sardinia   Pontecagnano

Francavilla Marittima

Huelva

Cádiz   Málaga

Messina
Naxos
Catana
Leontini
Sicily
Gela
Utica   Megara Hyblaia
Carthage   Syracuse

N

0   200 miles

0   200 kilometers

Berezan

Istros

Sinope

Apollonia

Incoronata/
Metaponto

Taranto

Siris
Sibaris

Otranto

Bouthroton

Kerkyra

Croton

Torre Galli

Canale

Methoni

Thasos

Sigeion

Smyrna

Gordion

Phrygia

Thebes

Euboia

Lefkandi

Boiotia

Delphi

Oropos

Perachora

Attica

Corinth

Athens

Olympia

Ithaka

Megara

Argive Heraion

Sparta

Sardis

Ionia

Lydia

Ephesus

Samos

Miletus

Caria

Delos

Naxos

Thera

Kythnos

Rhodes

Lycia

Eleftherna

Knossos

Kommos

Crete

Tarsus

Mersin

Cilicia

Carchemish

Amuq Plain

Al Mina

Ras
el-Bassit

Patina/
Unqi

Tell Tayinat

Tell Sukas

Cyprus

Salamis

Kition

Amathous

Tyre

Tel Kabri

Tabbat
el-Hammam

Cyrene

Mesad Hashavyahu

Ashkelon

Tell Dafana

Naukratis

Memphis

Saqqara

Egypt

Boiotia

Euboia

+ Mt. Kithairon

Mt. Parnes +

Oinoe
Marathon

Acharnai
Kifissia
Menidi
Eleusis
Chalandri
Draphi
Pallini
Pikermi
Loutsa
Vouvra
Spata
Salamis
Athens
Brauron

H y m e t t o s

Trachones
Elliniko
Kiapha
Thiti
Merenda
Aliki Glyphada
Lathouriza
Kalyvia
Kouvara

Aigina

Olympos
Anavyssos
Thorikos
Palaia
Phokaia
Profitis Ilias
Sounion

Achilleos 4
Aigaleos
Academy
Dipylon
Mitrodorou and Geminou K.10
Themistokleous 4
Peiraios 1893 excavation
Sapfous 10-12
Peiraios street drain excavation
Agiou Dimitriou 20
Karameikos
Ermou 90
Karameikos Station
Kriezi 23-24
Acropolis
Tavros
Agora
Olympieion
Aristonikou 4
Palaia Kokkinia
Athens
Meïntani 12-14
Kynosarges
Peiraios 57
Kallithea

Analatos

Mounichia
Phaleron

H y m e t t o s

Piraeus

0   2 miles

0   2 kilometers

Trachones

0   8 miles

0   8 kilometers

CHAPTER 1

The Margins

This book recovers a style of painting that does not fit neatly into our histories of Greek art but that can offer new perspectives on Athens, its place in the Mediterranean, and the people who lived there. The style has been called crude, awkward, and, on occasion, just ugly (Figure 1.1).[1] Compared to a troubled adolescent, it has been cautiously eyed as an unruly teen yet to attain the stature and poise of mature Greek art.[2] Produced in the region of Athens (i.e., Attica) and generally known as Protoattic, this style, made primarily in the seventh century BC—following the rigorous Late Geometric style of the eighth century (Figure 1.2) and before the refined black-figure technique of the sixth century (Figure 1.3)—can suffer as much from neglect as abuse.[3] Too different in appearance from both, it often becomes relegated to a prelude or an afterword, or ignored altogether. Take, for example, the exhibit *The Countless Aspects of Beauty* at the National Archaeological Museum in Athens in 2018, which showcased art from the Neolithic period to late antiquity, but omitted Protoattic altogether.[4] Perhaps nothing so clearly indicates the challenge in making the style conform as the prevalent label still used in textbooks to categorize and describe much of the seventh-century style made in Attica, and elsewhere in Greece: "Orientalizing." It is just not Greek enough.

The beguiling aesthetics of a regional style whose middle phase is classified simply as the "Wild Style" compels us to look again. And some of the very same authors who critique the style as ungainly also recognize in it something unusual, remarkable, and noteworthy.[5] Exuberance erupts across the surface of the vases (Figure 1.4).[6] With several hands and workshops active, and a variety of "personal" styles visible, this art of the seventh century could be seen to mark a watershed in Greek history, as the first time that makers and buyers were confronted with pronounced stylistic choices (compare Figures 1.1, 1.4–1.5, Plates 1 and 2).[7] This is a period, and a phenomenon, that merits scrutiny. And we must look at this pottery again, and more

Figure 1.1. Protoattic amphora from Phaleron attributed to the Group of the Wild Style. Athens, National Museum 222. Photo John Blazejewski / Princeton University, after *Corpus Vasorum Antiquorum* Athens 2, plate 5.

closely, if we want to understand some of the major developments in Greek culture that took place at the same time as these vases were made and used. Since very few written sources survive, pottery is the best body of evidence for broader investigations of society at a time when the city-state or *polis* developed, new interpersonal relationships formed, and Greek communities engaged with Mediterranean connectivity. But it is a complicated source of evidence, which has been used for social analysis primarily through recourse to the problematic concept of Orientalizing and structuralist models emphasizing elite agency. In this book, I work to loosen Protoattic from an Orientalizing paradigm and to recover the importance of the margins and the marginalized. To do so, the book moves from historiography through a variety of contexts—the cemetery, the workshop, the symposium, and the sanctuary—bringing the historical, geographic, and social margins into sharper focus and looking at how art and people interacted in the construction of subjectivities and communities.

This book aims to intervene in the ways that we use material culture to approach two important areas of study: the Mediterranean and social history. Recent research tends to emphasize the level of connectivity in the early Mediterranean.[8] From a macroperspective, trade and mobility steadily increased in the early first millennium BC and have attracted considerable scrutiny. Extensive and intensive long-distance movement and exchange challenge the traditional boundaries that have been drawn delimiting separate cultures. At the same time, much of this research has underscored the diverse and fragmented nature of the communities on the Mediterranean coastline.[9] It is now time for close (micro-)regional analysis, such as this book offers for Attica, to complement our new models of the Mediterranean and to assess the engagement of specific places with wider Mediterranean currents.[10]

A smaller scale of analysis is also now necessary to put objects more firmly back into the discussion. Surprisingly, material culture has played a relatively minor role in the macroscale approaches that offer histories *of* rather than *in* the Mediterranean.[11] Above all, objects have served as indexes of mobility and intercultural encounters, that is, as evidence for connectivity. The ancient Mediterranean is filling with ships and people, but seems oddly empty of art. Pick up nearly any fat book on the Mediterranean and you are likely to find maps and diagrams rather than pictures of things.[12] This is symptomatic of a move away from interpretations or discussions of individual objects as the geographic scope of analysis has expanded.

Figure 1.2. Attic Late Geometric pyxis. Athens, Agora P 5062. Photo courtesy of the American School of Classical Studies at Athens: Agora Excavations.

More than simply putting objects back onto the page, I hope to shift the way in which we use objects for social analysis. From tying the appearance of the Wild Style to social disorder, to reading visual subject matter as a symptom of Orientalizing behavior, to parsing the hybridity of an object as evidence of intercultural interaction, objects have been seen to reflect social structure. They become a type of mirror for observing the results of analyses that usually have been performed on the basis of other evidence. The most recent book on Orientalizing veers toward this passive methodology, interpreting objects as "tools" in the hands of social groups.[13] Another way to use objects has been more quantitative. In Attica, this has been especially common in the treatment of mortuary remains and, more recently, of settlement patterns.[14] In all of these trends, the object tends to take second place, serving to confirm a social model or being reduced to a datum point. A richer history of the object is needed that pays attention to shape, iconography, and technique, to producer as well as user, to context, and to the object's role interacting between and among people, sites, and activities, with a degree of agency granted to the object itself. This book aims to change our views of what Greek art looked like and, just as importantly, what it did. It will argue for the mutually constitutive relationship of objects and people in a time of social and cultural instability.

Figure 1.3. Attic black-figure dinos attributed to the Gorgon Painter. Paris, Musée du Louvre E 874. Photo © RMN-Grand Palais / Art Resource, NY.

A broader conceptualization of the object affords a place in analysis for the margins and the marginalized in the Mediterranean. One of the legacies of the concept of an Orientalizing style and an Orientalizing period, explored more in chapter 2, has been an obsession with the elite, in Attica and elsewhere.[15] In nearly all studies of seventh-century Athens, particularly those focused on material culture, the elite are the drivers of historical development. As the procurers of imports, the deployers of hybrid art, or the buriers of the dead, they are imagined the agents of cultural change.[16] In fact, no style of Greek art has been so closely associated with the elite as seventh-century art, with the connotations of luxury and decadence that its Orientalizing label implies. This is one of the traps that Orientalizing sets. With the scope and detail achievable through regional analysis, it is possible to recover a range of objects and contexts that challenge conventional thinking. A regional level of analysis, focus on objects, expansion of the canon beyond "masterpieces," and emphasis on object-person interactions at multiple social levels offers a way to reassess the vase-painting of seventh-century Attica in its Mediterranean context.

Figure 1.4. Protoattic kotyle. Athens, Agora P 7023. Illustration by Piet de Jong. Photo courtesy of the American School of Classical Studies at Athens: Agora Excavations.

In this book, I deploy "margins" in three ways. I look at historiography to see how periodization occurred and what sites and objects it placed at the margins of analysis. Next, I consider how Attica initially lay outside of the main seventh-century Mediterranean currents but belonged to unexpected networks, and how it gradually entered a more global world. From the geographic margins we move to the social margins, where I develop a framework that accommodates the marginalized as social actors and agents of artistic and cultural change. While these are admittedly three types of margins—historiographic, geographic, and social—they overlap and intersect in interesting and compelling ways. The concept of the "margins" provides a means to look at historiography, geography, and society in tandem. We will see that the marginalization of subelite "Phaleron Ware" (Figures 1.1, 1.6) and of the context of the Phaleron harbor in the periodization process facilitated an association of Protoattic with the elite, and that grappling with the marginal location of Attica in the Mediterranean provides a more accurate understanding of the geographical dynamics that underlie "Orientalizing" and, by implication, their social import.[17] "Margins" offer a challenge to rethink models of a highly interconnected Mediterranean centered on the powers of the Levant and driven by an elite and to reassess the type of objects we use to address questions of style and society. My argument in this book is that a remarkable Protoarchaic style of vase-painting emerged and operated within networks and practices in which the geographic and social margins played an intrinsic but overlooked role, and that this

Figure 1.5. Protoattic amphora attributed to the New York Nessos Painter, allegedly from Smyrna. New York, Metropolitan Museum of Art 11.210.1. Rogers Fund, 1911.

style had an impact on the way people thought of themselves and connected with one another.

Of these three, the socio(economic) margins probably will be controversial. Interpretations of changes in the Early Iron Age have focused above all on the elite, from Ian Morris's influential model of elite and middling ideologies and his distinctions between *agathoi* and *kakoi*, to Alain Duplouy's more recent formulation of the need for an ongoing performance of elite lifestyle, both of which will be discussed in more detail below.[18] Whereas archaeology as a practice and a discipline often can reveal the mundane and the nonelite, scholars generally maintain that surviving seventh-century material culture, which is not abundant, must belong to the elite or be derivative of the elite. In this book, a wide panorama of the material evidence, including a complete survey of the mortuary remains, reveals an abundance and variety of material that drives new interpretations. Together with the literary record, it suggests a period of social instability and a lack of widespread consensus over the norms for status display; society was stratified but not ranked, and there was an absence of cultural hegemony. The elite were unable to use material culture to assert and normalize an elevated social position—this is what I mean by an absence of cultural hegemony.[19] No doubt some people from the ancient world, perhaps in particular seventh-century At-

Figure 1.6. Protoattic Phaleron-type oinochoe from Phaleron (Grave 19), attributed to the Workshop of the Würzburg Group. Athens, National Museum 14957. Photo N. T. Arrington. Copyright © Hellenic Ministry of Culture and Sports / Archaeological Receipts Fund.

tica, are absent from the material record. They were too poor to deposit a clay vessel, too persecuted to bury their dead in a visible way. But there are others who left simple cups as votives or buried their dead with a few decorated vases in the recently rediscovered, massive cemetery of Phaleron. Such remains do not match the picture of Attica made primarily on the basis of the few spectacular burials in one cemetery, the Kerameikos. Sections of this book draw attention to this type of marginalized evidence that, from a comparative standpoint, seems to belong to a subelite. Yet an argument built merely on trying to identify subelite or nonelite remains would be open to numerous objections. One could always counter, for any object or assemblage, that we are still dealing with an elite social group, but one that was just not engaged in the performance of status in the ways that we might expect. So instead this book attempts not only to find evidence and actors that might qualify as subelite, but also to create a space in analysis for a role for subelite material culture and people. This entails building an approach that gives attention to the process of cultural change from below, to the generative role for mobility and immigrants, to the agency of artists, and to the use of objects outside of social contexts defined solely in terms of status. Creating this space also entails calling attention to how elite-dominated models fail to account for all the evidence.

Our surviving material evidence, as always, is but a small fragment of what once existed, rather than the result of practices of exclusion or social rationing. I do not deny that status and status display and performance were at work in the seventh century, but through attention to historiography, contexts, and a wide variety of evidence, I seek to step outside of the elite/nonelite or inside/outside picture and to develop an interpretive framework stressing the relationship between material culture and the formation of subjectivities and communities, a framework that can accommodate the margins. Going forward, I generally avoid the tempting term "nonelite" because it presumes an impossibly clear definition in economic terms and only serves to reify a notion of the elite. Instead, the concept of the margins and the marginalized recovers a place that was real but that depended on one's perspective and experience.

The remainder of this introduction helps situate the rest of the book in a few ways. First, it contextualizes this book with reference to studies of Greece and the Near East and to broader approaches toward the Mediterranean and "globalization" in order to discuss at greater length what a focus on Attica offers. Then, it examines the notion of style, which has fallen out of favor in much art historical and archaeological analysis, to consider how it is a valid subject of study, while also recognizing its limits and constraints. Next, this chapter moves on to describe the political context of Attica in the Late Geometric period (late eighth century) and through the seventh century and the evidence for social mobility, and discusses how there were multiple vectors for participation in communities at a time when the *polis* was coming into being. Finally, it provides a brief overview of the main characteristics of Protoattic pottery, advocating for the use of Protoattic over Orientalizing/sub-Geometric. A synopsis of the book concludes this introductory chapter.

GREECE AND THE NEAR EAST: THE NEED FOR A (MICRO-) REGIONAL PERSPECTIVE

The modern flight of refugees to Europe by way of the Greek islands serves as a powerful reminder of the place of the Aegean as a causeway for travel across the Mediterranean. These recent events also unfortunately emphasize differences between west and east. As much as the Greek islands are stepping stones, they also can become physical barriers and symbols of cultural polarities. Scholarship has not always helped bridge the geographical and conceptual divide. As Edward Said has argued, eastern cultures have been used to create representations of the Other in western attempts to understand itself.[20] Too often, the Near East becomes synonymous with luxury, despotism, decadence, and the exotic. These perceptions have dominated interpretations of the seventh century BC, when Greek communities imported, adapted, and transformed eastern goods and cultural practices in a phenomenon that has been called "Orientalizing."[21]

The so-called Orientalizing style is most apparent in vases and best discerned through a contrast with the preceding Geometric style (contrast, e.g., Figures 1.1, 1.4–1.6 with Figure 1.2). The seventh-century vases are painterly rather than linear and have more abundant vegetal motifs and more varied figural iconography, including specific and identifiable myths. "Orientalizing" applies to more than vases.[22] Metal objects, ivory figurines, and gemstones, too, have received the label "Orientalizing." Indexes include techniques—such as the use of granulation, application of incision, and adoption of terra-cotta molds—as well as iconography—such as the depiction of sphinxes or lion hunts. But the products are not particularly close to any Near Eastern models, and scholars tend to emphasize that they are adaptations rather than copies. The development of the Greek alphabet offers a useful analogy for the transformative process. In the eighth century, Phoenician letters were adopted and supplemented to provide Greek speakers with a new written language, much as "Orientalizing" objects modified non-Greek elements to present a new visual language. The example of the alphabet suggests that the cultural interaction touched on more than art alone. Many scholars perceive a deep cultural indebtedness to and inclination toward the Near East in the Early Iron Age. Greek myths, legends, lifestyles, and more have been traced to the direction of the rising sun. Across the Mediterranean, from Cyprus to Spain, "Orientalizing" often is applied not just to an artistic style but to an entire period (ca. seventh century, but late eighth to late seventh and even early sixth depending on the region) and to a phenomenon of cultural change.[23]

If we want to study more closely this cross-cultural interaction between Greece and the Near East, however, we encounter a serious methodological problem. The very formulation of the research topic reinforces the geographical binary, essentializes cultures, and only cleaves Greece farther from the eastern Mediterranean. Despite being an intercultural research agenda, the framework from the outset posits a unified "Greece" and a monolithic "East."[24] Yet city and regional identities prevailed in Aegean lands at this time. There was no single Greek region or Greek *polis*.[25] Likewise, the Near East, or what people once called "the Orient," was composed of Anatolian empires, North Syrian city-states, Phoenician city-states, the Neo-Assyrian empire, and more. Egypt is generally included in the Near East, even though it more accurately lies to the south of Greece.

A solution that Sarah Morris proposed to the east–west divide was to highlight the continuity of communication between the areas. For her, Greek cities were closely connected to the Near East, part of their orbit and part of their world system. Orientalizing, she wrote, is "a dimension of Greek culture rather than a phase."[26] Only with the invasions of the Persians in the early fifth century did a cleavage between east and west develop, as Greek identity coalesced in the face of an existential threat.[27] This viewpoint productively draws the Greek city-states closer to their neighbors.

Perspectives that focus on the whole Mediterranean increasingly inform analysis of the connections between Greek and Near Eastern cultures and attempt to avoid geographical cleavages.[28] The modern phenomenon of globalization no doubt encourages us to see connectivity in the past, and some studies explicitly address ancient globalization.[29] The term is employed to a variety of ends. Some scholars discuss a growing homogeneity of the first millennium Mediterranean and pay attention to the causes and manifestations of connectivity, particularly trade in commodities and elite interaction.[30] Others, sometimes using the rubric of "glocalization," stress instead the variegated local responses to broader trends as (the sense of) space and time compressed.[31] This approach stems in part from postcolonial concerns with indigenous agency and can frame interaction in terms of cultural clashes, with sharp distinctions rather than uniformity resulting from so-called globalization.[32]

The coexistence of fragmentation and connectivity has been brought to the fore by Peregrine Horden and Nicholas Purcell's *The Corrupting Sea: A Study of Mediterranean History* (2000), which focuses on microecologies and argues that there was unity in disunity, with the sea the main connector. The authors have received criticism for a lack of attention to change, political structures, society, and culture.[33] But their formulation of a decentralized model of the Mediterranean is powerful, their stress on connectivity and mobility will endure, and their emphasis on economic rather than status motivations heralds an important shift.[34]

The variety and complexity of the seventh-century material record make a regional focus of analysis now necessary.[35] This is particularly apparent if we want to incorporate material culture more explicitly into the Mediterranean. For all the talk of the connectivity of the first millennium Mediterranean, for all the focus on a history *of* rather than *in* the Mediterranean, and for all the discussion of globalization, there is no single Early Iron Age Mediterranean style. The identification of seventh-century regional styles of vase-painting is one of the accomplishments of scholarship. It is possible to distinguish Corinthian from Cycladic, Attic from Cretan, Rhodian from Euboian, and so on. As the styles suggest, all regions of Greece, and indeed of the Mediterranean, had different forms of engagement with Near Eastern cultures and with each other, and different local needs and traditions. Crete produced a very early "Orientalizing" style on pottery and metalwork and seems to have been the destination and home of traveling and immigrant Phoenicians and North Syrians. Rhodes cornered the market in mass-produced Egyptianizing faience products. Distinctive

Spartan lead figurines reveal connections to Levantine models and may reflect the adoption of religious ideas. Corinth exported unguents in distinctive "Orientaliz-ing" vases, where the iconography may be related to the contents of the vessels. The number and types of Near Eastern imports varied across the Aegean as well. The sanctuary of Hera at Samos explodes with imports, while Argos has a mere trickle. Transmissions in material culture also need to be placed alongside other cultural developments with care. Myths or philosophy, for example, may have crossed the Mediterranean in different ways and at different times than artifacts and styles.[36] To treat the whole period and the whole cultural phenomenon with one term with the same implications everywhere risks distorting the evidence. Ann Gunter, for exam-ple, has offered an interpretation of Orientalizing as Assyrianizing, which is a model that works well for Cyprus, where communities had experience with the Neo-Assyrian empire but is less effective at explaining art in other Greek regions.[37] We need to examine how specific (micro-)regions engaged with the broader Mediterra-nean and to elucidate the role of objects and styles in the transmission, communica-tion, and production of meaning, leaving open the possibility for eastern connections all the while contextualizing so-called Orientalizing objects in a broader treatment of material culture and its interaction with human agents.

The recent scholarship on ancient globalization and connectivity stems in no small part from new archaeological evidence, to which this book also responds. For example, where the extent of Phoenician activity once was debated, excavations have provided incontrovertible evidence for early Levantine presence in the far west. In Spain, excavations at Huelva have placed their activity in the ninth and possibly even tenth century, and radiocarbon results at Carthage point to a late ninth century date there.[38] On the southern coast of Crete, a tripartite Phoenician shrine of the eighth century with ninth-century Phoenician ceramics provides dramatic evidence for Phoenician movement and local impact, and tombs from inland Eleftherna in-clude distinctive Phoenician funerary monuments.[39] Burials with Phoenician goods exist at Salamis on Cyprus in the eleventh century,[40] and Kition was under Assyrian control in the late eighth century.[41] Pottery from Cyprus appears at an early date on Crete, in the Dodecanese, and at Lefkandi.[42] At Lefkandi, excavations continue to brighten the Dark Ages. Work in the settlement at Lefkandi has closed a gap between the Bronze Age and the Iron Age by demonstrating architectural con-tinuity from LH IIIC through the Geometric period, with a surprising degree of community organization.[43] At Methoni, archaeologists have uncovered an early trading entrepôt connected to the Near East and producing luxury goods. A re-markable deposit contained 191 incised vases, considerably enlarging the corpus of early Greek writing.[44] Studies of chemical and lead isotopes from Geometric tri-pod cauldrons at Olympia show that the copper came from Faynan (Jordan).[45] Ship-wrecks discovered in the waters of the Mediterranean have clarified how goods were conveyed around the seas.[46] Studies of old excavation material have been no less dramatic than the excavations. At Gordion, it now seems clear that a destruction level once dated circa 700 actually belongs about a hundred years earlier, with considerable consequences for the possible role of the city in intercultural exchange and for Mediterranean and European chronology.[47] These are just a few highlights of the ways archaeology constantly modifies our view of antiquity. As more material comes to light, museums have disseminated data and viewpoints. Landmark exhibits and conferences on Crete and Cyprus and in Athens, Venice, and New York provided the opportunity to draw together old material and new finds from controlled excavations.[48] Thematic essays from a range of specialists gave useful syntheses and timely interpretations. Two other books have brought together scholars to focus explicitly on the seventh century.[49]

The signs of movement across the Mediterranean tempt one to emphasize connectivity and to speak of globalization—but is that an accurate picture at every local level? A regional approach to this connected world can integrate a place into the early Mediterranean world while remaining sensitive to moments when particular geographical areas, particular nodes and links, became salient. It also avoids creating monolithic entities of Greece and the Near East. Attica provides an appropriate case study for a regional approach for a number of reasons. There are sufficient archaeological data and contexts from the seventh century to examine, which can be placed in dialogue with the literary record. Pottery provides the most abundant and important body of evidence, for it displays the most significant changes in style from the Geometric period through the seventh century and offers the best contexts. Moreover, ceramics, produced in large quantities of nonelite raw materials, are some of the objects most receptive to cultural change. Potters and painters working in the medium continued historical traditions and processes, but the pliable clay also was amenable to imitating and emulating other styles and media. In recent years, much material has accumulated. In addition to the discoveries from sporadic rescue excavations, finds from the Early Iron Age have emerged from the preparation for new metro lines and for the construction of the Stavros Niarchos Foundation Cultural Center in Phaleron. Old finds neglected in storerooms have received welcome attention as well, from such sites as the cemetery of Merenda (ancient Myrrhinous), the sanctuary of Artemis Mounichia in the Piraeus, and the sanctuary of Zeus Parnessios on Mount Parnes.[50] Giulia Rocco's extensive catalog of Protoattic pottery has gathered much of the seventh-century ceramic material from disparate sites and museums and organized it according to painter hands. Annette Haug has made a comprehensive survey of changes in subject matter. And Annarita Doronzio and Eirini Dimitriadou have examined the settlement data from Athens.[51] Yet when compared to other periods of Greek and especially Attic art, the seventh century, and especially its material culture, has received surprisingly little attention. Attica's Geometric and sixth-century styles have an important place in the historiography of Greek art, but Protoattic has largely been reserved for the connoisseur's eye or for quantitative and spatial analysis.

STYLE: TOWARD AN APPROACH

Discussion of seventh-century Attica (and Greece more broadly) often has relied on an Orientalizing paradigm that emerges from a belief in the existence of an Orientalizing style.[52] That is, the term *Orientalizing* is simultaneously descriptive—capturing the visual appearance of some but not all art of the time—and interpretive—explaining the changes in style through the alleged cultural contact embedded in the descriptive term itself. The presence of an Orientalizing style is taken to be a sign of a person's, group's, or culture's orientation toward the exoticism, power, and luxury proffered by the Near East and symptomatic of a package of cultural change taking place top-down. Few other classifications of Greek art do such interpretive work, and this is what makes Orientalizing so interesting and at the same time so problematic. "Geometric" applied to the preceding eighth century (and earlier) describes only the rectilinear appearance of the pottery; "black-figure" of the sixth century refers to a technique.[53] The methodological move from a description of a style as Orientalizing to an interpretation of a period is more often assumed than demonstrated. While inviting a link between description and explanation/interpretation, the word "Orientalizing" also renders the nature of that link vague. As Nicholas Purcell eloquently put it, "the term appears to exist in a kind of middle voice. It hovers between identifying active and passive participants. Do you get Orientalized? Can you Orientalize someone else?"[54] For these reasons and others, Purcell advocated abandoning the term.[55]

Archaeologists and art historians have long used a concept of style not only to classify but also, at least since Johann Winckelmann, to seek insights on the character of a people and a time.[56] The Classical style of the Greeks, for example, was thought to emanate from their natural environment, religious beliefs, and political freedom. Stylistic differences between periods could be explained through differences in collective mentalities and dispositions. Another strand of art history, exemplified by Alois Riegl and Heinrich Wölfflin, focused more explicitly on the internal evolution of styles across broad tracts of time with a formalist perspective that did not take considerable account of historical contexts.[57] Most art historians now recognize the teleological fallacies and circular reasoning inherent in both these approaches and criticize the way in which they essentialize cultures and distort the historical record. They are aware that style can become a scholarly construct, and as a result, style per se is less a subject of study than it once was.[58] Archaeologists, too, once eager to use style to demarcate cultural borders or to measure communication, have turned away.[59] Some scholars even argue that style does not exist, or at least not in the way that we think it does.[60] Other critics have argued that style is purely relational; it does not inhere in an object but is applied to it by scholars. We identify a set of attributes shared among a group of objects but not held by all of them, and (arbitrarily) use that set to distinguish objects from one another.[61] So style can do little more than classify according to a scheme that scholarship applies (e.g., Romanesque vs. Gothic); style is in the eye of the modern beholder.

Such skepticism is salutary and draws attention to the distinction that often needs to be made between style as a method of classification and style as a tool for interpretation.[62] But dismissing style or the label Orientalizing cannot sweep away the formal changes that occurred in the Aegean in the seventh century that are most manifest in ceramics and that vary according to region. The juxtaposition of eighth- and seventh-century vases demonstrates that a change in form occurred. Yet clearly seventh-century pottery needs to be approached in a way that, to the degree possible, avoids some of the pitfalls of both style more broadly and Orientalizing more narrowly. In this book, I take a few different approaches to address this problem and to broaden the notion of style at work. Let us define style as an affective mode of making and doing that participates in a system of meaning.[63] The term "Orientalizing" needs to be approached critically, starting from a historiographic perspective that asks why we began to use the term at all (chapter 2) and what the implications have been. Then, expanding the canon and incorporating a wider range of objects will reveal over the course of the book a plurality of styles operative in the seventh century that occur in "high" as well as "low" art. In analyzing these Protoattic pieces, rather than relying exclusively on iconography, which is usually the barometer for "Orientalizing," I devote attention to other aspects of form, facture, and process. Finally, the definition of style used here includes ways of doing on the part of the user, looking at the performative aspects of style and examining the object in its use contexts as an extension of the user's body. The style of a vase could posit a new interaction with the artist, user, and/or viewer, creating new possibilities for the expression of subjectivity and for relations of the individual to the group. At the same time, these uses recursively could make demands and expectations on the production of style itself, affecting its appearance.

This type of analysis aims to probe the relationship between formal (including stylistic) changes and both the production and consumption of vases. Scholars instead tend to focus on one or the other. On the one hand (production), scholars might look at artists and workshop organization or try to deduce the origins of an import or the ultimate source of an iconographic motif.[64] They are interested in identifying individual hands or in using objects and styles to trace cultural movement, usually in terms of passive diffusion.[65] They maintain close attention to objects, emphasizing the role of individual painters, and they tend to assume that boundaries between cultural entities are distinct, identifiable, and stable. On the other hand (consumption), scholars might look at how objects were purchased and used. They are interested in how imports were redeployed in local contexts and how images or motifs were transformed through transcultural exchange.[66] Much has been gained by such approaches, particularly in underscoring the ideological possibilities of objects, but the sharp edge of style has been made blunt.[67] Analyses of consumption tend to leave the object and its problems, contradictions, and difficulties aside, as it becomes a mere tool for social actors to wield.[68] This book tries to bridge the gap between the two approaches and examines style from the perspective of both its production and consumption.[69] It assesses, on the one hand, artists, workshops, processes, and traditions, and, on the other, purchasing groups, display contexts, and users. The aim is to place production and consumption in dialogue and to situate them socially and ideologically. I want to talk about style without resorting either to "communication" (like many archaeologists) or "hands" (like many art historians) in order to show how it participated in processes of meaning-making and how it related to social structure.

One result of this multifaceted approach to style is, I hope, something of a rapprochement between archaeology and art history. Although the topic of style cuts across archaeology and art history, the disciplines interact little over the subject.[70] Interdisciplinarity may have become a mainstay of academic work, but these two fields still seem in many respects surprisingly far apart. Few archaeologists seem to know about the work of Gottfried Semper or Alois Riegl, while ancient art historians do not usually consider style outside of a canon of so-called masterpieces. The chasm between fields did not always exist. The materialist orientation of the earliest archaeologists brought them in close contact with the objects of art history, while a pioneer in art history, Riegl, was inspired in large part by engagement with excavated material. Protoattic pottery offers unique opportunities to draw on the data and theoretical literature from both fields. As a ceramic style, it falls into the more traditional domain of archaeologists, for whom pottery represents the vast majority of surviving evidence. As a ware replete with complex imagery and made by assertive artistic personalities, it demands the arsenal of art historians. From archaeology, I draw on a long tradition of engagement with contexts and assemblages as well as on scholarship about networks and agency. From art history, I draw on the Peircian language of semiotics, Wölfflin's contrast between linear and painterly, and subjectivity.

Other media will enter our discussion, but this is predominantly a book about pottery, which requires some justification. I already mentioned some of the reasons above. It is on pottery that the stylistic changes are most evident and where there is sufficient evidence in terms of the quantity of finds and in terms of the contexts for a relatively fine-grained analysis. They also allow consideration of a range of social levels of use. And in the seventh century it is only with vases that we can speak about artists with any type of precision, making investigation of mobility and subjectivity feasible. Last, but not least, ceramics allow a study of historiography and periodization (chapter 2). Given the complexity of the relations between Greece and the Near East, ceramics are the most abundant and promising source of evidence for an investigation of style, its uses, and its connections to a Mediterranean world. However, this book is not directed specifically at pottery specialists, although I hope that they find some value in it. Instead, I aim to use pottery to address broader art historical, archaeological, and social questions, all the while retaining a focus on objects. Such an approach would not be unusual for sixth- or fifth-century vase-painting, which have benefited from a variety of methodologies, but Protoarchaic pottery remains the domain of the specialist. Maybe the limited number of figural scenes, the relative lack of textual sources, or the seventh-century's awkward place between the anthropological methods applied to Geometric and Sir John Beazley's methods (see chapter 5) applied to later Archaic render Protoattic less accessible and less relevant. Or it just does not look Greek enough.

ATTICA IN THE SEVENTH CENTURY: HISTORICAL CONTEXT

This book is not a historical or political study of the rise of the state, which is a topic of interest to many classicists and archaeologists looking at this time period. But in order to provide some necessary background for the rest of this book, this section will sketch out the history of Attica from the eighth into the seventh century, investigating the cohesiveness of the region, the emergence of political institutions, and the rise of social conflict. It will measure continuity and change from the Late Geometric into the Early Archaic periods.

According to historical sources, the mythical king Theseus united Attica politically, abolishing local council chambers (*bouleteria*) and magistrates (*archai*) and centering political authority in Athens. There is no scholarly consensus about when this event known as a *synoikismos* occurred, with proposals ranging from the Bronze Age to the eighth century, and it is possible that it is a story fabricated much later.[71] Nevertheless, Attica shared a dialect and material culture, and can be considered a region as early as the Protogeometric period (tenth century). And by the end of the eighth century, as the landscape filled in with settlements, Athens emerged as a dominant center, with smaller settlements agglomerated around it.[72] Athens was located in a place ideal for access to, and control over, Attica itself, whereas most of the other major settlements in Attica (Acharnai, Eleusis, Brauron, Marathon, and Thorikos) were located so as to offer access to places outside of Attica.[73] The emergence of Athens as the central urban settlement illustrates the degree to which the region was becoming united and integrated politically, socially, and culturally in the eighth century. Another indication of centralization is the scale and nature of cult activity on the Athenian Acropolis.[74]

In Attica in the second half of the eighth century, an increase in the number of cemeteries, burials, sites, and wells strongly suggests a rise in population as well as prosperity.[75] Many of the settlements were located inland and, together with the production of small ceramic granaries and the frequent depiction of horses, might indicate a landed source of wealth for some families. But ships are represented on vases, too. Iconography seems to indicate some new degree of connectivity with the rest of the Mediterranean, with motifs on gold bands and ceramics demonstrating Near Eastern links.[76] Imports support this view.[77] The style of some objects and the skills necessary for working some materials, such as gold and ivory, suggest the presence of a few foreign craftspeople. Connections are also attested through the adoption of the alphabet and its use on vases. Attic fine ware itself, however, circulated in smaller numbers than in the previous period (i.e., Middle Geometric).

Some aspects of the seventh-century archaeological record represent a break with developments in the Late Geometric period.[78] In Attica, many sites with eighth-century material have no trace of seventh-century remains, and several wells in the agora were closed. The number of graves drops, the amount of metal and especially weapons in the graves plummets, and beginning in the late eighth century, the burial rate of children rises, who occasionally were interred in their own burial plots or cemetery areas. Unlike many regions, Attica, with a few exceptions, did not invest in monumental urban sanctuaries in the seventh century. Instead, hill sanctuaries and places between communities received most ritual activity.[79] Conversely, cemeteries were comparatively more prosperous than elsewhere in central Greece. Ancient tombs also became a focus of interest in Attica (and elsewhere), with some Bronze Age graves receiving dedications and sometimes cult activity.[80]

The changes in the archaeological record, especially the number of graves, have been explained through a drought and epidemic, a war, or shifts in social structure and ideology.[81] There were probably several factors. It is unlikely that we are simply witnessing the material effects of depopulation, for there are too many reorientations in material practice and settlement pattern for a demographic explanation alone to suffice, and it seems possible there was instead a rise in population. (For example, while the overall number of sites drops, new ones appear.[82]) The demographic explanation also cannot account for the continuing low number of graves in the sixth century, when we know that population size was considerable.

Despite the disruption in some parts of the archaeological record, Annarita Doronzio and Eirini Dimitriadou recently have emphasized settlement continuity and a pattern of increased urbanization into and across the seventh century.[83] The *polis* or city-state is widely conceived now as the result not of a single moment of invention but of a long process of development, which continued throughout the seventh century.[84] There was an urban nucleus focused on the Acropolis, with other more dispersed hamlets in the vicinity.[85] Cult activity not only emphasized a center (the Acropolis) but also knit together the region, with sanctuaries in the city linking to ritual spaces outside of it. The rise in sanctuaries in Athens and Attica, the continuing prominence of the Acropolis in Athens, and the gradual transformation of the region of the later Classical agora, all of which will be discussed in more detail in chapter 6, are also signs that the community, its spaces, and its institutions were developing.

Historical sources are not as clear as we would like but attest to the presence of political institutions. There was an *archon*, *polemarchos*, and *basileus*. Such political appointments at first were made on the basis of wealth and birth.[86] We hear that the archonship became annual around 683/2,[87] and former *archontes* comprised the powerful Council of the Areopagus.[88] Among the political positions were *thesmothetai*, responsible in some way for legal affairs.[89] The function of another group of magistrates called *naukraroi* is vague. Perhaps they were forty-eight people responsible for financing the fleet who, by extension, had some control over the city finances.[90]

The city-state was not just a set of legal institutions, though. Alain Duplouy, Josine Blok, and Paulin Ismard, among others, have put aside Aristotelian notions of citizenship to examine the criteria for belonging in a community and the means of making claims to that community.[91] Ismard has drawn attention to the various types of associations that enabled people to contribute to and engage with a community.[92] Although he focuses on later periods, many of these mechanisms already existed in the seventh century. In particular, *phratriai* ("brotherhoods") were organizations with religious functions that possibly related also to a local regional identity. *Orgeones* may already have been in existence, groups that worshipped minor deities and heroes.[93] *Phylai* (tribes) once may have been tied to a specific region but eventually extended across Attica, linking it together. Citizens were distributed into four tribes, each subdivided into three *trittyes*. Eventually, these groups helped organize participation in the military. *Phratriai* and *phylai* both appear in Drakon's law code of the late seventh century, traditionally dated 621/0, and other groups already may have been in place, too.[94] They offered personal and regional networks that knit people and places together. Pursuing this turn from looking at the *polis* exclusively as a legal institution and toward thinking about the number of smaller groups that composed it, subsequent chapters of this book will consider the conditions for subjectivity and the formation of communities that material culture mediated.

Mobility and connectivity at the regional level contrasts with Attic engagement with the rest of the Mediterranean. Unlike other regions, it took only a small part in colonizing ventures to the west or the Black Sea. But it was not isolated. Attic produce (probably oil and wine) was conveyed far and wide in so-called SOS amphoras, containers for oil and/or wine that are named after the distinctive marks on the neck and that appear at many Mediterranean sites (Figure 1.7, and Figures 3.1, 3.9, 6.17).[95] We also hear of a few military conflicts against Aigina,[96] Megara (over Salamis),[97] and Sigeion in the Troad.[98] The date of the first is unclear; the late eighth century is possible. The others occurred in the later seventh century. The conflict at Sigeion is important for marking a new stage of more intensive and extensive Attic connections with the Mediterranean. The site is located near the mouth of the Hellespont, and Athens fought with Mytilene to maintain its hold. (This is the battle in which Alcaeus famously lost his shield.) Adding to the Panhellenic nature of the event, Periander of Corinth served as arbiter, awarding Sigeion to Athens. The conflict would have required a navy or the use of private ships (cf. Figure 4.30) and demonstrates the city's ability to muster resources, define its territory, and engage with the broader Mediterranean world at least by the end of the seventh century.

Although a small group of people held political power in Athens, unlike several other prominent Greek cities, it did not experience tyranny in the seventh century.

A man named Cylon tried to establish single rule, and the story of his attempted coup provides tantalizing insights on Athenian political and social structures.[99] An Olympic victor and a son-in-law of the tyrant at Megara, he seized the Acropolis around 630 (as early as 640 and as late as 624/3[100]), but he was driven out by a combination of magistrates, leading families, and others. Thucydides qualifies that people resisted the attempted tyranny en masse (πανδημεί).[101] The murder of Cylon's followers in a sanctuary led to the expulsion of the Alcmaeonidae, one of the leading families. While it is hard to know how much to trust the historical sources, they suggest intense competition among some elite families, the presence of some civic institutions, and a variety of actors.

By the early sixth century at the latest, social conflict divided the region. The author of the *Athenian Constitution* describes a long conflict between the many (*plethos*) and the rich.[102] Historians and archaeologists have explained the conflict as a result of wealthy landowners seizing profits and enslaving the poor.[103] Increasing population would have put pressure on the sub-elite, while new market opportunities would have encouraged the rich to intensify land use and maximize their revenues. Solon (archon in 594/3) was appointed to resolve the disputes, and his poetry describes a situation in which people suffered from extensive debt bondage. Some people had been sold into servitude or fled the region so long ago (i.e., presumably within the seventh century) that they had lost their native dialect. Poor men worked the land with their wives and children in a burdensome sharecropping system. Other people apparently had enriched themselves but were disqualified from civic offices on the basis of their birth, and so were economically mobile but not politically recognized. Solon instituted a number of reforms, including ending debt bondage, changing the qualifications for political office from wealth and birth to wealth alone, and establishing four property classes.[104] He seems to have been responding to mobility that was both social—the newly poor and newly rich—and physical—those who had lost their land or left the region.

Figure 1.7. Attic SOS amphora, late 8th century, representative of a type that also was produced and circulated in the 7th century. Athens, Agora P 23883. Photo courtesy of the American School of Classical Studies at Athens: Agora Excavations.

IN DEFENSE OF PROTOATTIC

With its focus on pot-person interaction, this is a somewhat unconventional book about ceramics, and an introduction may help clarify material that will be encountered again in more detail. So at the risk of oversimplifying the Protoattic style, an overview of its principal characteristics might be helpful at this point.[105] This section also will explain at greater length why I use a generous definition of the style, employing "Protoattic" to collapse a distinction often drawn between Orientalizing and sub-Geometric.

The beginning of Protoattic is often placed circa 710.[106] In a seminal article on Protoattic pottery, John M. Cook explained that it differed from Geometric in terms of shape, ornament, composition, and technique.[107] Shapes became more slim, some vessel forms dropped out from the repertoire, and new ones appeared. Ornaments he designated Orientalizing became more common. The surface of the vase was no longer strictly organized into decorative areas, but displayed "coordinated action." Lines that had been straight started to curve more frequently. Incision and the use of reservation also were employed. Other scholars have emphasized some of these characteristics of the style over others. Robert M. Cook (discussing Orientalizing more broadly) stressed the loosening of composition and the experiments with reservation and incision, and underlined "a freer use of curve and a more organic sense of form."[108] For Theodora Rombos, Protoattic principally heralded the elongation of vase shapes and the introduction of Orientalizing ornaments.[109] For

Figure 1.8. Attic Late Geometric amphora by the Dipylon Master. Athens, National Museum 804. Photo courtesy of Hans R. Goette.

Figure 1.9. Protoattic amphora by the Polyphemus Painter, or the Polyphemus Amphora, from Eleusis. Eleusis, Archaeological Museum. Photo https://commons.wikimedia.org/w/index.php?curid=55630622.

Eva Brann, plant ornament and outline painting were essential components of the new style.[110]

A comparison may help discern some of the changes. The Late Geometric Dipylon Amphora and the Protoattic Polyphemus Amphora are both from mortuary contexts, the first marking a grave, the second holding the remains of a child (Figures 1.8 and 1.9).[111] About a hundred years separates them. When compared to the Geometric amphora, the Protoattic amphora appears slimmer, particularly the lower half of the body. In terms of subject matter, the depiction of the laying out of the dead on the Dipylon Amphora was popular in Late Geometric but fell out of favor in the Protoattic period.[112] Although funerary iconography appeared in Protoattic art, it was much less common. Another popular Geometric theme, battles, also decreased in popularity. Motifs typical of the period on the Polyphemus Amphora include the guilloche, rosettes, hooked rays, and palmettes. The lion hunt can be traced back ultimately to Near Eastern sources, and the heads of the Gorgons resemble metalwork with Levantine connections (Figure 1.10).[113] Coordinated action pervades the scenes, which reveal a new interest in myth and narrative: Odysseus blinds the cyclops (Polyphemus), a lion pounces on a boar, and Perseus beheads Medusa. Figures are rendered with curved and rounded lines, and the techniques of incision and reservation, as well as added white, are employed.

Seventh-century Attic cases with less figuration and less ornate ornament are sometimes relegated to a class of "sub-Geometric" pottery and excluded from analysis of seventh-century material culture.[114] In most cases, though, the usefulness of these categories collapses. A few examples will demonstrate the problem, from a few different angles. The oinochoe in figure 1.6, from the Phaleron cemetery, is decorated mostly with lines and bands and usually would be classified as sub-Geometric. But on the neck, a griffin is in the new style, and the vase has a Protoattic hand assigned: the Workshop of the Würzburg Group. The shape, moreover, finds its closest parallels in Cypro-Phoenician pottery and metalwork (Figure 4.37). So classing it as sub-Geometric and excluding it from a style defined only in Orientalizing terms seems short-sighted. Another example is a vase with a dipinto speaking the name of the owner (Figure 6.8, Plate 14), which we will discuss at length in chapter 6. It transforms Geometric patterns into fish among waves. The manipulation of figure and ornament and the combination of different techniques (outline and incision) are sophisticated, but the vase's closest parallels in terms of shape and most of the iconography are with Attic Geometric rather than any Near Eastern culture. A strict definition of Protoattic only as Orientalizing would have to leave it out, but it is a complex piece that merits attention. The kotyle in figure 1.4 illustrates another dimension to the problem. It seems very "Orientalizing," with the rich, curvilinear vegetal ornament often associated with the term. But most of the ornament cannot be directly traced to Levantine sources, while the shape shows very close affinities instead to Corinth, which is probably the source of most of the ornament, too. So at first it seems Orientalizing rather than sub-Geometric,

Figure 1.10. Gilt silver cup from the Bernardini Tomb, Praeneste, early 7th century. Rome, Museo Nazionale Etrusco di Villa Giulia 61566. Photo © MIBACT. Museo Nazionale Etrusco di Villa Giulia—Roma.

but there is not much Levantine about it. Assemblages further demonstrate the difficulties in making sharp distinctions in stylistic categories. The burial of a child in the Kerameikos contained predominantly what one might designate sub-Geometric vessels (Figure 4.17).[115] The amphora that held the remains of the child, however, is attributed to the Group of the Wild Style, which produced much Orientalizing work. In addition, in a pyre associated with the burial lay an ivory figurine of Near Eastern manufacture, which is one of the few imports in Athens in the seventh century. The assemblage, then, seems Orientalizing, but most of the vases are sub-Geometric.[116] These examples should demonstrate the need for a more capacious approach to seventh-century vase-painting than a narrow concept of Orientalizing alone or, worse, Orientalizing versus sub-Geometric.

As these examples also show, despite shifts in subject matter from the eighth into the seventh centuries, often the iconography is not as overtly "Oriental" as the period term leads one to expect. I want to suggest that the most important change from Geometric into Protoattic is not iconography but a change in approach to the surface of the vase—in the relationship of the maker (and, consequently, also the user) to the object. We see this shift above all in the predominance of a freehand approach, which we will explore, along with the implications for society and subjectivity, in chapter 5.

In terms of shapes, various forms were used, some old, some new. Large and small vases were decorated. Some types are more common, like amphoras and standed bowls, others more rare, like feeders or model granaries. The pots had a variety of uses. In cemeteries, they marked graves, contained the remains of the dead, accompanied the dead, or were deposited near graves. They were associated with burials of the rich and poor, adults and children (see chapter 4). Vases, figurines, and plaques in the Protoattic style also were dedicated at sanctuaries, as we will see in chapter 6. There is less settlement than grave or sanctuary evidence from seventh-century Attica, but the agora well deposits and the morphology of some of the shapes seem to indicate that Protoattic had a domestic function, too. Chapter 6 will explore how such vases were used in the symposium.

John M. Cook in 1934–35 organized Protoattic into a classical tripartite scheme of early, middle, and late. In general terms, the earliest vases may be characterized by the persistence of Geometric forms and filling motifs (Figures 1.1, 1.6). A "Wild Style" with larger figures, expansive brushstrokes, and a fondness for ovoid kraters characterizes much but certainly not all of the work beginning around 680 (Figures 1.5, 1.9, and Figure 2.18 for an ovoid krater). On the latest pieces (closer to 620–610), the use of incision and added purple increases (Figure 1.11).[117] However, Giulia Rocco's study has demonstrated that the evolution is not predictable and the chronology not clear-cut, which is one reason why I avoid giving narrow date ranges in this book. There are unfortunately too few fixed points to establish a reliable scheme for close stylistic dating, with the possible exception of the start of Protoattic.[118] The end of Protoattic is somewhat arbitrary, since the subsequent style of black-figure is really a technique. Some scholars would place the vase in figure 1.11 into earliest black-figure rather than Late Protoattic.[119] Assemblages from a cemetery in the Piraeus also show that outline drawing was popular at the same time as increasing incision, further blurring the end of Protoattic (Figures 4.30, 5.5, Plate 9).[120]

One of the challenges to any close dating is that Protoattic pottery was produced in much smaller numbers than the preceding and subsequent styles (Late Geometric or Archaic). At the same time, it evinces a greater stylistic diversity than either. Artist hands are idiosyncratic, and in some cases identifiable through connoisseurship (Rocco's study of artists divides the corpus into fifty-four hands or groups and their workshops), but do not form stylistic lineages that can be traced over time. Despite their artistic personalities, however, the painters did not sign their works.[121] We will look at this phenomenon in more detail in chapter 5.

Some of the artists may have traveled within Attica and even abroad. Most tantalizing is a vase at Metaponto (Italy) decorated in the Protoattic style but made in local clay (Figures 3.11, 3.12). Painters may have immigrated to Attica as well. There are close affinities between Protoattic and Cycladic, and in the absence of substantial Cycladic imports, the connections are probably best understood through the movement of people rather than goods.[122] We will also see how strong the connections were between Protoattic and Corinthian pottery, with some affinities again best explained through the circulation of people. Very few of the Attic vases themselves were exported, however, and there was certainly no export "market" as such. Outside Attica, Protoattic has only been found at Aigina, Argos, Boiotia (especially Oropos and Thebes), Megara, Perachora, Thasos, Thera, Kythnos, Delos, Rhodes, Samos, Smyrna, Etruria, and Cádiz. While this list might seem long, the finds usually consist of only a few items, often just one, and there is a notable increase in the later seventh century, and a veritable explosion when it comes to sixth-century black-figure.[123] Finds are more pervasively distributed throughout Attica and concentrate in Athens and its vicinity, where four contexts stand out: Aigina, Phaleron, the area of the later (Classical) agora, and the Kerameikos. Cemetery contexts predominate, which are the most likely to preserve ceramics in the archaeological record and accord-

Figure 1.11. Late Protoattic or early black-figure amphora by the Piraeus Painter from a grave in Piraeus. Athens, National Museum 353. Photo Giannis Patrikianos. Copyright © Hellenic Ministry of Culture and Sports / Archaeological Receipts Fund.

ingly have received the most scrutiny. This book aims to provide a more comprehensive analysis of the ware by also looking at the sanctuary contexts and the domestic uses of the vases.

SYNOPSIS

Before moving forward, we need to look back. Chapter 2 provides a historiography of Protoattic in order to expose the interpretive frameworks that have been used and that continue to inform our conceptions of the style and the period. The process of periodization has had consequences for how we think about seventh-century

Attica and its material culture and for the types of objects that inform our discussions. We will examine how a style that once was associated with the Phaleron cemetery in Attica and included low-quality objects became associated with a vague, exotic east. Chapter 3 looks closely at this alleged eastern connection and uses style to examine the relationship of seventh-century Attica to the rest of the Mediterranean. Elaborating a concept of "horizons" and using network analysis, it reveals a surprising set of links and nodes in which the western Mediterranean was just as formative as the eastern. Chapter 4 examines the implications of this more capacious view of Protoattic ceramics and starts to more explicitly consider the relationship between style and social status. A complete survey of the burial evidence corrects prevalent views of the invisibility of seventh-century burials and the exclusive agency of the elite. Ceramics that were both decorated and undecorated enabled the engagement of mourners with one another and the mortuary ritual. Innovation in style occurred in nonelite contexts and was appropriated and elaborated in elite contexts. This is a different way of thinking about cultural change and about the role of objects in building communities. Chapter 5 offers another perspective on the relationship between style and society, investigating how the Protoattic style and the artist were mutually constitutive. The contexts of production and consumption and the new techniques and approaches to the vase that the Protoattic style entailed created possibilities for the realization and expression of subjectivity, conceived as an experience and articulation of selfhood and agency, which was not restricted to political identity or citizenship. Chapter 6 explores the relationship between style and subjectivity on the part of the user of the vase in two contexts that have received considerable scrutiny—symposia and sanctuaries. Returning to some of the arguments in chapters 4 and 5, it elucidates the social range of actors, the opportunities for status distinction, and the (few) instances when eastern Mediterranean cultures became salient in cultural practice. At a period of continuing development of the city-state, pottery allowed people to connect to multiple types of communities and to explore subjectivity. The final chapter (chapter 7) offers a summary, considers implications of the book's argument for other regions of Greece in the seventh century and for Attica in the sixth century, and concludes by returning to the Phaleron cemetery and to the controversy over how it might be preserved.

CHAPTER 2

From Phaleron Ware to Exotica

A Historiography of Protoattic

WHY LOOK BACK?

To disrupt the traditional narratives about seventh-century Athens and its material culture, I start with historiography. A critical reassessment of the formation of Protoattic and Orientalizing as concepts and as corpora can decouple the material culture from its assumed relationship with the Near East and the elite and recover objects that illuminate the margins. It will bring back into discussion the subelite Phaleron cemetery, which once was so closely associated with Protoattic that the pottery was called Phaleron Ware. Renewed excavations at Phaleron (2013–18), including the discovery of stunning mass burials, have brought this cemetery back into the public eye. This chapter tracks the twists and turns by which pottery that once was called Phaleron Ware became associated with an exotic-oriented elite and argues that we need to recover contexts, perspectives, and narratives that have been sidelined in scholarship, sometimes unknowingly.

The pottery studied in this book is typically organized under two rubrics: Protoattic and Orientalizing. Both terms can describe a style as well as a period, with "Protoattic" restricted to Attica, and "Orientalizing" applied more broadly to art from across the Mediterranean. Both terms are inventions of the nineteenth century, and the result of excavation, looting, curation, publication, and debate. This chapter tells the story of how these terms came into existence and examines the implications of the construction of a period. The process was cumulative and aggregative as scholars responded to one another, to new finds, and to their intellectual and sociopolitical contexts. Our current approaches have a trajectory, and while origins might not offer clear explanations, they can illuminate the roads that have led to our current positions and open up new paths.

The terms Protoattic and (Greek) Orientalizing are intertwined in many ways, but my focus here is above all on Protoattic. I will trace the discovery, publication, and reception of the pottery to elucidate the interpretive frameworks into which the vases were placed and to examine how approaches have developed and changed over time. A historiography of Protoattic touches more broadly on the problem of Orientalizing and additionally on Geometric art and even on Greek art and archaeology as a whole. Scholarly attempts to classify Protoattic were enmeshed in much bigger debates about Greek exceptionalism, as we will see. But I should be clear that I am not attempting to offer here a comprehensive history of Orientalizing or Orientalism, but rather I am looking at the intersecting historiographies of Protoattic and Orientalizing. Those studies already exist, although they are inevitably selective. A survey would include Martin Bernal, whose critique of classical scholarship and argument for pervasive Near Eastern, especially Egyptian, influence on Greece shook the field but largely neglected both material culture and the first millennium BC.[1] Edward Said, in his pathbreaking study of Orientalism, left aside Germany, the focus of Suzanne Marchand's penetrating work.[2] Frederick Bohrer offered a useful examination of the European reception of ancient Near Eastern civilizations, their monuments, and their aesthetics.[3] Smaller in scope but no less useful, Corinna Riva and Nicholas Vella used the historiography of Cypro-Phoenician bowls as a window onto Orientalizing, and Ann Gunter offered a concise historiography of Orientalizing and placed it in the context of European reactions to "Oriental" imports.[4] In different ways, these scholars and others all demonstrate the vexed relationship that intellectuals have charted between studies of Greek and eastern Mediterranean cultures within the political currents that often surround interpretations.[5]

The present study, too, is selective. It draws attention to one specific category of art, in the hopes that, through close analysis, it can offer a different vantage point.[6] With this ware, we can watch a corpus form and examine the changing scholarly discourse. So rather than framing this chapter as a history of Orientalizing per se, I examine the construction and deployment of that concept in the course of a historiography of regional ceramic production. Many of the conclusions have relevance beyond Protoattic itself.

The name "Protoattic" and the way it has been deployed are results of processes of classification and periodization, which are far from rote exercises. They profoundly shape the way that we organize material and think about a time period, its people, and its products. Recent studies of Greek periodization have made these points, but they have focused on the Early Iron Age and on its varied terminology, especially the deployment of the concept of a Dark Age.[7] They have left aside the equally pressing problem of the periodization of Orientalizing or regional styles. Periodization can serve evolutionary and teleological pursuits by constructing narratives of one period leading to another in a smooth progression. Along these lines, some scholars consider Protoattic art under Near Eastern influence a critical step leading to the Classical floruit of the fifth and fourth centuries. Conversely, periodization can mean distinguishing material as different or "Other" from works produced in the periods that precede and follow it. That is to say, some scholars use periodization to relegate objects that do not seem sufficiently Greek to an "Orientalizing" period. Whichever path one chooses (and there are others, as we will see), there are consequences to periodization.

Classification and periodization are themselves products of intellectual and social trends. In the earliest treatments of Greek material culture, there was little to no concern for periodization. Instead, synchronic approaches informed both the organization and study of material, as the heterogeneous and eclectic plaster cast collections combining Greek and Roman works from multiple periods make all too evident. A drive toward greater organization of the material and toward classification emerged in the nineteenth century for several reasons. Excavations, often on vast scales, produced enormous amounts of material that needed to be organized in some way. Meanwhile, new and growing museums required organizational schemes for the didactic grouping of material.[8] As objects accumulated and the appetite for Greek art became insatiable, eventually reaching university curricula, comprehensive handbooks were needed for narratives that explained the interrelation of the parts. They required clear distinctions and sharp geographic and chronological divisions. Informing the periodization process, of course, were intellectual trends, such as Darwinism or, more specific to art history, formalism, with its resistance to external developments. The historical and political contexts also cannot be neglected, such as the impact of nationalism or Protestantism.

The historiography of Protoattic, and its intersections with Orientalizing, has many threads, and I cannot hope to be comprehensive but to isolate the major trends all the while recovering a diversity of viewpoints. This chapter aims to demonstrate that while much early research was receptive to non-Hellenic dimensions of Greek art, efforts to fit Protoattic into art historical narratives, together with a strong predilection for the Classical style, pushed non-Hellenic cultures aside. Just as importantly, the classification process created a corpus that narrowed down an initially large and diverse amount of material to alleged masterpieces from select contexts and named artists. More recent approaches that focus on consumption in many cases continue to use the corpus and the intellectual framework built over the course of centuries of study, accepting and emphasizing the alleged Orientalizing aspects of Protoattic.[9] The legacy of the periodization process continues to inform interpretations of Protoattic.

THE FIRST FINDS AND THE BEGINNING OF ORIENTALIZING

Scholarship on Greek art in general and pottery in particular suffered in the eighteenth and nineteenth centuries from lack of access to Greece. Under Ottoman rule until the 1820s, for many years Greece was off travelers' itineraries. Eighteenth-century

Figure 2.1. Protoattic oinochoe attributed to the Group of the Buffalo Krateriskos, from a grave near the Dipylon Gate. Toulouse, Musée Saint-Raymond 26086. Photo Materia Viva, courtesy of the Musée Saint-Raymond Toulouse.

publications such as James Stuart and Nicholas Revett's *The Antiquities of Athens* (1762–1816) or David le Roy's *Les ruines des plus beaux monuments de la Grèce* (1758) were exceptional and focused on monumental remains. Classical archaeologists, perhaps most notably Johann Winckelmann, developed their viewpoints at a physical distance, relying on literary sources and focusing on gems and sculpture, especially Roman copies. As Greece opened up, many scholars preferred still not to visit but to fashion their conceptions from afar. There were, consequently, some serious misunderstandings about Greek art, especially pottery.[10] At first, Greek vases found in Italy were even considered Etruscan. When Greek authorship was acknowledged, many people still thought the pots had been made on Italian soil by immigrant artists. Eventually, their identification as imports was secured. But more difficult to assess, indeed to recognize at all, were Greek regional types rarely found in Italy, such as Protoattic. A history of Greek art based on literary sources and Italian discoveries could provide little place for objects that were not exported in considerable quantity. Consequently, Protoattic pottery arrived late into the repertoire of Greek art.

It was Otto Magnus von Stackelberg who, in 1837, unknowingly documented the first Protoattic find: an oinochoe discovered by the Dipylon Gate on the road to Eleusis, later in the possession of Louis François Sébastien Fauvel, and now in Toulouse (Figure 2.1).[11] Stackelberg illustrated it along with two Geometric vases and described all of them as examples of the oldest type of Greek pottery. Otto Jahn's landmark conspectus of pottery in 1854 still makes no mention of an independent seventh-century Athenian ware. The Burgon Krater, a Protoattic vase brought from Athens to London by Thomas Burgon in 1813, was classed in 1858 by Samuel Birch along with Corinthian pottery into a vague Early Archaic phase (Figure 2.2).[12]

Figure 2.2. Protoattic krater by the Painter of the Burgon Krater. London, British Museum 1842.7-28.827. Photo © The Trustees of the British Museum.

Only as finds began to emerge from the Phaleron cemetery south of Athens, albeit with few if any official reports, did the picture sharpen. In 1869, Albert Dumont published the oinochoe in figure 2.3 (Plate 3) and coined the term Phaleron Ware to describe vases of this style.[13] He was not certain about the date, but he suggested that these pots were not as ancient as they seemed and may have been imitations of older vessels. We now know that they include the earliest examples of Protoattic. Despite the mistake, Dumont's article represents the first publication of an Attic style distinct from preceding Geometric pottery and from contemporary ware from other cities (such as Corinth). The term "Phaleron Ware" would gain currency, particularly for the early and middle phases of Protoattic, and for vases miniature in size (especially oinochoai) or with sub-Geometric decoration. Many (but not all) were from Phaleron itself, which served as the main harbor for Athens until Themistokles shifted it to Piraeus, and it had thousands of burials.[14] We will look at the cemetery more closely in chapters 4 and 7. The site was extensively looted in the nineteenth and twentieth century and was the source of many unprovenanced Protoattic vases in museums. Konstantinos Kourouniotis in 1911 remarked on the extensive damage the site already had suffered.[15]

Adolf Furtwängler was aware of these vases and underlined that they were very different from Geometric pottery, which itself was still not well understood.[16] In 1880, he expanded the group of "Phaleron-Vasen," adding an amphora found on the slopes of Mount Hymettos and acquired by the museum in Berlin (Figure 2.4, Plate 4), which contained a small oinochoe and the bones of a child.[17] Shortly thereafter, he published a (much later) louterion with Perseus from Aigina (Figure 2.5), but he was still at a loss for close parallels. He compared it to "the later Geometric so-called

Figure 2.3. Protoattic Phaleron-type oinochoe from Phaleron, attributed to the Group of Kerameikos 18/XIX. Athens, National Museum 304. Photo Eleutherios Galanopoulos. Copyright © Hellenic Ministry of Culture and Sports / Archaeological Receipts Fund.

Phaleron vases," to Corinthian, Chalkidian, and Rhodian pottery, to the Burgon vase, and to a fragment from Menidi.[18] He concluded: "Our vase, however, appears to be without considerable successors; I at least do not know a single vessel really corresponding to ours."[19] It is now attributed to the Nessos Painter, and scholars would place it in the period of the latest Protoattic or earliest black-figure.

The quantity of comparable material remained small for several years. Otto Benndorf's 1883 publication of Greek and Italian vases included only two images of seventh-century Attic vases: one from Aigina and one from Phaleron.[20] Maxime Collignon's manual of Greek archaeology published in the same year and translated into English in 1886 represents the state of the field at the time and demonstrates the absence of seventh-century Attic vases from the repertoire of Greek art.[21]

This all changed in 1887, when Böhlau published the first and foundational study of late eighth- and seventh-century Athenian pottery (using the term "frühattisch") and embraced Orientalizing at Athens as a period. His goal, he explained, was to fill the gap between the Dipylon vases (i.e., Athenian Geometric pottery) and the François Vase (from the sixth century) and to show how "a completely idiosyncratic Orientalizing style" developed out of Attic Geometric, with influence from the Near East as well as from Mycenaean art.[22] He was mostly concerned with the earliest phase of what we now call Protoattic and devoted much attention to vases from

Figure 2.4. Protoattic amphora from a grave on Mount Hymettos attributed to the Group of the Wild Style. Berlin, Staatliche Museen, Antikensammlung F 56. Photo bpk Bildagentur / Antikensammlung, Staatliche Museen, Berlin / Art Resource, NY.

Figure 2.5. Late Protoattic louterion attributed to the Nessos Painter. Berlin, Staatliche Museen, Antikensammlung F 1682. Photo bpk Bildagentur / Antikensammlung, Staatliche Museen, Berlin / Art Resource, NY.

Phaleron or that he considered of the Phaleron style. He illustrated three large vessels—the Hymettos Amphora (Figure 2.4), a hydria later made the name-vase of the Analatos Painter (Figure 2.6),[23] and a louterion from Thebes—and a large selection of smaller vases (e.g., Figure 2.7).[24]

At this point, we need to step back to consider what Böhlau meant by "Orientalizing," where the term came from, and how it was used in the nineteenth century, for the term was coming into vogue at the same time as Protoattic vases were being discovered. Starting in the eighteenth century if not earlier, Hellenists were in general open to the influence of Near Eastern cultures in the west, much more so than today, when disciplinary and institutional boundaries are sharp and hyperspecialization rules. Pliny, Herodotus, and the Bible informed them that cultures flourished in Egypt and the Near East long before Greece, and they expected culture to diffuse.[25] Steeped in literature, they knew that Greek art receives little attention in Homer, while Phoenician crafts are prized; the Greek god Hephaistos even is said to have made a Sidonian krater.[26] The Roman antiquarians they admired also acknowledged the role of non-Hellenic culture in Greek art. Pliny, for example, attributes the invention of outline drawing to an Egyptian (or a Corinthian).[27] So, few hesitated to seek origins outside of Greece for culture, myth, and

Figure 2.6. Protoattic hydria from Analatos, by the Analatos Painter. Athens, National Museum 313. Photo Giannis Patrikianos. Copyright © Hellenic Ministry of Culture and Sports / Archaeological Receipts Fund.

art. Widespread biblical literacy meant that most antiquarians and scholars had some level of familiarity with Near Eastern cultures, and research in linguistics had revealed indisputable connections. For all these reasons, and more, there was considerable scholarly interest in an Orient that included Egypt and the Levant and extended to India and China. By the nineteenth century, there was increasing relegation of the study of the Orient to Orientalists, particularly in the area of philology, but scholars of Greek art were still relatively open to outside influence on Greece.

Figure 2.7. Protoattic mug from Phaleron attributed to the Painter of the Boston Amphora. London, British Museum 1865.7-20.7. Photo John Blazejewski / Princeton University, after Böhlau 1887, 50, figs. 9–10.

Excavations in the Near East, especially Paul-Émile Botta's and Austen Henry Layard's work in Assyria, fueled interest (Figure 2.8).[28] Finds were exhibited in the Louvre and the British Museum, and Layard's book, *Nineveh and Its Remains* (1849), may be considered the first archaeological blockbuster. The Great Exhibition of 1851 in London and the Expositions Universelles in Paris in 1867 and 1889 put non-Hellenic cultures on display as buildings and architectural spaces were reimagined

Figure 2.8. Austen Henry Layard's expedition to Nineveh. Photo John Blazejewski / Princeton University, after *The Monuments of Nineveh*, vol. 2, plate 51.

Figure 2.9. *La Mort de Sardanapale* by Eugène Delacroix, exhibited at the Salon of 1827–28. Musée du Louvre RF 2346. Photo © RMN-Grand Palais / Art Resource, NY.

and recreated. In biblically literate European societies, interest in these geographically remote but culturally relevant lands was fueled by these excavations, exhibitions, books (popular and scholarly), and art, with scholar and layperson affected.

But the western gaze was not detached, disengaged, and innocent.[29] As Napoleon's conquest of Egypt in 1798 and the subsequent publication of the *Description de l'Égypte* (1809–28) opened Near Eastern cultures to probing eyes and nationalist pursuits, it also ushered in a voyeurism and "Othering." As an example, consider the historical exoticism on view in Eugène Delacroix's *La Mort de Sardanapale*, exhibited at the Salon of 1827–28 (Figure 2.9), showing a decadent king reclining in opulent luxury as his city crumbles around him.[30] Here the Orient provides, among other things, a stage for ocular pleasure and a political commentary on monarchy, serving the purposes of its western audience and reinforcing stereotypes, creating a fantasy despite its historical and realistic veneer. Layard's book also contributed to cultural tropes. The picture of the author scrambling down a rock face to examine reliefs exudes a spirit of adventure and expounds the superiority of western knowledge. In such images, which convey in unusually clear terms the nationalist and often racist undercurrents of the time, the Orient could serve as an Other against which the Occident constructed a sense of itself and as a framework for colonialist notions of superiority. Scholars of Greek art lived and worked in this environment.

Many of them repeated and contributed to such Orientalist worldviews, consciously or not. Memories of Ottoman forces occupying Greece exacerbated the tendencies.

There were different responses to Near Eastern cultures, from admiration to disgust to neglect, and views varied according to nationality, class, education, and outlook.[31] Some scholars thought that all culture and civilization had diffused, especially in terms of religious beliefs, practices, and symbols.[32] On the other side were figures such as Carl Otfried Müller and Heinrich Brunn, who insisted on Hellenic exceptionalism and essentialism and associated art with cultural mentalities that they considered peerless.[33] Anti-Semitic attitudes also had a role to play in the development of scholarly approaches toward Near Eastern cultures, but in some cases these attitudes drove people to privilege one Near Eastern region over another, rather than to reject non-Hellenes entirely.

Despite rampant biases, the importance of the excavations in the Near East for the history of Greek art was quickly recognized in many circles. In his autobiography, Layard records that on the occasion of his 1848 presentation to the Académie des Inscriptions et Belles Lettres, "M. Lenormand [sic] remarked to the Académie that hereafter no one could venture to enter upon the subject of Greek Art or Mythology without being thoroughly acquainted with the details of Nimrud."[34] Jean de Witte in 1865 confirms that Layard did not overvalue the esteem of his contributions:

> Later, [after the discoveries at Vulci], the discoveries of the antiquities of Nineveh, the excavations done on the spot and in the environs of the ancient and opulent capital of the Assyrian empire by misters Botta, Flandi, Layard, and Place furnished precious conceptions on an art that we hardly knew: we recognized connections between this art and that of the Greeks, and from that time a whole new horizon opened itself up to research. It seems certain today that the Greeks, from a very early period, tried to imitate the painted vases that the Phoenicians transported through commerce to the ends of the earth, whether these wares were products of their industry, or whether they took them from other regions of the Near East.[35]

Gottfried Semper was among those deeply impressed by the public exhibitions at the Louvre and the British Museum, and he maintained that Near Eastern motifs helped regenerate Greek art.[36] Although elaborating a different argument for the evolution of style than Semper, Alois Riegl, too, underscored the continuous relationship between western and eastern art, beginning with his studies on Oriental carpets.[37]

The lavish publications of Layard's discoveries, with ornamental patterns enlarged and represented in vibrant color, encouraged and facilitated comparisons of Near Eastern art with vases and bronze finds recently unearthed in the west. Motifs from the wall reliefs, such as rosettes, could be identified among the western finds and offered sources for the iconography that had so bewildered scholars of Greek art. Silver bowls, such as those found in the Regolini-Galassi tomb in 1836, suddenly had excellent parallels in Assyria.[38] And it was not only the iconography that offered clues. The friezelike composition of wall reliefs recalled the description of the shield of Achilles in Homer.[39] Scholars thought that with more excavation, publication, and close study, they would be able to pin down the origins of the influences on Greek art. It was a period of academic positivism and optimistic confidence. One day, they maintained, they could distinguish whether influences were more Egyptian or Babylonian or Neo-Assyrian or Hittite or Urartian.

As discoveries and displays opened the door to diffusion, scholars sought to deduce its routes. At first they looked to Ionian Greek cities in the eastern Mediterranean, conceived as gateways for goods and influences. Samuel Birch in 1858 explained: "The first traces of Grecian art and refinement appeared upon the coast of Asia Minor. The Greeks, there placed in contact with the old and magnificent monarchies of Asia, became imbued with the love of luxuries unknown to those of their race who inhabited the bleaker shores of the Peloponnese."[40] Ionia, broadly conceived, would hold a prominent role in scholars' minds for many years to come.[41] But discoveries on Rhodes, Cyprus, and Thera of pottery and jewelry and metal bowls that shared affinities with the decorative motifs from the Near East offered new pathways less restricted to Ionians.[42]

A landmark publication for conceptions of diffusion was *Melische Thongefässe* (1862), by Alexander Conze. This enormous book presented only three vases, but they were reproduced at a one-to-one scale in spectacular color drawings (Figure 2.10). Conze maintained that these vases in Athenian collections but allegedly from Melos belonged to the oldest period of Greek pottery painting. He sought parallels in oriental "Kunstweise," specifically Assyrian, for the filling motifs, the animal friezes, and the composition, and he concluded that the vases were either inspired by Assyrian imports or made/influenced by Phoenicians who were involved in vase production before Dorians came to the islands. The quality and size of the publication and its vibrant illustrations ensured a wide and lasting impact.

In these discussions of diffusion, however, scholars had not identified an explicitly "Oriental" style (although the word "Orient" was certainly current in academic and popular discourse). Eduard Gerhard in 1831 used a tripartite classification that made outside influence evident, classifying Greek pottery in one of three ways: Egyptianizing (*la egiziana maniera*), Archaic, and Perfect.[43] The terms "Egyptian" and "Egyptianizing" were used widely, but they started to encounter two problems. First, scholars increasingly recognized that much of this pottery was actually Corinthian. This led some people, like Gerhard, to favor the term "Egyptianizing," with the suffix signaling that the vases were not, in fact, Egyptian.[44] Second, the excavations in the Near East showed that many of the influences behind the work were not Egyptian after all. Consequently, some scholars sought increasing precision in terminology. Otto Jahn's mid-nineteenth-century state-of-the-field chronicles a profusion of terms. In addition to Egyptian and Egyptianizing, pseudo-Egyptian, Egyptian-Babylonian, Phoenician, Phoenician-Babylonian, pseudo-Phoenician,

TAFEL I.

Figure 2.10. A plate from Conze 1862. Photo John Blazejewski / Princeton University.

Greek-Phoenician, and Carthaginian were all possible terms that could be used.[45] On Rhodes, Auguste Salzmann classified what would later be called "Orientalizing" as "style dorien," "style primitif," "style asiatique" (including sixth-century finds), "style phénicien," "style égyptien," and "style assyrien."[46] Other scholars instead sought out a broader period designation. So Birch laid out a scheme in which a linear and geometric phase was followed by a phase with floral motifs, birds, and real as well as mythological animals.[47] Birch advocated for a broad "Archaic Style."[48] And in 1863, for the first time, a "style oriental" (also referred to as "style asiatique") appeared, at the pen of Jean de Witte.[49] Following the presentation of a "style primitive," he wrote:

> We give the name of vases in an asiatic or oriental style to a large group of vases enriched by paintings more or less complicated. . . . Some archaeologists give them the name of Corinthian vases, because many small vases of this sort have been found in tombs around Corinth. But today since a large number of places on the Greek continent, the islands, the shores of Asia, Sicily, and Italy have furnished vases of exactly the same type, it seems this designation needs to be abandoned and a more general one substituted. They have also received the name *Phoenician, Greco-Phoenician,* or *pseudo-Phoenician vases.* We prefer *vases of the Asiatic or Oriental style.*[50]

So the qualification "Oriental" emerged in the context of continued misunderstandings about Corinthian pottery and to replace the earlier "Egyptian." It simplified a bewildering variety of nomenclature and served as a stopgap until iconographic research and diffusion studies could pinpoint more precise origins for the style. Now, de Witte used "style oriental" rather than "style orientalisant" (Oriental rather than Orientalizing), but the terms were virtually synonymous at first.[51] As with "Egyptianizing," the "-izing" suffix served to indicate that the objects were not, actually, Egyptian, or in this case, Oriental.[52] The way in which many scholars today use "-izing" to indicate a more widespread eastward cultural orientation was not present in the earliest scholarship; the "-izing" was an act of classification at first.

Compared to such erroneous labels as Tyrrhenian-Phoenician, the simpler terminology may have seemed an improvement, and it gained traction. But there were consequences. It is in Conze's treatise *Zur Geschichte der Anfänge griechischer Kunst* (1870) that "Orientalizing" appears for the first time in a sustained discussion of Greek pottery. It was used as one part of an opposing pair rather than as a step in a continuous development, as de Witte and others had conceived. This change depended on research into another style that was slow to be correctly identified: Geometric. It was recognized as early in date, and there were even reports from Athens reaching scholars in Italy that the vases in this style were found particularly deep in the ground.[53] But the style was so different from black-figure that many people had trouble believing it was Greek at all. At first, Geometric vases were grouped along with later pottery as Egyptian or Egyptianizing.[54] Some observers, including Fauvel, considered Geometric vases to be Phoenician.[55] Furtwängler was more cautious but long hesitated to call them Hellenic.[56]

Conze drew comparisons with (lowercase *g*) geometric styles elsewhere and influentially argued that the origins of Greek Geometric pottery lay in northern Europe; the style represented the Indo-Germanic roots of the inhabitants of Greece.[57] Accordingly, Orientalizing was a subsequent, later style, and could serve as a foil to Geometric. He characterized Orientalizing through its ornamentation and portrayal of animals but especially through the pronounced role of vegetal motifs on the pottery.[58] The name Orientalizing, he freely admitted, was rather vague but preferable to other terminology such as Corinthian or Phoenicianizing, and it served his purpose of making a contrast with Geometric.[59] Conze, like Semper, developed an interpretive framework wherein an Orientalizing style led to a purely Greek style. Without Orientalizing, he thought, Greek art was inconceivable. It represented a fertilizing process, as the Geometric style—which Conze incorrectly thought lacked any human forms—was infused with figures and mythical scenes.[60] New discoveries would require some modification to his views, but an oppositional framework was now operative. It depended on the use of a vague term, Orientalizing, in place of a search for terminology with specific cultural attributes; on the reification of the Geometric period and its association with immigrant Dorians; and on the historical and political associations of the Orient. While providing a conceptual space for non-Hellenic influences, the framework also displaced the origins of Greek art from Egypt to Greek soil, relegating the Near East (including Egypt) to a period set apart.

The discovery of Bronze Age material was the first complication for these narratives of Orientalizing.[61] The deep antiquity of the prehistoric remains at first was not recognized. Mycenaean finds of the 1860s at Rhodes, for example, were classified by the British Museum as Greco-Phoenician.[62] But in 1874, Heinrich Schliemann uncovered Bronze Age remains at Mycenae. He quickly published his work, and excavations by Christos Tsountas at Mycenae and in the Cyclades produced even more stratified material.[63] These early finds posed an interesting problem to the existing narratives of Greek art, because they added a new stage to the history, and because many pieces exhibited styles that in their curvilinear and vegetal decoration looked surprisingly Orientalizing.[64] Confronted with the Bronze Age, it became difficult to advance an evolutionary scheme of development in which Geometric necessarily ceded to Orientalizing in a predestined step toward the Classical style. Yet at the same time, the prehistoric finds offered a solution to scholars hesitant to see external influences on Greek art by providing early examples of Orientalizing art that were Greek. As Riegl wrote: "Mycenaean art now looms as the direct predecessor of the Hellenic art that we know more closely from the historical period. The Dipylon [i.e., Geometric] Style, and whatever else separated the two periods, was only an obscure interlude, a haze cast over a development already well underway."[65]

The impact of the new discoveries and Conze's writing are evident in Furtwängler's influential publication of eighth- and seventh-century bronzes from Olympia. He classified the remains into two "sharply separated groups" (*scharf geschiedene Gruppen*), one with Geometric and linear motifs, the other with plants and so-called Oriental animal motifs.[66] But he maintained that the Geometric and Orientalizing styles were concurrent.[67] He also was not convinced that Geometric art was Greek. He took into account Bronze Age finds by modifying the diffusion model to argue that the current of Orientalizing decoration passed from Mycenaean art to "Melian" vases and later to Rhodian vases.[68] In other words, what seemed Oriental was actually indigenous, and there was no need for Geometric to interfere between Mycenaean and mainland Orientalizing. In his publication of Mycenaean vases, too, he insisted that, unlike other forms of Mycenaean art, the vases resisted foreign influences.[69]

We can now return to Böhlau, and to his use of Orientalizing for describing seventh-century Attic vases. He was not satisfied with the term, and like many scholars he used it as a placeholder as he sought more precise origins of influences. He thought that the forms originated from Greek colonies in Ionia, and he followed Furtwängler in accepting the survival of Mycenaean elements.[70] But unlike Furtwängler, Böhlau's acceptance of Geometric as a distinctive phase in Attic art led to a model in which Geometric pottery gradually succumbed to foreign influences:

It is a long and rather belabored process that we see decided on our vases: for a long time the Geometric style in all its severity held out beside the eastern import streaming in with increasing strength, until this succeeded in gradually undermining the Geometric style's rule and eventually overthrowing it.[71]

Böhlau thus for the first time brought together a group of seventh-century Attic vases, defined them as Attic, and recognized their place after Geometric. Like Conze, he applied a framework of stylistic conflict—Böhlau's language is physical, almost violent—and like Furtwängler, he emphasized indigenous influences. Where Geometric art once had been considered Phoenician or Indo-European, it represented for him a purely Greek form that was assaulted by foreign influence.

A CANON TAKES SHAPE

The next phase of study after Böhlau is characterized by the beginning of large-scale excavations in Greece, the accumulation of more material, the composition of major syntheses of Greek art and vase-painting, and continuing debates over chronology, influences, and Orientalizing. To measure the changes, we can look at the state of the field before the avalanche of discoveries. Carl Otfried Müller's textbook published in 1830 and later revised, translated into French in 1842 and English in 1847 (revised in 1852), offers a convenient starting point. As the number of translations suggests, the book had impact. It is symptomatic of its time in devoting only three pages to vase-painting and in making no mention of early Attic production.[72] The companion plates to the textbook illustrated no vase earlier than the sixth century BC.[73] Olivier Rayet and Maxime Collignon's 1888 publication devoted to the history of Greek vases included two chapters on Orientalizing, but privileged material from the islands and from Corinth. Attic material was not discussed at any length, and only the Burgon Krater was illustrated.[74] Dumont and Chaplain's extensive 1888 pottery survey devoted more attention to Athens, with a chapter titled "Type ancien d'Athènes: Type de Phalère," but the only vase illustrated was the oinochoe from Phaleron, which Dumont had published when he coined the term "Phaleron Ware" in 1869 (Figure 2.3).[75]

Discoveries over the next decades would gradually change this picture, augmenting the number of finds and giving Athens a firmer place in the history of Greek vases. The pace of excavation in Attica and nearby regions increased, and material from all phases of Protoattic accumulated. Notable findspots were, in the order of their publication: Peiraios Street in Athens (Figure 2.11);[76] Vourva (e.g., Figure 2.12);[77] Phaleron (e.g., Figure 2.13);[78] Aigina (e.g., Figure 6.9);[79] Piraeus (Figure 1.11);[80] the Argive Heraion (e.g., Figure 2.14);[81] south of the Ilissos River in Athens (Kynosarges, Figure 2.15);[82] Eleusis;[83] and the Athenian Acropolis.[84] The ambitious excavations in the agora and in the Kerameikos were particularly important for establishing chronologies and developing a corpus, with plentiful finds accompanied by assiduous publication.[85] Most stunning were the funeral trenches from the Kerameikos, first found in 1932, providing unexpected contexts with high-quality vessels (Figure 2.16).

Museums, too, played a part in changes, and although we deplore the looting that they encouraged, their contribution to historiography cannot be neglected. They acquired new pieces, published collections, and organized displays and exhibitions that contributed to the development of a corpus and toward the refinement of geographical distinctions. New material included a krater in Munich (Figure 2.17),[86] an amphora in New York (Figure 1.5), finds from Aigina in Berlin (Figures 5.19, 6.10),[87] and the collection in Cambridge (Figure 2.18).[88] As they published these vases and placed them into galleries, museums were confronted with the task of selection and classification, deciding which objects to display and where and investigating how they might be integrated into a history of Greek art.

Despite the new discoveries, seventh-century Attic vases still presented problems of identification, and their origin and date were not always recognized. The Protoattic finds from the Argive Heraion, for example, were considered Argive. The accumulation of material only gradually brought clarity, and as scholars added new pieces to the repertoire, they occasionally took stock of the whole corpus, suggesting chronological sequences and divisions.[89] Terminology remained mixed. Dumont had developed the term Phaleron Ware (1869) and Böhlau had employed

Figure 2.11. Late Protoattic amphora from Athens (Peiraios Street) by the Nessos Painter. Athens, National Museum 1002. Photo Giannis Patrikianos. Copyright © Hellenic Ministry of Culture and Sports / Archaeological Receipts Fund.

"frühattisch" (1887). It was Louis Couve (and not Cecil Smith, as often claimed) who coined the term Protoattic ("proto-attique") in his 1893 publication of the amphora with wild boars from Phaleron (Figure 1.1).[90] Not everyone adopted this label. Some preferred "frühattisch" or early Athenian.[91] Many others continued to use Phaleron Ware to refer to seventh-century Athenian pottery in general, to its earliest period, or to miniature vases, especially oinochoai.[92] The latest phase of Protoattic and the earliest black-figure also caused problems and were sometimes labeled according to representative pieces. For instance, the publication of Acropolis vases

Figure 2.12. Late Protoattic krater from Vourva. Athens, National Museum 993. Copyright © Hellenic Ministry of Culture and Sports / Archaeological Receipts Fund.

included a "Group of the Nettos Amphora" to refer to vases produced late in the seventh century and similar in style to figure 2.11.[93]

The new finds of Greek vases, of which Protoattic vases were only one component, together with the variegated terminology, created an increased need for new syntheses, but the process was slow and the treatment of Athens still mixed. Heinrich Brunn's important textbook of 1893 demonstrated a clear debt to Böhlau's recent publication, and seventh-century Attic vases (grouped together with the Dipylon style) here took pride of place over subsequent discussions of Melos, Thera, Rhodes, Naukratis, and Corinth.[94] But at first few authors followed this lead, and major treatises on Greek art could still omit seventh-century Attic vases altogether. Percy Gardner's 1905 and 1914 introductions to Greek art contained none. The enormous, encyclopedic, ten-volume work by Georges Perrot and Charles Chipiez, *Histoire de l'art dans l'antiquité* (1882–1914), devoted only two pages to them. The Burgon Krater (Figure 2.2) was illustrated and treated as an example of the shape, and the Ram Jug (Figure 6.9) was illustrated but considered possibly Argive.[95] The *Dictionnaire des antiquités grecques et romaines* (1877–1919) illustrated the Analatos hydria (Figure 2.6) and the amphora from Hymmetos (Figure 2.4), but lamented the quality.[96] Even in the 1920s, Protoattic vases could be left out of handbooks on Greek vase-painting.[97]

Major syntheses that focused on vase-painting shifted the discourse. The influential books by Ernst Buschor, *Griechische Vasenmalerei* (1913), and Ernst Pfuhl, *Malerei und Zeichnung der Griechen* (1923), marked turning points in the history of early Greek art and finally gave seventh-century Attic vases a lasting place within a chronological, geographic, and stylistic frame-work. The format of a manual-like synthesis demanded strict periodization, and both schol-ars drew sharp lines. Geometric was now ac-cepted as a clearly defined style closely associ-ated with Athens. In describing how it interfaced with seventh-century production, they moved away from Böhlau and instead followed Hein-rich Brunn. Whereas Böhlau had posited a con-flict between Geometric art and non-Hellenic influences, Brunn a few years later had countered with the suggestion that Geometric art was able to appropriate and integrate foreign forms rather than battle them.[98] Buschor and Pfuhl extended this type of "fertilizing" view adopted from Brunn. When the Geometric style was tired out, they argued, the Orient provided new impetus. Buschor wrote:

> Oriental works of art, which this lively traffic brought before the Greeks' eyes, forcefully stimulated their imagination. The abundance of decorative motifs, especially from the world of plants and fantastic animals, and the supe-riority of oriental art in the representation of figural forms tore Greek vase painting com-pletely away from Geometric monotony and pointed to new paths.[99]

Similarly, Pfuhl:

> When the driving force of the Dipylon style was exhausted and its tautness loosened and its abundance declined, then gradually east-ern elements penetrated into Attic ceram-ics. . . . Attic potters behaved suddenly like kids on Christmas morning in front of a cornuco-pia of new riches.[100]

Figure 2.13. Protoattic Phaleron-type oinochoe from Phaleron, attributed to the Workshop of the Passas Painter. London, British Museum 1865.7-20.1. Photo N. T. Arrington.

More than before, seventh-century vase-painting was associated with Oriental-izing and became a distinct, separate phase of Greek art. One consequence of brack-eting off Orientalizing into a specific time period was that scholars now also downplayed the possible role of the Bronze Age in the development of Greek art.[101] Mycenaean influence was still present in Gisela Richter's 1912 analysis of the New

Figure 2.14. Fragments of a Protoattic stand from the Argive Heraion. Athens, National Museum 27967α–στ. Not all preserved fragments of the object are shown in this photograph. Photo N. T. Arrington. Copyright © Hellenic Ministry of Culture and Sports / Archaeological Receipts Fund.

York Nessos Amphora but was absent from both Buschor's and Pfuhl's syntheses.[102] Frederik Poulsen's 1912 landmark monograph, *Der Orient und die frühgriechische Kunst*, highlighting the influence of the Near East and arguing for discontinuity with the Bronze Age, no doubt encouraged the shift. The development of the Bronze Age as an independent specialty or subdiscipline likely also contributed to the new paradigm.

As the pottery from various regions of Greece started to become distinguishable from one other, they offered different sources for influence.[103] One of these regions was Corinth, where scholarship had made enormous progress. Although Friis Johansen erroneously considered the ware Sikyonian, he nevertheless provided a clear and influential chronological framework, improving on views that it was Egyptian or Near Eastern, as once Jahn had chronicled.[104] He also offered some observations on Orientalizing, arguing that "Orientalizing" was not the most accurate term for the Greek style.[105] Very few motifs, he noted, were borrowed directly from the east. Ionia did not offer a simple solution, either, for continued excavation in Asia Minor had failed to find clear connections between western Orientalizing and eastern wares.[106] Instead, he argued, excavations on Crete and Cyprus had revealed that those islands were important stepping stones for the development Greek art.[107] Humfry Payne's landmark publication of Corinthian pottery in 1931 also underlined the role of Crete for conveying Orientalizing motifs and vase shapes, such as the aryballos.[108] Payne included the island with three forces at work in the development of style in the Archaic period—eastern Greece, Crete, and Corinth—and claimed that "the early Protocorinthian patterns are, indeed, more purely Hellenic than those of any contemporary school."[109] He detected a change from Protocorinthian to Corinthian styles, when there was more trade with the Near East, and more direct contact visible in vase iconography.[110] For Payne, therefore, any Orientalizing style was more likely to lie in the sixth century than the seventh century. Whether or not scholars accepted these models, all of this work on Protocorinthian

meant that scholars looking at Protoattic now had a secure source of influence for Athenian pottery, which
was Greek ("purely Hellenic," as Payne put it). Burr,
publishing a Protoattic votive deposit from the agora a
couple of years after Payne's book appeared, noted the
presence of much Middle Protocorinthian in the deposit and surmised "that Attic potters were familiar
with Protocorinthian and presumably learned much
from it."[111]

The accumulation of vases, therefore, and the
writing of syntheses entailed the refining, but also the
hardening of a period, with Bronze Age and non-
Hellenic influences bracketed out of the history of
Greek art. Another major impact of the new finds was
that as more vases were found that could be identified
specifically as Attic, a canon took shape privileging
high-quality objects and excluding more humble
products. The shift is evident in both terminology and
the choice of vases to illustrate, and it had lasting consequences. Dumont had coined "Phaleron Ware" on
the basis of a specific find (Figure 2.3), and Couve used
a find from Phaleron when he employed the term
"proto-attique" for the first time (Figure 1.1). Pottery
from Phaleron was the foundation of Böhlau's study,
and the term Phaleron Ware (or a version thereof) was
used by Furtwängler, Smith, Dumont, Collignon, Hackl,
and Herford.[112] Buschor, however, organized seventh-
and early sixth-century vase-painting into three parts—

Figure 2.15. Late Protoattic amphora from
Kynosarges, by the Kynosarges Painter.
Athens, National Museum 14497. Photo John
Blazejewski / Princeton University, after Smith
1902, pl. 4.

Phaleron Ware, the Nessos vase style, and the Vourva style—without illustrating
the Phaleron vases. Pfuhl provided some illustrations of the vases, but his extensive and exhaustive bibliography at the end of his discussion explicitly leaves out
Phaleron.[113] This trend continued in both textbooks and surveys. Hans Diepolder
in *Griechische Vasen* (1947) illustrates no Phaleron vases, Andreas Rumpf's *Malerei
und Zeichnung* (1953) has no discussion of finds from Phaleron, and Friedrich
Matz's influential textbook *Geschichte der griechischen Kunst* (1950) has only one
image from Phaleron out of more than twenty-five Protoattic vases and no discussion of Phaleron as a term or a context.[114] Today, acknowledged masterpieces form
a recognizable and coherent repertoire, with named painters. John Boardman's survey
of Greek vase-painting illustrates a vase by the Analatos Painter, the Polyphemus
Amphora, and a set of vases from an offering trench in the Kerameikos.[115] Richard
Neer's textbook on Greek art illustrates the same vase by the Analatos Painter, the
Polyphemus Amphora, and the Ram Jug.[116] Mark Stansbury-O'Donnell's textbook

Figure 2.16. Protoattic vases from funeral trench (Opferrinne) ζ in the Kerameikos. See table 1, Kerameikos VI-13. Photo courtesy of the Deutsches Archäologisches Institut, Athens (Karl Kübler, D-DAI-ATH-Kerameikos-04549).

just shows the Polyphemus Amphora.[117] There is also sufficient material now to talk about Orientalizing without much mention of Greek ceramics, as in Ann Gunter's *Greek Art and the Orient*, illustrating one Wild Goat amphora, and one Late Geometric amphora.[118]

Vases from excavations in the Kerameikos, the agora, and Eleusis or acquired by museums, particularly the Aigina material in Berlin, were more impressive than many of the pieces that had been found earlier, when finds from the relatively poor Phaleron cemetery had guided research. The new canon favored objects with complex depictions of human figures, elaborate ornamentation, and mythical scenes. As new objects were added to the repertoire of Protoattic, others were excised from discussion, along with their contexts.[119] Paradoxically, while one might have expected the accumulation of material from excavations to increase the variety of objects available to the field, it contributed to a shift in the types of objects that were analyzed. The change in canon would influence the way the period was seen. For Böhlau, with Phaleron at hand, seventh-century Attic vases had been made for rich and poor alike.[120] Yet this broad audience was in the process of narrowing to a refined, luxury-loving clientele.[121] But before examining some of these consequences of periodization, we need to look at how intellectual and aesthetic trends promoting the Classical style affected the Protoattic canon and its reception.

TO MAKE PROTOARCHAIC ART . . . CLASSICAL

The surveys and syntheses of the late eighteenth and early nineteenth centuries were trying to solve chronological and geographical problems of vase-painting. But there was a third problem they addressed as well, implicitly and explicitly: aesthetics. The

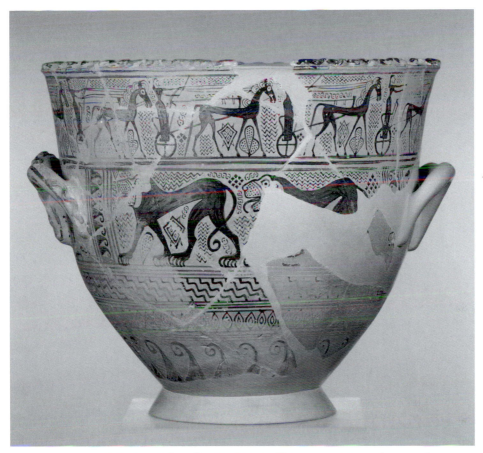

Figure 2.17. Protoattic krater attributed to the Analatos Painter. Munich, Antikensammlungen 6077. Photo State Collection of Antiquities and Glyptothek Munich.

Dictionnaire des antiquités grecques et romaines (1877–1919) made the issue clear when it described Protoattic with unusually frank disparaging terms: "the drawing [of the Hymettos Amphora, figure 2.4] reveals a childish inexperience that makes Orientalizing Athenian figures rank among some of the ugliest Greek pottery."[122] Behind this claim that the pottery is ugly lies a distaste toward art that did not meet expectations of what Greek styles should look like. Nineteenth-century discoveries in the Near East already had provoked many critical reactions. Henry Rawlinson pointedly wrote to Layard, "your winged God is not the Apollo Belvedere."[123] These aesthetic critiques accompanied a broader disparagement of non-Greek cultures. Gisela Richter, for instance, contrasted Near Eastern and Greek art and made the revealing comment that the ancient Greeks were closer in spirit to her audience: "In order to properly appreciate Greek art we must also understand the Greek spirit," she wrote in her handbook to the Metropolitan Museum's collection. "This is not difficult; for there is an essential likeness between the Greeks and ourselves.

Figure 2.18. Protoattic ovoid krater. Cambridge, Fitzwilliam Museum 7/25. Photo © Fitzwilliam Museum, Cambridge / Art Resource, NY.

No such adjustment is necessary as in the study, for instance, of an Oriental and alien civilization."[124] In this context, "Orientalizing" was not a compliment. For many observers, the problem was simply that the seventh-century style did not look Greek enough. It was too far removed in appearance from the Classical style, which was prized in the early twentieth century as the pinnacle of Greek (and human) artistic achievement, the summit to which preceding styles led and from which later styles declined, and to which Near Eastern art could not compare. Whereas both eighth- and sixth-century Greek art exhibited the balance and control that scholars associated with Classical Greece—and, by extension, all of Greek art—seventh-century art was wild, foreign.

So, part of the process of creating a corpus of seventh-century vases entailed making it conform to the aesthetic standards and ideals that informed conceptions of the rest of Greek art by removing pieces from the canon that seemed less Classical (or, as they might have put it, less beautiful), and by privileging those that shared some affinities with the later styles. Scholars increasingly prioritized those vases that had the most Classical characteristics: a vase such as figure 2.6 rather than figure 2.7. This development can be hard to pinpoint in the secondary literature, but there are occasions when the language that scholars employ reveals their prejudices and exposes their agenda: when they either use the term "Classical" itself, or when they use a vocabulary that associates seventh-century art with the balance, control, and moderation associated with the Classical style. For example, in John M. Cook's seminal article of 1934–35 (more on this article in a moment), he protested: "Few writers on Protoattic have failed to call attention to the 'fermentation' which follows the collapse of Geometric. To stress this is unfair; Protoattic progresses steadily and soberly."[125] In other words, the Classical qualities of Protoattic can be highlighted as a response to critics. Cook went further and invented terminology that linked seventh-century art explicitly

with the Classical style. He grouped those painters associated with a newly baptized Analatos Painter into a "Classical Tradition" and placed others "Outside."
This invented "Classical Tradition" suggests artistic continuity and puts a qualify-
ing label on Protoattic. It is perhaps no surprise that Cook did not hesitate to judge
the quality of the painting relegated to the category "Outside," disparaging pottery
from Phaleron, describing figure 1.1 as a "miserable amphora" and castigating the
Hymettos Amphora (Figure 2.4) as "ugly."[126] Such language, and the refusal to illustrate the maligned objects, pushed certain vases out of the repertoire, fashioned
a more tame appearance to Protoattic, and wrapped the discourse in classically infused prose. The quality of the corpus not only had changed, as we saw in the last
section. So had the very character of the pieces represented and the language used
to describe them.

Despite Cook's attempts to rehabilitate the ware, Protoattic was still insufficiently
Classical for most observers. The connoisseur Sir John Beazley, in his book on sixth-
century pottery, relegated Protoattic to a chapter appropriately titled, "The Road to
Black Figure." In his account, Protoattic forms the antithesis of Classical forms
manifested in both Geometric and black-figure. Describing a very Late Geometric
or Early Protoattic vase, Beazley tellingly wrote, "The *classic* control of the [Geo-
metric] prothesis vase in Athens has given way to a furious energy."[127] Such frenzy
lasted until the latest period of Protoattic, a phase he describes as "a *classic* period
in one sense, the first since the high Geometric style of the prothesis vase. Imagination no longer tends to outrun skill of hand and grasp of form."[128] The essential
point here is that the word "classic" was deployed as a modifier for both Geometric
and black-figure, but not Protoattic.

Martin Robertson's review of a publication of vases from Aigina reiterates the
classicizing language and standard:

> Beazley has lately remarked that the painters of the Nessos [Figure 2.11] and Chi-
> maera circle represent a "classic" phase of vase-painting, the first in Attica since
> high Geometric. Beside the Chimaera vase the Ram Jug [Figure 6.9], for all its
> charm, looks naive and uneasy; but contemporary Protocorinthian, like the ani-
> mal oenochoe 273 or the Bellerophon kotyle, is sure and strong and beautiful—
> already "classical." The troubled adolescence of seventh-century Attic presaged
> a greater future, but the greater achievement at the time is unquestionably
> Corinth's.[129]

Robertson evidently recognized the classicizing language in Beazley, which was
applied to Geometric and black-figure, and which he extended to Protocorinthian,
making a contrast with ungainly, anticlassical Protoattic. This was not only happening in English-language scholarship. For example, Andreas Rumpf, in an extensive survey of Greek pottery, expressed his Classical tastes, albeit with less
explicit language.[130] He rejected the term Orientalizing altogether, instead dividing
the period into two phases: Idaean and Daidalic. The second phase, he maintained,

brought "discipline" and "order" to the unruly Idaean, words that are again associated with the Classical style.

The attempts to classicize seventh-century painting affected more than the corpus and terminology. They also intersected with a new approach, namely, an effort to make Protoattic conform to a history of Greek art that increasingly was conceived as a history of artists. Beazley's work on Attic black- and red-figure vase-painters had shifted how people wrote about Greek art and what scholars and public valued.[131] In attributing thousands of unsigned pots to individual hands, he created a new chronological as well as conceptual framework. The search for artists had characterized the study of sculpture; now it could be applied to pottery as well, and Greek art could be placed into a grand western narrative of human achievement. As James Whitley, among others, has noted, the method is not atheoretical, and it offers more than a process of cataloging alone.[132] Beazley's connoisseurial skill provoked admiration and emulation among many scholars, who turned to untried fields, such as Corinthian pottery or black-figure lekythoi, in search of hands.[133] Protoattic, the period immediately preceding Beazley's black-figure, was ripe for attention. John M. Cook took up Beazley's unspoken challenge and sought to organize all of Protoattic into named personalities, in the seminal 1934–35 article mentioned above.[134] Leaving aside discussions of Orientalizing or foreign influences, he sought instead to fill the gap between Geometric and black-figure with a narrative of artistic excellence. The contrast in approach with Böhlau is striking. Böhlau named no artist; Cook baptized artists and used them to provide chronological order. He began by naming the Analatos Painter (Figure 2.6), and he added several others, especially the Ram Jug Painter (Figure 6.9). It needs to be stressed that artists provided as much a conceptual and theoretical framework as a chronological one. Cook structured the history of Protoattic around personalities, who became agents for change. And they were also a mechanism for inserting Protoattic into a broader, and ultimately Classical, narrative of Greek art. The term "Protoattic" itself suggests that the period is no more than a prelude.

The intersection of classicizing impulses, the search for the artist, and social interpretations can be seen in the treatment of the figure of the Analatos Painter, an Early Protoattic artistic personality with a conservative style and a member of Cook's "Classical Tradition." While Cook left the origins of Protoattic vague in his 1934–35 article,[135] a few years later he solved the problem by anointing one person the founder of Protoattic: the Analatos Painter.[136] This view has been widely accepted.[137] A comprehensive study of the artist goes so far as to say that "he *is* Early Protoattic" and continues to claim, "this exact match between an individual and artistic movement is rare."[138] Establishing this restrained artist's work as the touchstone placed emphasis on balance and clarity in an otherwise unruly phase of vase-painting, fulfilling scholars' classicizing desires. According to Ronald Hood, the Analatos Painter "kept his head when other Late Geometric artists were losing theirs . . . in a sense, by preserving high standards of draughtsmanship while pioneering Protoattic, he was the savior of Athenian vase painting."[139] There are social implications to this model. Attributing stylistic change to a single individual allows the transition to be monopolized by a lone figure who works for a small clientele.[140] His clients can be select people whose distinctive and refined tastes played no small part in driving the new style. Cook went even further and imagined an elevated social status for the Analatos Painter himself, making him a member of the elite. "If we look for an explanation of this phenomenon [of rapid change in the late 8th century]," he wrote, "Homer and the Analatos Painter may together serve to indicate one possible factor, that an essential part was played by a small number of leading personalities, men of high culture who had the necessary skill and taste to do things ἐπισταμένως [skillfully, expertly]."[141] In fact, however, there were multiple artists at work in Early Protoattic, and the Analatos Painter was not the most innovative. He experimented very little with the new techniques of outline, incision, and added color, and his iconographic repertoire remained deeply conservative. Vases by the Passas Painter, the Group of the Buffalo Krateriskos, and the Würzburg Group accompany early Protocorinthian pottery and thus date to the earliest period of Protoattic, and they set on a more progressive path, which would make a more lasting impact on the style than the Analatos Painter.[142]

The search for artists, which Beazley launched and which Cook followed, displaced other research questions as focus shifted from outside influences to the interrelations of painters. Gisela Richter, in her 1912 publication of the New York Nessos Amphora (Figure 1.5), concluded her discussion of influences with a sharp turn to the individual: "stronger than any influences of past and foreign arts was, as we have seen, a new-born and highly individual artistic sense, which was stimulated perhaps by outside influences, but is unmistakable in its vigorous originality."[143] Dorothy Burr Thompson also championed the independence and freedom of the individual artist:

> Not only is the Attic potter free to choose what he will from the repertory of other styles, but he is free to re-observe the subjects, making them somewhat his own. With strange independence he avoids copying pattern for its own sake. This tendency toward naturalism is what carried the Athenian artist through the decorative period of his art, in which the Rhodian and Corinthian far excelled him, to the peculiarly Attic creations of the Black-figured and Red-figured styles.[144]

In this formulation, not only does the artist drive artistic change, but "naturalism," a watchword for the Greek Classical style, paves their way forward.

As soon as the evolution of style became a question of personalities and hands, there was little need to explore the origins or significance of Near Eastern influence. The concept of Orientalizing thereby was dramatically simplified and no longer the subject of critical examination by art historians.[145] For decades, most subsequent publications on Protoattic, especially those written in English, were concerned first and foremost with painter hands.[146] Museum publications, such as the important *Corpus Vasorum Antiquorum* of Berlin, added attributions.[147] So, too, did excavations, such as Wilhelm Kraiker's publication of pottery from Aigina, George Mylonas's publication of the Polyphemus Amphora, or Semni Karouzou's publication of pottery from Vari.[148] Eva Brann's publications of the material from the agora devoted more attention to hands than to contexts, and even John M. Cook thought that she may have been too eager to find the Analatos Painter in minute fragments.[149] The process of attribution only intensified the narrowing of the canon to higher-quality objects and vases with figural drawing, which are more susceptible to the connoisseur's gaze. This meant sidelining a significant quantity of material because it was not prone to attribution.[150] Needless to say, Cook was uninterested in vases from Phaleron and argued against the use of the term for a style rather than for vases from a specific findspot.[151] Already in 1942, Rodney Young could complain, "The published articles dealing with Proto-Attic ware are either stylistic studies based on a few important pieces in various museums or publications of large groups of vases and fragments found together but extending over too long a period of time to allow of a detailed study of the development."[152] He presented assemblages from the Phaleron cemetery, mainly to sort out chronological problems. Despite his interests, he felt the need to disparage the painters as "second-rate," lacking in skill and imagination.[153]

There were reactions to the search for artistic personalities, but they were not altogether productive. Hans Diepolder wrote a short history of vases on the basis of the collection in Berlin.[154] His formalist approach avoids discussion of painters, but he also does not discuss external influences, for he considers pottery from the Geometric period onward purely Greek. His selection of material reveals the ossification of a canon that had been underway for decades. Karl Kübler, working on the finds from the Kerameikos, discussed Protoattic in competition with Protocorinthian, offered new insights on Protoattic technique and style, and advanced very narrow dates, but he largely rejected workshop connections altogether, despite the abundant material at his disposal.[155] Compared to Cook's lucid article, Kübler's vast monographs on the Kerameikos, where vases are published more often by type rather than by grave assemblage, are difficult to use, and his dating is problematic. He also published a short and informative monograph on Protoattic painting, with some interesting observations, but despite his connections to an excavation, he devoted surprisingly little attention to context.[156]

Now, not everyone accepted the privileging of the Classical style. For some scholars, discoveries on Crete offered a refuge from the contemporary worship of the alleged control, order, and balance of the fifth and fourth centuries BC. They argued for Cretan influence over the mainland, not only in the Bronze Age but also throughout subsequent periods.[157] In a book for the general reader, Charles Hawes and Harriet Boyd Hawes, the latter the excavator of Gournia, wrote, "Egypt may have been foster-mother to classical Greece, but the mother, never forgotten by her child, was Crete."[158] For Sir Arthur Evans, Minoan civilization was the primary mover in the ancient Aegean and an antidote to the contemporary privileging of Classical culture.[159] But most scholars interested specifically in Protoarchaic art were becoming increasingly myopic, and if there had been a time when the seventh century could be studied in tandem with the Bronze Age, it was now joining a narrative linked to the sixth and subsequent centuries, part of a prelude to the Classical.

THE TURN TO CONSUMPTION, AND ITS CONSEQUENCES

In the second half of the twentieth century and into the twenty-first century, as some scholars, such as Karl Kübler or Sarah Morris, continued to study the production of Protoattic pottery, and as Giulia Rocco brought John M. Cook's work on attribution to fruition, other scholars started to move in a new direction.[160] They began to study ceramics with an eye to social history. Studies moved away from production—who made a vase, where, and how—to consumption—who used a vase, where, and how. Anthropological and historical approaches took the lead over connoisseurship and other more art historical methods, and for the first time find contexts became the center of attention.[161] Where an object was found became more important than the object itself, and the "-izing" part of "Orientalizing" carried new sociocultural significance.

Ian Morris's work on the relationship between burial and social structure is representative of the change in focus, and it made a lasting impact on the study of seventh-century material culture.[162] (His approach and his results will be discussed at greater length in chapter 4, on cemeteries.) In the context of a study across several regions and centuries, he drew attention to an oddity in the seventh-century Attic archaeological record: the decrease in burials. Arguing that burials recovered by archaeologists reflected access to formalized funerary treatment rather than demographics, he used mortuary evidence to reconstruct a distinctive phase in the history of *polis* formation and class warfare. For Morris, the Athenian elite in the seventh century were able to claw back privileges to formal burial, marking a retreat of the *polis*, and a step backward in the formation of a community organized on principles of equality. Quantitative analysis formed the main support for his argument, but he also invoked Protoattic pottery, seeing the Orientalizing style as symptomatic of an elite power grab.

Morris's work prompted a number of responses and reactions.[163] There were criticisms, to be sure, but not about the effort to use material culture to address social questions, and many scholars have continued to explore the connection between pottery and society.[164] We can follow some of the import of the turn in James Whitley's significant article published shortly after Morris, where he followed and also extended Morris's approach, championing a "contextual archaeology."[165] He explained that in his method "the shape and decoration of material culture, and the nature of that society's 'depositional practices,' are seen as being related, as being the product of a particular social structure or social order."[166] On the basis of quantitative analysis and ethnography, he argued that Protoattic pottery, like high-status burial, was rationed by occasion and status.[167] Like Morris, he used the Orientalizing label to describe much Protoattic pottery and to link it with an elite, and, like Morris, he focused on contexts and uses: on consumption.

These approaches, and others like them, are deeply informed by structuralism, wherein the underlying logic and order of a society is sought by looking at large-scale patterns and trends and by emphasizing oppositions, such as formal versus informal burial. One consequence, however, of structuralist approaches seeking to recover significance and meaning by mapping paired concepts, is a tendency toward the reification of Orientalizing as scholars accept the period label and make it into a clear and distinct category. This binary is particularly evident in Whitley's article, where sub-Geometric and Orientalizing/Protoattic styles are separated in analysis, even though the distinction is often very hard to draw.[168] In some ways, the operation structuralism demands resembles periodization, as objects (or contexts or behavior) are slotted into one category or another, with that category serving to define the main characteristics of the object. The consequence for Protoattic has been to encourage the acceptance of the concept of Orientalizing, with a new emphasis on "-izing" as a signal of a social inclination. Where Orientalizing as a style, period, and phenomenon once was disputed, it often now is accepted unquestioningly and used as a tool of analysis. Classification is essential to these studies, without the terms of that classification, or the long histories of debate, receiving much attention. An extreme version of this problem is the conflation of Orientalizing with Near Eastern objects. For Ian Morris, there is no significant difference between a Greek object in an Orientalizing style and an import.[169] Both are treated as exotic goods and as symbols of status, power, and prestige.

The impact of structuralism is also evident in the distinction that many authors in the later twentieth century and still today draw between elite and nonelite. On one side, authors could group formal burial, the elite, and Orientalizing pottery; on the other, informal burial, the nonelite, and sub-Geometric pottery or the absence of pottery. The categories provided a way to map the conceptual universe of the ancient Athenians and to measure change. For Morris, the binary was reinforced by a Marxist perspective that saw development in terms of class conflict.[170] While this specific political orientation is not always present in subsequent studies, the sharp distinction between elite and nonelite tends to persist as well as the notion that a Protoattic vase offers a means to recover an elite context and, with it, elite behavior.[171]

In their pursuit of the order, logic, and meaning underlying the social use of material culture, many scholars, like Morris and Whitley, have used quantitative analyses, embracing the scientific turn of New or Processual Archaeology. However, studies that need reliable numbers depend on publications with data, or at least publications that can be used to generate data. Other scholars who have moved away from strictly statistical approaches but still focus on interpretations of contexts also rely on the thorough publication of archaeological material. But there is only one seventh-century cemetery that has been excavated with sufficient care and published in significant detail to afford detailed contextual analysis: the Kerameikos. Morris and Whitley, to be sure, looked at other contexts as well, and Whitley in particular incorporated statistics drawn from well deposits in the agora. But it is perhaps no surprise that their interpretations rely on the Kerameikos, with its rich primary deposits. Subsequent studies, such as those of Sanne Houby-Nielsen, Erich Kistler, and Thomas Brisart, have dealt exclusively with the Kerameikos. In comparison, other cemeteries remain published only in preliminary reports, were looted before they could be studied in detail, or suffer from other publication shortcomings. (I discuss this problem in more detail in chapter 4.) And cemeteries were privileged over other contexts for social analyses because of the attention that Morris drew to mortuary behavior and because cemetery contexts tend to have greater archaeological integrity. Although the agora has enjoyed good publication, the seventh-century material is primarily from secondary deposits (especially wells). Several scholars recently have started to argue that the obsession with mortuary material may have skewed our perceptions of seventh-century Attica,[172] and others who work on cemeteries, such as Alexandra Alexandridou, are now looking well beyond Athens.[173]

The turn to consumption has entailed, perhaps inadvertently, that objects themselves tend to be lost from analysis, as they are essentialized by periodization, relegated to categories/types, and used to explain or elucidate a context. The details of what a specific vase looks like do not matter very much. The title of Ian Morris's chapter, "The Art of Citizenship," might lead readers to expect at least one image of an object.[174] They will be disappointed. In social analyses, vases are often the means to an end. A vase becomes a datum point rather than the main subject of study.

While an emphasis on context does provide a much needed perspective, it is important to recognize that it is generally only one type of context that receives attention: the context of final deposition. The way objects were used before they were placed in the location where archaeologists found them remains underscrutinized. So one might say that studies of consumption have made objects disappear from analysis and also rendered them inert, since their importance lies in their final resting place in the dirt. Chapters 4–6 of this book attempt to remedy this shortcoming by focusing on pot-person interactions in multiple contexts.

There are, of course, exceptions. Most notably, Robin Osborne explicitly tried to link quantitative and qualitative analysis, including a discussion of "the manner of artistic expression" in an important article on seventh-century Attica.[175] He considered how scenes on Protoattic pottery challenged the role of tradition and community as a source of value, and he attempted to wed the analysis of images to the historical issues archaeologists were addressing through their tabulation of data.[176] But his work is exceptional, I think, and Whitley's accusation that Osborne was too art historical is very revealing about the changes in scholarly emphasis under the influence of New Archaeology, when data reigned.[177]

Periodization persists. Once the categories have been constructed, they exert a lasting influence on interpretations, long after structuralism has fallen out of fashion, and they often are accepted without question. Thomas Brisart's 2011 book, *Un art citoyen: Recherches sur l'orientalisation des artisanats en Grèce proto-archaïque*, exemplifies how scholarship has opened new fields of inquiry but remains in the chains of periodization. Consumption for him is no longer a quantitative approach but a qualitative examination of how Near Eastern models were transformed and manipulated to meet Greek needs in specific political and historical contexts.[178] Although he rejects the term "Orientalizing" for a period, he accepts it as a stylistic label that can be applied across Greece.[179] He explains the origins of Orientalizing art, which he defines as objects that make ostensible references to Near Eastern cultures but that are recognizably Greek, within the context of the emergence of the Greek city-state and its appropriation of traditional modes of elite status display, such as warfare. He excludes from the category of Protoattic any object that he does not deem Orientalizing.[180] Protoattic, in other words, is defined in purely Orientalizing terms: "What does this style consist of? We have said it, one of its major characteristics is its receptivity to oriental influences."[181] With a wave of the hand he thus dismisses the extensive discussions about what, exactly, these "Oriental" influences may have been, which preoccupied scholars for so long, and he also neglects the research that once suggested closer affinities with Mycenaean, Protocorinthian, or Cretan pottery. Although he recognizes the plurality of Near Eastern cultures that existed, he maintains that Greeks thought of all of them as rich and prosperous, thus justifying his essentializing deployment of the term "Orientalizing."[182] In his reading, style serves as a tool for the elaboration of social status. To perform this analysis in Attica, he discusses only the Kerameikos, where he claims that the majority of "chefs-d'oeuvre" (a very telling word) of Protoattic were found.[183] His survey of find contexts does not mention Phaleron.[184]

SHIFTING THE ORIENTALIZING PARADIGM

The turn to context and consumption has drawn welcome attention to the odd material record of seventh-century Athens. The turn also showcases how styles, motifs, and technologies can be redeployed in new contexts and to new ends. But the spectrum of Protoattic vase shapes, imagery, and contexts has been filtered out, and a thin corpus of Protoattic has been adopted, with objects marshaled for quantitative analysis, or with sustained discussion only of those high-quality objects that have figural imagery and elaborate scenes most amenable to interpretation.[185] Although many modern scholars reject the search for the artist and no longer lionize the Classical style, they have not turned back to the repertoire and contexts that once existed. Instead, they have accepted the corpus that, as we have seen, had become increasingly reified in large part through the search for the artist and "pure" Greek art, and they have accepted a periodization scheme that once was highly fraught. The change is evident in the fate of pottery once associated with Phaleron. The first vase published as Protoattic was from Phaleron (Figure 1.1), and vases from this cemetery so dominated research that Phaleron Ware or the Phaleron style was synonymous with Early Protoattic. Yet the pottery is absent from almost all later twentieth- and twenty-first-century studies, and by the time of Robert M. Cook's opus *Greek Painted Pottery*, now in its third edition, Phaleron appears only in the glossary, with the telling modifier, "Obsolete."[186] Protoattic has been equated with Orientalizing, and the period label does much of the interpretive work. Even when the word "Orientalizing" is not employed, an Orientalizing paradigm persists, with the Near East the primary source of influence and the pottery connected to the elite pursuit of status.

In some ways, we need to return to the eighteenth and nineteenth centuries, when there was greater openness to multiple influences on Greek art, matched with greater skepticism about the precise nature of that influence and the language we should use to describe it. We also need to put production and consumption in dialogue. To move forward, the next chapter looks at the broader Mediterranean context for Protoattic to decouple it from an exclusive connection with Near Eastern cultures and to show the variety of horizons that it could draw on. The subsequent chapters advocate for a return to a broader canon (chapters 4, 6) and, aware of the pitfalls of the early twentieth century, seek to acknowledge the role of the artist without lionizing the artist or privileging a Classical style (chapter 5). They also pursue a richer understanding of context than most consumption studies have sought. This entails two moves. Firstly, looking at more contexts, namely, all the cemeteries and burial plots of Attica (chapter 4), as well as evidence for commensal activity and religious rituals (chapter 5). Secondly, shifting focus away from the moment of final deposition to the interaction of people with objects across a longer life history of the object. This means moving beyond the typical focus of social history, with emphasis on the development of citizenship and the *polis* under the rubric of structuralist or quantitative approaches. Instead, with close attention to the vases themselves, I ask how pottery contributed to a fragmented social structure and how it shaped subjectivity in a variety of social settings. Posing the questions in this way allows a return to Phaleron and affords a space for the margins and the marginalized.

CHAPTER 3

The Place of Athens in the Mediterranean

Horizons and Networks

WHICH WAY IS THE ORIENT?

This chapter puts seventh-century Athens and Attica into their wider Mediterranean context through an examination of imports, exports, textual sources, and style. The period has been dominated by Orientalizing and the geographic orientation embedded within the word—which is one of the pitfalls of the label and why this book uses a more expansive definition of Protoattic. Even when scholars used to acknowledge a range of Near Eastern cultures, trying to pin down Urartian or Phoenician or North Syrian influences on Greek art, the geographic orientation of these influences still lay generally eastward. This eastern orientation persists. The way scholars thought these influences moved, through diffusion, with people and products flowing smoothly and steadily from the east toward the west, also persists. Martin West describes a similar model in the opening of his important book on the connection of Greek poetry to the east, writing that "culture, like all forms of gas, tends to spread out from where it is densest into adjacent areas where it is less dense."[1] More recently, Massimo Botto has penned an informative chapter on the Levant and Etruria but maintained the theoretical angle, as evident in the title: "The Diffusion of Near Eastern Cultures."[2] And the title of a landmark exhibit at the Metropolitan Museum is similarly revealing: *Assyria to Iberia*.[3] This east–west orientation is deeply engrained in popular thought—*ex oriente lux*, after all—and continues to inform interpretations, even as people have moved away from explanations based on diffusion.[4] When scholars use anthropological models of consumption or embrace a trans-Mediterranean scale, Near Eastern cultures are still the main engines of change in the Mediterranean, with the more advanced Neo-Assyrian empire and the more mobile Phoenicians propelling the movement and acquisition of goods and ideas.

To challenge conventional thinking on the place of Athens and Attica in the Mediterranean, with implications beyond that one region, I will deploy two concepts in this chapter: horizons and networks. I use "horizons" to refer to spaces at once physical and conceptual. "Horizons" are where the known and the unknown, the familiar and the unfamiliar meet. They are actual physical features of perceived landscapes and seascapes but mutable depending on place, time, and weather, and altogether dependent on individual perspective. To gaze at a horizon is, on the one hand, to stand in a place and to measure distance with the eye. On the other hand, it compels one to imagine what lies beyond, drawing on knowledge learned firsthand and from those people, things, and stories that have crossed it. These two types of horizons, the geographic and the cognitive, are interlinked, with material traveling across the horizon to inform conceptions of what lies beyond. In this chapter, I deploy the term to organize discussion of three separate directions people could experience and conceive first- or second-hand: the east, the west, and the past. Together they contributed to peoples' mental maps, shaping the ways they imagined the world. I examine trade routes, settlement patterns, the transfer of motifs and styles, and encounters with the past to chart these geographies. How did objects participate in the creation of these horizons, and how did changing horizons influence the production and consumption of objects and their styles?

The way in which Attica was linked up to the different horizons is perceptible through a network rather than a diffusion model.[5] The deployment of networks hardly needs justification any longer, and Mediterranean-wide perspectives and emphases on connectivity have provided an opening to network thinking.[6] The implicit role of the Near East as the main driver of change, however, has discouraged attempts at network thinking in this time period. In the discussion that follows, I suggest that they help reveal how the west rather than the east may be the proximate source of much of the materials and styles scholars associate with Orientalizing, disrupting the Orientalizing paradigm. One strength of network approaches is that they can reveal these types of unexpected trajectories and surprising connections. Networks also allow us to consider the different types of nodes and links that allowed for horizon crossing and to think through the interaction of people, objects, and places. Analysis will show the important role of sites at the macro- as well as the meso-scale (such as Corinth, a critical link for Athens to the rest of the Mediterranean) and help recover the agency of the subelite in cultural change. A more detailed discussion of the contexts, actors, and objects will take place in the subsequent chapters (chapters 4–6).

There are, of course, other horizons that I am not addressing. Most glaring in its absence is the northern horizon and possible connections of Attica with such areas as Thessaly, Macedonia, and Thrace. The Attic production and distribution of SOS amphoras suggest a close relationship with Euboia, a region that may have provided a conduit for Attic connections toward the north.[7] There are also links between Attica and Boiotia (e.g., Figure 5.7). I leave that horizon aside here because my main goal is to disorient the east–west paradigm, and because most traffic across the Mediterranean in the seventh century was moving between west and east, by sea rather than by land. As I will discuss in chapter 7, in the sixth century, the picture changed, with Athens taking advantage of its position between south and north to connect with northern mainland Greece, Asia Minor, and the Black Sea.

The location of Attica in the Mediterranean makes a network perspective essential, because it was not ideally positioned to receive considerable east–west flow (see the maps on frontmatter pages xii–xiv). The main east–west long-distance trade route would touch at Cyprus, Crete, Sicily, and Sardinia, as evident from the geographical position of those places as well as their material records. More localized routes could link up with this major artery, for example, routes linking Cyprus with Rhodes, Crete with the Cyclades, or Sardinia with Etruria. The situation had not changed much in the fourteenth century AD, as the records in Genoese ships' logs show.[8] Attica is not on the trans-Mediterranean route, not on the way to the primary metal-producing regions of Etruria and Iberia, nor even on a direct route to the mountains of Thrace. Attica certainly was not isolated. But when compared with the locations of such eighth- and seventh-century hubs as Rhodes, Cyprus, Crete, Corinth, or Euboia, it was marginal. Moreover, the dominant city of Athens was located in an inland position best suited for connections to the rest of Attica, not the outside world.[9] The regional nodes for external connectivity might have been the southeastern tip of Attica, at Sounion, and along the northeast coast, where the region was oriented toward the Euboian Gulf. Eventually, in the sixth century, Athens (and Attica) would occupy a prominent place in Mediterranean geography, able to take advantage of its position between Corinth and Euboia and between Aigina and Boiotia as those polities developed. In the seventh century, however, this was not yet the case, and Protoattic has only been found outside of Attica and Aigina in very small numbers.[10] It is all the more useful, therefore, to consider in what ways this place that lay outside of the main east–west routes may have linked up to a wider world. Why should there be any trace of "Orientalizing" in its art at all, and how might it have arrived?

The marginal place of Athens in the seventh-century Mediterranean is one reason why the focus specifically on the region of Attica and its connectivity is useful. Another is that the studies of the Mediterranean that emphasize connectivity tend to treat Greece as a single entity rather than as a collection of different cities and regions each possessing different horizons. From a bird's-eye perspective, one can write a relatively straightforward story about the dependence of Greek culture on

Near Eastern cultures. One could look at Greek myth and medicine and epic, even at the Greek alphabet itself, as many have done.[11] But from the perspective on the ground, as it were, it is abundantly clear that the experience of regions with Near Eastern cultures and the mechanisms of interaction differed. This has implications for how we use literary sources. We should not deploy a few canonical texts to generalize about connectivity for all of Greece, using the contours of the modern nation-state to set the geographic parameters. I will use some textual sources to help map out various horizons and networks, but it is objects that constitute our most reliable evidence for analysis at the regional level.

THE EASTERN HORIZON

The Levant and Egypt are the geographic regions most often associated with the Orientalizing phenomenon, even though Egypt more accurately lies to the southeast of Athens.[12] For the sake of clarity, discussion of Athenian contacts across this eastern horizon will be divided into three parts. Firstly, we will evaluate the import record at Athens from the eighth and seventh centuries. Secondly, we will look at exports, inscriptions, and historical sources indicating Greek activity in the Levant and Egypt and evaluate how Athens might fit into the picture. Thirdly, we will turn to the evidence presented by Attic style and iconography, again looking at both the eighth and seventh centuries. By weighing these three categories of evidence, we can evaluate the quantity and quality of links between Athens and the Near East, which will serve as a basis for comparison with connectivity with the west and with the past, treated in the next sections. Who sailed across the eastern horizon, and to what end? What types of goods were imported and exported, and how were they used? Were the connections pervasive and lasting or more sporadic and fleeting? As mentioned, the evidence from material culture is more precise than the conclusions that can be drawn from texts. In a separate section below, I address Homer, but other authors who have been adduced to discuss Greek relations with the Near East, such as Sappho, Xenophanes, and Phocylides, are from the late seventh or sixth century, and are better treated as part of a separate phenomenon that relates specifically to Lydia (see further chapter 6, on the symposium), rather than synchronically.

There are some Near Eastern imports to Athens in the Late Geometric period, mostly figurines and amulets from graves.[13] Five bronze artifacts from the Acropolis may have been deposited in the eighth century, but the stylistic dating is not close and contexts do not help.[14] The presence of Near Eastern craftsmen or of Greeks who trained with them is suggested by ivory and gold objects in Athens made in a mixed style.[15] These foreign materials required skills more likely systematically learned firsthand rather than imitated, but they were not produced in large numbers. Outside of Athens, at Sounion, a Levantine bronze pendant of the storm god,[16] scarabs from Rhodes and the Nile delta, Egyptian figurines and amulets, two Lyre-Player seals, and other gems and seals were deposited.[17]

In the seventh century, Near Eastern imports to Athens do not increase notably. There are three bronze bowls, one belt, and one ivory figurine from the Kerameikos (Figure 4.17) and, from the Acropolis, one Cypriot bronze candelabrum, one ivory figurine, and one Egyptian figurine of Harpokrates.[18] Imports to the Acropolis from Crete, which could be a source of "Orientalizing" art, consist of a stand and two bronze figurines.[19] Outside of Athens, "Egyptian" faience amulets and figurines from Sounion appear in the seventh century (and into the sixth century), but many of them are actually Greek.[20]

Let us turn to exports.[21] Because of the difficulty in recovering ethnicity in the archaeological record, and because Athenians may well have joined other Greeks on expeditions, my discussion here is not limited to Attic activity. This is not the place to enter into the vexed question of how to use material culture to identify Greeks,[22] but a balanced review of the evidence suggests that even a generous interpretation of the archaeological and historical material only concedes a few Greek adventurers, traders, and mercenaries and a few small clusters of settlers in the Levant in the seventh century.[23] Al Mina is the exception in the regional record.[24] Yet even if this site were an enclave of settled Greek traders, activity here was sanctioned—and simultaneously restricted—by the local political structure. Apart from Al Mina, there may be some Greek presence in Syria at Tell Tayinat (from the late ninth century), Tell Sukas (from ca. 670), and perhaps at Ras el-Bassit (from the late eighth century) and Tabbat el-Hammam (from ca. 700). In Cilicia, too, there may be Greek presence at Tarsus and Mersin from the early seventh century. In the southern Levant, there is evidence of mercenary activity at a few sites in the seventh century (especially Tel Kabri, Mesad Hashavyahu, and Ashkelon), probably more specifically the late seventh century. Likewise from the late seventh century, an Ionian bronze shield and greave at Carchemish may have belonged to a mercenary in Necho II's army, which occupied the city in 605.[25]

The historical record provides some additional evidence that can supplement this archaeological picture.[26] Neo-Assyrian documents mention raids on the Phoenician coast as early as the 740s by Ionians, a broad ethnic category that could include Dorians of Rhodes and non-Greeks of Anatolia. They appear again in Sargon II's annals, which record Neo-Assyrian success over the Ionians off the coasts of Cilicia and Phoenicia in 715. For the early seventh century, a Hellenistic source mentions that Sennacherib defeated Ionian warships. For the late seventh century, Alcaeus records that his brother Antimenidas served as a mercenary in the Babylonian army. Until the late seventh century, therefore, Greek settlement and mercenary and pirate activity in the Levant is present but limited.[27]

Greek mercenaries may have been more numerous in Egypt.[28] Psammetichos (r. 664–610) employed Ionians and Carians to seize power and then settled them in a region on the Nile delta called "The Camps" (*Stratopeda*).[29] According to Herodotus, they were engaged in plundering before they chanced to enter mercenary employment, but Diodorus instead writes that Psammetichos enjoyed trade connections with Phoenicians and Greeks and intentionally summoned Carians and Ionians

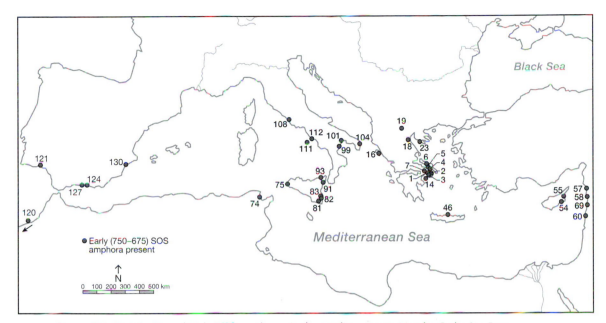

Figure 3.1. Distribution of early SOS amphoras in the Mediterranean. Map by Catherine Pratt. From Pratt 2015, reproduced with permission. Numbers refer to her catalog.

as mercenaries. Other historical testimony for mercenary activity in Egypt is provided by Prism A (or the so-called Rassam Prism) of the Assyrian king Assurbanipal, which states that king Gyges of Lydia sent military aid to Psammetichos, which may have included Greeks from Asia Minor.[30]

It is difficult to evaluate the numbers of mercenaries active in Egypt and the possible consequences for Greco-Egyptian relations.[31] On the one hand, Diodorus emphasizes Psammetichos's welcome of foreigners and notes that he opened emporia, provided security, and made alliances with Athens and other Greek cities.[32] On the other hand, he qualifies the welcome as "unprecedented," suggesting that Egypt had been difficult for Greeks to penetrate, and it is possible that such sociopolitical conditions did not change rapidly. It seems significant that the Greek mercenaries were settled in a locale, "The Camps," rather than left to integrate more broadly and widely into society. Trade activity similarly seems to have been controlled. The emporion at Naukratis is an important case, where Greek material first appears late during Psammetichos's reign, and where subsequently Amasis granted land to Greeks for settlement, trade, and worship.[33] The site certainly facilitated Greek and Egyptian interaction, and there are signs of cohabitation, but since all trade had to move through Naukratis, the Egyptians also were able to use the site to control and limit Greek access.[34] Greek pottery appears at many other sites in Egypt but differs in number and kind.[35] At Saqqara, however, there are gravestones for Carians as early as the seventh century, perhaps indicating mercenaries.[36] Starting in the seventh century, there are also dedications of Egyptian bronze statuettes at Egyptian temples bearing Carian and Greek inscriptions.[37] In balance, contact between

Figure 3.2. Tondo of an Attic Late Geometric shallow bowl. Athens, National Museum 784. Photo George Fafalis. Copyright © Hellenic Ministry of Culture and Sports / Archaeological Receipts Fund.

Figure 3.3. Tondo of an Attic Late Geometric shallow bowl. Edinburgh, National Museum of Scotland 1956.422. Photo copyright Edinburgh, National Museum of Scotland.

Greece and Egypt once again appears to be somewhat limited overall but from a comparative perspective more intense than Greek activity in the Levant. It may only have taken off in the late seventh century; there are no Greek ceramics in Egypt necessarily earlier than the last quarter of the seventh century.[38]

Judging the evidence for Greek links with the Near East in the seventh century weak, Alexander Fantalkin provocatively proposed that instead of an Orientalizing revolution, a "Great Divide" lay between mainland Greece and the Levant.[39] He argued that Tiglath-Pileser III's annexation of the Syro-Anatolian city-state Patina/Unqi in 738/7 marked a return of Neo-Assyrian hegemony to the littoral and a tight control of economic markets and trade routes in the Levant. The concept of a "Great Divide," however, seems to overstate the case, for the evidence summarized above does suggest some connections between Greeks and Near Eastern communities, particularly if one includes Cilicia and Egypt in the analysis. Although both are excluded from Fantalkin's model, they are routinely part of treatments of the eastern Mediterranean in this period. But Fantalkin is probably correct to draw attention to the fact that the extent of connectivity is more limited than "Orientalizing" as a period label implies. The social and political conditions of Neo-Assyrian—and one should add Egyptian—power constrained as much as they enabled trade and movement.

Figure 3.4. Protoattic oinochoe attributed to the Workshop of the Ram Jug Painter, from the Tholos cemetery. Athens, Agora P 4611. Photo courtesy of the American School of Classical Studies at Athens: Agora Excavations.

The engagement more specifically of Attica with the eastern Mediterranean was even more slight, with a drop in connectivity from the eighth into the seventh centuries suggested by both imports and exports. A 1988 study of Attic fine-ware pottery on Cyprus, for example, documented twenty-five pieces from Middle Geometric and only three from Late Geometric, with none from the seventh century.[40] A 2003 study of pottery distribution in the Levant, omitting Al Mina and the sites in the Amuq plain, documented eight and a possible further two vases from Attic Middle Geometric and only one possible fragment from Late Geometric.[41] I know of no seventh-century Attic fine ware from the Levant. The closest one gets is the New York Nessos Amphora, allegedly acquired in Smyrna (Figure 1.5). The pattern repeats with the distribution of Attic SOS amphoras (Figure 1.7). Catherine Pratt has recently gathered the material and demonstrated that the early group, dating

Figure 3.5. Protoattic amphora attributed to the Workshop of the Würzburg Group. Boulder, Colorado, University Museum 22317. Photo copyright Boulder, Colorado, University Museum.

Figure 3.6. Levantine ivory vessel, late 2nd–early 1st millennium BC. New York, Metropolitan Museum of Art 50.198.2. Purchase, Joseph Pulitzer Bequest, 1950.

from the mid-eighth- to the mid-seventh-century BC, is only attested at two sites in Cyprus and four in the Levant (Figure 3.1).[42] There are none from Egypt. Apart from Diodorus's mention of an alliance, there is no evidence of direct interaction between Athens and Egypt in the seventh century.

Iconography and style complete this picture drawn on the basis of the record of imports and exports and the historical testimony. For Late Geometric art, subject matter such as animal friezes, "rattle players," the sacred tree, exotic animals like sphinxes, the *prothesis* (laying out of the dead), and battle scenes have been traced to the Near East.[43] Shapes like the dinos drew on a Near Eastern repertoire as well. The closest parallels between Attic Geometric art and the Near East are a series of Late

Geometric shallow terra-cotta bowls that imitate in form, composition, and iconography Cypro-Phoenician metal bowls (Figures 3.2–3.3).[44] Yet the production of these bowls actually ceases in the seventh century. This cesura seems symptomatic of the flight of other Near Eastern elements from the repertoire. The "rattle players" disappear, too, as do many of the battle scenes and, with a few exceptions, all of the *prothesis* scenes. Gold bands originally made in an "Orientalizing" style become over the course of the eighth century increasingly Geometric, another sign of the shift.[45]

In comparison to Late Geometric, Protoattic bears fewer direct traces of Near Eastern pedigree. Such exotic creatures as sphinxes recall Levantine and Neo-Assyrian art (Figure 3.4), but it is difficult to prove a direct link even for them.[46] Similarly, vegetal motifs abound in variety and may have been drawn from circulating Near Eastern objects such as ivories, but it is hard to find a clear prototype. Other typical Levantine iconography is simply absent from Protoattic vases, such as the Mistress of Animals.[47] Any of the typical "Orientalizing" motifs, as we will see, could arrive through different routes than an east–west trajectory; dependence must be demonstrated rather

Figure 3.7. Late Geometric krater from Cyprus by the (Euboian) Cesnola Painter. New York, Metropolitan Museum of Art 74.51.965. The Cesnola Collection, Purchased by subscription, 1874–76.

than assumed. For example, the rampant goat is a motif that appears in Protoattic art (Figure 3.5) and that has parallels in the Levant (Figure 3.6), and it would be classified as "Orientalizing."[48] But it also was a favorite subject of the Late Geometric Cesnola Painter, a Euboian (it seems) whose work circulated widely (Figure 3.7, this example found in Cyprus), and it was a not uncommon motif in southern Italy.[49] How do we know if the motif came to Athens in the seventh century via Italy or Euboia, or via the Levant? In cases like this, the ultimate origin of an iconographic motif may be meaningless, its proximate origin (the Cyclades, Rhodes, Euboia, Corinth, and such) more significant for the people who looked at

Figure 3.8. Protoattic standed bowl from Kerameikos funeral trench (Opferrinne) γ, attributed to the Painter of Opferrinne γ II. Athens, Kerameikos 138. Photo courtesy of the Deutsches Archäologisches Institut, Athens (DAI-ATH-Kerameikos-02696).

the images and used the objects. When the product is Greek and the connections to Near Eastern models faint, and when even the existence of those models in Athens is in doubt, we should be careful to presume that someone using an object we have categorized as "Orientalizing" actually intended it to be seen as such.

In comparison to iconography, seventh-century vase *shapes* may preserve more direct traces of influence from the Near East, in particular the oinochoe with tapering neck (often called a Phaleron oinochoe) (Figures 1.6, 2.3, 2.13, 4.22–4.25), which has parallels in Phoenician pottery (Figure 4.37), vases with lotus bud attachments (Figure 3.8), and dinoi (Figure 5.4).[50] But here, too, the parallels should not be pressed too hard. Like the iconographic motifs, they could arrive from a secondary origin.

Gathered together, the archaeological and historical data show surprisingly little evidence for deep and sustained interaction between Greece and the Levant and Egypt in the seventh century, and even less when we look at Attica in particular. In comparison with the eighth century, there is a drop in connectivity with the Levant, and while Egypt was opening for opportunities, particularly for mercenaries, activity at the outset was limited. In comparison with the sixth century, there was also little engagement with the coast of west Anatolia. At those sites where Greek trading focused—Al Mina and Naukratis—commerce was controlled and restricted, and the main participants among Greeks were Corinthians and East Greeks. This commercial exchange certainly opened pathways, but it did not lead to a flood of Near Eastern imports to Athens, and any dedications of returning mercenaries were heterogeneous and unsystematic and generally made at sites outside of Attica.[51] The quantity and quality of contact with the eastern Mediterranean contrasts with the interaction Greeks, including Athenians, experienced and imagined in the western Mediterranean, to which we now turn.

THE WESTERN HORIZON

The main source of material evidence for Athenian participation in trade networks are SOS amphoras, and their distribution pattern leads us away from the east and toward the west, especially Sicily and Italy (Figures 3.1, 3.9). Although they were not necessarily carried by Athenians, they reveal ways in which Attica connected to wider networks. According to Pratt's valuable analysis, thirteen sites in Sicily and Italy imported the early amphora type, with dense concentrations at Pithekoussai, Cerveteri, and Megara Hyblaia.[52] The numbers eclipse the eastern distribution and urge us to consider the ways in which Athens may have been connected to western networks of trade and communication that centered on Sicily and Italy. Here Greek interaction differed in both degree and kind from Greek experience with east Mediterranean peoples and cultures. People from many regions of Greece traveled west in considerable number, and many of them permanently settled.[53] Although the term "colonization," which is used to describe this movement, has been justly criticized for its anachronism and its implicit notions of formal organization and Greek cultural superiority, the label provides a useful qualitative contrast with Greek activity in the eastern Mediterranean, where engagement and interaction were more limited and restricted. In many groups, large and small, Greeks traveled to Sicily and Italy in search of land, profit, and opportunity, and they interacted extensively and intimately with one another and with the local populations. In trading goods, building cities, establishing sanctuaries, burying their dead, and creating objects, they brought new ideas and practices and also adapted to, learned from, and blended with local traditions.

Athens did not formally partake in this phase of colonization (I maintain the word for the sake of convenience and contrast). As the distribution of SOS amphoras suggests, however, there are some indications of Attic engagement with the

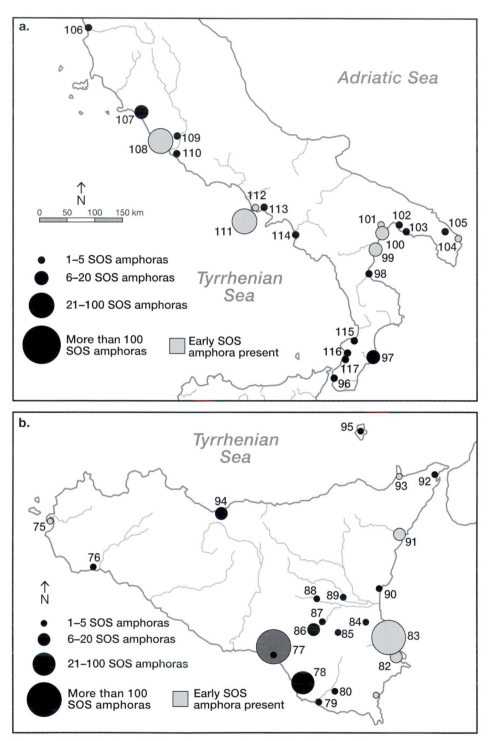

Figure 3.9. Distribution of SOS amphoras in Italy and Sicily. Map by Catherine Pratt. From Pratt 2015, reproduced with permission. Numbers refer to catalog.

westward circulation of people and goods. And according to one ancient source (Ephoros), Theokles, the founder of Naxos, the first Greek colony in Sicily, was an Athenian.[54] The fourth-century historian tells us that Theokles could not persuade Athenians to join him, so he led Chalkidians and Cycladic Naxians and some Dorians including Megarians. From Naxos, Theokles went on to found two more colonies: Leontini and Catana. The pro-Athenian Ephoros should perhaps not be trusted, but the composite nature of colonial expeditions could allow for some degree of Athenian participation. Trade, too, was a way for the city to engage, and the distribution of fine-ware ceramics complements the evidence of the SOS amphoras with a quantity unmatched in the Levant and Egypt. The earliest Attic and Atticizing fine-ware ceramics are Middle Geometric II–Late Geometric I skyphoi at Pontecagnano, Cumae, Capua, Veii, and Tarquinia, and also a jug and a pyxis from Veii.[55] Slightly later, the Late Geometric IIb Workshop of Athens 897 made a spouted krater found at Ortygia (in Syracuse), a neck-handled amphora from Pithekoussai, and an oinochoe from a grave at Canale (possibly produced locally).[56] Also from Canale is an amphora with a deer looking backward, with Attic parallels.[57] At Megara Hyblaia, spouted kraters or louteria from domestic contexts and dating from the second half of the eighth into the second half of the seventh centuries were both imported from Athens and produced locally in shapes and styles so close to Attic that they suggest the movement of artists.[58] Finally, a vase fragment on display in the Museo Archeologico Regionale Paolo Orsi (Syracuse) from the railway excavations appears to be Attic Late Geometric II, but it may also be a local production.[59]

There is compelling evidence for the movement of Attic artists, at the Timpone della Motta at Francavilla Marittima. In particular, the iconography and style of a Late Geometric stamnoid pyxis, now in a private collection, has very close parallels with Attic workshops (Figure 3.10).[60] On one side, women bring a jug and drinking cup to an enthroned goddess (?), while on the other, a citharoed accompanies helmeted men with raised hands. A fragment of the lid preserves a man with a sword holding a woman's hand, perhaps dancing. Once considered Attic, Attic provincial, or Boiotian, now the painter is thought to be a person with Athenian training located in Calabria, who has been dubbed either the Francavilla Painter or the Master of the Group of the Basel/Toledo Kraters. At Timpone della Motta, the stamnoid pyxis was dedicated in a sacred context along with other wares made by immigrant artists beginning in the second quarter of the eighth century, predominantly Euboian, working near the preexisting sanctuary.[61] The iconography conforms to the local cultic context, where hydriskai and small cups were deposited in great quantity, while the style finds undeniable Attic parallels, evident through a comparison with the tondo of the cup in figure 3.2. The sanctuary context demonstrates the mobility of Greek artisans and their integration into preexisting markets and their response to local cult needs.

Figure 3.10. Late Geometric pyxis from Timpone della Motta at Francavilla Marittima, by an Attic painter or a painter with strong Attic connections, dubbed the Francavilla Painter or the Master of the Group of the Basel/Toledo Kraters. Photo John Blazejewski / Princeton University, after Denoyelle and Iozzo, 2009, 42, fig. 23.

Literary sources support this view of mobility. In particular, Pliny states that the Bacchiad Demaratus, the father of the future king of Rome, Tarquinius Priscus, fled his Corinthian homeland for Italy accompanied by three artists: Eucheir, Diopos, and Eugrammos.[62] The context of the passage seems to relate to the introduction of terra-cotta (*plastice*) to Italy, while elsewhere, Pliny (allegedly following Aristotle) attributes to a Eucheir (not necessarily the same person) the invention of painting in Greece.[63] These stories may be apocryphal, yet they still preserve grains of truth, especially the possibility that artists could travel. For Demaratus, political events compelled flight, but one can imagine many other scenarios in which artists would migrate, with or without such an elite patron. Early Iron Age Greece lacked the palatial power structures that kept artists tied to a patronage system, and while some vase-painters may have been enslaved persons, the general picture is one of greater regional mobility than artistic production on estates. New foundations overseas could be appealing, with their markets and opportunities. Clay was relatively plentiful in the Mediterranean, and a move did not require painter or potter to bring a large array of resources or materials. On site, he would need a kiln, but it might be small in scale. He could expect to find a welcome in settlements for which ceramics were indispensable to both urban and rural life. The ceramicist was as necessary to new foundations as the carpenter or the priest.

Excavations at Incoronata near Metaponto have provided startling new data on the mobility of Greek, including Attic, craftsmen.[64] Known for many years, the rich deposits of ceramics from Incoronata once were associated with domestic or trading activity divided into two distinct stratigraphic phases: a first, pre-Greek phase, violently replaced in the early seventh century by a second, Greek phase of occupation. More recent excavations by the University of Rennes, however, have forced a revision of this stark picture. Indigenous activity at the site began in the late ninth century, and Greek imports appeared in the eighth century, without any signs of violence. In the late eighth and seventh centuries, the production of local Greek-style pottery, so-called colonial ware, took place alongside production in more indigenous styles. Inscriptions on pots as well as style and technique point to the presence of Greek craftsmen. As at Timpone della Motta, ritual contexts were a draw for them. Ceramic production took place close to an apsidal building that was a ritual center or home of a local leader, and which was demolished or dismantled in the late seventh or early sixth century. A focal point of ritual was none other than the base of an Attic SOS amphora set in the ground of the apsidal structure to receive libations.

Among the many pieces of "colonial ware" at the site, one merits particular scrutiny. In one of the pits with ritual destruction debris were found a dinos with the earliest depiction of Bellerophon fighting the Chimera (Figures 3.11, 3.12).[65] Commentators agree that the clay is local, but the painting has been attributed to various Attic artists: the Analatos Painter, the Checkerboard Painter, or the Group of the Thebes Louterion. The unmistakable Protoattic aspects include the profile of Bellerophon's face; the dot filler for his cloak and the lion's muzzle; the lion's stance, with lolling tongue and raised paw; the central palmette and volute ornament; and the mixture of silhouette, outline, and incision. Other elements of the vase, however, conform more closely to the local context. The dinos shape enjoyed greater popularity in Italian contexts than in Greece, and the composition of Bellerophon and the Chimera recalls the heraldic horses on local wares. The sparse use of the filling ornament and the employment of the concave triangle on the sides also are indigenous characteristics. In sum, this seems to be a vessel produced locally but made by an Athenian or someone very close to an Athenian, who had a solid grasp of the local Oinotrian market. It is testimony that at Incoronata, as at Francavilla Marittima, the Greek craftsmen included Athenians, or at the very least persons

Figure 3.11. Protoattic dinos from Metoponto, variously attributed to the Analatos Painter, the Checkerboard Painter, or the Group of the Thebes Louterion. Metaponto 298.978.9. Photo James Glazier.

with very strong connections to Athenian modes of production, who responded to local demands and cultural contexts.[66] It might be tempting to designate such a vessel a "hybrid," but this word implies that elements can be traced back to two "pure" parents, whereas Protoattic was itself highly eclectic (as we will see), and ultimately, the term creates more problems than it solves.

Figure 3.12. Detail of Figure 3.11. Photo James Glazier.

Other objects from Italy, particularly Etruria, suggest that a cross-cultural artistic dynamic was not unusual and that Athens had some role to play.[67] Marina Martelli has emphasized the Attic side of the prolific Narce Painter, active in Etruria in the early seventh century.[68] For example, compare the checkerboard lozenge, outline crosses, and lion on a vase now in Budapest with Attic production (Figure 3.13, Plate 5).[69] The birds and horses, however, as well as the vase shape and the prevalence of silhouette technique, concede to local taste. More distant iconographically from Attic sources, but with a shared interest in figuration, in vivid energetic images, and in monumentality, are the large vases by the prolific Painter of the Cranes (Figure 3.14) and the remarkable Heptachord Painter (Figure 3.15).[70]

Finally, there are indisputable Attic elements in the famous Aristonothos Krater, which shows on one side the blinding of Polyphemus by Odysseus and his companions and on the other a battle between Greeks and Etruscans (on the basis of their ship types) (Figure 3.16, Plate 6).[71] The profiles of the figures, the form of their limbs, and the use of black and white for the large rosette are some of the Attic characteristics, while the vase shape and much of the ornament, such as the rays, respond to the local context. The vase supplies one of the earliest artist signatures, "Aristonothos epoiesen," which may be translated, "the noble bastard made it." Thus both name and style declare a mixed pedigree. Might Aristonothos have been the son of an Athenian and a native Italian? We can only speculate, but it is certainly interesting that one of the earliest Greek signatures features so prominently on a vase of heterogenous style, bearing scenes of cross-cultural contact and deposited in an Etruscan cemetery. We will return to the figure of the artist in chapter 5.

Figure 3.13. Italian olla attributed to the Narce Painter, 7th century BC. Budapest, Szépművészeti Múzeum. Photo © László Mátyus, Museum of Fine Arts, Budapest.

Aristonothos's path to Italy may have been very different from the route traveled by the craftsmen who allegedly accompanied Demaratus, and his name as well as the mixed styles in figures 3.10–3.16 question the validity of applying ethnic labels to artists at all. Yet the search for ethnic origins of overseas products has a long history with implications for how pottery in the west has been treated in scholarship. Alan Blakeway in two landmark articles in the 1930s noted the variety of dynamics at work and tried to identify four classes of pottery: "Imported Geometric"; "Local Geometric pottery made and painted by Greek craftsmen"; "Local Geometric pottery made by locals, imitating Greek models both in shape and in decoration"; and "Local Geometric pottery of Barbarian shape and workmanship, but with painted decoration derived, but not strictly copied, from Greek Geometric designs."[72] But often it is not evident to which category a piece of "colonial ware" belongs, and distinctions should not be pressed too hard, as a name like "Aristonothos" suggests. Objects like the pyxis from Timpone della Motta, the dinos from Metaponto, and the Aristonothos Krater seem inconceivable from artists who did not reside at some point in Athens, while someone like the Narce Painter may have looked closely at Attic drawing. But in all cases, our evidence is limited. More importantly, attempting to draw a sharp distinction between Greek and indigenous overlooks the porosity between the two categories and can lead to false dichotomies. Blakeway's use of the word "Barbarian" is characteristic of the ways in which Italy was conceived as a backward region awaiting the enlightenment of Hellenization. Scholars now instead recognize the strength and vibrancy of the local communities throughout Italy and Sicily, which were experiencing state formation

Figure 3.14. Italian amphora attributed to the Painter of the Cranes. Cerveteri 105391. Photo John Blazejewski / Princeton University, after Martelli, 1987a, 86, fig. 33.

Figure 3.15. Italian biconical krater by the Heptachord Painter. Museo Archeologico Nazionale di Tarquinia 127942. Photo Mauro Benedetti © MIBACT. Museo Nazionale Etrusco di Villa Giulia.

and social stratification long before Greeks arrived.[73] Local communities possessed sophisticated metalworking skills, complex mortuary practices, and strong connections with one another and with Near Eastern communities; a link between Villanovans and Sardinia was particularly robust already in the Early Iron Age.[74] As the ritual contexts at Timpone della Motta and Incoronata demonstrate, local communities were informed and active consumers of Greek products, and Greek artists had to adapt and conform to local needs and desires, integrating their wares into interconnected markets. While most scholarship no longer discusses a straightforward Hellenization of the West, the field of Greek archaeology has been slower to recognize overseas art production as a subject of worthwhile inquiry, often relegating it to the category of the provincial. Thomas James Dunbabin did not think there was any colonial pottery production.[75] Now it has been identified, but if it is included in textbooks, it is discussed as an aberration and deviation from allegedly pure Greek norms; Blakeway's "Barbarians" lurk.[76]

If we leave anachronistic notions of barbarians behind, Italy and Sicily emerge as dynamic places of cross-cultural interaction and vibrant artistic production and innovation.[77] A painter at Incoronata, for example, encountered local Oinotrian pottery in addition to imports from Corinth, the Cyclades, and East Greece as well as local production by potters hailing from different cities in Greece and Italy. Traveling

Figure 3.16. Krater from Etruria signed by Aristonothos. Rome, Musei Capitolini 172. Photo courtesy of the museum.

Figure 3.17. "Colonial-style" vase made in Megara Hyblaia and found at Selinus. Paris, Musée du Louvre CA 3837. Photo © RMN-Grand Palais / Art Resource, NY.

artists looked to old and new models for inspiration as they adapted their production for new clientele and uses. The movement of people, goods, and ideas fomented a stimulating environment for artistic and cultural growth. The results, here and elsewhere in Italy and Sicily, were eclectic. "Colonial ware"—made at Taranto, Incoronata/Metaponto, Siris, Croton, Sibaris, Megara Hyblaia (Figure 3.17), Syracuse (Figure 3.18), Gela, Leontini, and more—betrays a variety of influences: Euboian (particularly dominant in the eighth century), Corinthian, Cycladic, East

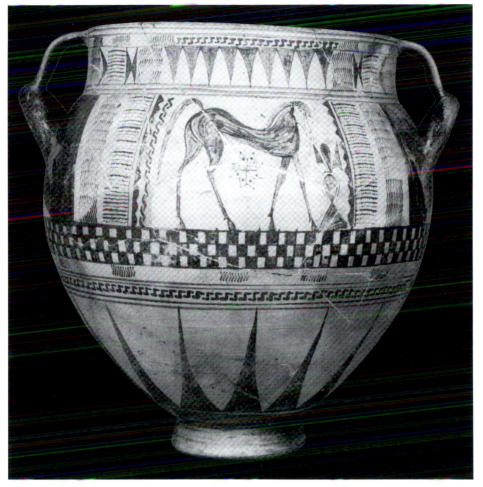

Figure 3.18. "Colonial-style" krater from Syracuse in an Argive style. Syracuse, Museo Archeologico Regionale Paolo Orsi 13893. Photo John Blazejewski / Princeton University, after Denoyelle and Iozzo 2009, 55, fig. 54.

Greek, Argive, and Attic.[78] The products, never very numerous, stand out from indigenous wares in the use of the potter's wheel, the presence of figuration, and the application of polychromy. In the creation of this eclectic style, the role of Athenian artists and objects cannot be excluded.[79]

THE HORIZON OF ANTIQUITY

Any effort to delineate the physical and conceptual horizons operative in the seventh century needs to move beyond Cartesian frameworks of space and to evaluate interaction with the past, too. For seventh-century Athenians, Bronze Age and Early Iron Age structures and tumuli were still visible, while graves and other subterranean features lurked below their feet. Remains of the past might be uncovered with a plow or unearthed when digging foundations, encountered in a home, sanctuary, or rural landscape. The past was inescapable. Interest in this horizon grew in the second half of the eighth century, particularly in Attica. Much of the activity took place at tombs, which have been the subject of the most scholarly study, in part because of their possible connection to epic heroes. In this chapter, however, tomb cult is treated as one component of a broader encounter with the material remains of the past.

The clearest example of tomb cult in Attica is at Menidi (ancient Acharnai), where offerings were made in the dromos of a Late Helladic IIIA2 or Late Helladic IIIB tholos beginning in Late Geometric II and continuing into the fifth century.[80] There was also tomb cult at Thorikos. A Late Helladic IIB oval tholos tomb received cult activity inside and outside the grave from the seventh into the fifth centuries.[81] At a smaller scale, a stone slab associated with the dromos of a Mycenaean grave at Aliki Glyphada had evidence of burning and was associated with a Late Geometric II lidded pyxis.[82]

Mere disturbance of earlier tombs seems to have been more common than such overt cult activity, and intrusions into earlier tombs began before the Late Geometric period. In the agora, Protogeometric and Middle Geometric tombs were dug into the dromoi of Mycenaean chamber tombs, and a Geometric ash urn was placed in the Bronze Age Tomb of the Niches.[83] Less respectfully, on Dimitrakopoulou Street (south of the Acropolis) a Mycenaean chamber tomb was looted in the Geometric period.[84]

More often, however, tombs were respected and left inviolate, implying that they were visible or marked.[85] Surveying the evidence for Bronze Age and Early Iron Age tombs in the agora, John Papadopoulos surmised that by the Late Geometric period the north slope of the Areopagus had become so crowded with burials that mortuary activity moved west.[86] The shift implies that buriers were aware of the remains of the past and generally respectful of the dead, even if they did not usually engage in such cult activity as we see at Menidi.

On some occasions, however, reverence for the past took a more monumental and built form. The evidence is never straightforward and has received numerous interpretations.[87] At the Academy to the northwest of Athens, a seven-room Late Geometric house (possibly used into the early seventh century) contained ash deposits that used to be interpreted as sacrificial remains. Close to the house lay an Early Helladic apsidal building, and 150 m from the apsidal building was a Protogeometric–Early or Middle Geometric votive deposit. Geometric and seventh-century cult activity in the house may have been related to the imagined inhabitant of the apsidal building (the hero Akademos?) or to Late Geometric and Archaic graves in the vicinity.[88] A recent excavation along with close examination of old excavation diaries, however, have suggested that the cult activity was actually domestic.[89] Another so-called sacred house in Athens has also received attention. In the agora, an oval structure 5 × 11 m was built in the Late Geometric period over four Early Geometric and Middle Geometric graves, with additional Middle Geometric graves in the vicinity.[90] It is not clear if the structure was intended for domestic or cult activity, but subsequently Protoattic ceramics, including votives, were deposited against the outer wall of the house. Other seventh-century cult activity in the area may have focused on the Late Geometric structure, the underlying tombs, or the other tombs in the vicinity.

Interaction with the tombs of the long-departed occurred elsewhere in Attica, too. At Eleusis, a Geometric enclosure about 9 × 12 m was placed over and around 8.5 Middle Helladic–Late Helladic cist tombs.[91] There are no signs of votives or cult activity to support George Mylonas's association of the enclosure with the Heroön of the Seven Against Thebes, but the structure does represent a tangible connection with the remote past. Nearby, Mycenean chamber tombs were disturbed and reused, and in at least one case there is clear evidence for respect for the dead: in the seventh century, a child burial in a pithos intruded on a Middle Helladic adult inhumation, and it appears that the buriers reassembled the disturbed cranium, deposited an oinochoe, and changed the direction of their trench.[92] Respect for the more recent dead is manifest in a series of built structures at Eleusis, which once again raise the issue of the "Sacred House."[93] Outside of the Late Classical temenos, a late eighth-century male inhumation lay under a tumulus in front of the porch of a megaron (10 × 14.5 m) of similar date. Between the two were the remains of successive offering pyres with vases, ashes, bones, and shell. The megaron seems to have gone out of use in the late eighth or early seventh century, replaced by a house-like structure, which included extensive traces of ritual activity and was used until the end of the seventh century. In the early sixth century, a naiskos followed by an altar were placed over both the "house" and the tumulus, and later in the Archaic period, a peribolos enclosed all the remains, with a poros temple (possibly from the Classical period) placed on top of the naiskos. The continuity in cult activity suggests a veneration for the deceased under the tumulus.

Regular burial of the dead was a more mundane manifestation of a similar phenomenon of temporal horizon crossing as people went to cemeteries and saw the tombs of their family members and others and participated in acts of remembrance. Grave markers stood as reminders of departed persons. Libations to the dead, such as those afforded by holes in the bottom of Geometric grave markers, allowed mourners to access in some way the deceased. Presumably many graves were untended over the decades and centuries, and their neglect served as stark reminders of the passing of time and the gulf separating past and present. Tombs also might show the passage of time through their use of styles that were now out of fashion.

From the random encounter with earlier remains to monumental and ritual engagement with the dead of the recent and distant past, interaction with antiquity occurred after a hiatus with the Bronze Age. With the exception of the gradual evolution of vase shapes, there is little evidence for continuity in material culture from the Bronze Age through the Protoarchaic period. Instead, the eighth and seventh centuries witness the *reuse* of objects, the *revival* of shapes, and a *reawakened interest* in similar iconography and style. Each of these components of the Early Iron Age orientation toward the past may be documented in the material record.

At Athens, reuse included spaces such as the Menidi tomb as well as objects, like Middle Helladic objects placed in a Late Geometric grave or a Mycenaean figurine placed in a seventh-century deposit.[94] The reused antiques were not always so precious. In the agora, six Mycenaean goblet stems were cut down for use as simple bobbins.[95] The process of revival affected above all vase shapes, especially seventh-century cups and Geometric spouted bowls (or louteria), both looking back to the Mycenaean period.[96] It is interesting that many of the cups are relatively simple, sub-Geometric cups (e.g., Figures 6.14, 6.18, Plate 15), although of course there may have been other revivals in metal that do not survive.

Evaluating a reawakened interest in style and iconography is more difficult. When Mycenaean and Minoan art were first identified, strong similarities were noted between Bronze Age and so-called Orientalizing art, and the Bronze Age was marshaled to dispel any foreign influences on Protoarchaic Greek art (chapter 2). Now there is much more caution. Some scholars, most notably Jack Leonard Benson, advocate for close formal parallels between Bronze Age and Geometric and seventh-century art and for continuity in artistic and ritual traditions.[97] But most of the shared motifs have closer parallels with Near Eastern or other regional Greek iconographies than Mycenaean, and the lack of a clear connection contrasts with the evident debt of Cretan production to Minoan art.[98] There may have been an occasional point of contact, but it is difficult to maintain that the Bronze Age was a major source of inspiration for the new seventh-century Attic style.

A more pronounced impact of the Bronze Age may be seen in subject matter. The encounter with ruins, the veneration of the dead, and the circulation of stories likely contributed to the heroic imagery that characterizes much of Late Geometric art, with its warfare and ships and processions.[99] And while much of this repertoire recedes in popularity in Protoattic, the seventh century witnesses clearly identifiable mythical figures in Attic vase-painting, such as Odysseus, Herakles, Agamemnon, and Iphigeneia. The "heroic" veneer of Late Geometric may have faded from vase-painting, but the horizon of the past actually came into sharper focus in the seventh century, as vague allusions to heroic activity were supplanted by references to more specific mythical events.

WESTERN CONNECTIONS: FROM DIFFUSION TO NETWORK THINKING

While it is relatively straightforward to imagine how Athenians might encounter the past through ruins, burials, objects, and stories, and while links between the Aegean and the eastern Mediterranean have received considerable scrutiny, the ways in which Athens was integrated into ceramic production and consumption in the western Mediterranean are less obvious. The historical and material evidence surveyed above for the presence of Athenian objects and persons in the west does not suggest that Italy or Sicily were teeming with Attic presence. Obviously, not every vase with Attic stylistic influence found in the west represents direct contact, and SOS amphoras may not have been transported by Athenians. Also, Attica was not full of imports from the west.[100] So traces are faint, links weak. It is just such weak links, however, that social scientists have demonstrated can possess significant strength, capable of connecting small world networks distant from each other.[101] But what exactly were the nodes, and what were the links in a network that incorporated Attica, Italy, and Sicily?

We can model two types of networks. In the first, sites functioned as nodes, with traders and travelers serving as links and objects circulating from site to site through these links. We have seen how multicultural overseas sites like Incoronata facilitated exposure to new objects and ideas, and such interaction could occur at many sites in the west (e.g., Pithekoussai). Sites in Greece could also function as nodes in this network. For example, the port of Phaleron in Attica was a site where local residents might see the traders and goods traveling with the SOS amphoras, no matter who was transporting them. A short row away, the island of Aigina was another place of intersecting routes and a setting for dynamic Protoattic consumption. At a larger geographic scale, the panhellenic sanctuaries were places where western and mainland Greeks interacted intensively, and where western Greeks and possibly Etruscans made dedications, bringing western wares to mainland Greek eyes, and vice-versa.[102] Sanctuaries as arenas for the dedications of Near Eastern objects are well known but less often acknowledged as settings for western dedications as well. For example, Pausanias (5.12.5) says the first non-Greek to honor Zeus with a votive at Olympia was the Etruscan king Arimnestos,[103] and Samos was a sanctuary with western as well as eastern dedications.

As these sanctuaries demonstrate, this network can also accommodate eastern links. Aigina, for instance, allowed Attica to connect indirectly to Egypt through its participation in settlement at Naukratis. But as we have seen, a site like Pithekoussai or Incoronata entailed a different type of interaction than Naukratis or Al Mina. In Italy and Sicily, there was more extensive and more intensive interaction among people of various cultures than in Egypt and the Levant, where the number of Greeks involved was lower and the activity was driven more by itinerant merchants and mercenaries than settlers. The links with the west in this network were more substantive than the Near East, with more opportunities for the circulation of peoples and goods.

We might also model a second type of network, perhaps more abstract, in which the objects themselves functioned as the nodes, with producers and consumers serving as the links between them.[104] In this formulation, the objects elicit the attention of patrons, purchasers, and painters and spark admiration, desire, and competition. Objects assume a degree of agency. They are responsible for enticing viewership, for creating conditions for dedication and use, and for sparking imitation, emulation, or the rejection of artistic styles. For example, artists such as the Narce Painter might see Attic paintings and try to adapt the iconography and technique, thus serving as a link between nodes composed of objects made in a variety of styles. Or a consumer might see a vase on his travels, imagine a local use for it, desire to dedicate a similar product, and commission a local vase in a new style.

Participation in both of these networks was direct, through interaction at sites like Phaleron or Incoronata and with objects such as SOS amphoras or Italian vases, but also indirect. For Athens, Corinth and its ceramics provided an important indirect entry to broader networks.[105] Widely distributed across the Mediterranean, pottery from Corinth reached Athens in the late eighth and seventh centuries in large numbers. At Athens, a variety of shapes were imported and also imitated and adopted into the local repertoire. Deposits without Corinthian or Corinthianizing material are exceptional. Eva Brann noted that in the agora, from the last quarter of the eighth century onward, "almost every well group contains fairly large amounts of Protocorinthian and Early Corinthian pottery, usually about one-tenth of the whole lot," and Corinthian imports outnumbered all other imports combined.[106] Graves, rich and poor alike, also contained abundant Corinthian material and imitations. Two representative examples will suffice to illustrate the situation. Phaleron Grave 27, a pot burial for a child, contained nine objects, of which three (a kotyle, an aryballos, and a pyxis) are certainly Corinthian imports, two are likely Corinthian imports (an oinochoe and an amphora), and one is an Attic imitation of a Corinthian skyphos (Figure 3.19; the amphora and the Corinthianizing skyphos are missing from the photograph; see also Figure 4.21).[107] In the Kerameikos, an assemblage often used to illustrate Orientalizing instead showcases the preponderance of Corinthian ceramics in the Attic repertoire (Figure 3.20).[108] In Opferplatz α/IV, associated with a cremation burial, were deposited seven Corinthian objects (a jug, a kotyle, two lidded bowls, a pyxis, and two aryballoi—the last three objects are not in the figure). In the same assemblage, a lidded bowl (inv. 1155) and kotyle (inv. 1270) are imitations of Corinthian models, while two more lidded bowls (inv. 1151 and 1158) and an additional kotyle (inv. 1152) are Corinthian in shape but Protoattic in decoration. These two assemblages are representative of the demand for Corinthian wares in Athens and demonstrate how they influenced local production. These Corinthian links were present from the very beginning, with Early Protoattic imitations of Early Protocorinthian globular aryballoi and kotylai.[109] It seems likely that some Corinthian potters set up shop in Athens.[110] Corinth itself was highly interconnected with Mediterranean networks, and its ceramics illustrate "Orientalizing" motifs, particularly on aryballoi. Often what we designate Orientalizing in Attica might be more appropriately called Corinthianizing. In the eyes of an Athenian user, an object like a molded aryballos with "Orientalizing" decoration and a Daedalic head would likely appear much more Corinthian than Levantine (Figure 3.21).[111]

The meso-scale network connecting Greek regions and their painters and objects to one another is just as significant as the trans-Mediterranean networks that so often are emphasized. As the case of Corinthian ceramics shows, technologies and ideas could reach Athens through the mediation of Greek cities. Corinth was the most significant regional player, but Euboia, the Cyclades, and Aigina also could

Figure 3.19. Selection from a grave assemblage from the Phaleron cemetery (Grave 27), including Protocorinthian vases. Athens, National Museum 14959 (the same inventory number for all objects). Photo Eleutherios Galanopoulos. Copyright © Hellenic Ministry of Culture and Sports / Archaeological Receipts Fund.

connect Athens to other nodes and horizons. Francis Croissant and Anne Coulié have both stressed the competitive and emulative nature of Greek artistic production, with artists drawing on outside sources to distinguish themselves from each other and to rival one another.[112]

The networks described here connected Athens to the east as well as the west, but as the evidence for the different "horizons" suggests, the principal locus for connectivity lay toward the west. This is where we see the most intense settlement, circulation of goods, and cross-cultural production. By focusing on art, of course, one risks distorting the historical record. Were one to focus on mercenary activity, for example, one would underline the importance of Egypt and the dedication by mercenaries of non-Greek goods in Greek sanctuaries. There were multiple vectors and modes of interaction between Greece and the eastern Mediterranean. What style reveals, however, is the largely unrecognized participation of people and objects in networks located to the west of Athens. This style is most traceable in pottery, which is the material that survives best in the archaeological record and that through the intensity of its production best measures change over time. It is of course possible that material such as textiles that do not survive would tell a different story.

To diagram these networks of ceramic production and consumption would be scientistic and misleading; they are most effective as ways to think through the problem of seventh-century Mediterranean styles, and they should be imagined as coexisting and overlapping. One of the advantages to these network views is that they avoid the simplistic use of pots to form ethnic distribution maps. Both networks instead use ceramics to suggest the manifold ways in which Athens was connected with the Mediterranean through people, sites, and objects. Artisans, traders, travelers,

Figure 3.20. Selection of vases and figurines from Kerameikos offering place (Opferplatz) α/IV. (see table 1, Grave VI-4). Not to scale. Photos courtesy of the Deutsches Archäologisches Institut, Athens (Hermann Wagner, [D-DAI-ATH-Kerameikos-04934, 04937, 04938, 04939A, 04940, 04944, 04945, 04946, 04948, 04969, 04961, 04987, 04992, 04997, 05760, 05764]).

Figure 3.20. continued

Figure 3.21. Protoattic aryballos, a Corinthian shape. Athens, National Museum 2378. Photo Eleutherios Galanopoulos. Copyright © Hellenic Ministry of Culture and Sports / Archaeological Receipts Fund.

and objects transmitted ideas, techniques, and ways of thinking and doing as people circulated through different cultural and physical settings, exchanged objects, and moved from one small world to another. Style in this understanding does more than merely fossilize interaction—it contributes to the construction of individual subjectivities and community, as will be discussed at greater length in subsequent chapters. For now, it is important to stress another strength of these network models, which is that they are not restricted to elite actors and elite objects.[113] Travelers and traders rather than any type of "landed gentry" played a critical role. This is not to deny that the elite had a function, but it is to refuse them the place of primary agents of transmission and change. The networks were not controlled, manipulated, or monopolized by a small group of actors but expansive in terms of scale, multifaceted in terms of links and nodes, and open in terms of participants. Merchants, painters, and pots were just as important as any Demaratus.

THE "ORIENTAL" WEST

It is problematic that the stylistic and periodic label "Orientalizing," so firmly *oriented* toward the east, belies the extent of Levantine penetration into the west. New discoveries in Iberia, especially at the site of Huelva, have moved up the dates for Levantine long-distance trading earlier than the traditional archaeological chronology of the late eighth century.[114] Earlier dates than many archaeologists once accepted are also emerging from Cádiz, Utica, Carthage, and Sant'Imbenia (Sardinia). There is still disagreement over chronology, with some scholars putting Levantine activity in the west as early

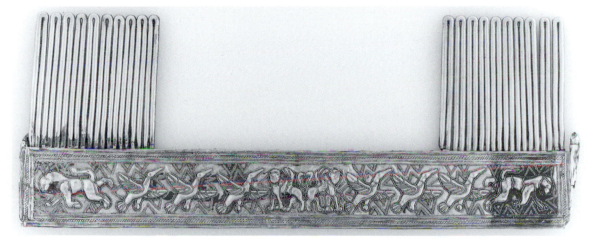

Figure 3.22. Gold clasp from the Bernardini Tomb, Praeneste, early 7th century. Rome, Museo Nazionale Etrusco di Villa Giulia 61553. Photo © MIBACT. Museo Nazionale Etrusco di Villa Giulia—Roma.

as the tenth century, a few even in the eleventh century. In the current state of knowledge, a late ninth-century date for Levantine activity in the west seems the most likely, and a late ninth-century foundation for Carthage seems increasingly possible.[115] Even a conservative date in the early eighth century substantially revises the chronology of westward movement and places the archaeological foundation dates closer to those obtained from literary sources.

Levantines sailed west early, and they did not enter a void. Research has stressed that Sardinia was an early and active player in the Mediterranean, and that Villanovan communities were well developed and well connected.[116] The links among Iberia, north Africa, Sardinia, and Etruria integrated Italy and Sicily with western Levantine trade networks and through them with Cyprus, Crete, and the Levant, long before Greek colonies were established on western shores. Levantine products reached Italy in the ninth (if not the late tenth) and first half of the eighth centuries, and they may well have come from western foundations or western trade routes. The evidence includes faience, ivory, and bronze from the cemetery of Torre Galli; shallow carinated bronze bowls from Tomb S of the Macchiabate necropolis at Francavilla Marittima and Tomb 132 at Castel di Decima; two pendants, a scarab, and a jug from Tarquinia; and pendants and a Cypriot bronze cauldron from Capua.[117] This is around the same time that Greek products started to arrive in Italy and Sicily, too, but in comparison they were more limited in number and variety and even may have been transported by Levantines.[118] The identity of the carriers is less important than the existence of early western foundations and trade routes that connected Sicily and Italy westward to places and objects that have been designated culturally as "Oriental." These nodes and links contributed to the decentralized movement of ideas, people, and material culture.

Figure 3.23. Gold plaque from the Bernardini Tomb, Praeneste, early 7th century. Rome, Museo Nazionale Etrusco di Villa Giulia 61545. Photo © MIBACT. Museo Nazionale Etrusco di Villa Giulia—Roma.

The new chronological framework means that Greek colonists in the late eighth and seventh centuries encountered peoples in Italy and Sicily who already had a history of deploying and manipulating goods we now tend to associate with the eastern Mediterranean and who possessed a more extensive Levantine orientation to their material culture than contemporary Greeks. We need not return to those views, going back at least to Thomas Dempster, writing in the seventeenth century, that Etruscans were immigrants from the eastern Mediterranean and the progenitors of Mediterranean cultural achievements.[119] But in comparison to Greece in general and Athens in particular, Italy and Sicily were more linked, directly and indirectly, with the Near East and consumed goods in an informed, selective, and deliberate manner. These communities and their objects became important nodes in the networks by which Athenians may have encountered Near Eastern cultures. In northern Italy, the use of these objects and iconographies was particularly spectacular, with the so-called princely tombs dwarfing any of the sumptuary displays in seventh-century Greece.[120] Here and as far south as Pontecagnano, the elite drew on a Levantine iconographic repertoire to create a set of shared symbols of power. In the Bernardini tomb from the Colombella necropolis at Praeneste, for example, "excavated" in 1876, over one hundred objects were deposited with the dead, including imports as well as objects of local manufacture.[121] Precious metals of exquisite workmanship abounded, such as a gilt silver cup with snake protomes; a gold clasp with sphinxes, birds, and

Figure 3.24. Cypro-phoenician gilt silver bowl from the Bernardini Tomb, Praeneste, early 7th century. Rome, Museo Nazionale Etrusco di Villa Giulia 61565. Photo © MIBACT. Museo Nazionale Etrusco di Villa Giulia—Roma.

lions; a gold plaque with chimeras, lions, sirens, and horses; and a so-called Cypro-Phoenician bowl (Figures 1.10, 3.22–3.24).[122] Many of these and other works were produced locally, and in some cases the exceptional technical knowledge suggests the close involvement of immigrant craftsmen. The repetition of objects and images in different grave assemblages implies that the elite deployed them in ways that were meaningful and understandable to each other and to the broader population. Elements of the elite visual repertoire present in the seventh century included double axes, scepters, thrones, stools, fans, and trumpets (*litui*).[123] Such a focused and deliberate use of exotica contrasts with the eclectic Greek approach in the same period, as we will see in the next chapter. The objects in Figures 1.10, 3.22–3.24 were ostensibly, ostentatiously, and recognizably Neo-Assyrian and Levantine.

Drinking assemblages, too, drew on an eastern Mediterranean repertoire, integrating foreign imports into local feasting rituals. Some drinking wares were Greek, with cups particularly popular, but Levantine objects also were used. These included sympotic wares and transport amphoras presumably carrying Levantine wine. At ancient Ficana, a deposit near the foundations of a monumental building included mixing bowls on stands, ollas, pyxides, chalices, and plates, most of them in a red impasto imitating Phoenician wares.[124] The shapes, too, of the chalices and plates find their closest parallels in Assyria and Phoenicia. This is a striking example of Levantine and Assyrian rather than Greek paraphernalia incorporated into local practice. Evidently the indigenous populations did not require Greek intermediaries to learn how to drink wine.

To meet the demand for their products, as mentioned above, Levantine goldsmiths, bronze workers, ivory carvers, stone sculptors, and their descendants set up shop in Iberia, Italy, and Sicily.[125] They brought with them the skills necessary for working materials unfamiliar to local craftsmen. Fine gold work and ivory carving, for example, could not be learned by imitation alone. In some cases, artisans also likely brought the materials, like ivory, and they may have worked in close relationship with elite patrons.

Artists were not the only Levantines to settle. According to Thucydides (6.2.6), Phoenicians populated the west coast of Sicily before the Greeks arrived, and at Motya, Phoenician occupation is attested from the late eighth century. A site like Pithekoussai, an island off the Bay of Naples, shows the rich potential for western contexts to promote cross-cultural interaction, with material evidence pointing to Levantines, Syrians, and Greeks living side-by-side and intermarrying with the local population.[126] Greek as well as Aramaic writing appears in the material record, and pottery of various types was used, including Phoenician-style plates and lamps.

At a time when few Greeks set foot in the Levant or Egypt, Italy and Sicily were the primary places they encountered "Oriental" cultures and wares. Through their interaction with a network of colonies and trade, Athenians intersected with a small world with a high number of immigrants, a considerable quantity of Levantine goods, and an intensive and extensive use of Near Eastern imagery for status display. Italian communities were connected with the Mediterranean more systematically than the Greek mainland, largely through their engagement with Levantine communities in the west and through the settlement of Levantine communities on their soil. In many ways, from the perspective of an Athenian, the Orient lay toward the west.

TWO UNEXPECTED TRAJECTORIES: ODYSSEUS AND COLAEUS

The texts of Homer and Herodotus lend some support to this reconfigured geography and decentered Mediterranean. Despite their mythical content, Homer's poems relate to aspects of eighth-century reality, including the way listeners thought of time and place, in order to create a world that the audience could imagine.[127] Similarly, Herodotus relates stories from the Protoarchaic period that conveyed some seventh-century realities of the Mediterranean. The poet and the historian provide evidence for interconnections and information on the existence of routes, which have been studied at length. Here I want to examine how they sketch out the geographic horizons of their listeners. Both texts emerged from actual conceptions of space and time and also shaped the expectations and perceptions of their audiences. In particular, the travels of Homer's Odysseus and Herodotus's Colaeus illuminate some ways people may have thought of horizons, geography in the Mediterranean, and movement across the waters.

In Homer, a revealing distinction emerges between places that can be grouped roughly into the modern scholarly notion of the Near East and those which lie to the west.[128] For the Achaean warriors, the eastern Mediterranean was relatively well known. The peoples are designated specifically as Trojans, Phrygians, Lycians, and Phoenicians rather than described with any vague "Oriental" language. Greeks had besieged Troy for years and grown intimate with the landscape, and the Trojans were characterized in Homer in much the same cultural terms as the Achaeans.[129] Places such as Cyprus, Crete, Phoenicia, or Egypt were distant sources of wealth, but recognizable and reachable.[130] They were destinations for trade, and close guest friendships with their inhabitants were entirely possible. Some of these peoples, particularly the Phoenicians, might be maligned in the poems, but they were also praised, and the eastern locales themselves held no particular threatening danger.[131] Menelaus, for example, traveled to Crete, Cyprus, Phoenicia, Egypt, Ethiopia, and Libya and returned home rich, having weathered few perils apart from wrestling Proteus.[132] It was entirely within the realm of the imaginable for a Homeric character to encounter a traveler from these places, and it is revealing that when Odysseus deceived someone with a travel narrative intended to be plausible, he located his wanderings and travails in the east.[133]

Contrast Menelaus's travels eastward (broadly conceived), which sound like a long trading voyage, with Odysseus's journeys, through an altogether different terrain, physically as well as conceptually. Now, there is much disagreement over Odysseus's specific itinerary, and some of his destinations probably do not possess an actual geographic reality. As early as Thucydides, however, commentators have located many of his wanderings in the west, in particular identifying Scylla and Charybdis as the straits of Messina, and placing the lands of the cyclopes and Laestrygonians on Sicily, with the cyclopes emblematic of proto-urban, pre-farming communities.[134] In addition to Thucydides, there is good textual support within Homer to indicate that listeners would have imagined him wandering in the west. From the home of the cyclopes, for example, Odysseus and his men reach Aeolus, whence the text informs the listener they sailed home for ten days with a wind blowing *from* the west.[135] Ogygia, the island of Calypso, is placed in the midst of the sea or ocean, surely still in the west.[136] From Ogygia, Odysseus travels twenty days to

Scheria, the land of the Phaeacians, keeping the Ursa Major constellation to his left, so he must be traveling eastward to reach home.[137]

The precise location of Odysseus's wanderings will continue to be debated, but there is no doubt that his home, Ithaka, was located somewhere in northwestern Greece, poised for westward interactions. Also debated is the date at which cult related to the *nostoi* began, which eventually flourished in Italy and securely tied the west to heroic returns. In Hesiod's *Theogony*, Odysseus is the progenitor of Agrios and Latinos, rulers over the Tyrrhenians. But Martin West disputes the authenticity of the passage, and most *nostoi* cults seem to begin no earlier than the sixth century BC.[138] The evidence for early cult activity related to epic in the west should not be pressed, although it would be most convenient for my argument. The importance of Homer's text remains in the contrast it posits between the relatively well-known eastern Mediterranean and the exotic, adventurous, dangerous, beguiling west.[139] It upsets our traditional geographies with their straightforward association of "Oriental" with "exotic."

The travels of the historical figure Colaeus the Samian reported in Herodotus provide an interesting complement to those of Odysseus.[140] Heading from near Cyrene to Egypt, he was blown off course and landed at Tartessos, most likely located in modern Spain.[141] According to Herodotus, he profited from trade enormously, more than any other Greek except for Sostratus of Aigina. Returning to the Aegean with their wealth, Colaeus and his shipmates dedicated a bronze protome griffin bowl over 10 feet tall at the sanctuary of Hera on Samos. The object does not survive, but the type is relatively well known and often considered a paradigm of Orientalizing art because of the combination of Greek and Near Eastern forms. In Herodotus, however, the object is qualified unambiguously as Argive in style. Colaeus's trajectory, source of wealth, and dedication destabilize traditional geographies of the Mediterranean. For Colaeus, the west unexpectedly provided a landfall of wealth, from which the crew dedicated an ostensibly Orientalizing object, but which Herodotus instead describes as Greek. The story exposes the ways in which the west could be the catalyst for what scholars have called an Orientalizing phenomenon.

FEEDBACK FROM THE WEST

These stories help illustrate how network thinking precludes any unidirectional movement of goods and ideas—the type of east to west flows implicit in the term Orientalizing—and opens up the possibility for unexpected geographical trajectories. Another advantage to networks is that they allow us to consider feedback. In place of the one-way transmission or diffusion of goods and ideas from the eastern Mediterranean to Greece, and in place of a similarly east–west colonialist process of Hellenization in Italy, a more open and multifaceted system of communication existed, with transmission occurring in both directions along a link. Attica participated in a Mediterranean network and was acted on by that network.[142] The concept of feedback in network thinking means that there are implications of the horizons, links, and nodes described up to this point for the Protoattic style. An encounter with "Orientalizing" objects could occur in or from the west, furnishing shapes and iconography with an ultimate eastern pedigree. For example, although "Oriental" models are often sought for a seventh-century Protoattic bowl with lotus terminations from the Kerameikos (Figure 3.8), similar objects appear in eighth-century Italian contexts, where they arrived through links with Sardinia.[143] Near Eastern prototypes and models for Athenian products may have arrived in Greece via Sicily and Italy or been encountered in trade or settlement contexts in the west.

Figure 3.25. Greek-Italian oinochoe from Cumae. Naples, National Archaeological Museum 128199. Photo Giorgio Alabno, by permission of the Ministry for Cultural Heritage and Activities and Tourism—National Archaeological Museum of Naples.

There are more explicit links to Greek-Italian pottery production itself. Most striking (yet unacknowledged) are the parallels between Protoattic pottery and the Cumae Group, an Early/Middle Protocorinthian workshop active in Italy.[144] Products of the workshop have been found at Corinth, Aigina, the Argive Heraion, Aetos, and Afrati (Crete), but the group owes its name to finds at Cumae (Figure 3.25), where it enjoyed the broadest reception.[145] The style of painting differs markedly from mainland Corinthian. In place of the miniature technique characteristic of Corinth, the Cumae Group favors broad and expansive ornament, especially tendrils and tassels, applied to the bellies of oinochoai. Since the discovery of the pieces at Cumae, more oinochoai of a similar Greek-Italian style have appeared at other sites, revealing that the Cumae Group was but one facet of a much broader production of oinochoai bearing vegetal ornament, fish, and snakes (Figures 3.26, 3.27, 3.28).[146] In grave assemblages, they are often the only vessels to receive such decoration,

Figure 3.26. Greek-Italian oinochoe, from Pontecagnano. Pontecagnano, National Archaeological Museum 162963. Photo N. T. Arrington.

Figure 3.27. Greek-Italian oinochoe, from Tarquinia. Tarquinia, National Museum RC 2102. Photo John Blazejewski / Princeton University after *Corpus Vasorum Antiquorum* Tarquinia 3, plate 5.

perhaps because of their important ritual function of pouring a libation at the tomb or quenching a funerary pyre, but examples also survive from domestic contexts.[147] Intriguing formal and iconographic parallels of these oinochoai with vases in the Protoattic style occur. On the belly of a hydria by the Mesogeia Painter, for example, tendrils and palmettes break free from the surrounding Geometric ornament in a manner that recalls the Italian oinochoai (Figure 5.11). In the Kerameikos, one Attic oinochoe displays an enormous blossoming plant (Figure 3.29).[148] Athenian artists may have seen or heard of the Greek-Italian oinochoai abroad or at home; there is an example from a grave at Kallithea in Attica.[149]

The Polyphemus Amphora, treated in more detail in the next chapter, may also betray specific iconographic debts to art from Italy (Figure 1.9). The head of one Gorgon with snakes has been compared to metal cauldrons, but snake protomes occur only in Etruria (Figure 1.10).[150] If such metal protomes provided the Polyphemus Painter with his pictorial inspiration for the depiction of the monster, then it is most likely that the influence originated in Etruria.

We can also examine feedback by looking beyond shapes and iconography and more holistically at style as a way of making—as an approach to the surface of the vase. There are three aspects of the Protoattic style that may reflect the constitutive role for western contexts, markets, and practices. First, the Protoattic experimentation with polychromy and the single brush finds good parallels in Italian pottery. In both regions, painters ventured to depart from the multiple brush and from the application of decoration while the potters' wheel was turning, instead exposing their hands and the process of facture, as will be discussed more in chapter 5. Second, the monumentality of Protoattic vases, so different from contemporary Protocorinthian pottery, finds an echo in such Italian vases as the amphoras by the Painter of the Cranes and the Heptachord Painter (Figures 3.14, 3.15). And third, the eclecticism of Protoattic recalls

Figure 3.28. Greek-Italian oinochoe, from Pithekoussai. Ischia, Archaeological Museum of Pithecusae 168828. Photo John Blazejewski / Princeton University after Buchner and Ridgway 1993, plate 242.

Figure 3.29. Protoattic oinochoe from the Kerameikos (Grave VI-62), attributed to the Group of the Wild Style. Kerameikos 81. Photo courtesy of the Deutsches Archäologisches Institut, Athens (D-DAI-ATH-Kerameikos-02716).

Italic production. Corinthian and Cycladic stylistic elements alternatively dominated, with the Cycladic in a vase like the amphora attributed to the Passas Painter (Figure 3.30), Corinthian in a vase like the mug attributed to the Kerameikos Mugs Group (Figure 3.31).[151] This stylistic heterogeneity contrasts with the homogeneity of both preceding Geometric and subsequent black-figure wares. In all these ways, the Protoattic style can be conceived as part of a broader world of painterly production in the Mediterranean, with more similarities to artwork in the west than to purported Near Eastern models. No doubt there were Near Eastern influences as well, and Athenian pottery participated in eastern Mediterranean networks, with imported objects and dedications at sanctuaries providing some stimulus, but, in balance, the Near East did not offer the same impact on the painting style in Athens and elsewhere in Greece.

By any measure, Protoattic iconography and style do not suggest close and consistent interaction between western and Greek painters, on the model, for

Figure 3.30. Protoattic amphora attributed to the Passas Painter. New York, Metropolitan Museum of Art 21.88.18. Rogers Fund, 1921.

Figure 3.31. Protoattic mug from funeral trench (Opferrinne) β in the Kerameikos (Grave VI-9), attributed to the Kerameikos Mugs Group. Kerameikos 73. Photo courtesy of the Deutsches Archäologisches Institut, Athens (D-DAI-ATH-Kerameikos-02739).

example, of sustained workshop collaboration. The parallels between the wares should not be overemphasized—but nor can they be dismissed out of hand. From the perspective of Attica, a picture emerges of a weak link with Italy and Sicily through a network of ceramic production, transportation, and consumption mediated by objects, people, and sites. Network thinking allows us to imagine the connections between a marginal area like Athens with those processes and ideas occurring in the fervent atmosphere of the western Mediterranean and to suggest that links across a broad geographic scale, even at second or third hand, carried important implications for stylistic and cultural change.

THE PERIPHERIES OF A GLOBAL MEDITERRANEAN

Alongside the astonishing long-distance connections that survived the collapse of the Bronze Age palatial economies lay broken links. A history of a "global" Mediterranean must, in part, account for isolation and consider the ways in which people on different shores learned about one another, slowly. The Assyrian king Assurbanipal, closely linked to supply chains stretching from the Levant to Iberia, could nevertheless claim that no one in his court could interpret for a Lydian messenger.[152] If globalization is to retain heuristic value for the ancient world, it needs to be conceived as a process and to account for gaps as well as connectivity.

Today's capital of modern Greece once lay at the margins of the main seventh-century communication currents. The distribution of SOS amphoras, the import record, the small number of fine-ware exports, and artistic styles show that links were present, but the region was only weakly connected to Mediterranean networks. The dynamics of these networks nevertheless are important because they reveal unexpected trajectories for people, goods, and ideas. In place of the geography that is implicit in the term "Orientalizing," that subtends analysis of cultural change in the Mediterranean, and that implies passive diffusion, analysis of Attica shows a system of overlapping and interlocking networks of circulation and exchange, at different scales, which provided access to worlds across geographic and temporal horizons to a range of social actors. In this model, there is a place for the Neo-Assyrian empire, the Levant, Egypt, and the Bronze Age past, but the west, especially Italy and Sicily, played a critical role. In and through the west, Greeks encountered Levantine cultures and extravagant elite display, and to the (farther) west they attributed the properties of the exotic and the unknown. In the west, Greeks settled and engaged closely with peoples and sites, markets and producers, in multicultural contexts. While the role of Italy and Sicily in "Orientalizing" support the idea of a global Mediterranean, it is important to emphasize the heterogeneity of the regional Greek experiences with the Mediterraneanizing process rather than embrace the homogenizing view that sometimes accompanies discussions of globalization. The networks by which Attica participated in the Mediterranean were shared across the Aegean, but each region interfaced with those networks in different ways.

An important way in which Attica interfaced was through meso-scale intermediaries. Engagement with sanctuaries and with regions like Corinth and Euboia and Aigina was fundamental to its ability to link up to a larger network. In addition, competition and emulation among Greek potters and painters contributed to the movement of goods and the evolution of style. Corinth seems to have been the region most intimately connected to Near Eastern cultures as well as the west, like Euboia was in the eighth century. There may have been a more palpable Corinthianizing than "Orientalizing" current in seventh-century Attic material culture.

Studies of the Mediterranean have emphasized the trader, the warrior, and the patron. But it is possible that the roving, socially marginalized artist was more consequential for the development of intercultural connections. Artists brought their traditions and outlooks with them across the horizons, and sometimes also their materials.[153] They had flexibility to move (as refugees or entrepreneurs), ability to adopt and adapt to local culture, sensitivity to cultural differences in producing and consuming material culture, and opportunities to create enduring objects, which were themselves mobile.

The distribution of these objects has provided data on routes, and the changes in shapes and styles have provided evidence for the connection of places with one another. But this chapter has suggested that objects were more than symptoms of cultural change and more than reflections of processes that occurred in society. As one of the network models proposed above suggested, they could be catalysts. Objects themselves could connect users with remote places and with the past, they could entrance travelers and artists into new markets, and they could suggest that new and different ways of imagining the world were possible. The objects did not merely emerge from a network of connectivity but formed integral components. The remainder of this book devotes more attention to the interaction of people with objects in specific contexts and explores how different horizons could come into view depending on the particular object and how it was used.

CHAPTER 4

Interaction at the Grave

Style, Practice, and Status

MORE THAN A PAINTING

It is easy to forget that the object in figures 1.9 and 4.1 is a vase.[1] The painting arrests attention. On the body, the Gorgons pursue Perseus; on the shoulder, a lion attacks a boar; and on the neck, Odysseus and his men blind the drunken cyclops, Polyphemus. From the rush of the Gorgons to the pounce of the lion to the thrust of Odysseus, the painting pulses with motion and energy. The smooth and fluid brushstrokes and the dazzling variety of twisting, curling, whirling ornament add to the image's enchanting pull on the viewer. The painting is sophisticated, advanced for its time. The painter configured Gorgon bodies before a visual tradition for them existed, drawing on foreign metal bowls, textual sources, and imagination. The scene on the neck is no less complex, collapsing narrative time, as the sleeping cyclops drinks. The composition, the mythological subject matter, the bold use of contrasting colors, the free application of the brush, and the discernible hand of an artist make it appropriate to think of the image as a painting, as a work of art, and to seek out other images by the hand of the same artist, anointed the Polyphemus Painter (cf. Figure 6.10). And yet it is also a thing, a vase. The flat image in a book, just like PowerPoint in a classroom, belies the three-dimensional aspect of the painting and occludes the materiality of its vehicle and frame. The large and spherical clay amphora served as the container for the body of a dead child (Figure 4.2). Discovered in 1954 at Eleusis, it lay on its side, the mouth covered by schist slabs, and contained bones and a small incised handmade vase (Figure 4.3). To look only at the image leaves the picture, as it were, incomplete.[2] We need to put the vase back into vase-painting: to explore the contexts of such ceramic objects, to devote attention to their

Figure 4.1. Detail of neck of Figure 1.9. Photo N. T. Arrington.

shapes and functions, and to pursue their long and complex object biographies.[3] We need to include in our analysis objects that are not richly decorated—objects such as the small handmade vase found inside the Polyphemus Amphora or, elsewhere, a cooking pot used as a burial urn.[4] And finally, we need to consider how these objects interacted with the people and groups who used them.

This chapter examines the intersection of seventh-century ceramics with burial rituals. For many scholars, this choice might seem perverse. Typically, this period has been characterized by a dearth of mortuary evidence, with the drop in burial numbers and goods receiving emphasis. But while archaeologists looking at cemeteries tend to focus on burial deposits themselves, which leave the most observable marks in the archaeological record, closer attention to a wider range of mortuary contexts and materials can broaden the temporal scope of our analysis beyond the moment the body was disposed. With a comprehensive survey of the evidence across the burial plots and cemeteries of Athens and Attica, and with attention to a range of funeral rites, discussion can dwell less on the alleged problems of invisibility of the period, and instead investigate how vases participated in mortuary rituals. The approach here entails extending our notion of style beyond iconography and form alone, to use or practice. As bodily extensions of mourners, catalysts for ritual action, and components of assemblages, vases connected the living, the corpse, and sites of commemoration.

The first step in investigating the place of ceramics in burial rites is to abandon the canon that was created in the process of periodization described in chapter 2 and gather anew the evidence. Expanding the traditional corpus of seventh-century vases and surveying all burial evidence will render funeral practices more visible to us. Unexpectedly, it will also lead us to the margins of society, to subelite contexts, and compel revising our notions of how the style emerged.

The social margins are far from the typical place where scholars locate Protoattic; a close link with the elite is widely assumed, and the limited burial evidence has

Figure 4.2. Archaeological context of Figures 1.9 and 4.1. Photo John Blazejewski / Princeton University after Mylonas 1975, vol. 3, plate Γ, figs. 222–23.

helped forge this link. Most influential for the study of seventh-century Attica has been Ian Morris's conception of "formal burial," meaning burials that can be identified and recovered by archaeologists, and that signaled authority over resources and access to communal membership. According to Morris, in the eighth century, as the Athenian *polis* took shape, a wide social group enjoyed formal burial, but in the

Figure 4.3. Handmade ("Argive monochrome") aryballos found along with the Polyphemus Amphora. Photo: John Blazejewski / Princeton University after Mylonas 1975, vol. 3, plate Γ, fig. 224.

seventh century, the elite clawed back privileges to formal burial, and the *polis* as a community of citizens retreated.[5] All seventh-century burials for Morris belonged to his *agathoi*, and all pottery therein was elite. A second influential and representative interpretation has been James Whitley's argument that Protoattic pottery was rationed by status.[6] Both Morris and Whitley (along with many others) emphasize the elite use of Protoattic and advocate a top-down model of cultural change. But it is troubling that neither clearly articulates just how burial was restricted or pottery was rationed.[7] No doubt material culture, including pottery, participated in the expression of social organization in seventh-century Athens and Attica. But what if social structure was not yet fixed and established? What if no structure existed for structuralist analysis to uncover? A period marked by the development of urbanization, sanctuaries, tomb cults, overseas settlement, immigration, and literacy might well be a period without a dominant ideology or an established symbolic cultural hegemony. At the very least, it merits a reevaluation of the evidence. This move is all the more necessary as our views of the Protoarchaic city have changed, and scholars are more inclined to see a gradual process of political development than a single moment of invention or emergence, with continuity in the seventh century rather than decline.[8]

If one approach toward the Polyphemus Amphora truncates the object by treating it as a painting divorced from a material frame, those structuralist approaches that have made headway on social questions risk making the vase a mere statistic.[9] While they draw attention to (final) context, they show little regard for shape, assemblage, or decoration, as the object becomes transformed into a number in a table. Tellingly, there are no images of Protoattic vases in Morris's seminal investigation of Greek burial. What a vase looked like or how it felt, the ways it invited and enabled use, the objects it resembled, hardly matter. This move shortens the life of an object to its moment of final deposition. In addition, by forcing the vase into a predetermined category, the variety of shapes, images, and depositional practices at work are neglected. It trades on an essentializing notion of style, with Protoattic equated with Orientalizing, and with Orientalizing conceived as a set of formal characteristics that inheres to the vessel itself: there is something about the shape or iconography or composition that makes a clear semantic gesture toward Near Eastern cultures. Analysis thus falls into one of the traps of defining a period in terms of a ceramic style, by letting a descriptive label do the interpretive work (chapter 2), and it also neglects the multiple networks and horizons that we explored in the previous chapter.

Might it be possible to put the vase as a three-dimensional, tangible form back into the discussion of the seventh century? To move away from mere statistics and to recover the richness and variety of the period's material record, without descending to rote visual analysis or mere connoisseurship? At stake is how we integrate objects into the lived experiences of people long gone, and how we write social, political, and cultural history on the basis of style.

The first section of this chapter gathers, for the first time, all the mortuary evidence for the period, documenting every (known) burial in Attica from the latest Geometric period into the late seventh century, when early Corinthian pottery appears. It becomes clear that several aspects of the traditional scholarly narratives of this period are incorrect. There are unexpected age distributions, glimmers of wealth in surprising places, and many graves from subelite contexts. While there remains a drop in burials from Late Geometric into Protoattic, I explore reasons beside social structure for the discrepancy in numbers and show that the Kerameikos cemetery has distorted perceptions of the period. Next, leaving aside for the moment issues of status display that have dominated discussions, I examine how vases as objects and not just images moved between workshop, home, and grave, investigate their role in the hands of mourners, and trace the funeral rituals that they enabled and enacted. This approach can accommodate coarse ware as well as fine ware and reveals how ceramics extended human activity and connected time and place. With this framework in mind, we can turn back to a consideration of status display, which was operative in cemeteries, but not the main factor governing the production and consumption of Protoattic. Indeed, the evidence of the burial contexts and the characteristics of the Protoattic style itself compel a critical reassessment of the association of decorated vases with the elite, along with the very terms "elite" and "aristocratic." I advocate for a period of social disorder and instability in the seventh century and conclude by placing subelite and elite contexts and objects in dialogue, offering a model for the origin and development of the style in which the marginalized had some agency, and style itself could participate in social change and contestation.

THE LANDSCAPE OF COMMEMORATION

Table 1 on pages 227–52 lists all the burials coterminous with the production of Protoattic pottery, from the late eighth to the late seventh century (excluding burials containing only Late Geometric or Early Corinthian pottery). This table corrects and updates previous lists of graves, and it includes more information on the assemblages,

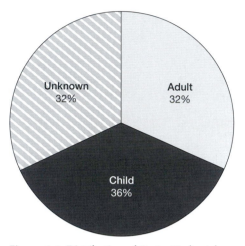

Figure 4.4. Distribution of Protoattic burials according to age. Graph N. T. Arrington.

so that other scholars can (re)evaluate my conclusions.[10] Some readers may wish to refine the dating scheme at work. I have not provided narrow date ranges within the seventh century, because I am not confident that our current understanding of ceramics allows such precision to be applied consistently, and alterations to a few numbers in this sample size could prompt considerable interpretive changes.[11] For similar reasons, although I generate below some charts and statistics on the basis of this table, the uneven way the data have been gathered and transmitted through the excavation and publication process means that the numbers should not be considered *the* definitive representation of the ancient burial record. Any attempt at statistics for this time period and this body of evidence is bound to be flawed. Nevertheless, the numbers and figures can provide a general picture, reveal some important trends, and counteract several common assumptions about seventh-century Attic burials.

Unlike other compilations of seventh-century funeral evidence, this table systematically includes vases from museums with an alleged Attic mortuary provenance. Every volume of the *Corpus Vasorum Antiquorum* has been reviewed.[12] To my knowledge, none of these objects entered the art market after 1970 (the date of the landmark UNESCO convention restricting acquisitions), and including this data here does not condone illicit archaeological activity. On the contrary, it demonstrates the degree to which looting has disturbed vital archaeological contexts.

The table and the data therein are a necessary response to the canonization that periodization created, and they offer the starting point for a survey of the types of burials, grave markers, and rituals in the seventh century. It is important to go over the evidence in order to get a better sense of the burial processes, the mechanisms of interaction and participation, and the factors affecting archaeological visibility.

The table shows that the two most common types of burial in the seventh century were inhumations in vases for infants and young children and primary cremations for juveniles and adults (Figure 4.4).[13] (Unfortunately, the osteological data are insufficient to make comments about the sex of the deceased, and gender identifications based on grave goods are not reliable.) The practice of inhuming in burial urns first appeared in the Late Protogeometric period but only became common for infants/young children in Late Geometric I. In the seventh century, amphoras, pithoi, hydriai, and jugs served as urns, sometimes made of painted fine ware such as the Polyphemus Amphora, more often of undecorated cook or coarse ware (Figure 4.5). Usually sherds were removed from the vessel wall to fit the corpse inside the urn, and the urn was laid on its side in a pit. (The base of the Polyphemus Amphora instead

Figure 4.5. Pot burial 1 from Palaia Kokkinia. Piraeus, Archaeological Museum 16517. Photo courtesy of Georgios Spyropoulos.

seems to have been cut for the insertion of the corpse, and then sealed with lead clamps.[14]) The mouth of the urn was covered by a stone slab (usually schist) or by another vessel (fragmentary or complete). Grave goods were placed inside and/or outside the burial urn.

The immolation of corpses, specifically secondary cremation, had long been known in Athens and Attica. Then Late Geometric I saw a shift toward inhumation, and by Late Geometric II it was the most common way to dispose of the adult dead.[15] In the seventh century, however, the cremation of adults became the norm, and now specifically primary cremation. Yet the depth of the primary cremation pit varied considerably, with implications for the ritual. For a shallow pit as little as 0.20 m deep, the fuel must have been piled high above ground to enable immolation (Figure 4.6).[16] Alternatively, a pit 1.45 m deep could have contained ample fuel within itself (Figure 4.7).[17] The evidence for primary cremation can be elusive in the pyres, especially from shallow pyres. Burnt soil, charred pit walls, and bones are not always reported from burials referred to as pyres in excavation reports. The cursory nature of publications and the methods of recovery (such as a lack of sieving) may explain some of the missing information, but it is also likely that some of these pyres represent ceremonial pyres—pyres used in funeral rites, but not for burning the dead.

Figure 4.6. Pyre 1 (cremation burial) from Palaia Kokkinia. Photo courtesy of Georgios Spyropoulos.

Figure 4.7. Excavations in the cemetery of the Kerameikos with graves VI-19 and VI-23 and funeral trenches (Opferrinnen) γ and ζ. Photo courtesy of the Deutsches Archäologisches Institut, Athens (D-DAI-ATH-Kerameikos-02314). Annotations by N. T. Arrington.

While jar burials and primary cremations dominate the archaeological record, there were other forms of burial in the seventh century, too, and this variety needs to be underlined.[18] There are several examples of inhumations in pits, shafts (defined here as a pit over a meter deep), or cists rather than vessels, predominantly but not exclusively Early Protoattic in date, from the agora,[19] the Kerameikos,[20] Kallithea,[21] and Thorikos.[22] Traces of a wooden sarcophagus occasionally are preserved.[23] From Peiraios Street, an adult rather than a child was buried in a vessel, a large pithos.[24] There are some instances of secondary cremation, too. At Eleusis, the cremated remains of a ten-year-old were placed in an amphora attributed to the Group of the Wild Style, its mouth covered by a Late Geometric shallow bowl.[25] In the Kerameikos, the cremated remains of presumably three different individuals were placed in three bronze urns.[26] Secondary cremations for adults in urns and pits persisted at Trachones from Late Geometric into Early Protoattic, where the bodies were not completely burned, perhaps for lack of fuel.[27]

Particularly noteworthy and sensational are the mass inhumation burials found in the cemetery of Phaleron in 1915 and 2016, the same cemetery that produced the abundant finds discussed in chapter 2, many of them looted, and that once bestowed the name Phaleron Ware on Protoattic pottery. The first discovery was a mass burial of 17 or 18 men with chained necks, hands, and feet, including five individuals with arrow points in their chests (Figures 4.8-4.9).[28] The bodies were laid two or more

Figure 4.8. Mass burial in Phaleron, discovered in 1915. Photo John Blazejewski / Princeton University after Keramopoullos 1923, fig. 12.

Figure 4.9. Skeletons from the mass burial in Phaleron discovered in 1915. Photo John Blazejewski / Princeton University after Keramopoullos 1923, figs. 7–8.

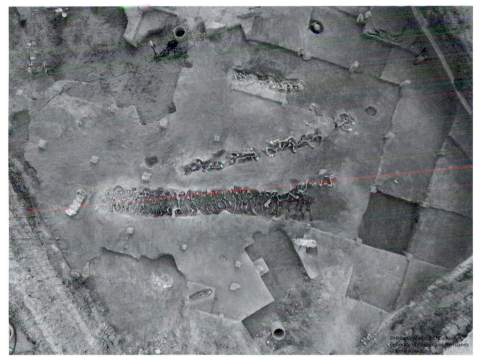

Figure 4.10. Mass burials in Phaleron, discovered in 2016 at the Stavros Niarchos Foundation Cultural Center. Photo courtesy of Stella Chryssoulaki.

deep in a trench 4.8 × 2.5 m. Necks, hands, and legs were attached to wooden planks, and it is likely that they suffered a form of capital punishment. Unfortunately there is no secure date for the burial. The more recently discovered mass burials, however, have been dated to the seventh century on the basis of Protoattic ceramics in one of the trenches (Figures 4.10–4.11).[29] Altogether, three trenches contained seventy-eight to seventy-nine male adults, predominantly young adults and juveniles, some of them face down, and some with hands chained or bound behind their backs, or with arms lifted over their heads. One of the individuals had an arrowhead in the chest, and another had a dagger near the shin.[30] Media reports noted the otherwise good health of the bones (unusual for this cemetery), and there has been speculation that they were elite killed when Cylon attempted to establish a tyranny in the city.[31] The bioarchaeological field analysis concluded that there were thirty-nine "likely or possible perimortem fractions."[32] Moreover, the body positions of three individuals made it seem like they were killed on the spot and fell "like dominoes."[33] The authors are cautious, but they suggest the following possible explanation for the bodies in the mass graves:

> A hypothetical scenario is that a majority of the captives, probably in poor physical condition, e.g., starved, dehydrated, and beaten but otherwise in good general health, were brought to Phaleron in shackles, some of them plausibly tied to a frame with ropes, as suggested by their positions. The individuals may have been pushed to the

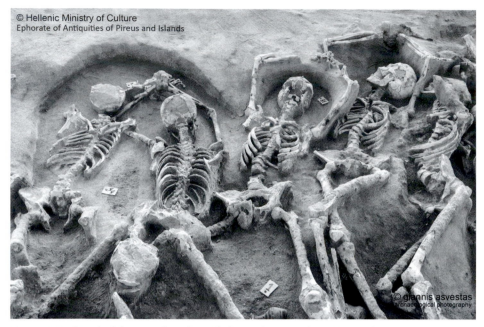

Figure 4.11. Detail of the mass burials in Phaleron discovered in 2016, with a Protoattic Phaleron oinochoe visible at the bottom of the image. Photo courtesy of Stella Chryssoulaki.

ground, some of them perhaps kneeling, before fatal blows/punches to the head of the individuals not already dead were inflicted before the bodies were covered.[34]

We will return to this cemetery later in this chapter and in the conclusion.

Compared to the Geometric period, the markers for graves during the seventh century are more elusive but not altogether absent. The best documented markers, not surprisingly, are in the meticulously excavated Kerameikos and took several forms. The most conspicuous involved physical transformations of the very earth of the landscape, with low mounds (1–1.5 m high, 4–10 m wide) erected over the grave, circular and rectangular in shape, and sometimes topped by a krater (often the so-called "kotyle krater" or "skyphos krater" shape, and smaller than the Late Geometric ceramic grave markers) or a stele (Figures 4.12–4.13).[35] Stray finds of vessels within other cemeteries may represent the remains of such funeral markers. Built mud brick structures also could mark a grave and became more common in the Kerameikos as space for mounds decreased.[36] Tumuli were used elsewhere as well to designate graves, such as Vari, and mounds could become themselves the siting for a grave, with seventh-century burials placed on or cut into mounds at Anavyssos and Palaia Phokaia.[37] Simple stone markers also could articulate the landscape. An upright stone marked burial VI at Eleusis,[38] and a marker distinguished one of the mass burials at Phaleron.[39] At Oinoe, jar burial στ lay under a small mound of stones, and some of the built structures above the graves may date to the seventh century.[40] Other markers in burial plots may have been made of perishable material,

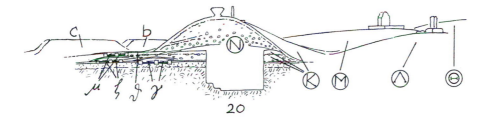

Figure 4.12. Stratigraphy in the Kerameikos cemetery. Photo John Blazejewski / Princeton University after Kübler 1970, Beilage 19.

Figure 4.13. Protoattic krater from Mound N in the Kerameikos (Grave VI-20). Kerameikos 152. Photo courtesy of the Deutsches Archäologisches Institut, Athens (D-DAI-ATH-Kerameikos-02561).

such as wood, which would not survive. Stone sepulchral sculpture only seems to have emerged at the end of the century and probably established a new material and form of grave marker rather than a new idea of how the landscape could be transformed into a place for commemoration.[41] At the end of the century, we also find plaques that may have decorated tomb precincts (Figures 4.14–4.15, Plate 7), illustrating some of the funeral rites that took place.[42]

The funeral trenches (Opferrinnen) in the Kerameikos are the most visible aspect of seventh-century funeral rituals, even if numerically they are not the most prevalent (Figures 4.7, 4.12, 4.16).[43] The ritual began in Late Geometric II, in the Kerameikos.

Figure 4.14. Attic funerary plaque, late 7th century, from Olympos. New York, Metropolitan Museum of Art 14.146.3a. Rogers Fund, 1914.

Figure 4.15. Attic funerary plaque, late 7th century, from Olympos. New York, Metropolitan Museum of Art 14.146.3b. Rogers Fund, 1914.

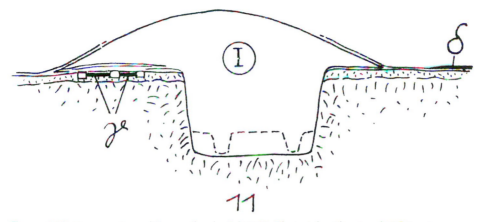

Figure 4.16. Cross section of Kerameikos burial VI-11. Photo John Blazejewski / Princeton University after Kübler 1970, Beilage 8.

In the seventh century, it is only attested in the Kerameikos and possibly at Vari.[44] The longest trench is 12 m, and not completely preserved. The trenches were narrow (ca. 0.50–1 m) and shallow (ca. 0.05–0.20 m), with the sides and a center strip delineated with mud bricks. On a wooden platform, vases and small animals such as birds were burnt while the tomb was still open. The ritual occurred at nearly the same time as the burial, which was usually a primary cremation in a separate pit. Then a mound usually covered both the burial and the offering trench. Interpretations of the ritual have varied, with scholars stressing the cultic or banqueting orientations of the ritual, which I will address below, when we consider in more detail the role of vases in Attic cemeteries.

The trenches should be treated as part of a broader phenomenon of other rituals at the tomb that have received less attention. Perhaps most understudied are those pyres that seem unrelated to the cremation of a corpse, and which had a more ceremonial function (for lack of a better word).[45] In the Kerameikos, several were located outside of the tumulus and designated as "Opferplätzen."[46] But there are others. They are too small to have been used for cremation, or they do not contain bones. And when found in close association with inhumations in jar burials, pyres likely performed a different function than cremation.[47] In the Kerameikos, a pyre with ashes and the head of an ivory figurine overlay the inhumation of a child in a jar (Figure 4.17).[48] At Oinoe, pyres were closely associated with jar burials—adjacent or below, and in one case above—and very thin.[49] The variety of the stratigraphic relationships of the pyres to the jar burials at Oinoe suggests there was no single ritual activity but different practices that took place before or after deposition. An array of activities surrounding depositions at Eleusis also can be traced. A pyre with charcoal and the unburnt bones of a hare or rabbit lay under a secondary cremation, and above the burial was a second pit 0.40 m deep containing ash and burnt sherds. At the edge of the grave, the upright base of a vessel may have received libations.[50] In

Figure 4.17. Burial assemblage from the Kerameikos, north of the Sacred Way. The ivory is from a pyre above the burial. The amphora (Kerameikos 2718) is attributed to the Group of the Wild Style. Photo John Blazejewski / Princeton University after Vierneisel 1964, fig. 29.

the same cemetery, a small pyre (diameter 0.80 m, depth 0.10 m) adjacent to a jar burial contained the burnt bones of a lamb, and a third pyre was found near two seventh-century jar inhumations.[51] At Phaleron, a pyre with Protoattic sherds lay above an adult inhumation in a stone cist.[52] All of these pyres are the traces of complex, multistage, variegated rituals that mourners performed to commemorate the dead.

VISIBILITY AND VARIABILITY IN THE BURIAL RECORD

Studies of ceramics and society in the seventh century have focused on the funeral trenches of the Kerameikos, for good reasons. Just as the discovery of the sumptuous vases in the cemetery modified the canon (chapter 2), so too did their contexts shift attention. Excavations revealed a spectacular rite involving the destruction of splendid vases by attributable painters. Meticulous publication has only increased the trenches' utility. Yet too often these trenches have formed the basis for broad generalizations about the seventh century, mortuary rituals, and Protoattic pottery, with the trenches characterized as typical and representative of burial practices

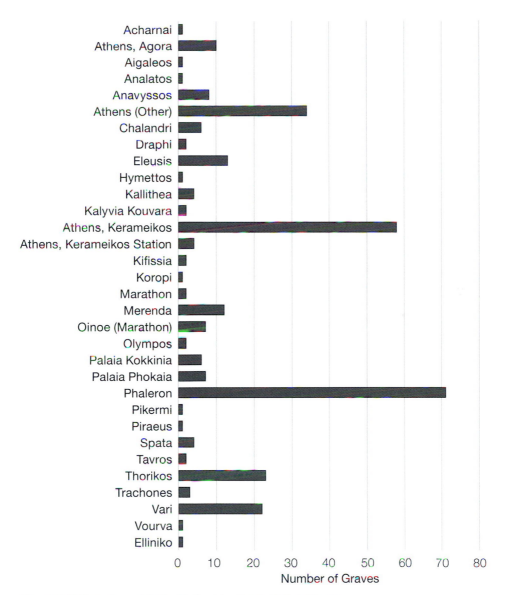

Figure 4.18. Locations of Protoattic burials. Graph N. T. Arrington.

and set against an otherwise largely invisible background of absent or "informal" burials.[53] Scholars discussing the seventh century tend to emphasize a drop in burial numbers, the termination of burial plots and cemeteries, the separation of child and adult burials, and the general poverty of burial assemblages, with elite funeral trenches shining as meaningful beacons in the darkness.

Gathering all of the evidence for seventh-century graves and looking outside of the Kerameikos clarifies the situation. There are nine funeral trenches coterminous with the production of Protoattic pottery, an additional two if one includes the LG IIb funeral trenches. With the possible exception of Vari, all are from the Kerameikos.[54]

Clearly this is an unusual practice, and Erich Kistler and Annarita Doronzio link it with a specific burying group using the Agia Triada burial plot of the Kerameikos.[55] In the Kerameikos alone, there are a further fifty burials, and in Athens and Attica, there are more than three hundred, from a variety of sites (Figure 4.18). The Kerameikos represents 19.5 percent of the burials, but this number would drop if other sites had better publication. In table 1 and figure 4.18, for example, Elliniko has only one entry, but there was an unspecified number of burials. The 1911 excavations by Kourouniotis at Phaleron are also only one entry in the table and the graph, because although he found sixty-eight graves, they cannot reliably be assigned to periods. Current excavations have added around eighty seventh-century burials to Phaleron, which are not yet included in my tabulation, as I await the promised publication.[56] Phaleron currently has 24 percent of the total burials; if one added the eighty, it would more than double the number of documented graves from Phaleron, giving it nearly three times as many burials as the Kerameikos and about half of the total number of seventh-century burials.

Burials for both children and adults are relatively evenly balanced in terms of numbers (38 percent and 33 percent, respectively, Figure 4.19), and do not seem as physically separated as scholars have maintained. Morris claimed that Phaleron was a cemetery primarily for children, but the evidence shows otherwise.[57] Moreover, while the Kerameikos finds promote the view that adults were accompanied by the most grave goods in the form of funeral trench offerings, the data show that actually children in Athens and Attica enjoyed grave goods more often than adults. As we survey the evidence presented above and in table 1, the seventh century seems not so invisible after all.

The case for visibility, however, should not be overstated, and compared to the late eighth century, there are indeed fewer seventh-century burials. Morris in 1987 recorded 388 burials for the Late Geometric period, a number that has only grown as excavations throughout Athens and Attica have continued to add graves to the tally.[58] Some of the reasons for the drop in the seventh century should be explored before returning to an analysis of the role of ceramics within the burial rituals. Demographic arguments have been widely dismissed; what merits attention is the way people buried and the way we recover burials. I will begin with the latter, which has not received as much attention as it should.

The spatial and temporal constraints placed on rescue excavations complicate their ability to recover seventh-century burials. At Oinoe, for example, it is certain that the cemetery extended beyond the confines of the narrow excavation (4–8 m wide, 30 m long), where archaeologists uncovered over thirty burials, including at least nine from the seventh century.[59] But the excavation was prompted by the construction of a water pipe and could not pursue the complete cemetery. In other cases, the goals of the excavators simply did not include questions and issues related to the seventh century, leading to underreporting. This problem was particularly pronounced in the nineteenth and early twentieth century, when interest for the period was dampened by distaste for the aesthetics of the seventh-century style, making it unlikely excavators would either search for the material or include it in the documentation of their results. It was costly and time consuming enough to illustrate and publish any vase; why devote attention to something so anticlassical? The 1896–97 excavations by the British School in Athens at Kynosarges are a case in point for the methods of the period and their skewed results. The project aimed to provide the school with some archaeological experience before it embarked on campaigns on Melos.[60] The only vase published from those excavations was the

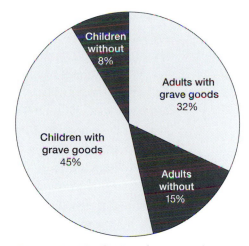

Figure 4.19. Distribution of grave goods in Protoattic burials. Graph N. T. Arrington.

Kynosarges Amphora (Figure 2.15), and most of the vases went to the owner of the site, according to Greek law of the time.[61] About a decade later, J. P. Droop published several Protoattic vases from the excavation, and nearly a hundred years later, once priorities and interests had changed, J. N. Coldstream returned to the material in detail.[62] Eventually, scholars were able to add eleven vases to the original one and to demonstrate that there was more than one Protoattic grave, but all objects still lack a specific context. We do not know how many graves there were, and we have no idea how many Protoattic vases were lost to the archaeological record.

Even more destructive of context than irregular publication was the looting of archaeological sites, which is by no means a contemporary phenomenon. The earliest archaeological reports from Greece already condemn wide-scale looting, including cemeteries rich in Protoattic material. Writing in 1921, Alexandros Philadelpheus reported that the cemetery at Spata had been victim to looting for years and that few unplundered tombs remained from what was once a large cemetery.[63] Vases were salvaged from Vari only because Humfry Payne, Michael Vlastos, and the National Archaeological Museum intervened in 1935 to stop plundering. Much material was lost, and the context of the material that remained is very difficult to piece together.[64] Unfortunately, this case is not exceptional. Many of the defining pieces of the Protoattic canon lack good contexts. The name-vase of the Analatos Painter, for example, a hydria from Analatos and the first Protoattic vase to be attributed, was essentially looted (Figure 2.6).[65] Table 1 indicates that 26 percent of all Attic seventh-century burials are only known through ceramic evidence, from vases that were reportedly found in tombs. The vases stem from excavations, where the vases were found but the graves destroyed or not reported in detail (such as Kourouniotis's excavations at Phaleron) or from museum collections that allege a mortuary provenience.

When we do possess information on contexts, the detail that publications supply varies considerably. Brief reports rarely document all burials and finds or provide data and illustrations that allow readers to check and evaluate writers' claims. It is not just a matter of needing more pages and figures; the study process that a comprehensive final publication demands can add considerable seventh-century material to a site, and even document the century when it was otherwise neglected or thought to be missing. Consider, for example, Maria Xagorari-Gleissner's publication of the material from Merenda (ancient Myrrinous). Following field seasons in 1960–61, the excavator, Ioannis Papadimitriou, reported only Late Geometric and early sixth- to fifth-century finds.[66] Xagorari-Gleissner's work, conducted decades after the dig, revealed that there were three seventh-century grave deposits, and a further six seventh-century vases and one figurine.[67] The 1967 and 1968 excavations at the site have still not received a full publication, and the preliminary reports briefly mention the upper portion of a Protoattic amphora and Protoattic sherds in fills.[68] How many more seventh-century graves here, and elsewhere, await? Merenda is not an isolated incident. The sad reality is that the majority of Attic cemeteries have not been published in a manner that makes it possible to confidently use statistics for the seventh century. Outliers, such as the Kerameikos and agora cemeteries, hold a dominant place in the historiography of the field. The data in figure 4.18 show that only sites that have received something close to a final publication (with the exception of Vari) have 3 percent or more of the total burials. In other words, the charts are in many ways just a reflection of which sites have received publication.

The cemetery at Phaleron has suffered from many of the problems discussed here and can illustrate the variety of issues we confront when trying to draw conclusions about society on the basis of burial evidence. Gregorios Bournias first excavated the cemetery in 1863, and he allegedly found 179 vases from a variety of periods, including Protoattic, that have not been published systematically.[69] When Konstantinos Kourouniotis excavated the Phaleron cemetery in 1911, he already reported many signs of looting and speculated that most if not all of the "Phaleron vases" in collections came from the site.[70] While his work salvaged important information on the cemetery, the material published was very selective, and it was presented without contexts. Of the sixty-eight burials he reported, not one assemblage can be reconstructed, and we do not know how many dated to the seventh century. Stratis Pelekidis excavated more of the cemetery in 1915, and his data are useful, but the scope of his rescue excavation was limited. Construction of the Stavros Niarchos Foundation Cultural Center prompted the archaeological work of 2012–20, which has been much more comprehensive methodologically. The information provided to the press has been tantalizing, and the final publication is eagerly awaited. Until then, the conclusions we can draw are limited. In the latest campaign, up to 2017 (for which numbers are available), nearly 10,000 m² had been excavated, with about 1,800 graves (not exclusively seventh century) discovered.[71]

Figure 4.20. Protoattic standed bowl attributed to the Vulture Painter, from an Attic grave. New York, Metropolitan Museum of Art 10.210.5. Rogers Fund, 1910.

The cemetery is 200 m wide, possibly over 500 m.[72] But once again the project's scope was limited by the salvage nature of the work, as I will discuss in the conclusion.

The problems described here affect many chronological periods, but the seventh century in particular. As described in chapter 2, the period often was not the main research interest of archaeologists, and its artwork was widely considered unappealing, and so the material was less likely to make its way into a preliminary report or a final publication. There are two other issues relatively unique to the seventh century that reduce its visibility in the archaeological record. First is the difficulty in dating seventh-century pottery. Geometric idioms persisted well into the seventh century, when sub-Geometric vases were made (Figure 4.20).[73] In more cases than one, a burial has been dated Late Geometric, but the illustrated objects allow us to redate it to the Early Protoattic period. So Ian Morris classified a pit burial at

Aristonikou 4 as Late Geometric, following the date provided in the publication report, but the illustrated vases demonstrate it is actually Early Protoattic.[74] At Meïntani 12–14, two pit burials were dated to Late Geometric, but the vases accompanying the report are instead Protoattic.[75] Denise Callipolitis-Feytmans dated three graves from Kallithea to Late Geometric, which J. N. Coldstream later revised to sub-Geometric contemporary with Early Protoattic.[76] These are only a few examples of a more pervasive problem, and when the images of the grave goods are not published, the errors cannot be corrected.

The second problem relatively unique to the seventh century is the placement of ceramics out of the burial and the prevalence of shallow cremation pyres, which often did not contain terra-cotta grave goods. Yet to dismiss these as "informal" burials would be a mistake. The fuel, labor, and time required for primary cremation were substantial. With or without a deep pit, the ritual created a highly visible funeral spectacle, the flames heating mourners as dead flesh burned, the smell spreading, the smoke visible from afar.[77] But since pyres could be made close to or on the surface, they were easily disturbed and even obliterated by later burial activity. At Eleusis, for example, all the recovered burials (with one exception) were jar inhumations so close to the surface that one suspects any shallow pyres would have been lost.[78] And indeed, many Protoattic vases from Eleusis come from fills or otherwise do not have a specific mortuary context. Protoattic sherds also exist at the Areopagus cemetery in the agora, where there are no identified seventh-century burials, and Rodney Young hypothesized that the shallow depth of the graves and later activity could account for the absence.[79] North of the Olympieion, a small excavation square (0.60 × 1.00 m) in 1956 recovered seventh-century sherds likely from burials that were destroyed by the leveling for the temple and by aggressive nineteenth-century excavations.[80] It is worth recalling that many of the seventh-century dates for graves in the Kerameikos were only ascertainable through careful stratigraphic analysis, not through the preservation of grave goods.

Although table 1 does not restore numeric equivalency between Late Geometric and Protoattic, a consideration of the data demonstrates variability in the mortuary record, starts to indicate some reasons other than social status for fluctuations in numbers, and exposes pitfalls to quantitative approaches. Most of the burials in Attica clearly are neither the funeral trenches of the Kerameikos nor derivative. A major difficulty to mortuary recovery is the drop in the number of recoverable grave goods placed in the tomb, but this should not necessarily be explained as a sign of poverty or of "informal" burials. The evidence demonstrates a considerable variety in burial practices in the seventh century in which consistent symbols of rank cannot be identified.[81] Some burials are exceptionally humble, yet Morris's views demand that any burial with material goods from the seventh century be associated with the elite. Morris partly addressed this problem by expanding the concept of *agathoi* to embrace 25 to 50 percent of the population, consisting of "aristocrats and wealthy but non-governing peasants."[82] A more likely solution is that there was considerable variety in the way everyone buried their dead, with factors other than wealth and status determining the form the burials took. So before turning more specifically to the issue of social status, I want to take a different approach than scholars usually adopt for the seventh-century ceramic record and first look more specifically at the objects themselves in their broader mortuary contexts. Examining the interaction of people with pots beyond the moment of final deposition and outside of questions exclusively of social status, let us look at the ways they enabled engagement with people, objects, and funeral rites.

VASES IN MOTION: PARTICIPATION AND INTERACTION IN FUNERAL RITUALS

The vases deposited at the tomb were of several types: repurposed domestic vessels made of fine ware, cook ware, or coarse ware; single vases purchased or imported specifically for the funeral; or special commissions of whole sets, often with some miniature vases included. Some shapes may have contained food, such as the standed bowls or the Corinthian(izing) pyxides. Others likely contained unguents, such as aryballoi (Figure 4.21) or long-neck incised juglets.[83] Still other vase shapes were used for libations: cups, terra-cotta phialai,[84] and especially oinochoai (Figures 4.22–4.25).[85]

Figure 4.21. Protocorinthian vases from Phaleron (Grave 11): aryballoi, pxyis, kotylai. Athens, National Museum 14953 (one inventory number for all finds). Copyright © Hellenic Ministry of Culture and Sports / Archaeological Receipts Fund.

Figure 4.22. Protoattic Phaleron-type oinochoe, from Phaleron (Grave 48), attributed to the Group of the Wild Style. Athens, National Museum 14965. Photo N. T. Arrington. Copyright © Hellenic Ministry of Culture and Sports / Archaeological Receipts Fund.

When miniature, they may have been too small for actual use and only evoked libations. Figurines also were deposited but in much smaller numbers, perhaps because they lacked the range of functions and associations of multipurpose pots (Figures 4.26–4.27, Plate 8).[86] In terms of style, "Orientalizing," sub-Geometric, Corinthian, Corinthianizing, and cook ware and coarse ware were used together.

Interpretations of the ceramics have focused on the funerary trenches of the Kerameikos and have offered several suggestions, often making a connection with tomb or hero cults and/ or with sympotic behavior.[87] Ronald Hampe thought they were tomb offerings, part of the cult of the dead, offered perhaps at the event later known as *ta enata*.[88] Anna Maria d'Onofrio emphasized the heroic connotations of the ritual and saw a role for dining and consumption at the grave.[89] In three separate articles, Sanne Houby-Nielsen shifted discussion toward the objects as reflections of the lifestyle, qualities, and virtues of the aristocratic deceased.[90]

The objects referred to banqueting, and she located them in the context of changes in the religious sphere marked by the appearance of temples with altars and the rise of hero cults. James Whitley related the contexts to behavior and society, with "depositional practices" a "product" of a social structure.[91] Protoattic pottery in the trenches, he argued, resulted from social rationing by occasion and status, a style for the elite. In a second article, he emphasized the cultic character of the grave goods, making parallels between tomb cults in and outside of Athens, and the graves in the Kerameikos and Vari.[92] Erich Kistler drew a distinction between the ceremony in the Kerameikos, contemporary with burial, and funeral trenches elsewhere that lay outside of the tumulus. Developing and extending Houby-Nielsen's view, he argued that the Kerameikos ritual and the pottery style made an effective display of Near Eastern banqueting.[93] Alexandra Alexandridou's research has focused on practices outside of Athens (Vari, Vourva, Marathon), much of it sixth century, and has argued that in the countryside the funerary trenches were part of postfunerary cultic activity, a result of local elite conservatism and land claims.[94] Thomas Brisart developed some of these views, especially Houby-Nielsen's and Kistler's, and argued that the vases were not offerings to the dead but status symbols.[95]

These interpretations, which in many respects overlap, have much to recommend them, but they are incomplete and insufficient explanations of the function of vases within the rich variety of the seventh-century burial rituals in Attica described above. With the exception of Whitley, they attempt to account for vases in only one specific ritual, which, it must be emphasized, does not in fact "trickle down" to the rest of the burying population. There are no miniature funeral trenches in Athens and Attica, no trenches that imitate on a smaller scale the Kerameikos remains, with either a smaller trench or fewer grave goods. The practice is not even that widespread in the Kerameikos itself, limited to the Agia Triada burial plot. And while the relationship of the trench deposits to banqueting is compelling, it is not evident how that metaphor would be transferable to a child burial. When we look closer at the Kerameikos, too, not all the vases in the offering trenches are sympotic. More disturbing, the vases

Figure 4.23. Protoattic Phaleron-type oinochoe, probably from Phaleron. Oxford University, Ashmolean Museum of Art and Archaeology 1887.3402. Image © Ashmolean Museum, University of Oxford.

are not all textbook examples of Orientalizing pottery. Some images may be curvilinear and replete with vegetal motifs, and they may be attributable to Protoattic painters, but the iconography only very rarely and exceptionally makes any allusion to the Levant. Some shapes, such as thymateria or standed dinoi, are relatively clear in their pretensions, but they are not ubiquitous. Nor are there any Near Eastern imports accompanying the vessels, as we might expect were the Levant so important to the burying community. Instead, the trenches contain Corinthian imports, and in fact the style of the Attic vases is more often Corinthianizing than Orientalizing (see also chapter 3).

Let us try another approach that incorporates funeral rituals other than the trenches. Rather than ask, "What do the vases mean," let us consider practice, and ask, "What do the vases do?" The first question implies that the significance of the

Figure 4.24. Protoattic Phaleron-type oinochoe. Athens, National Museum 310. Photo N. T. Arrington.

objects lies within the vases themselves. It presumes that an object simply "is," and that through its static ontology it can "mean" something. So scholars have sought an object's meaning through an analogy with language, treating material culture as a text that can be read, searching for semiotic references, symbolism, and (concealed) structures of signification that will reveal a logical and systematic relationship between material culture and concepts. In this approach, meaning lurks within an object for the scholar to discover.[96] Along these lines, scholars have overemphasized the Orientalizing aspects of Protoattic pottery, which have been defined in formal terms (i.e., style) with social implications. A seventh-century Protoattic vase in a funeral trench automatically becomes a gesture toward the cultures of the Near East.

Over the last few decades, anthropologists and archaeologists increasingly have criticized this search for the meaning of or within an object, asking not what an object is but what it does. Many of these approaches have emphasized the effect of objects on viewers and users from a phenomenological perspective.[97] The notion of practice, however, allows us to take a slightly different direction and to follow those scholars who have attempted to break down the Cartesian mind-body duality and to integrate mind, action, and matter. Jean-Pierre Warnier, for example, argues for a praxeological approach, which "considers material culture not only in terms of its sign value within a system of communication but in terms of its practical value in a system of agency," stressing how objects are props, conduits, supports, and articulations of human activity.[98] With such an approach, the question shifts yet again, from, "What do objects do," to "What do objects and humans do together," or "What do objects afford, invite, and enable humans to do?"

Our focus can then turn from object agency to human-object interaction. The work of Carl Knappett has been influential for me here. In *Thinking through Material Culture: An Interdisciplinary Perspective* (2005), he draws on Peircian semiotics to develop a useful framework for interpreting how people use material culture, which accounts for objects' formal and physical properties. Unlike many studies of materiality that, paradoxically, seem to leave the object itself behind, his work explic-

itly weds traditional art historical terminology to anthropological analysis. Particularly useful for addressing the role of
seventh-century vases, as we will see, is his deployment of
the Peircian terms "iconicity" and "indexicality," with iconicity describing the physical similarity among artifacts and
indexicality pinpointing formal relationships dependent on
contiguity, causality, and factorality.[99] In a subsequent book,
*An Archaeology of Interaction: Network Perspectives on Material
Culture and Society* (2011), he theorizes the ways in which people
interact specifically with assemblages, and he uses network
analysis to assess different scales of interaction and to look
at chronological change. He argues that objects uniquely enable human interaction and existence across space and time,
with proximate and present objects capable of referencing
absent and distant types.

Of course, not all of these approaches are immediately
relevant to the problem of seventh-century vases in Athens,
but with their help, we can turn now from the question,
"What do the vases mean?" to look at the ways in which the
vases participated in the socially mediated production of
meaning through activity performed at the hands of human
actors. Vases of a variety of shapes, fabrics, and styles were
used in many ways and at multiple times in the funeral ritual, even in the seventh century, when scholars speak of the

Figure 4.25. Protoattic Phaleron-type
oinochoe, from Phaleron, attributed
to the Workshop of the Passas Painter.
Athens, National Museum 307.
Photo N. T. Arrington.

absence of goods from the graves themselves. As objects rather than mere images,
they interfaced among humans, the dead, and other objects at the tomb at several
points in time. We can broaden our view of funeral rituals beyond the moment of
interment and put vases into the long process of burying and commemorating
the dead.

When someone died, the process of gathering objects for burial began, as mourners visited workshops to make purchases or to request special commissions, or
selected material from the home to repurpose. In preparing the corpse, vases were
used to hold water and unguents for cleaning and anointing the body. Touching
and caring for the corpse, with the mediation of vases, helped the living to process
the finality of the biological body. Pottery might also have been used prior to interment for commensal rituals at the home, as people gathered to lament the dead. And
vases may have been placed near the corpse on view in the house (the *prothesis*),
as was the case in later periods. In the cemetery, a vase could be the tomb itself,
serving as a funeral urn. People had to manipulate these repurposed vases, to break
them carefully to fit in the corpse, and to place the sherds back in position. Transported to the cemetery along with the corpse, vases could be used in several ways.

Figure 4.26. Horse figurine from the Palaia Kokkinia burial plot (Pyre 1). Piraeus, Archaeological Museum 15843. Photo Eleni Papathanasiou, courtesy of Georgios Spyropoulos.

At approximately the same time as burial, vases might be destroyed in funerary trenches, or placed nearby in an offering place, or burned on a ceremonial pyre. They may have contained offerings given to the dead, or liquids poured in libation, or other materials used for ritual purposes such as wine for quenching a fire. Following a cremation, vases or figurines could be placed on a cooled pyre, allowing a survivor to connect to the ashes. And finally a vase could serve as the marker on a burial mound. The use of objects to engage with the funeral, however, did not end with burial. Vases probably were used for ritual meals at the tomb that took place while the grave was open or after it was closed, and commemorative meals could also take place back at home (the *perideipnon*).[100] Finally, at some period following the deposition of the body, possibly a fixed period such as the *triakostia*, more vases could be used at or near the grave for making libations, anointing the tomb, partaking in meals, or just breaking.[101]

When we have traces of these activities, the use of vases never appears haphazard, and we can discern some of the care and concern of the hands behind them. Whether placed, smashed, or burned, they were used deliberately. The curation of the objects is particularly apparent in some well-preserved grave assemblages, where it is not uncommon to find vases carefully placed upside down or nestled inside one another, such as the assemblage from an inhumation in a jar at Palaia Kokkinia, with an aryballos inside a louterion, placed next to an upright stand (Figure 4.28).[102] At Thorikos, deposits at the mouth and base of the burial jar partially mirrored each other, with a juglet, olpe or oinochoe, skyphos, and cup at each end (Figure 4.29).[103]

Mourners used pottery to announce their state of mourning, to navigate the emotional trauma of the loss of life, to come to terms with biological death, to process and cope with the departure of loved ones, to celebrate and remember, and to affirm the persistence and continuity of the burying group. The popularity of the oinochoe, a vessel for pouring libations, underscores the performative role for vases at the seventh-century tomb.[104] Placed next to graves and often upright, they represent the trace of a mourner who brought the object from home, who performed a final offering, and who carefully set the object in a final resting place. The vases that were purchased,

Figure 4.27. Figurines from Vari (Grave 27), attributed to the Protoattic Painter of Opferrinne ζ/XIV. Athens, National Museum 26747. Photo Irini Miari. Copyright © Hellenic Ministry of Culture and Sports / Archaeological Receipts Fund.

Figure 4.28. Pot Burial 2 from Palaia Kokkinia. Photo courtesy of Georgios Spyropoulos.

Figure 4.29. Pot burial from Thorikos West Cemetery (T 203). Photo Courtesy of the Thorikos—EBSA archive.

held, poured, and deposited became extensions of their bodies and mechanisms for engagement with rituals and death, allowing them to touch the corpse, to reach into the grave, to express sorrow, to dine together, and to remember.

While the actions at the home and grave were performed by individuals, the practices were shared, and a group rather than a single person buried the dead and cohered through rituals.[105] Through using, depositing, and viewing objects, a community of mourners coalesced. They shared the customs of burial and took part in the ritual together. Even if not every person touched an object at the tomb, they witnessed the objects moving between the living and the dead, the home and the grave, through the hands of several persons. The vases allowed people to reestablish their social communities ruptured by death and the loss of family members by sharing in the funeral rite. Van Gennep's conceptualization of the rites of passage is useful here, and we can imagine the ways in which objects helped people to separate from and reintegrate into society. The importance of affirming social bonds in the face of loss may have been particularly acute at a time when the civic institutions of the *polis* were emerging and new, suprafamilial communities coalescing.[106]

Decoration on the vases distinguished the object, heightening the emotional and social valence of the activity that people performed. It might allow the crossing of specific horizons, through allusions to the east, the west, or the past. Depending on how the vases were used, certain aspects of the imagery and the style could come into focus. At the funeral trench, in making allusions to the symposium through practice, mourners could gesture toward the Levant, Etruria, or the Mediterranean. Decorated vases here and elsewhere allowed participants to connect to an extensive geographical-scape and time-scape, which was more open-ended than "Orientalizing" and part of an intricate fabric of activity at the grave.

Domestic vessels—especially the amphoras, hydrias, and pithoi repurposed as inhumation urns—crossed a certain horizon, too, through their close links with the home. When these vases served as burial containers for inhumations, they enwrapped the corpse with a physical shell and provided a vivid means to connect the mourners, the corpse, and the house. As icons and indexes (drawing on Knappett's redeployment of the terms), the vases' shape, fabric, and decoration referenced other similar objects still in the *oikos*, the domestic goods they once held, and the household activities with which they were once associated. The vase bestowed a warmth and affection on the dead child and affirmed their belonging to the domestic unit. Used in burials, as types the pots still belonged to a broad assemblage of domestic goods, and they brought their earlier "lives" with them. Unlike the vases commissioned for burial, the vases from the home came with their biographies.[107] Viewers and users at the tomb would immediately apprehend the wider network of goods to which they belonged: the burial urn resembled and echoed the domestic vessel. By sharing formal and visual properties with domestic goods, the funeral objects knit tomb and

Figure 4.30. Late Protoattic louterion from the Palaia Kokkinia burial plot (Pot Burial 2), close to the Painter of Opferrinne ζ/XIV. Piraeus, Archaeological Museum 14260. Photo Jeff Vanderpool, courtesy of Georgios Spyropoulos.

hearth together. As the repurposed domestic vessels colored conceptions of the deceased, they also shaped the way that family members used domestic goods back at the home, who interacted with objects that shared formal properties with a vase that now held a corpse. The pithos in the cellar that they used on a daily basis now was a potential tomb. So like a vase rich with "Orientalizing" imagery, a cook pot, too, provided a broader and more meaningful frame of reference for mourners and served as a mechanism for extending the temporal, geographical, and emotional import of burial, helping mourners to bury the deceased with the home, and to remember the deceased in their daily rituals. By the end of the Protoattic period, mourners could hang at the tomb plaques with an image of the laying out of the dead at the home, a vivid intermingling of *oikos* and sepulcher (Figures 4.14–4.15).[108]

Associations of coarse- and cook-ware vases with women strengthened this link with the house. The large storage jars repurposed for burial were associated with wealth and abundance, and just as importantly they held close connections to the female body through use, materials, and shape.[109] Within the Hippocratic corpus and among later anatomists, the uterus was described as a vase.[110] Some cook-ware jars included nipples, making an iconic link between the body of the vase and the female form.[111] To bury the deceased—usually a child—in such domestic jars was in some sense to return them to the female body and to the womb.

If domestic pottery allowed a localized type of horizon-crossing, a more long-distance, temporal horizon-crossing was possible at tomb cults. They were one manifestation of graves as sites of memory where objects could bridge space and time and draw people together. As we saw in chapter 3, the precise number of tomb cults and the identities of the people honored is disputed and probably impossible to recover reliably. Yet at these tombs from the distant past, people used rituals to connect to the deceased, to the land, and to one another. The dead may have been conceived as ancestors, as heroes, or as inhabitants of the land; I am not convinced we can know for sure. But it is interesting that there is overlap between tomb cult and funeral activity at grave sites. Some scholars, as we have seen, connect at least some of the funeral trenches to the worship of the deceased. And outside of the funeral trenches, too, some of the same types of ritual objects were used in both places. At a child inhumation in Palaia Kokkinia, for example, fragments of four standed louteria were buried with the deceased, a type of ritual libation bowl also found in the Protoarchaic deposit at the Bronze Age tomb of Menidi (Figure 4.30).[112] Tomb cults throw into relief the ways in which objects could enable meaningful participation in a variety of funeral rituals and link participants with each other and with the deceased across horizons near and far.

Figure 4.31. Late Geometric I oinochoe from Grave 48 in the Kerameikos, by the Concentric Circle Group. Kerameikos 1327. Photo courtesy of the Deutsches Archäologisches Institut, Athens (Émile Seraf, D-DAI-ATH-Kerameikos-05376).

SOCIAL DISORDER AND THE ABSENCE OF CULTURAL HEGEMONY

As we look outside of the Kerameikos at a wider variety of graves and assemblages, and as we consider the many ways in which vases operated in mortuary contexts, the link of Protoattic ceramics with elite display weakens. Evidently there were other concerns. In addition, close consideration of contexts reveals an inconsistency in the alleged terms of display. A sequence of overlapping burials in the Kerameikos cemetery demonstrates some of the problems with conventional models. The first in this stratigraphic sequence (Late Geometric I), Grave 48, was an inhumation with an amphora, two cups, a high-rimmed bowl, and an oinochoe by the Concentric Circle Group, which was modeled on Cypriot examples (Figure 4.31).[113] This seems to be a burying group, therefore, with connections toward the Levant and a tendency toward "Orientalizing." Grave 49 (Late Geometric II) cut it, a cremation containing

Figure 4.32. Late Geometric II bird askos from Grave 49. Kerameikos 1351. Photo courtesy of the Deutsches Archäologisches Institut, Athens (Hermann Wagner, D-DAI-ATH-Kerameikos-05551).

Figure 4.33. Late Geometric II dinos from a funeral trench (Opferrinne 1), attributed to the Workshop of Athens 894 or near it. Kerameikos 1354. Photo courtesy of the Deutsches Archäologisches Institut, Athens (Kurt Gebauer, D-DAI-ATH-Kerameikos-05558).

three kantharoi, three kalathoi, two high-rimmed bowls, an oinochoe, three askoi (Figure 4.32), a bronze bracelet, and an iron knife.[114] With the quantity of grave goods, the askoi, and the metals, this grave, too, would seem to testify to an elite burying group, which the next funeral activity in the sequence seems to confirm: a funeral trench with fourteen vases, most of them by the Late Geometric II Workshop of Athens 894 or near it, including four dinoi on high stands with bird appliqués, a type of vase for mixing wine that imitates Near Eastern metal vases and that makes the banqueting allusions scholars like to see in subsequent seventh-century graves (Figure 4.33).[115] Yet the picture changes with the next two burials in the sequence. Grave 99, a child inhumation in a wooden sarcophagus, cuts the offering trench, and the grave goods are remarkably austere: two kotylai, one oinochoe, and one Protocorinthian aryballos, with plain decoration (Figure 4.34).[116] Finally, Grave 100, a jar burial for a child, cuts Grave 99 and contains one kotyle, one oinochoe, and one cup, without a trace of the contemporary "Orientalizing" style (Figure 4.35).[117] Why did this burying group depart from the Near Eastern idioms they were beginning to use? It is hard to imagine that new families were using this space, given the close chronological succession of burials and the continuity of place. Did Graves 99 and 100 belong to families that were no longer elite, or to people who no longer wanted to use objects with Near Eastern connotations? Or might our assumptions about style, status, and display be misplaced?

This disruption in burial practices, with the absence of consistent modes for representing status, finds a parallel in the change in style of the vases themselves. Geometric vases were relatively uniform in appearance and shared a formal repertoire, from their shape to their subject matter to their facture. Composed of linear ornaments, they were highly organized objects, with much of their aesthetics dependent on repetition. The facture of the vases, with decoration often made with a multiple brush, contributed to the uniform appearance of the vase's decoration and to visual similarities among painters. Only a few workshops have been identified. Protoattic, in contrast, had a myriad of individual hands and highly idiosyncratic styles. The introduction of vegetal ornament provided a rich repertoire for artists, yielding considerable diversity in iconography, with sub-Geometric forms also a possibility. The preference for freehand painting away from the potter's wheel changed the whole approach to the vase. There were also new techniques, such as incision and added color. Meanwhile, the size of vases decreased. (See further chapter 5 on these changes.)

Protoattic did not mark a retreat from order and a descent into chaos, as some scholars who privilege the Classical style have thought,[118] but it did represent a new variety and variability in which there were few norms and standards—much as there were few conventions for the burial of the dead.[119] Vase shapes waxed and waned in popularity, and highly individualized painters emerged without leaving any lasting workshop tradition behind. The Protoattic style created more possibilities for representation than Geometric, and as the Kerameikos sequence

Figure 4.34. Early Protocorinthian aryballos and kotyle from Grave V-99 in the Kerameikos, late 8th or early 7th century. Photos courtesy of the Deutsches Archäologisches Institut, Athens (Hermann Wagner, D-DAI-ATH-Kerameikos-05541A, -05441B).

above suggests, consumers did not agree on when or how to use the style, if at all. Imports and new modes of representation could threaten the entrenched symbolic order in traditional societies just as much as they could offer new vectors for power.[120]

One cause of the heterarchy in style and in burial rituals was the development of communities in the eighth century, producing civic institutions that created new

Figure 4.35. Kotyle and cup from Grave V-100 in the Kerameikos, early 7th century. Photo courtesy of the Deutsches Archäologisches Institut, Athens (D-DAI-ATH-Kerameikos-05539).

mechanisms for power and influence and alternative modes of status acquisition.[121] Some scholars, for example, have traced a shift from military values to leisure values among the elite in the seventh century, which they perceive in the decline of martial subject matter on Protoattic vases and the absence of weapons from graves.[122] The change may be related to the increase in mass, hoplite warfare that a *polis* community demanded.[123]

But competition was not within a closed elite, and there are also traces of demographic shifts, with new groups contributing to the diversity in style and practice.[124] The seventh century may witness fewer burials than the eighth century, but there were new burial plots. The wealthiest Late Geometric cemeteries of Athens were no longer so prominent, the Agia Triada burial plot in the Kerameikos attained new preeminence, and other more modest burial plots appeared. This shifting mortuary landscape probably responds to a filling-in of the landscape, with less space available for burial as settlements grew, to a growing distinction between the space of the dead and the living, and to the burial practices of new groups, who had not been interring in the eighth century.[125] The previous chapter argued for connectivity, including immigration, between Athens and the rest of the Mediterranean, and such groups may have contributed to the new burial plots, much as they contributed to a new painting style. The decline in archaeologically visible burials is a result more of historiographic problems, changes in burial types, debates about how to bury and commemorate the dead, and a rise in simple cremations than an indication of elite-only access to burials. The elite of the seventh century lacked cultural hegemony in a period marked by a pervasive spirit of experimentation.

The closer we look at the term "elite," which subtends all analysis of Protoattic pottery and social status, the more nebulous it appears. The very flexibility of the term endows it with heuristic value, allowing researchers to designate myriad behaviors as elite, with Morris guessing that as much as 50 percent of the Athenian population could be among his *agathoi*.[126] The breadth of this category, which should by definition be circumscribed, suggests something is amiss. And once we try to pinpoint qualifications for elite status, we immediately encounter difficulties. Burials preserved in the archaeological record (i.e., "formal burial"), as we have seen, do not necessarily correlate with status, with humble and rich burials side by side. So how might we define an elite in Greece? On the basis of wealth? Political influence? Culture? Where might someone like Hesiod rank? As an immigrant, he could not have belonged to an established family dynasty. Yet he managed a prosperous farm with the assistance of servile labor. He wrote treatises at a time when few were literate, and he traveled to compete (and win) in poetic competitions, with his work sufficiently prized that a manuscript tradition survives to this day. But he also worked the land himself and claimed to be lower than *basileis*. Economic, political, and cultural markers do not neatly correlate.

Even more problematic than the term "elite" is the related concept of a Greek aristocracy. Fisher and van Wees have discussed the weaknesses and limitations of this notion of hereditary status in ancient Greece, and Alain Duplouy has persuasively argued that status in ancient Greece was constantly (re-)achieved rather than momentarily ascribed.[127] He demonstrates that the elite sought social distinction and prestige through various strategies (which he designates "modes de reconnaissance social"), including marriage, funeral monuments, dedications, collecting, leisure activities, and genealogy, and they thereby continually reaffirmed and maintained their rank. There were no stable and fixed classes or aristocracies, Duplouy emphasizes, and status was constantly performed. His views were influential on Thomas Brisart's treatment of Orientalizing art as a social tool in the context of the emergence of the Greek city-state, alternatively serving as a means for distinction or as a mechanism for integration, depending on the type of *polis*.[128] However, Duplouy may place too little weight on the importance of family and institutional (i.e., civic) structures.[129] Much depends on how we interpret the few literary sources at our disposal. To what extent does Homer represent ideals rather than realities, and to what extent do Classical passages about the seventh century reflect their later contexts? Some of the texts, especially the pseudo-Aristotelian *Constitution of Athens*, suggest that considerable power lay in the hands of a small number of people on the basis of wealth and birth.[130] According to Herodotus, *naukraroi* (presidents of the naval board), compelled the Cylonian conspirators to remove themselves from the Acropolis around 630, and specifically the family of the Alcmaeonidae were among those who killed the suppliants.[131] Thucydides describes a different distribution of power, with Athenians streaming in from the countryside to lay siege to the Acropolis, but he goes on to relate that nine archons were left in charge of the situation.

Chapter 1 described some of the state institutions that seem already to have existed in the seventh century and the importance of birth for attaining political power. So we should not discount the role that families could have on status and political power already in the seventh century, all the while recognizing that there were no Greek aristocracies, and that social standing was in flux and in need of performance—but without an agreed set of conventions for using material culture.

Defining a nonelite is, if anything, only more problematic than defining an elite. Defining them in economic terms as "the poor," as an aggregate social/political group measured against an arbitrary, unmet economic threshold, is anachronistic and unnecessarily restrictive.[132] Our concept of the nonelite should be as fluid as our concept of the elite. It should relate as much to an experience or perception of a subelite status for cultural and social reasons as to a relationship to economic resources—hence, my preference for the term "marginalized."

The textual record of the late seventh and sixth centuries, predominantly poetic fragments, supplements the picture of social disorder perceptible in the archaeological record, with a lack of established visual systems for representing status, and supports the possibility that people could move in and out of the margins. Archaic literature was obsessed with the question of status and who had it. Who was elite? On what grounds? And what was their authority? While the writers had their own audiences and agendas and can only be used with caution, they transmit the impression of social disorder rather than clear and accepted social distinctions. Theognis, for example, laments, "Many base men are rich and good men are poor. But we will not exchange wealth for virtue, since virtue always lasts, but now one, now another has money."[133] His poetry is riddled with similar references to changes in wealth and social status and the difficulty in assessing virtue.[134] More specifically in reference to Attica, Solon uses identical language at one point, stating, "Now one man, now another has money."[135] Usually the stress in the sources falls on downward social mobility and the specter of poverty.[136] Writers do not always enumerate the causes, but on occasion they specifically mention war, illness, or lack of sons.[137] We can imagine other causes, too, such as shipwreck or poor harvests, which were particularly likely given the high climactic variability of the microregions of Greece. The movement of wealth, however, could go both ways, as the passages from Theognis and Solon imply (and critique).[138] Archilochos says that the gods often raise people up as well as knock them down,[139] and Semonides speaks of the widespread expectation that peoples' lots will improve, if only to criticize such deluded thinking: "Yet hope and confidence nourish all in our eagerness for the impossible. Some wait for the morrow to come, others for the revolving seasons, and there is no one who does not expect that he will arrive at the next year as the friend of wealth and prosperity."[140] Solon records a similar sentiment: "If someone is lacking means and is constrained by the effects of poverty, he thinks that he will assuredly acquire much money. Everyone has a different pursuit."[141] Interestingly, he specifies how people might climb out of misery, enumerating a variety of

occupations: fishing, farming, craftsmanship, poetry, prophecy, and medicine.[142] While these are hardly the activities that scholars tend to associate with
the elite, with the exceptions of farming and poetry, Solon thought the list would
resonate with his listeners. Solon's early sixth-century reforms at Athens, changing the qualifications for office from wealth and birth to just wealth, must have
responded in part to the demands of an emergent prosperous group.[143] By the end
of the seventh century, it is reasonably clear from the texts that social conflict
divided Attica, with land increasingly in the hands of few, and with many poor
people working the land, some in debt bondage.[144] Funerals became such a source
of contention that laws attributed to Solon limited display in mourning (specifically self-lacerating, weeping, and sacrificing an ox) in addition to restrictions on
the amount of garments one could bring, the number of aulos players, the participation of women outside the close family, and visiting the tombs of nonfamily
members on days other than funerals.[145]

In place of a static social order of elite and nonelite, or *agathoi* and *kakoi*, the
location and types of burials, the new pottery style and shapes, the variety of uses
of material culture, and the textual sources indicate that the seventh century was
marked by social instability and fluidity, in both directions. Protoattic pottery both
responded to and participated in the social disruption of the time period. In a
context of increased social complexity, with the rise in population numbers, de-
limitation of sacred space, increased Mediterranean connectivity, and urbanization, Protoattic pottery opened up new possibilities of meaning and disrupted the
signification system through shapes, iconography, and style. The elite did not have
a clear set of symbols to use for displaying status, or an agreed-on, consistent way
of burying the dead, and they were not a fixed group. The pottery offered people of
multiple means, not only the exceedingly wealthy, a mechanism for burying and
mourning their dead and using material culture to engage with rites of mourning
and to connect with one another.

APPROPRIATION AND TRANSFORMATION:
A MODEL FOR CHANGE FROM BELOW

In order to gauge the consumption of pottery among the elite and at the margins,
I will compare and contrast the Kerameikos and Phaleron cemeteries. This is not to
suggest that the categories of elite and marginalized were fixed but to suggest that
there was a meaningful difference between the way that status was and was not performed in both cemeteries. The Kerameikos cemetery is an elite context, and Phaleron
marginal, in the sense that the first has a comparatively much more time-consuming
and elaborate funeral outlay. The Kerameikos was home to the most ostentatious
burials of the seventh century, those with funeral trenches. At Phaleron, the majority
of burials lacked grave goods, disease and hardship characterized the bone evidence, and no funeral trenches were used (Figure 4.36, Plate 10). It was a large space,

Figure 4.36. Excavations at the Phaleron cemetery, Stavros Niarchos Foundation Cultural Center. Photo courtesy of Stella Chryssoulaki.

with hundreds if not thousands of burials. Not least, the presence of mass, deviant burials, perhaps suffering from capital punishment, indicates that it was a place for the interment of the politically marginalized.

Yet Phaleron was a site where Protoattic was deposited—in such numbers that the style originally was called Phaleron Ware (chapter 2). One of the most prevalent shapes deposited here, the oinochoe with a tapering neck, has close parallels with oinochoai with an exclusively funerary use from the Levant and Cyprus.[146] The vases were made in metal and red impasto and characterized by a conical neck. Not only did they circulate widely across the Mediterranean, but they also were locally produced in the west—as far west as Iberia. Some of the closest parallels for the Phaleron jugs are oinochoai from Tarquinia and Caere from the first half of the seventh century (Figure 4.37, and compare Figures 1.6, 2.3, 2.13, 4.22–4.25).[147] Much of the decoration is relatively simple or sub-Geometric, but there are also examples of figural decoration and so-called Orientalizing ornamentation. The presence of decorated ceramics in Phaleron militates against the view that the style was strictly associated with the elite or socially rationed. Nevertheless, some scholars might attempt to explain away Protoattic in such a poor cemetery through a model of trickle-down cultural development in which nonelite simply imitated the elite. This view, rarely challenged, dominates interpretations of Early Iron Age Greek cultural change in general.[148] The presence of Protoattic in a subelite context would only testify to the power of conspicuous

Figure 4.37. Cypro-phoenician bronze oinochoe from Pontecagnano. Pontecagnano 928. Photo John Blazejewski / Princeton University after d'Agostino 1977, plate 19.

consumption and extravagant display, which compelled imitation, emulation, and derivation. The motor of innovation and cultural change would remain at the top of the social echelon.[149]

As we have seen, however, the opulent funeral trenches of the Kerameikos are relatively unique and did not lead to wide-scale imitation. It is not possible to establish clear and consistent criteria for the ranking of burials in this period characterized by heterogeneous practices, or to find traces of derivation. Doubtless an elite was more connected to international trends (and more horizons) than those with fewer resources at their disposal, and doubtless they engaged in status competition with peers and sought to distinguish themselves from each other and the subelite, particularly in a period of social mobility when the threat of becoming marginalized was palpable. Protoattic, however, was not the obvious recourse, for reasons described above. The grave sequence we traced in the Kerameikos, with sub-Geometric appearing at the very time that more ornate Protoattic was accessible, is symptomatic of the hesitation among elite groups in using a new pottery style that departed in terms of size, style, and subject matter from prior standards of status display. We have also seen how the concerns of burial communities were not always first and foremost with status, but with using objects to negotiate the trauma of death and to help the community mourn and heal.

Is a radical alternative possible: that a so-called Orientalizing style in Athens and Attica started at the margins, among those who buried at Phaleron? Chronological contexts suggest this is possible. Not only is Protoattic pottery present at Phaleron, but the cemetery also has some of the earliest Protoattic vases from secure contexts. A comparison to the Kerameikos is instructive: while Early Protoattic exists in the Kerameikos, such as in the offering place designated Opferplatz α/IV, seventh-century ceramics do not appear in funeral trenches until the Middle Protoattic period, long after it had been used at Phaleron.[150] A consideration of painters' hands points in a similar direction. Many scholars have emphasized the role for one painter, the Analatos Painter, in the creation of the Protoattic style.[151] This framework of an individual genius suits conventional explanations of cultural change and also allows for the close interaction of one painter with an ostensibly elite clientele, further supporting the model of top-down change. However, the evidence indicates that several painters were working in the Protoattic style just as early if not earlier than the Analatos Painter, including those disparaged by Cook as "non-Classical." The Analatos Painter was hardly the most innovative but one of the more conservative of the first painters, one who continued to use Late Geometric style and iconography. The "non-Classical" painters, such as the Passas Painter and the Würzburg Group, were more forward and are particularly well documented at Phaleron and other marginalized contexts (Figure 1.6).[152] Taken together, the evidence from chronology, contexts, and artists suggests that it is certainly possible that this style ultimately associated with the elite began in very different social circles.

Although this is not how we usually conceive of cultural change, the social margins could be the crucible for the development of a new style. The types of communities represented by the Phaleron cemetery were not homogenous. And on the basis of Phaleron as well as other archaeological contexts, together with the texts adumbrated above, we can deduce that these marginalized were not without agency. Even when poor in resources, as an aggregate they had a power of consumption.[153] Moreover, they likely included such nonpropertied individuals as immigrants, travelers, tradespeople, and possibly mercenaries, from multiple backgrounds, with a variety of traditions and tastes, and holding an array of ideas about how to bury the dead.[154] They lived and buried in a harbor town, which may have been more open to travelers and their different tastes and ideas.

Heterogenous demand could prompt innovation and experimentation among producers, and nonelite objects provided an ideal vehicle for flexibly responding to new needs. Compared to the massive Geometric grave markers decorated in an intricate, time-consuming style and fired in an enormous kiln, a small Protoattic vase could be thrown in little time by one person and painted with a few strokes.

On these smaller, more humble vessels, the artist was much more likely to take a risk and to try something new, catering to a broad (if not large) audience.

There are parallels in other periods and media for this type of innovation at the margins of the artistic canon. For example, Meyer Schapiro described how a variety of styles could coexist on the same object, and not always where one might expect them. He drew attention to medieval manuscripts, where the more developed style was located on the borders, and commented that "in medieval art the sculptor or painter is often bolder where he is less bound to an external requirement; he even seeks out and appropriates the regions of freedom."[155] The so-called Phaleron Ware, produced for subelite, heterogeneous, international and immigrant communities, were the type of objects on which Geometric could give way to new ideas about painting. The vases represent what Schapiro called "the unhomogeneous, unstable aspect [of style], the obscure tendencies toward new forms."[156]

When we consider all the factors behind the beginning of the style and the characteristics of the style itself, the audience and objects at the margins emerge as catalysts for stylistic change. Yet there was still an important role for the elite in the development of the style, if not its genesis. They placed the style that began at the margins in new contexts, with elaborate forms and distinctive uses. In the Kerameikos, vases were made with much more labor than those at Phaleron. Intricate ornamentation, striking coloration, and complex figuration on larger vases demanded more labor (Figure 3.31) and could invoke the latest Corinthian trends, a Levantine horizon, or nostalgically look back to Geometric models. Plastic attachments transformed the vases into quasi-sculptures that were spectacular in appearance and impossible to use for anything other than a funeral dedication (Figure 4.38).[157] The objects became manifestly nonutilitarian, morphed into objects of display and conspicuous consumption. The role of practice played a fundamental role in this elaboration and distancing effect, in the funeral trenches evoking a symposium and making international associations.[158] In other words, form and practice at the funeral ceremony transformed and appropriated the pictorial style for the elite.

This model of cultural change, with an appropriation from below, has some modern echoes. Some scholars have discussed a somewhat similar phenomenon of "poor chic" or "shabby chic"—going back at least to Marie Antoinette's Hameau, a recreation of rural architecture on the grounds of Versailles—in which symbols of the working- or underclass are made stylish and recreational.[159] Everyday examples are all around us: jeans torn for effect, combat boots that will never see battle, or sport utility vehicles that stay on asphalt. As in the seventh century, these utilitarian objects are transformed through materials, form, and practice into objects of desire that no longer serve their original function and no longer appeal to the people who initially used them. Consider the striking example of the X-Class pickup truck designed by Mercedes and launched in 2017. Promotional material carefully

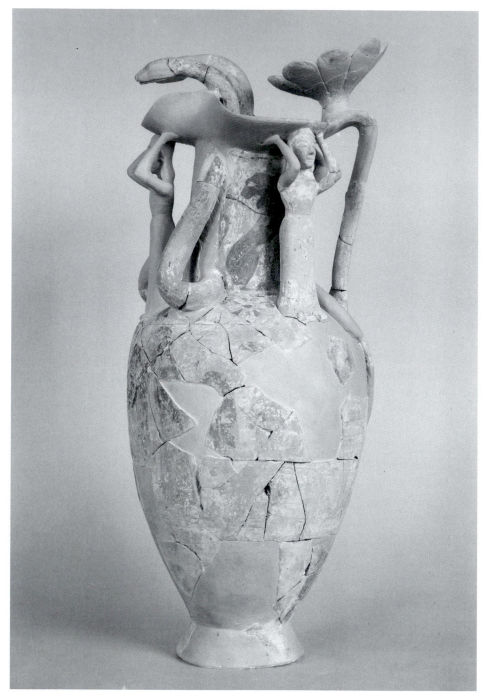

Figure 4.38. Protoattic oinochoe with attached figural mourners, from Kerameikos funeral trench (Opferrinne) γ. Kerameikos 149, attributed to the Painter of Opferrinne γ I. Photo courtesy of the Deutsches Archäologisches Institut, Athens (Hermann Wagner, D-DAI-ATH-Kerameikos-03439).

avoided the word "truck," declaring it "the world's first true premium pickup for the modern urban lifestyle." Targeted at "families with an active lifestyle and an affinity to premium products" and "successful adventurers who live in an urban environment," the pickup promised to inspire "trend-conscious individualists." "It will absorb bumps in a superior fashion, making it a perfect fit for the urban environment."[160] The vehicle has a clear formal affinity to the utilitarian pickup trucks from which it derived but is transformed through name, materials, and style into a new breed of vehicle targeted at a different clientele for new contexts.

There are obvious differences between these modern examples and ancient ceramics. Today these appropriations occur in part because of the values of authenticity or ruggedness associated with nonelite and utilitarian objects. Drawing attention to the ubiquity of this phenomenon, however, should unsettle our conventional narratives about how culture changed in antiquity. Thinking about these modern examples may help us reflect on how an Athenian looked on a decorated amphora such as the one in Figure 4.1.

To recover the genesis of the Protoattic style among the subelite, therefore, does not entail a romantic declaration of nonelite agency. Instead, it exposes the insidious ways in which elite appropriate and distort forms of cultural life, alienating the subelite from the very products that they helped generate and shaping a group into the marginalized. The elaborated forms and distinctive practices rendered stark the wealth and leisure of the elite as they attempted to define the terms of their community and to forge a gulf between themselves and others. It was a process in which both sides looked to each other, but rather than display at the top leading to imitation below, innovation below was followed by appropriation above.

The fluidity of the process was abetted by the inconsistency in the use of symbols to assert rank and status, by the overall heterarchy in the use of vases in burial rituals, and by the disruptive properties of the Protoattic style itself, which broke with past conventions of representation and offered new opportunities for painting and use. The elite did not agree on the terms of the discourse or how to use pottery, because the definition of elite was not fixed and because of the new style. The resultant discord bears some similarities to a framework that Ian Morris advocated, pointing to evidence, particularly in the literary record, for elite debates over sources of authority and legitimacy.[161] He distinguished middling (elite) from elitists, the first who looked to the community, the second who looked outside of it. His approach captures some of the social tensions but is too rigid and binary when compared to the variety we see in the material record of the seventh century. It assumes a fixed group of elite and a fixed resource of status symbols, and it renders those who considered themselves marginalized completely absent in the process of cultural transformation. So, too, Duplouy's notion of status performances operates at the level of the elite. Instead, I advocate a tug and pull in which the elite usurp styles developed below, and in which a boundary between elite and subelite was never very clear. The process was not restricted to vase-painting, and chapter 6 will look at the elite elaboration and appropriation of writing and wine consumption, too.

DISSENT AND RESISTANCE

Despite their grab, the elite never had a monopoly on the Protoattic style, and lurking beneath every Protoattic object lay its subelite genesis. Protoattic, with its new ways and modes of making and imaging, had opened new possibilities. By making a break with the past and departing from Geometric customs and idioms, it was poised to subvert norms of representation and social order. The funeral trench ritual exposes how much the elite needed practice to render the style elitist; the ritual looks desperate. The objects alone were insufficient for their status claims, too open to different modes of signification and to misinterpretation. The elite burying community required a massive investment of labor in a spectacular display.

Can we hear other voices? Ian Morris wrote, "It has been well-nigh impossible for Greek historians to discover competing counter-ideologies."[162] But some vases preserve traces of dissent in the fluid social order and the chaotic symbolic world of the seventh century, as production and consumption continued at the social margins. A close look at a few objects suggests that we can pull back the veil of uniformity and conformity that a style label can cast over a period.

The first time a Protoattic object was recognized as Athenian and distinct from Geometric was when Albert Dumont published an oinochoe, almost certainly from the Phaleron cemetery, in 1869 (Figure 2.3, Figure 4.39).[163] It was a watershed in the study of Athenian pottery. But the object has fallen out of the canon and our handbooks, out of sync with the types of objects found in the Kerameikos and associated with a "Classical" style of seventh-century ceramics. This may be our first clue that a different dynamic was at work in this vase-painting, that it was (and is) unconventional. The painting, from the ornament to the figures, is rendered in fluid, loose, hasty strokes that could be interpreted as sloppy, or as a meaningful departure from the Geometric repertoire of straight lines, sharp angles, and compass-drawn circles. There is certainly nothing careless about the shape and potting of the vase, the organization of the ornament, or the ambition in figuration. On the neck, the loose mode of rendering combines with iconography to portray exaggerated physiognomies that approach modern conceptions of caricature. Two protomes of men have elaborately trimmed facial hair, one with a mustache, the other with a shaved upper lip. At least one seems to wear a diadem. The third figure is perhaps a woman in a long dress and wearing earrings, holding something in her hand that emits a stream of dots (see Figure 2.3). There are no parallels for this image, so it is hard to identify exactly what is happening, but it should not be dismissed as derivative, for it does not attempt to imitate any known vessel or type. The exaggerated physiognomies mock people of high social standing who wear jewelry and diadems and keep their facial hair coiffed. The style and mode of rendering deconstruct elite features.

Figure 4.39. Detail of Figure 2.3. Photo John Blazejewski / Princeton University after Dumont 1869, 218, where the figures are re-ordered and dots near the woman removed. Compare Figure 2.3.

I suspect that more examples of politically subversive images lurk at the margins of the canon, where norms and standards of representation were inverted, conventions displaced, and humor employed to mock social groups. Consider another vase from Phaleron, for example, with an important historiographic role: when it was published, the term "Protoattic" (French "proto-attique") was used for the first time. It is an amphora with fine banded lines on the lower body, boars on the upper body, tendrils on the shoulder, and an intriguing scene on the neck: winged creatures with Near Eastern pedigree flanking a sacred tree (Figures 1.1, 4.40).[164] The heraldic composition is familiar to art historians and immediately recognizable as a quintessential "Orientalizing" symbol that recalls genies on either side of a sacred tree. But something is off. The loose style of rendering, the posture of the winged figures, and their facial expression led Cook to dismiss the vase as a "miserable amphora."[165] Yet there is nothing amiss with the construction and firing of the vase itself, the careful banding on the belly, and the delicate loops on the shoulder, and once again the subject matter is ambitious. Might it be meaningfully irreverent, as a symbol of Near Eastern decadence becomes a bundle of volutes, and the genies no more than a pair of innocuous winged men slightly bewildered at the ornament placed between them?

Conventions and expectations are also subverted on a kotyle where, in place of a dog catching a hare, the prey leaps onto the pursuer (Figure 4.41).[166] Once again,

Figure 4.40. Detail of Figure 1.1.

Figure 4.41. Protoattic kotyle. Athens, Agora P 26556. Photo courtesy of the American School of Classical Studies at Athens: Agora Excavations.

loci of elite activity are inverted. The hunt, a leisure activity with connotations of high status, fails, as the hunter's companion becomes victim of the hunted. The iconography, moreover, plays with the trope of the lion hunt, with the rabbit assuming the position associated with the lion killing its prey known from the Levant and throughout Greece as a symbol of royal power.

There is always a risk of over-interpreting such images and searching for political meaning in a careless slip of the brush. But there is also a risk of not being open to the possibility of ambiguity and humor in vases created at the hands of marginalized craftsmen, for consumers at the margins, at a time of social mobility and growing strife. Every Protoattic vase, which marks a stylistic departure from the conservative Geometric modes of rendition and display, should be suspect.

THE MANY HANDS AT WORK

The Polyphemus Amphora, with which this chapter opened, should now look different. While many previous studies have focused on the hand at work on the vase (belonging to the Polyphemus Painter) and the exceptional image that it created, this chapter has added more hands to the history of this vase: the hands of those who purchased it, those who carefully cut out the base to insert the deceased, those who buried it amid a variety of rites, and those who tore their hair in grief. The vase takes its place in a cemetery among other burials, many of them lost when the upper strata of the site were disturbed. Sufficient evidence at the cemetery remains, however, to witness a complex set of depositional and postdepositional rituals, which extended the time of mourning and commemoration both before and beyond the act of burial itself. The ways in which vases were used multiplies. The small vase accompanying the dead in the Polyphemus Amphora probably contained unguents, which may have been used in the preparation of the corpse. Its handmade rather than wheel-made properties intensified the tactile connection between the living and the dead. The large amphora, usually held up as a paradig-matic example of Orientalizing, crossed multiple horizons through its shape and imagery, bridging cemetery and home, and invoking the west, the east, and the past. It extended the geographical-scape and time-scape of the grave, creating a powerful landscape of commemoration that seeped back into the *oikos*. The way in which the amphora was deposited and the rituals surrounding it would have brought out one aspect or another of its style, but unfortunately we have insuffi-cient evidence to judge, just as we can only speculate about the size of the burying group and its status. Like many of the other burials we have seen, the Eleusis vase contained a child, a person whose social status, from many perspectives, was low, despite the high quality of the vase. Yet through the burial a group could rein-force its solidarity and a family could declare its continuity as it sought to cohere despite the rending trauma of loss. In these rituals, status display became salient and tangible, as the vase transformed the mundane shape of the amphora through size and ornamentation into something distinct from the utilitarian and ubiqui-tous amphoras used for transportation. The stunning openwork handles, for ex-ample, render emphatic the impossibility of using the vase to hold wine. The labo-rious decoration and the complex myths further elevated and distinguished the object, making it sophisticated and recherché. The violence of the appropriation and transformation of subelite forms was matched by the violence of the scenes on the vase itself.

Cemeteries have provided the majority of the finds of Protoattic and also formed the basis of quantitative analysis of seventh-century ceramics and society, and so it was with cemeteries that we had to begin in order to offer a new model for cul-tural change, seventh-century society, and the role of material culture. Surveying the evidence has revealed a greater number of burials and a variety in burial ritu-als that finds echoes in the social flux that literary sources describe and critique. Cemeteries provide the best contexts for Protoattic, but this chapter has suggested that we also need to look at the longer lives of objects and at the many persons and hands with which they engaged. To develop this interactionist approach, we now turn more explicitly to the people who made, used, and viewed Protoattic pottery in different contexts.

CHAPTER 5

Artists and Their Styles

Production, Process, and Subjectivity

BEYOND CONNOISSEURSHIP

The history of art is not simply a history of inspired artists. But neither should the figure of the artist be left aside, as some social analyses and quantitative approaches have tended to do. With attention to social structure writ large, they can leave little room for individual agency, let alone for someone specifically making objects. In this chapter, we will look at how people at the margins creatively engaged with the new possibilities of style and in the process gave form to that style. This marks a turn from the previous chapter, where the interaction of people with objects was examined at the tomb and the implications for the relationship of style and society were considered. Here we pivot toward some of the individuals within society and look more closely at the engagement of makers with vases, techniques, and contexts of production. The approach still emphasizes interaction, mobility, and heterogeneity, but this chapter introduces the notion of subjectivity to explain some of the stakes and consequences.

Investigating artists might seem to be an invitation to engage in connoisseurship—the close analysis of the formal properties of vases with an eye to determining the hand behind them—but that is not my pursuit, and those readers seeking a traditional account of the figure of the artist will be disappointed. There are other books and articles for those accounts. For Protoattic, Giulia Rocco has written a definitive monograph making attributions.[1] Instead, through close looking at representative vases with attention to facture, and by contextualizing the artistic labor of Protoattic painters with their markets and social dynamics, I investigate what makes it possible to attribute vases in the seventh century at all, and what this can tell us about the interaction of artists with pots.

Attribution has a long history in classical archaeology. The study of Greek vase-painting forever has been stamped by Sir John Beazley's achievement of attributing hands.[2] Through the close study of shapes, motifs, formal details, and techniques, he was able to group together Archaic and Classical vases that shared such close similarities in style that they appeared to be made by the same person. He gave these people names, thereby elevating the study of humble, mostly anonymous ceramics to the status hitherto reserved for sculpture. As we saw in chapter 2, this method set the tone for much of the early twentieth-century treatment of Protoattic, and its influence continues to be felt. Many of the attributions of Protoattic have been convincing, and figures such as the Polyphemus Painter now populate the pages of textbooks. With names, we have an organizational and chronological structure to the material and we can discuss not only period and regional styles but also what is often called personal style. There are, however, drawbacks. I suggested in chapter 2 that the Classical tastes behind much of this pursuit and the privileging of higher-quality, figural, attributable vases have narrowed the corpus. The search for artist hands also makes methodological assumptions, positing a transparent relationship between people and their oeuvres, and conflating an artist's style with personality. Style can be (falsely) conceived as offering a straightforward window onto character, even though the way one paints does not necessarily reflect how one thinks. Also, with connoisseurship, the history of Greek art risks becoming a history of artists who are geniuses operating outside of social contexts. And once the attribution pursuit gathers momentum, it can be difficult to pause and reflect on the process. A sherd's value becomes measured by its ability to testify to an artist; few scholars resist looking for a famed artist in an unsigned sherd. Museums and excavators alike want names. Even John M. Cook, no critic of attribution in general, accused Eva Brann of spotting the Analatos Painter too many times in her publication of material from the agora.[3] She went further than name-spotting, and with the loose deployment of terms like "Close to the Analatos Painter" and "Follower of the Analatos Painter," she created a hierarchy in which one master inspired others. As so often, her deployment of attribution not only implicitly, and uncritically, situated the artist in a modern intellectual context—a narrative of change driven by single actors whose style exposes personality—it also constructed an ancient social context.

For these reasons, and more, attribution has received due criticism.[4] And yet the phenomenon of identifiable hands, the author-effect of vase-painting, should not be dismissed too quickly (Figure 5.1, Plate 11).[5] One might disapprove of the assumptions connoisseurship makes and the way in which personal names are used to describe a set of shared formal qualities, or castigate the relationship between connoisseurship and the art market, but for all the complaints, the formal qualities remain. Rather than criticize the process within the typical terms of the debate, I want to reflect

Figure 5.1. Protoattic oinochoe attributed to the Painter of the Burgon Krater (Figure 2.2), from Phaleron. Athens, National Museum 322. Photo Giannis Patrikianos. Copyright © Hellenic Ministry of Culture and Sports / Archaeological Receipts Fund.

on what makes Protoattic vases attributable in the first place.[6] Why is it possible to apply Beazley's method to seventh-century vases? And what are the implications for the Protoattic style, for painters, and for society?

I am aware that not all vases attributed to a single painter were necessarily by that person's hand. Behind the attribution of the Analatos Painter, for example, might be several actual persons.[7] This is especially true when the attribution concerns a "Workshop" or "Group" (more on these below). But what I am interested in here is the ways in which, when compared to Geometric art, the impression of hands—the author-effect, as it were—emerges in Protoattic as never before. Examining this effect entails moving beyond considering style as a mere reflection of historical and political events and instead looking at peoples' interaction with objects and style. In the rest of this chapter, I will first provide more evidence that it is worthwhile to ask questions about artistic personalities, which appear in startling and unexpected ways in the seventh century. I will suggest that the lens of subjectivity offers a productive framework for assessing the implications of the engagement of makers with objects, one another, and contexts of production, and that it can help explain why Protoattic vases look the way they do.

THE PARADOX OF THE SEVENTH-CENTURY ARTIST PERSONALITY

Not all vase-painting styles are as susceptible to attribution as Protoattic. In fact, Protoattic is uniquely susceptible and is the first vase-painting style to which connoisseurship can be applied somewhat consistently. As a point of comparison, take the Geometric style of painting. Despite the larger number of vases, there are fewer identified (and identifiable) artists. J. N. Coldstream might be considered the "Beazley" of Geometric vase-painting, and his connoisseurship organized a vast amount of material into regional styles. But he was able to identify only twenty-one painters and workshops in Attic Late Geometric and none in Middle Geometric.[8] In contrast, despite working with a smaller amount of material, Giulia Rocco identified over fifty hands or groups and their workshops working in the Protoattic style.[9] The cause is not a matter of scholarly inclination, for I have little doubt that Coldstream would have subdivided groups into smaller categories if only to render chronology more clear. Instead, it seems that there is something about Protoattic that makes it the first style of Greek vase-painting particularly amenable to the study of hands. It is a watershed in Greek art. Contemporary Corinthian and Cycladic vase-paintings of the seventh century are not nearly as attributable.

It is relatively easy for even a novice to detect the presence of painterly hands in Protoattic. Two sets of three vases will illustrate what personal styles look like. The first set is Early Protoattic in date and consists of vases by the Analatos Painter (Figure 2.17), the Passas Painter (Figure 3.30), and the Painter of Acropolis 345 (Figure 5.2).[10] It does not demand deep experience in the rudiments of connoisseurship to perceive the extreme stylistic differences among these objects and to conclude that different people made them. Contrast, for example, the different use of filling ornament on the vases by the Analatos Painter and the Passas Painter, with the Analatos Painter preferring to fill the space with chevrons and to articulate the baseline with stuffed vegetal ornaments and the Passas Painter more keen to leave the image field open and to punctuate the ground line with elongated triangles. A similar treatment of the ground line appears on the amphora by the Painter of Acropolis 345, but the triangles are different in shape, and the delicate legs and neck of the bird contrast with the heavier horses of the Passas Painter. These are

Figure 5.2. Protoattic amphora attributed to the Painter of Acropolis 345 from a grave at Eleusis. Eleusis, Archaeological Museum 935. Photo N. T. Arrington.

Figure 5.3. Protoattic stand attributed to the Group of Kerameikos LZB from grave Kerameikos LZB I. Kerameikos 4278. Photo courtesy of the Deutsches Archäologisches Institut, Athens (D-DAI-ATH-Kerameikos-07883).

products of three painters working at approximately the same time, yet the stylistic differences must have been as apparent to ancient viewers as they are to us. Our second set is traditionally dated to the Middle Protoattic period. We can compare vases attributed to the New York Nessos Painter (Figure 1.5), the Group of Kerameikos LZB (Figure 5.3),[11] and the Ram Jug Painter (Figure 6.9). Both the New York Nessos Painter and the Ram Jug Painter tackle ambitious mythical representations (Herakles and the centaur; Odysseus fleeing Polyphemus), with different approaches to the surface of the vase and different treatments of the human figure, ornament, and technique. The LZB Group, meanwhile, avoids figural representation altogether. In terms of technique, the New York Nessos Painter favors added white, the Group of Kerameikos LZB silhouette, and the Ram Jug Painter outline. In terms of iconography, floral elements for the first may be stuffed, for the second thick, for the third sparse and delicate. The differences among these vase-paintings are so patent that we do not even need to consider those modes of rendering that were unconscious habits, such as the depictions of ears or noses, which often feature in connoisseurship.

These six vases, obviously representative rather than comprehensive in their selection, highlight some of the visual characteristics of personal styles that set Protoattic apart from Geometric. They make it possible, at the least, to group together vases that share formal properties, and in many cases it is not too bold to see behind the shared formal properties a single hand at work. As the examples suggest, however, this organizational scheme does not produce a history of Protoattic art as a straightforward development of technique and style guided by a few prominent hands. Cook sought such a trajectory in his landmark 1934–35 article, when he organized Protoattic into early, middle, and late phases. But Rocco's reassessment of the material showed that much of this organizational scheme did not work, since there were multiple stylistic currents at the same time.[12] Among the Early Protoattic painters described above, for example, the Analatos Painter is closer to the Geometric Workshop of Athens 894, while the Passas Painter and Painter of Acropolis 345 are closer to Cycladic traditions. Rocco groups the New York Nessos Painter among the workshops in the Wild Style, the contemporary Ram Jug Painter betrays East Greek influences, and the Group of Tomb LZB has affinities with Corinthian production.[13] There are disagreements over the identification of artists and influences, as conflicting attributions indicate, but little debate that there are personalities to discuss.

Was the seventh century, then, an Age of the Artist? The first signature on a vase-painting does appear in the very late eighth century on Pithekoussai, after all.[14] And might we go even further, noticing the deployment of the first person in contemporary lyric poetry, and posit more ambitiously an Age of the Individual? There are a few reasons to resist such a simplistic formulation. Despite unique painting styles, many artists and workshops left little impact on subsequent generations. Brilliant painters appeared and vanished without leaving a legacy in the form of a subsequent pictorial tradition that we can follow. This contrasts with later Archaic and Classical production. One of the strengths of connoisseurship in later periods is that in black- and red-figure vase-painting we can trace the interactions of workshops and hands, seeing the relations between teachers and pupils and the gradual transformation of workshop and regional styles over time. This is not the case for the heterogeneous Protoattic styles.[15] So Protoattic presents a paradox that merits scrutiny: the vase-paintings are amenable to attribution, as never before, but they do not fit neatly and consistently into trajectories. Painterly personalities stand out, but in the end seem evanescent.

Despite their pronounced artistic personalities, most Protoattic vase-painters do not sign their works.[16] In Italy, the signature on an Italic vase with Attic connections of the name (or pseudo-name?) Aristonothos, "noble bastard," suggests that the relationship between a person and his work was not straightforward at this time (Figure 3.16).[17] The placement and deployment of the name, along with the name itself, are at once sophisticated and (deliberately?) misleading. Written retrograde, it is carefully designed to bend from the top of the figural scene down, separating the antagonists. Was it the painter's actual name, its placement on an object with mixed styles in a multicultural context an assertion of his own possibly multiethnic identity?[18] Could the Etruscan audience that used the vase even read this name inserted so aggressively into the mythical narrative? There are no obvious answers. In lyric and epic poetry, too, the use of the first person was not transparent, with the "I" capable of functioning as conceit, foil, or veil.[19]

In order to account for the apparent emergence of an individual while resisting oversimplification of the phenomenon or explanations in terms of sweeping changes in individual identity, we can use the lens of subjectivity. Subjectivity is an experience and expression of personhood and agency. It is not stable but shifts over time and in different relational contexts—with places and objects, and with other people. A discussion of subjectivity acknowledges the artists as people and agents in their social contexts, without resorting to anachronistic and romantic notions of the solitary and free genius. It recognizes that the artist was a craftsman working within the constraints of society and tradition. And unlike the terms individuality or identity, which often are imagined to be stable cores hidden within people, subjectivity is formed and expressed externally in relation to people, places, and objects.[20] The rest of this chapter examines the development and expression of artistic subjectivity from two angles: the organization of production, and style. The first angle entails looking at the ways artists interacted with people, places, and things. The second angle entails examining how artists interacted with the vase itself, with technique and ornament. The next chapter will turn more to the viewers and users of the vases.

THE CONTEXTS OF PRODUCTION

In seventh-century Attica, there was not yet a full-fledged ceramics "industry" in terms of the number of vases produced, the extent of trade, or the level of consumption. Although Protoattic pottery participated in Mediterranean ceramic and cultural networks (chapter 3), output was comparatively small when compared to contemporary Protocorinthian pottery and subsequent sixth-century Attic black-figure, when we can start to speak of a veritable "industry" in which potters and painters turned out objects in a predictable style for a predictable clientele, and artists started to specialize in shapes and iconography. In seventh-century Attica, there was not yet a robust export market for Attic pottery, and even the local market was fickle. Taste was as heterogeneous as the Protoattic style itself. People held different conceptions of what types of shapes and imagery were desirable and how ceramics could and should be used, as we saw in the preceding chapter. This challenging production context—the unpredictability of the clientele and the weakness of market demand—placed constraints on ancient craftsmen, limiting the amount of material they could produce and the impact that they could have.[21] One possible result of this context might have been stagnant artistic activity. But that is not what we see in the material record. Instead, despite the small number of vases, there was tremendous variety and vitality and several distinct painterly personalities. Apparently the production context, because of its very challenges, also opened opportunities. It created an environment in which vase-painters needed to be mobile, flexible, and innovative.

A group of five standed dinoi at Mainz illustrates some of the social dynamics that the tools of connoisseurship can uncover (Figure 5.4).[22] The impressive

Figure 5.4. Protoattic dinoi, from Athens. Left: attributed to the Analatos Painter (stand) and the Passas Painter (cauldron). Right: attributed to the Passas Painter. There are three more dinoi from the assemblage. Mainz, Sammlung der Universität 153–154. Photo John Blazejewski / Princeton University after *Corpus Vasorum Antiquorum* Mainz 1, plate 23.

standed dinoi are all a similar shape and size and allegedly were a single commission from the same funeral context. From afar, the similarities among them stand out. They imitate metal objects and resemble one another. On closer inspection, however, it is clear that at least three prominent artists of the time collaborated: the Analatos Painter, the Passas Painter, and the Mesogeia Painter. Moreover, on one vessel, the Passas Painter worked on the cauldron while the Analatos Painter made the stand. In this context, we see how the vases and the funeral context drew at least three different painters together and compelled interaction with one another, with their patron, and with the metal objects they imitated. The objects, assemblage, and setting became sites of interaction where intersubjectivity could take place.

Figure 5.5. Protoattic stand, from the Palaia Kokkinia burial plot (Pot Burial 2), close to the Painter of Opferrinne ζ/XIV. Piraeus, Archaeological Museum 14259. Photo Eleni Papathanasiou, Courtesy of Georgios Spyropoulos.

We see this evidence for interaction in multiple cemeteries, because funerals frequently demanded a series of vases produced in little time. Funeral rituals followed soon after death, and in the absence of shops bursting with wares, customers seem to have sought quick commissions. In some deposits, the majority of the vases are from one workshop, such as Opferplatz α/IV (Figure 3.20) or Tomb LZB I in the Kerameikos.[23] Other assemblages demonstrate multiple hands at work, like the Mainz vases. At least two hands painted the vases from Opferrinne γ in the Kerameikos.[24] In Opferrinne β, the Kerameikos Mugs Group and the Painter of Opferrinne β/IX are attested, while the kotyle krater marking the mound has been attributed to the Oresteia Painter.[25] Table 1 shows other examples of multiple artist hands in funeral assemblages. As at Mainz, generally the vases cohere as an assemblage and a set, despite the number of hands present. At Palaia Kokkinia, for example, a stand with an aulete, dancers, and a tripod (Figure 5.5) seems to be painted by a different hand than the other vases in the assemblage, but is linked to them through shared ornament and technique, such as the application of white rosettes on red bands (Figure 4.30).

Unfortunately, we lack the evidence to be precise about what happened, and when, to encourage such formal similarities. Maybe a customer visited a shop and selected several vases that resembled one another. More likely, given the low level of production, he or she visited a kiln and commissioned the potters and painters on hand to complete a set, leading to a variety of hands producing a similar style. Maybe a single potter cum painter operated the kiln and called on another painter to help him complete the commission. Or a father and son team worked together closely, one teaching the other his craft, the son producing only some of the figural images but all of the ornament. We will probably never know the precise social dynamics at work behind such commissions. Indisputable, however, are the signs of collaboration, interaction, and close looking between and among several artisans at work on funeral commissions.

Although many vases display an author-effect through pronounced personality, there are other moments when it is not clear that we are dealing with just one hand. One solution has been to draw lines around these looser formal links to make "workshop" designations. Rocco, for example, bestows on eleven painters "workshop" attributions (the Analatos Painter, the Mesogeia Painter, the N Painter, the Passas Painter, the Checkerboard Painter, the New York Nessos Painter, the Polyphemus Painter, the Ram Jug Painter, the Painter of Opferrinne γ I, the Painter of Opferrinne γ II, and the Pair Painter). What the designation "workshop" here indicates is a combination of stylistic affinity and distance. A piece attributed to the Workshop of the Ram Jug Painter, for example, is sufficiently close in style to the Ram Jug Painter that the connoisseur sees an association but not so close that the connoisseur believes it to be by the same hand. Now, some "workshop" labels might actually represent a physical reality—a space. When vases appear in the same fu-

Figure 5.6. Protoattic olpe, attributed to the Workshop of the Ram Jug Painter. Athens, Agora P 22550. Photo courtesy of the American School of Classical Studies at Athens: Agora Excavations.

neral context and are commissions from a group designated a "workshop," we can perhaps reliably conclude that painters worked side by side in the same space. The two hands behind one vase may well have painted in an architectural unit that included a kiln and a space in which painters could work. But usually we have no reason to assume that people in a connoisseur's "workshop" actually worked together in a workshop. When vases are assigned to a "workshop" through stylistic analysis and without contextual support, the scholar has made an interpretive move with social implications. The evidence has been classified in a particular, and peculiar, way, with a host of social implications. In the case of Rocco's classification, it suggests that there were eleven painters in Attica who were masters of workshops, with fixed production spaces. It creates the illusion that there was a widespread and acknowledged hierarchy among vase-painters, with weaker artists orbiting more accomplished and talented prodigies, recalling a Renaissance model of masters and apprentices. But on most occasions, the attribution of vases to a "workshop" really can mean no more than "close

Figure 5.7. Louterion from the Sanctuary of Herakles at Thebes, possibly by a Protoattic painter. Archaeological Museum of Thebes. Copyright © Hellenic Ministry of Culture and Sports / Archaeological Receipts Fund.

to" the style of a particular artist. Consider an oinochoe and an olpe from the agora that have been attributed to the Workshop of the Ram Jug Painter (Figures 3.4, 5.6).[26] If we compare them to the name-vase of the "master" (Figure 6.9), we see the similarities, such as the use of a thick outline, the sparse ornament, and the line from the chin up to the ear. We also see the differences, such as the treatment of the eyes and the choice of ornament. These vase-painters interacted with one another, with each other's objects, or with a broader network of painters and objects with similar techniques. A workshop relationship is not the only, or the best, way to explain the combination of similarities and differences.

The prevalence of the "workshop" designation in seventh-century connoisseurship actually suggests, rather than a permanent physical space, a high degree of horizontal mobility. The interaction of artists created the combination of similarities and differences that the designation attempts to capture. The use of the term "Group" rather than "Painter" in connoisseurship studies also points in this direction. More often than attributing a specific hand, Rocco actually prefers to deploy the term "Group," as in the Würzburg Group or the Kerameikos Mugs Group, which designates vases that share formal properties but that might be painted by multiple hands. Perhaps the painters worked together for an extended period of time, or perhaps they collaborated on a commission. Or perhaps one painter sought to imitate works he had seen, or was unconsciously influenced by a piece. The so-called Group of the Wild Style is little more than a grab bag of highly idiosyncratic and variegated hands, not a collective of persons who worked in one place and time.[27]

Artisan mobility is indeed corroborated at the regional level, with hands identified across Attica (such as the Nessos Painter active at Vari[28]) and even at the transregional level. Although some objects may have moved through trade and exchange, at the sanctuary of Herakles at Thebes next to the Elektra Gates (leading in the direction of Athens), the imagery in the Protoattic style on a few vases is so apt for the context that it likely was made there by a traveling painter (Figure 5.7).[29] There are also a few vases in museums that have a provenance from Boiotia or that are made from Boiotian fabric, but that are Protoattic in style.[30] In the opposite direction, the consumption of Protoattic on Aigina may have prompted some painters to produce vases on or for the island.[31] Even farther afield, a Protoattic painter appears to have been at work at Metaponto (Figures 3.11, 3.12). The roads ran in multiple directions, with painters coming to Attica, too. The strong Corinthianizing element to Protoattic pottery could stem in part from immigrant painters.[32] The many affinities between Protoattic and Cycladic painting could also relate to immigration, as Rocco has underlined.[33] Painters linked up to the local, meso-scale, and macroscale networks for the circulation of people, goods, and ideas in the seventh-century Mediterranean, as we saw in chapter 3. It is telling that the letters painted on three Protoattic vases (two of them Late Protoattic or earliest black-figure) are not in the Attic script (Figures 2.5, 2.11, 6.10).[34]

Until there is a definitive study of Protoattic shapes, it remains unclear how potters fit into this picture. The variety of shapes painted by attributable hands, however, does suggest that painters worked with several different potters, supporting a model of artisan mobility. One possible scenario is that potters owned the kilns and painters moved from one kiln to another, encountering different painters and collaborating with different potters depending on the type of vase, the place of a commission, or perhaps even the time of year.

Figure 5.8. Votive plaque attributed to the Workshop of the Ram Jug Painter. Athens, Agora T 175. Photo courtesy of the American School of Classical Studies at Athens: Agora Excavations.

An archaeological context from the agora illustrates the variety of activity that could take place at these kilns. A pit and irregular cutting containing kiln debris included production discards that were not limited to pottery but also included debris from terra-cotta figurines, lamps, loom weights, spindle whorls, beads, and buttons.[35] Elsewhere in the agora, a second kiln deposit with ceramic wasters also had a figurine waster, and two loom weights were found in the kiln itself.[36] The diversity of debris and production material within these kiln deposits suggests the variety of objects and artisans that a painter might encounter in a production

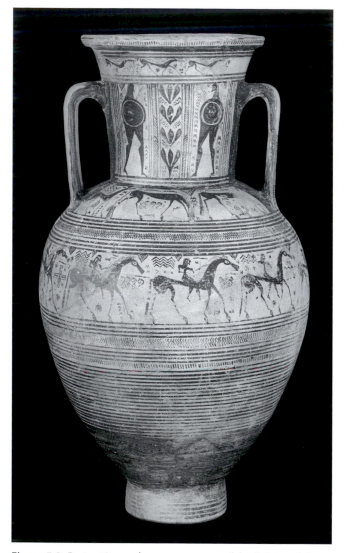

Figure 5.9. Protoattic amphora, name-vase of the Painter of the Boston Amphora 03.782. Boston, Museum of Fine Arts 03.782. Photo © 2021 Museum of Fine Arts, Boston.

context. The kilns in this period were not specialized, churning out a few types of vases, but were spaces for the production of many types of objects.

Notable is the presence of figurines in the same kilns producing vases. Vase-painters operated at least in the same milieu as figurine production and may have painted some of them. The Vari ekphora figurines, for example, have been attributed to a Protoattic vase-painter, the Painter of Opferrinne ζ/XIV (Figure 4.27).[37] Another vase-painter, the Ram Jug Painter or a related painter, seems to have decorated a stunning plaque from the agora showing a deity flanked by snakes, which conflates pictorial and plastic traditions (Figure 5.8, Plate 12).[38] The rich polychromy vies with vase-paintings, while the mold-made head draws on coroplastic traditions. The goddess emerges from the surface, breaking the two-dimensionality of the plaque to perform a divine epiphany. The techniques and processes for both vase-painting and figurine production combine on this object to yield a convincing, compelling representation at the hands of a versatile artist. So the label of "vase-painter" may inaccurately limit the range of the Ram Jug Painter's activity. Likewise, applied mourners, snakes, and flowers on an oinochoe from Opferrinne γ (and attributed to the Painter of Opferrinne γ I) vie with plastic traditions and make the object as much a figurine group as a container (Figure 4.38). On many vases from this funeral trench, paint was applied on a white ground after firing, following the technique of coroplasts.[39] There are many more examples of this interrelationship of vase-painting with figurines.

Given the relatively small number of Protoattic vase-paintings that survive, when compared to the ouput of black-figure and red-figure painters, it is possible that vase-painters worked in media other than terra-cotta, too. Temples were rising in Greece, and they needed painting. Also, the increased use of hoplites demanded shields and, with them, painted shield devices (cf. the decorated votive shield in Figure 6.19).[40] Might some of these people painting murals, architectural revetmens, and shields also have been vase-painters, and vice-versa? Such links are impossible to prove with the current state of the evidence but would help account for the small output of vase-painting from hands that otherwise seem experienced. For example, the Painter of the Boston Amphora 03.782 seems no stranger to the paintbrush (Figure 5.9),[41] but Rocco attributes only one other vase to this hand, and the formal connection seems tenuous (Figure 2.7). The Painter of the Burgon Krater (Figure 2.2) receives only one other attribution (Figure 5.1). The formal parallels here are more convincing, but the small number of attributions remains just as puzzling.[42]

Whether or not Protoattic vase-painters strayed far afield in their production, the ceramics demonstrate a degree of cross-media pollination. Many painters redeployed and reworked methods for decorating ivory and metal, particularly visible in the use of incision and in the choice of ornaments like the guilloche. Shapes, too, drew on other media, especially metals, such as the Mainz dinoi, which look to bronze prototypes. More than merely imitating, the vase-painters appropriated and transformed features and techniques. The Mainz dinoi, for example, with their lavish decoration, are visually stunning objects that vie with metal cauldrons. The Polyphemus Painter's name-vase is another good example. The incision and open-work handles recall metal vases, and the Gorgon heads riff bronze and silver bowls. These vases are emulative rather than derivative, as potter and painter used multiple stimuli to create distinctive, new, and compelling ceramic objects.

The formal properties underlying the connoisseurship designations "Workshop" and "Group," the kiln debris, and the vases themselves indicate shifting networks of horizontally mobile painters who were presented with many opportunities for interaction with people, contexts, and objects. These interactions had implications for the development and expression of the painters' subjectivity. As they operated in different physical environments—moving from kiln to kiln and market to market, working alongside various potters and painters and coroplasts—they saw and experienced a range of contexts, objects, and processes, prompting a variety of responses, including imitation, experimentation, and adaptation. Painters may have learned new skills, developed fresh ideas, or attempted to outdo the visual forms they encountered.

Competition is well documented among painters in later periods, such as the Late Archaic group of vase-painters known as the Pioneers, and already in the seventh century, Hesiod wrote of the rivalry among potters.[43] The competitive dynamic likely extended to seventh-century vase-painters. They observed the painters and vases and objects around them and actively engaged in material responses that required self-evaluation and self-reflection about what they might make and how they might do so. Just as the attributes of the Analatos Painter's work appear sharper to us through the traditional art-historical technique of juxtaposing one work by this hand with another object by someone else, so the painter laboring on the Mainz dinos would have recognized and developed the unique qualities of his own style alongside another painter. Or working in a diverse kiln context with a coroplast, he experienced other methods and techniques and pressed the limits of his medium. Horizontal mobility fostered a production atmosphere conducive to realizing the distinctive properties of vase-painters' craft and of their artistic personalities.

EXPERIMENTS WITH FIGURE AND ORNAMENT

Along with a change in the contexts and processes of production came new iconography. The seventh-century saw awakened interest in the representation of the human figure. No longer constructed in sharp, rectilinear forms that echoed the surrounding decoration, human figures stepped out from the ornamental field with a corporeality and physiognomy that allowed for the expression of individual styles. Connoisseurs have long favored figural drawings, where the rendition of body parts like ears and noses elicits a habitual mode of depiction that tends to remain relatively unique to a painter. Contrast, for example, the eyes and ears in figures 1.5 and 1.9. The New York Nessos Painter favored a sharp nose, thin mouth, and wide eye with arched eyebrow, while the Polyphemus Painter favored a bulbous nose, narrow eye, eyebrow with upturned ends, and two interlocking C's for the inner ear. The emergence of the figure is one reason why more Protoattic vases are attributable than Geometric.

But perhaps nothing distinguishes Protoattic from Geometric as much as the type of ornament enlivening the surface of a vase. While Geometric vases can be enticing and mesmerizing in their kaleidoscope of carefully arranged linear forms, Protoattic vases can be lush and wild, beguiling and disorienting. Lines become plants, and vegetal life erupts. Faced with new choices and possibilities, painters favored some ornament over others, developing and enhancing their own repertoire and fashioning their own style. But they were expansive in their tastes and could continuously draw on models circulating through trade and travel. Rocco's analysis of painters helpfully details the choices of ornament that people made, and a glance at her charts reveals the abundance at hand and the distinctive selections (Figure 5.10).

The taste for vegetal ornament compelled artists to rethink the relationship of decoration to figuration. They had to reconsider the ways in which vase-paintings worked. True, painters already in the eighth century had experimented with figuration and probed how ornament and figure might be distinguished or interrelated, but the process intensified in the seventh century.[44] The enrichment and expansion of the ornamental repertoire coincided with an increase in the amount of figural representation. As ornament adopted new forms, so did figuration. There were more compelling and complex narrative scenes in Protoattic compared to Geometric.

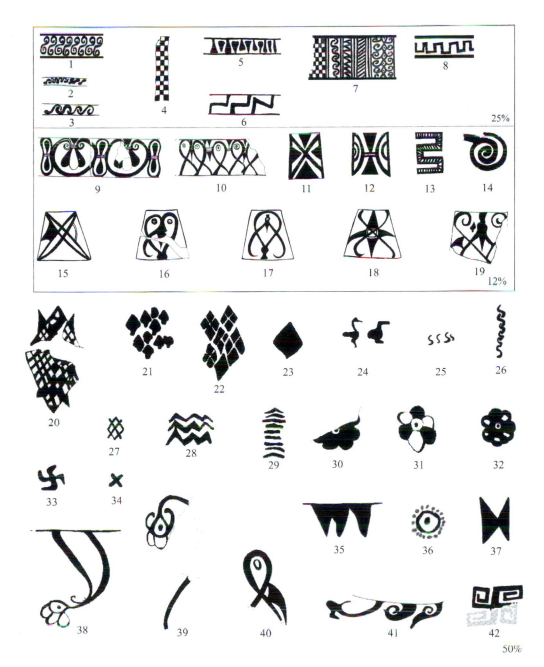

Figure 5.10. Ornamental repertoire of the Checkerboard Painter and the New York Nessos Painter, by Giulia Rocco. Photo John Blazejewski / Princeton University after Rocco 2008, figs. 15, 18, by permission of G. Rocco.

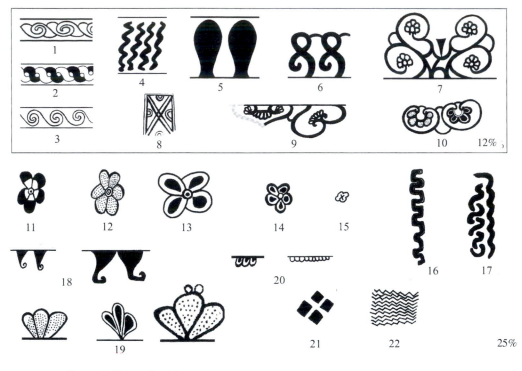

Figure 5.10. continued

These were not merely changes in iconography or composition; they fundamentally transformed what a vase could show, and how. Once a myth takes place on a vase, there are new possibilities for figure and frame. And once a groundline can sprout vegetation, it possesses a different valence. Make a line a plant, and all other lines are laden with semiotic possibilities.

An amphora attributed to the Mesogeia Painter shows some of the ways artists grappled with the new relationships between figure and ornament that the Protoattic style posited, which become clearer for us through a contrast with the Dipylon Amphora (Figures 5.11 and 1.8).[45] On the older vase, the figures are composed of shapes that echo the surrounding decoration; despite their narrative content, they are little more than pattern. On the later vase, in contrast, different types of ornament are juxtaposed with each other. Most striking is the way that the seventh-century painter has inserted lush, curvilinear ornament into the field that the Dipylon Painter used for a figural scene, focalizing the new vegetal ornament in the central panel of the vase. The composition creates a contrast with the framing rectilinear ornament that continues to assert a Geometric pedigree. The Analatos Painter devotes similar attention to deploying ornament as subject matter on an amphora in the Louvre (Figure 5.12), with palmettes, tendrils, and volutes in silhouette on the belly, and stippled (or "stuffed") on the shoulder.[46] The isolation of the ornament in these two registers and the varying technical treatment draw attention to the new forms and distinguish them from the surrounding rectilinear repertoire. In these two examples, ornament assumes the position on the vase once frequently reserved for figural forms (i.e., the main panel), and the experimentation with ornament occurs without the presence of narration. These artists seem aware of what makes the Protoattic style new and how it can mark a radical departure from previous norms of painting. The juxtaposition of the two styles of painting invites viewers to make the comparison.

In other cases, it is the relationship between figure and ornament that artists more closely probe. On the Polyphemus Amphora (Figure 1.9), the swirling ornament simultaneously articulates the surface of the vase and underscores the activity of the human and animal figures. The black and white rosettes, like pinwheels whirling in the wind, accompany the narrative rush. Ornament here complements the surface of the vase and figural action. But on the neck of the amphora, the artist

Figure 5.11. Protoattic hydria attributed to the Mesogeia Painter. From a grave at Kalyvia Kouvara. Athens, National Museum VS 67. Photo N. T. Arrington.

questions the bounds of ornament, as Odysseus's men grab the line defining the upper edge of the image field and transform it into a stake. Here lines are not decoration but devices that the depicted figures can manipulate. Similarly, on the name-vase of the Group of the Schliemann Krater and the Vari Loutrophoros (Figure 5.13), the vegetal ornament does more than decorate; it represents a lush landscape in which animals parade.[47] There is even a flowering branch supporting a bird. This is a far remove from the repetitive series of identical birds on Geometric vases.

Some scholars have argued that ornament in Geometric art, too, represented natural forms like plants.[48] I remain dubious. Geometric ornament performs a compelling visual function without needing recourse to an external signified. It enlivens the surface of the vase and creates a visual spectacle that can enchant.[49] If we resort to symbolism to read the iconography on a Geometric vase, we seek meaning outside of the vase itself rather than in the beguiling and complex interrelationship of patterns, which seems to have been the focus of the vase-painter. To seek a symbolic

Figure 5.12. Protoattic amphora attributed to the Analatos Painter. Paris, Musée du Louvre CA 1960. Photo © RMN-Grand Palais / Art Resource, NY.

reading for Geometric ornament is to insist on a teleological understanding of Greek art as striving toward naturalistic representation. If vase-painters were trying to make a Geometric vase symbolic, they certainly kept the meanings opaque. And even if one accepts that Geometric ornament could sometimes signify natural forms, such as plants, the Protoattic style still ushered in a disruptive way of conceiving the interrelationship of figure and ornament through its more abundant use of vegetation and its increase in narrative.

Perhaps no ornament better represents the opportunities and challenges of the seventh-century repertoire than the sacred tree. Although the form circulated in Aegean contexts in the eighth century (and earlier), it enjoyed greater popularity and wider reception in the seventh century.[50] Originally derived from Cypro-Levantine cultures, but

Figure 5.13. Protoattic krater by the Group of the Schliemann Krater and the Vari Loutrophoros. Athens, National Museum 17762. Photo: John Blazejewski / Princeton University after *Corpus Vasorum Antiquorum* Athens 2, plate 2.

also accessible to Greece via networks of mobility and trade from the western Mediterranean, the tree offered a particularly rich array of vegetal options— tendrils, palmettes, volutes. Many Protoattic ornaments can be traced back to a sacred tree, such as the tendrils and palmettes in figures 5.11 and 5.12. More significantly, the tree subverts modern tendencies to rank figure over ornament. In its original Near Eastern contexts, the sacred tree usually formed the focal point of an image and dominated figural fields in terms of both narrative importance and composition. Frequently placed between two figures, it loomed over them. With this motif, Greek artists confronted a very different conception of the relationship of pattern to signification, in which ornament represented a powerful sacred force. How much of the tree's original meaning was imported probably varied. On the amphora in Boston, the ornament in a panel between two warriors on the neck (Figure 5.9) recalls the sacred tree, and on the vases attributed to the Mesogeia Painter and the Analatos Painter, the sacred tree may have provided not only the forms but also the concept that vegetal ornament could take the place of figure (Figures 5.11–5.12). The new iconographies and artistic traditions nourished artistic trends while also destabilizing the representational field, demanding painters rethink their craft and their role in it.

The increase in figuration, the development of the ornamental repertoire, and the encounter with different modes of conceiving the connection between image and ornament contributed to the diversity of personal styles in the seventh century. The Protoattic artist faced a range of stylistic choices unprecedented in Greek art, confronting an array of ways of making that his Geometric predecessor did not know. A painter's vase might be more or less sub-Geometric, more or less Levantine, more or less Italic, more or less Corinthian, more or less Cycladic. Changes in the shape, size, and function of many vases at the turn of the century only encouraged a vase-painter to reach into the new palimpsest of style and to experiment, as new vehicles for the image stimulated new thinking about the way they could be decorated. There was an unparalleled palette available from which a personal style, and a sense of subjectivity, could emerge.

TECHNIQUE AND THE EMERGENCE OF THE PAINTER'S HAND

Vase-painters also faced an unprecedented set of choices in terms of techniques. They experimented with silhouette, outline, incision, and color. These choices were not necessarily exclusive of one another. Whereas Cook once tried to place developments in a chronological sequence—from less to more incision, less to more color—such a progression no longer fits the evidence.[51] Incision appeared already in Early Protoattic, while there were Late Protoattic vases without any (e.g., Figure 5.5). Some painters, early and late, applied more color than others. As in the depiction of figures and ornaments, there was a rich palette for artists to use.

Figure 5.14. Protocorinthian kotyle serving as a test piece or practice piece. Corinth, Archaeological Museum KP 182. Photo: Ino Ioannidou and Lenio Bartzioti, American School of Classical Studies at Athens: Corinth Excavations.

A significant development in technique in seventh-century Attica was the move away from decoration applied while the vase was still on the potter's wheel to more freehand painting. Although Geometric painters were familiar with freehand painting, they frequently applied decoration while the pot was slowly turning to ensure clean and even parallel lines. Geometric artists also exploited the use of a pivoted multiple brush.[52] A test-piece or practice-piece from Corinth shows how the multiple brush could create even and controlled lines (Figure 5.14).[53] The mechanic aesthetic extended to their freehand work, as they sought to match the uniformity and standardization of those patterns made with multiple brushes or on the wheel (Figure 5.15). The freehand work, in other words, was never very free. This aesthetic, and the processes behind it, entailed an obfuscation of the hand. It was an aesthetic that privileged pattern and uniformity, and that depended on the subordination of parts to the whole. No single line stands out. Instead, it is as if the Geometric vase were made in one moment, like a stamp on a piece of clay.

In Protoattic painting, in contrast, technique was more transparent, and the freehand technique quite liberal. To grasp the difference, contrast the meander (quintessential Geometric) or the straight ray (quintessential Corinthian) with the Protoattic hooked ray (Figures 5.15–5.16). The meander is a continuously moving, closed shape. Follow the line, and it will twist and turn, and begin again. There is no beginning or end to the pattern. Similarly, straight rays are uniform and repetitive, with one ray closely resembling the next. More like stamps than painted lines, they do not reveal where an artist started and stopped and bear little trace of their facture. The brush may have moved horizontally across the ray, or first articulated the outline and then filled it in; we cannot tell by looking. The process of creating both meanders and rays is deliberately opaque, yielding a harmony of pattern where no one stroke stands out.

By the seventh century, however, the so-called hooked ray had become popular, particularly in Attica, and is representative of the sea change in approaches to vase-painting. (There were also hooked rays in Protocorinthian and straight rays in Protoattic. The argument I am making is that the hooked rays are symptomatic of a new approach to the vase by many Protoattic vase-painters, but not the only approach, and not exclusive to Attica.) The apparently minor addition of a curvilinear stroke to the top of a ray carried significant ramifications. It marked the trace

Figure 5.15. Detail of the Dipylon Amphora (Figure 1.8). Photo N. T. Arrington.

Figure 5.16. Detail of a Protoattic kotyle (Figure 1.4). Photo N. T. Arrington.

Figure 5.17. Protoattic mug, attributed to the Group of the Wild Style. Athens, National Museum 1294. Photo John Blazejewski / Princeton University after Böhlau 1887, fig. 11.

of painterly movement, making that movement visible. The hook exposes the moment that the artist ended his stroke and draws attention to the directionality and process of painting. The form is repeatable but sufficiently complex that no two hooked rays will be identical, even on the same vase. The hooked ray is the painter's hand manifest. It was a sufficiently significant motif that it became thematized on some vases. On a mug, for example, hooked rays dominate the decorative scheme as the painter boldly declared the movement of his hand (Figure 5.17).[54] The popularity of the motif is symptomatic of a move from the mechanical to the free hand, from linear to painterly.

The semiotic notion of an index can help elucidate the shift here from Geometric to Protoattic modes of rendering. The index is a sign that relies on contiguity. The classic example is smoke and fire: the smoke indexes the fire. We do not need to see the fire, only the smoke, to know that the fire is there. In Protoattic vase-painting, a painterly stroke like the end of a hooked ray indexes the hand of the artist behind it. It allows the painter to express subjectivity and the viewer of the vase to see the traces of a subject at work. Whereas the Geometric stroke often indexes a tool, Protoattic indexes a body. Using the theoretical framework of agency rather than semiotics, we might say that the object causes the viewer to infer or abduct the artist behind the vase.

The import of this shift in technique and aesthetic can be seen by looking at other curvilinear strokes. Consider, for example, the enormous palmettes on the rim of a kotyle krater in Athens (Figure 5.18).[55] Tendrils and leaves spiral and billow in a manner unfathomable in Geometric art. Eschewing replication, the artist made each entwined palmette slightly different. The motion of the spirals closely mirrors the action of the painter's hand in a way that straight lines or compass-drawn circles do not: we can see where the brush began to make the spirals and where it stopped. The lower register of geometric rhomboid netting establishes a meaningful contrast between the painterly and the linear modes of representation, making the upper frieze stand out. A similar contrast appears on the hydria attributed to the Mesogeia Painter, where the register of vegetation occupies the main body of the vase (Figure 5.11). Surrounded by ornament made with the multiple brush and possibly on the wheel, the freehand tendrils and plants burst with

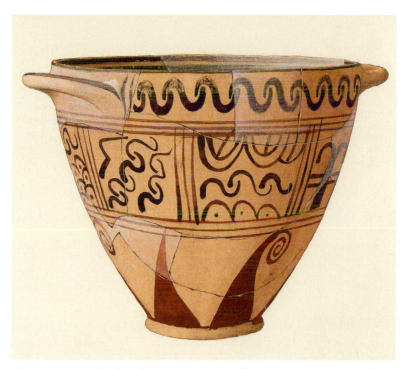

Plate 1. Protoattic kotyle. Athens, Agora P 7023. Illustration by Piet de Jong. Photo courtesy of the American School of Classical Studies at Athens: Agora Excavations.

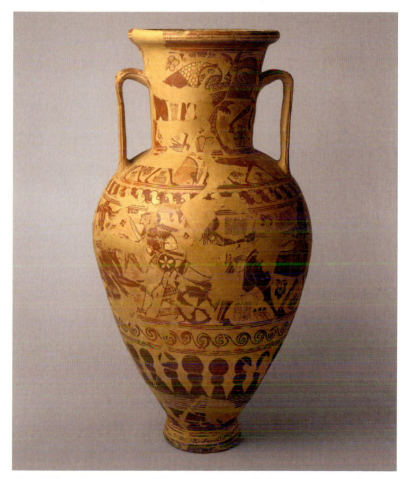

Plate 2. Protoattic amphora attributed to the New York Nessos Painter, allegedly from Smyrna. New York, Metropolitan Museum of Art 11.210.1. Rogers Fund, 1911.

Plate 3. Protoattic Phaleron-type oinochoe from Phaleron, attributed to the Group of Kerameikos 18/XIX. Athens, National Museum 304. Photo Eleutherios Galanopoulos. Copyright © Hellenic Ministry of Culture and Sports / Archaeological Receipts Fund.

Plate 4. Protoattic amphora from a grave on Mount Hymettos attributed to the Group of the Wild Style. Berlin, Staatliche Museen, Antikensammlung F 56. Photo bpk Bildagentur / Antikensammlung, Staatliche Museen, Berlin / Art Resource, NY. © Fitzwilliam Museum, Cambridge / Art Resource, NY.

Plate 5. Italian olla attributed to the Narce Painter, 7th century BC. Budapest, Szépművészeti Múzeum. Photo © László Mátyus, Museum of Fine Arts, Budapest.

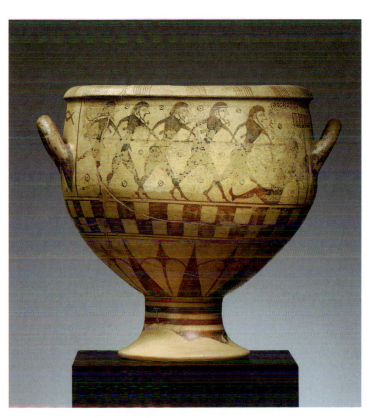

Plate 6. Krater from Etruria signed by Aristonothos. Rome, Musei Capitolini 172. Photo courtesy of the museum.

Plate 7. Attic funerary plaque, late 7th century, from Olympos. New York, Metropolitan Museum of Art 14.146.3a. Rogers Fund, 1914.

Plate 8. Figurines from Vari (Grave 27), attributed to the Protoattic Painter of Opferrinne ζ/XIV. Athens, National Museum 26747. Photo Irini Miari. Copyright © Hellenic Ministry of Culture and Sports / Archaeological Receipts Fund.

Plate 9. Late Protoattic louterion from the Palaia Kokkinia burial plot (Pot Burial 2), close to the Painter of Opferrinne ζ/XIV. Piraeus, Archaeological Museum 14260. Photo Jeff Vanderpool, courtesy of Georgios Spyropoulos.

Plate 10. Excavations at the Phaleron cemetery, Stavros Niarchos Foundation Cultural Center. Photo courtesy of Stella Chryssoulaki.

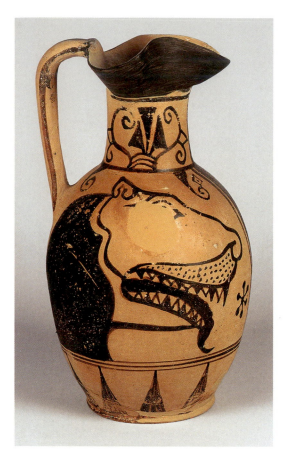

Plate 11. Protoattic oinochoe attributed to the Painter of the Burgon Krater. Athens, National Museum 322. Photo Giannis Patrikianos. Copyright © Hellenic Ministry of Culture and Sports / Archaeological Receipts Fund.

Plate 12. Votive plaque attributed to the Workshop of the Ram Jug Painter. Athens, Agora T 175. Photo courtesy of the American School of Classical Studies at Athens: Agora Excavations.

Plate 13. Protoattic kantharos. Athens, Agora P 531. Photo courtesy of the American School of Classical Studies at Athens: Agora Excavations.

Plate 14. Protoattic skyphos with dipinto. Athens, Agora P 7014. Photo courtesy of the American School of Classical Studies at Athens: Agora Excavations.

Plate 15. Inscribed Phaleron-type cup, 7th century. Athens, Agora P 26420. Photo courtesy of the American School of Classical Studies at Athens: Agora Excavations.

Plate 16. Protoattic loutrophoros from the Sanctuary of the Nymphs, attributed to the Group of Protomelian and Melian Inspiration. Acropolis Museum, Fetichie Tzami NA-57-Aα 456. Photo Yiannis Koulelis © Acropolis Museum, 2020.

Figure 5.18. Protoattic krater attributed to the Checkerboard Painter, from a cemetery at Spata. Athens, National Museum VS 188. Photo N. T. Arrington.

vitality, and our eye follows the path of the brush that curved over the surface and stopped, started, stopped, started. Again, we see process. On a standed bowl in Berlin (Figure 5.19), the geometric pattern on the body of the vase quivers and starts to dissolve, while on the stand, the line thickens considerably, the rich black shapes contrasting with the thinner lines above them and drawing attention to the versatility and dynamism of a brush.[56] The image need not be so complex to present a contrast with the Geometric mode of rending. On a kantharos from the agora, for example, a series of horizontal stripes surrounds the vase, but the painter made no attempt to apply the slip evenly (Figure 5.20, Plate 13).[57] On the contrary, it seems deliberately uneven. To call this sloppy or incompetent misses the point. The Geometric aesthetic disintegrates as the Protoattic painter's hand emerges. Where the handle meets the wall, two lines merge and overlap, and on the outer face of the handle, we can see where the painter lifted his hand to make the line in two strokes (Figure 5.21). This freehand painting could explode in energy and ex-uberance, as on the reverse of the neck of the Polyphemus Amphora (Figure 5.22),

Figure 5.19. Standed bowl attributed to the Checkerboard Painter. Berlin, Staatliche Museen, Antikensammlung A 39. Photo bpk Bildagentur / Antikensammlung, Staatliche Museen, Berlin / Art Resource, NY.

where volutes churn. On the reverse of the body, the painter used the overlapping lines to create a sense of depth and texture that was not possible in Geometric. Through close looking, it is possible to determine the sequence in which the artist laid down the paint. The lines provide a temporal dimension to the image and gesture to the body behind it.

"PERSONAL" STYLES

Through his engagement with markets, artists, objects, iconography, and techniques, the artist developed and expressed subjectivity as a creative agent and social person. In other words, and to return to the question posed near the beginning of this chapter, social and material conditions and the means of production and consumption of vase-painting made the artist-effect emerge in the past and render attribution possible in the present.

Figure 5.20. Protoattic kantharos. Athens, Agora P 531. Photo courtesy of the American School of Classical Studies at Athens: Agora Excavations.

There is no need to accept that every attribution of a vase-painter is correct, or even that the named artists represent actual persons. But behind the attribution process lie variegated styles that seem to us "personal" and that relate to artistic, social, and historical phenomena. Some of these personal styles may have been distributed across several actual persons, with the "Analatos Painter" representing several artists. Or several attributed painters may have been one person, with pieces attributed to the Analatos Painter and the Mesogeia Painter actually made by one hand. If so, it would only support the argument of horizontal mobility advanced here and reinforce the notion that subjectivity was

Figure 5.21. Protoattic kantharos. Athens, Agora P 531. Photo courtesy of the American School of Classical Studies at Athens: Agora Excavations.

shaped in the creation of Protoattic vases. Workshop and group attributions, which some scholars might consider a failure of connoisseurship, instead point to a social and artistic reality in which styles were distinct yet fluid, with a variety of influences on a person's work.

This was not a period of unfettered artist agency or free will, however. The objects and the techniques made certain demands on the artist, opening expressive possibilities but also setting constraints. Just as importantly, contexts of use and patrons made specific demands; not all was possible or desirable at all times. A funeral required certain shapes and images, a symposium (as we will see in the next chapter) others. Some shapes seem to have elicited particular approaches. For example, standed bowls tend to have more sub-Geometric decoration than oinochoai. The presence of dipinti on same vases, which were applied prior to firing, indicates that on some occasions at least there was a particularly close involvement of patrons

Figure 5.22. Reverse of the Polyphemus Amphora (Figure 1.9). Photo N. T. Arrington.

in the production process, especially when a person's name appears. Sanctuaries, too (treated in the next chapter), will reveal the role of context in shaping an artist's output.

But there was a place for artistic creativity in the face of a changing market and style. From the margins of society came creative agents facing an increasing number of choices in terms of iconography, technique, and style. They could dramatically reconceive what a vase might look like, and what it could do. Much as the Protoattic style offered challenges and opportunities to consumers using ceramics in funeral rites, it offered a medium for artists to think anew. Horizontally mobile, they were urged by patrons, contexts, and other artists to imitate and emulate, and to think critically about their world, their own work, and themselves. Through a process of experimentation that gives the Protoattic style such variety and visual interest, they worked through the possibilities of art and their own place as craftsmen.

CHAPTER 6

Drinking and Worshipping Together

Participation and Subjectivity in the Symposium and the Sanctuary

COMMUNITIES OF INDIVIDUALS

This chapter examines how people used material culture to participate in group activities and to shape their subjectivity in two ritual contexts: the symposium and the sanctuary. This marks a relatively new perspective on the Protoattic style, which has been studied with an eye to cemetery contexts and to the artist but rarely has been integrated into sympotic or cult contexts. It is true that the evidence is often fleeting and indirect. No Attic seventh-century equivalent of the Classical *andron* (a domestic drinking space) survives, or any other space or assemblage that can be associated directly and securely with the event. For sanctuaries, much of the material is poorly published, and often it is not possible to evaluate how objects were used across a site or how they may have related to architecture or other features. The symposium and the sanctuary also are each embroiled in complex scholarly debates, concerning the origin and nature of the symposium, the degree of centralization of cult activity, and the beginnings of the *polis*. These issues will have to be addressed in some detail below. With a clearer understanding of these rituals and their contexts in hand and a broad look at the material evidence, it will be possible to examine how people from a variety of social backgrounds used objects (especially but not exclusively vases) to participate, to connect to groups, and to perform their sense of self.

These two contexts complement each other in that the symposium elucidates how aspects of the Protoattic style could enable and shape participation in group events and the sanctuary more specifically clarifies the range of communities that people formed and the implications for the development of the *polis*. The communities in question are in some respects political, yet the evidence suggests that we need to move outside the usual frameworks of the *polis* and citizenship. Political identity is one obvious component of subjectivity that became particularly important in the seventh century as Athens continued to take form and dominate Attica, but it was not the only one. Gender, kinship, occupational activity, status, wealth, and regional belonging could be salient as well.

For these contexts to be accurately assessed, we need to be acutely aware of the assumptions that the Orientalizing paradigm described in chapter 2 has imposed. Both rituals consistently have been interpreted as closely associated with the elite and with Near Eastern cultures. Specifically, the symposium has been closely linked in scholarship with Neo-Assyrian and Levantine drinking practices, and cult sites have been considered a substitute for the eighth-century display that took place at the grave, serving as channels for the elite to lay claims to authority outside the *polis*. Holding Orientalizing readings at arm's length allows a more comprehensive and balanced assessment of the evidence and can accommodate objects and people at the social margins.

BETWEEN ATTIC RED-FIGURE AND LEVANTINE BOWLS

To set the scene, let us begin by looking at the close connection between vases and subjectivity at the symposium in the Late Archaic period to see what was possible in a period for which the evidence is more copious. Here, the first self-portrait in western art appears, on a late sixth-century stamnos made for a symposium and depicting a symposium (Figure 6.1).[1] Signed by Smikros (one of the Late Archaic painters known as the Pioneers), the image portrays a reclining figure labeled none other than Smikros enraptured by the music of an aulos. It is a remarkable example of how the symposium as a physical, ritualized setting and a pictorial device promoted the interaction of pottery, culture, and the performance of identity and status. These dynamics, and the role for ceramics, are clearly recognizable in the Late Archaic material record, even if interpretations of specific vases differ. Guy Hedreen has drawn attention to the ways in which Late Archaic vase-paintings such as Smikros's stamnos convey highly sophisticated and sometimes deliberately deceptive and misleading conceptions of the artist, on par with the tropes created by literary figures such as Odysseus or lyric poets such as Archilochos.[2] Hedreen argues that Smikros is none other than the painter Euphronios, coyly parading (on the vase) as Smikros at an elite event where potters and patrons were not frequent guests.[3] Whether or not this attractive reading is correct, it is undisputed that the Archaic-Classical symposium provided an ideal setting for ambiguity and inter-

Figure 6.1. Attic red-figure stamnos signed by Smikros, late 6th century. Brussels, Musées royaux d'art et d'histoire A717. Photo © RMAH, Brussels.

textuality, for the cultivation of riddle-like qualities in art and orality, and for the pursuit of urbane tastes. While Hedreen focuses on the subject of the artist who delights in creating subtle and playful images, other scholars have shown how Archaic and Classical symposia demanded that participants—those who used the pots—perform socially. In one compelling article, for example, Robin Osborne describes how the vases at symposia and the imagery on them enabled and elicited the projection of drinkers' identities, compelling them to ponder the types of behavior and tastes they could or should express.[4]

My question is to what extent this sophisticated interplay of people, objects, and images documented for the sixth and fifth centuries was operative in the seventh century, too. This line of inquiry has not been undertaken because there is no depiction of a symposium in Protoattic art, and certainly no close equivalent of the representation of Smikros. But if we look to the other chronological side of the seventh century, there is evidence from early first millennium Levantine bowls that

Figure 6.2. Silver-gilt Cypro-phoenician bowl, ca. 725–675. New York, Metropolitan Museum of Art 74.51.4554. The Cesnola Collection, Purchased by subscription, 1874–76.

objects used for the consumption of wine could mediate personhood and shape subjectivity in a considerably earlier period, too. These ninth- to seventh-century bronze bowls could be inscribed with names that declare ownership; the objects themselves "speak" and assert their connections to owners (Figure 6.2).[5] Marian Feldman has argued convincingly that the bowls were closely connected to bodies and, through drinking and funeral practices, could preserve and transmit memories.[6] Restricted to the interior of the bowl, images were accessible mainly to the person drinking, who peered deep inside and intimately encountered the enchanting, lush, and complex iconography. In Figure 6.2, one name was partly erased ("I am [the bowl] of Akestor, king of Paphos") and another added ("I am [the bowl] of Timokretes").[7] Writing contributed to the connection of the object to persons—to users and owners, both present and past. Circulating through high-value gifting and elite exchange, the bowls interwove object and human biographies.

These two sets of objects—Archaic sympotic vases and Levantine bowls—are neither points on a teleological progression nor moments in an unchanging continuum, but they suggest some of the possibilities for the ways in which objects may have operated in sympotic contexts in the seventh century. They offer impetus for thinking about a period that is usually omitted from discussions of drinking practices because the evidence is less direct. In the following sections, I will address this lacuna by first examining the origins and nature of the symposium and then closely examining a selection of vases to show how Protoattic pottery expressed and shaped subjectivity in the symposium through the interplay of figure and ornament, the depiction of myth, and the deployment of writing. As often as possible, each vase will be treated in its archaeological context.

NESTOR'S CUP

Let us inch closer to the Protoattic period and look at a remarkable example of material culture related to drinking that was produced only a few decades before the seventh century: a cup from Pithekoussai, a multicultural emporion in Sicily that included Greeks (Figure 6.3). Looking at this cup can help us understand some of the dynamics of the symposium coming into the seventh century and what Geometric pottery could and could not do. Found in a grave along with other vases related to wine consumption, the Rhodian or North Ionian drinking cup dating circa 720 is most notable for its remarkable inscription in three lines—the second two in hexameter—in the Euboian script. In the corpus of Greek inscriptions on vases, it is one of the earliest, longest, and most sophisticated texts:

Νέστορός ε[ἰμ]ι εὔποτ[ον] ποτέριον
ὃς δ᾽ ἂν τõδε πίεσι ποτερί[ο] αὐτίκα κε̃νον
ἵμερος hαιρέσει καλλιστε[φά]νο Ἀφροδίτες.

I am the delicious cup of Nestor
Whoever drinks this cup, straightway that man
the desire of beautiful-crowned Aphrodite will seize.[8]

The first word in the Greek is "Nestor" (in the genitive case), and along with the next word, "I am," anticipates a typical inscription of ownership, in which the object speaks. The third Greek word, however, "delicious" (literally "easy to drink" or "pleasant to the taste"), signals that more is at work here than naming alone, and the hexameter meter of the second line throws the script into a very different register. It offers a common formulation for a curse, "whoever drinks this cup," leading the reader to expect a terrible ending, such as "will be struck blind." But instead, the final line provides a gratifying surprise: the only thing that will strike the drinker are the pleasures of Aphrodite. In light of the jest in the final two lines, the "Nestor" of the first line is probably none other than the Homeric

Figure 6.3. "Nestor's cup," Late Geometric Rhodian or North Ionian inscribed skyphos, from Pithekoussai. Ischia, Museo Archeologico di Pithecusae 166788. Photo Marcus Cyron, CC BY-SA 4.0, https://commons.wikimedia.org/w/index.php?curid=68129777.

hero, and the cup claims to be the cup of Nestor described in the *Iliad* (11.632–637). But any knowledgeable drinker knew that Nestor's cup looked nothing like this clay vessel. In the poem, it is gold and so massive that people had trouble lifting it. The text repeatedly subverts expectations to surprise and delight readers and drinkers.[9] It assumes a literate and informed audience.

The cup testifies to the playfulness and good cheer (*euphrosyne*) operative in a commensal context and suggests the cultural pretensions of the users.[10] Through its intertextuality, riddle-like qualities, and eroticism it recalls the sophisticated literary games we know existed in later symposia, when Smikros reclines listening to an aulos. It also preserves the literate interaction of members of a group, presaging the games (particularly the *skolia*) of the sixth and fifth centuries, when drinkers one after another added verses to a spontaneous oral composition, creating a twisting and turning poem. The most successful compositions, like the epigram on Nestor's cup (as the clay vessel often is called), would surprise and delight participants with sophisticated wit. We might imagine that in the eighth century, one person composed the joke about the clay cup belonging to heroic Nestor, a second began the formulation for a curse, and the third crafted the delightful and unexpected ending. At the end of the banquet, the winsome poem was scratched on the cup as a memento of an evening well spent.

But what about the cup itself? While the inscription has received extensive discussion, the decoration of the cup has not merited a second glance. For all the playfulness of the text, the image is typical, conventional, and predictable. A main panel at the top is subdivided into four metopes containing diamonds, a stylized sacred tree, and meander hooks. The metopes are set over a low rectangular panel containing a zigzag. The decoration is well made, but not ambitious, and certainly not unexpected. To some extent the text adapts and conforms to the surface of the vase and its decoration.[11] It is inscribed within the long lower panel, an area selected perhaps because of the absence of ornamentation, with the one zigzag recalling the flow of written letters. But the inscription clearly was an addition to the surface of the cup, and the vase-painter could not anticipate that it would be made. Image and text on this vase seem as far afield as the clay cup itself from the golden vessel of the *Iliad*. Apart from the text, there is no concession of the decoration to the sympotic context—yet.

DEFINING THE SYMPOSIUM AND ITS PARTICIPANTS

We will return later to this question of sympotic imagery, but for now, let us address the problem of the date, characteristics, and participants of the symposium to better understand what drinking together was like in the seventh century. In terms of date, Nestor's cup seems to supply good evidence that the symposium existed by the Late Geometric period. There are now parallels from Methoni for other Geometric cups inscribed in relation to drinking.[12] But the date and location of the symposium's ultimate origins will depend on what one is looking for and what characteristics of communal drinking one emphasizes. Oswyn Murray influentially has emphasized the act of drinking while reclined as the marker of the symposium and sees an ultimately Near Eastern origin for the practice. He places the development in the context of the Orientalizing phenomenon, with a relatively rapid appearance at the end of the eighth century and notes that the multicultural context of Pithekoussai was the type of location where Greeks may have learned the custom from Levantines. For Murray, the mention of Aphrodite on Nestor's cup suggests that participants already were dining reclined. Moreover, he points out that the excavators of the tomb containing Nestor's cup maintained that the family had Semitic connections.[13] Like Murray, Hartmut Matthäus emphasizes reclining as the defining feature of the symposium but dates its export to Greece to the earlier eighth century, decades before Nestor's cup, with an important role for Crete in transmission from the Levant. The symposium is again part of an Orientalizing phenomenon, but one that begins earlier than the Orientalizing period of the seventh century.[14] More recently, Marek Węcowski has argued instead that movement "to the right" during the feast was the more distinctive "tracer element." He accepts Nestor's cup as evidence for the symposium but uses it to support his view of the ritual circulation of cups and conversation. In place of Near Eastern origins, he advocates for a more gradual and indigenous process starting in the beginning of the eighth or possibly late ninth century. He sees an important role for Athens, where there is a rise in tableware in graves from circa 850 onward, a preference for some types of drinking equipment in male graves, an appearance of multistory vases in the eighth century, and the invention of the kantharos shape in Middle Geometric II.[15]

Part of the difficulty in pinpointing an origin for the symposium in Greece is that not all wine consumption was sympotic, and feasts and banquets ("commensal politics") were long used as a means to establish and strengthen hierarchy in the Mediterranean, from at least the Bronze Age. Most scholars agree on a broad and general definition of the symposium as "a culture-oriented drinking occasion of simultaneously egalitarian and competitive character,"[16] but as we have seen, they differ on the details, which has implications for the date and the social dynamics. Wine consumption itself was relatively ubiquitous, occurring, for example, in indigenous Italian contexts before Greeks and Phoenicians imported anything resembling a sympotic practice and it could occur at multiple social levels, from elite to nonelite. To conceptualize what set the symposium apart from earlier drinking practices, Węcowski deploys Michael Dietler's three modes of "commensal politics."[17] The terms "empowering feast" and "patron feast" describe rituals for the acquisition and maintenance of power that had long histories in the Mediterranean. A third term, "diacritical feast," describes a mode of commensal politics "which involves the use of differentiated cuisine and styles of consumption as a diacritical symbolic device to naturalize and reify concepts of ranked differences in the status of social orders or classes."[18] Governed by style, taste, and exclusivity, the diacritical feast serves to define elite membership and channel social competition.[19] Such a mode of feasting is not fixed and static but evolves as a result of competition among participants and ongoing efforts to distinguish the feast from other modes of consumption. A symposium conceived as a diacritical feast would be for a select group within a larger community. Along these lines, Murray has emphasized the escapist nature of the symposium and related it to a shift in elite values from military and heroic prestige to leisure, and Ian Morris has exploited this view to advocate a conception of the symposium that was relatively anti-*polis*.[20] Węcowski instead sees a more productive social function to the diacritical feast, arguing that during a period of social mobility, the ritual allowed new elite to integrate into the upper echelons of society.[21] The feast oscillated between affirming equality and facilitating competition among members, who asserted their membership to the same group while also seeking through performative displays to distinguish themselves from one another. In all these views, we see the Orientalizing paradigm at work.

Perspectives, however, have started to change. Some recent scholarship has attempted to pull the symposium away from a strict relationship with a fixed elite or an aristocracy. Sean Corner, for example, advocates that the symposium offered a place away from private interests and class distinctions in which people from many backgrounds learned how to become citizens.[22] Even Murray has now clarified: "it is the instability of aristocratic control, the comparative absence of religious privilege, and the uncertain control of landed wealth in the face of trade and manufacture that meant that an aristocratic class never fully emerged in early Greece."[23] And he goes on to write that the symposium was "never an exclusive marker of social status, but rather an aspiration for those with leisure and wealth."[24] The feast can be seen now as a mechanism and tool for social claims and adaptation to new political and social realities, particularly as the city-state or *polis* and its institutions were forming, offering new vectors for political power and appropriating some of the traditional modes of status display. Whereas Dietler's "diacritical feast" assumes that rank is fixed albeit constantly reasserted, drinking together in the seventh century occurred in a more socially fluid setting.

A fundamental problem with a strictly elite view of the symposium is that there are plenty of subelite drinking vases. The material culture we will look at below includes vases that were relatively plain, with the exception of their graffiti, and even this type of basic literacy was not confined to an elite class.[25] The simple vases belonged to literate persons who engaged in commensal drinking practices that entailed humor, jest, and sex, and we have no reason not to think of these events as symposia, as social gatherings involving the consumption of alcohol. Even Nestor's cup comes from a subelite cemetery.[26] So I suggest a broader, more literal definition of symposium than a diacritical feast, as "the practice of drinking together in groups of men," which can accommodate ritualized drinking at various social levels in homes, cemeteries, and sanctuaries.[27] With this understanding, the diacritical feast was one form of symposium. Yet, inevitably, the more distinctive forms of drinking, the more elite ones, are more likely to be recognizable in the archaeological record and to be susceptible to interpretation. So rather than focus exclusively on the social margins of drinking, I instead use a range of objects to develop a model in which there is space for people at the margins to use material culture to participate in group dynamics.

THE SPINNING CUP

Several kantharoi illustrate the possible interactions between shapes, imagery, and drinking in seventh-century Athens. Somewhat antiquated in form, kantharoi reappeared in the Middle Geometric period and perhaps drew on Bronze Age prototypes (Figures 6.4 and 6.5).[28] Some ceramic examples also seem to imitate metal. The shape in the seventh century thus could be doubly prestigious in terms of its temporal and material allusions. Moreover, the high handles—the most distinctive aspect of the shape—transformed the drinking cup into a performance piece that could be used dramatically in several ways. The drinker could grasp both handles and lower his head into the bowl, framing his face with the handles. Or he could hold one handle and gracefully tip the cup toward his lips. Or he could attempt to balance the top-heavy cup from the base, displaying equilibrium and finesse amid the consumption of wine. The high handles made the antiquated shape unsuitable for dipping into a mixing bowl, so we should imagine the user extending it to someone else to fill, probably a slave, in a movement that asserted the leisure and status of the user. The shape, however, also was well suited for moving through a group, with the handles facilitating passing from hand to hand and sufficiently sturdy so that someone only had to grasp one to support the whole vessel.[29] Moving hand to hand, the vase would rotate around its own axis as it circulated through the group, like a planet spinning while in orbit. The imagery on a kantharos partially revealed itself to the person drinking from it—seeing now one side, now another—and to the participants in the symposium as it moved to and from the mixing bowl or around the room—seeing now one side, now another.

On some kantharoi, we can detect a deliberate and careful deployment of ornament that takes advantage of these viewing conditions to create a playful interaction between the two sides of the vessel. Before looking at these examples in detail, a few words about context are necessary. All the examples discussed here are from the area of the Classical agora; the area's use in the seventh century has been the subject of considerable debate. John Papadopoulos has drawn attention to the potters' debris and argued that the area was used primarily for potters' workshops and cemeteries, whereas settlement focused on the Acropolis.[30] Anna Maria d'Onofrio and Annarita Doronzio advocate for widespread, scattered hamlet settlement in Athens, with the intermingling of burial plots and habitation.[31] For them, the piecemeal mortuary record in the agora reflects a diffuse settlement pattern. In addition, they see a public space developing in the area of the Classical agora already in the seventh century, and they emphasize signs of cult activity, even seeing poliadic cult.[32] For the purposes of this chapter, it is worth noting that none of these activities—mortuary, sacred, or even workshop—precludes commensal activity in which vases could be used. And wells may have accompanied workshops but could also accompany homes, or homes cum workshops.[33] A close consideration of the material, attention to context, and capacious understanding of the symposium reveals material from the region of the Classical agora with sympotic connections. For the sake of convenience, as in previous chapters, I use "agora" to refer to the archaeological site and museum.

With these contexts in mind, we can turn back to the objects. A kantharos in the agora subtly contrasts the ornament on each side, with vertical zigzags over meanders on one side, and meanders over vertical zigzags on the other (Figure 6.4).[34] The drinker could compare the schemes, perhaps turning the cup to activate it. Or he might perceive one side of the decoration while he held the cup, another side when it was in someone else's hands. The movement of the spinning cup in the drinker's hands or to and through the hands of participants put the ornament into motion, creating a shifting and shimmering display that complemented the sympotic ambience and encouraged viewers to attend to, and perhaps to question, what they were seeing.

A second kantharos from the agora shares the conceit but engages in an even more sophisticated interplay of sides, taking advantage of the developments in the seventh century that probed the figure/ornament relationship, which we discussed in the previous chapter (Figure 6.5).[35] On one side, rays and interlaced diamonds frame the long necks and heads of water birds that have been created with an accomplished and confident stroke. The small reserved eye and the mere dash of a

Figure 6.4. Protoattic kantharos. Athens, Agora P 530. Photo courtesy of the American School of Classical Studies at Athens: Agora Excavations.

Figure 6.5. Protoattic kantharos. Athens, Agora P 579. Illustration by Piet de Jong. Photo courtesy of the American School of Classical Studies at Athens: Agora Excavations.

beak endow a curved line with a figural quality. Without a dash and a dot, they would lack such semantic weight. These animated lines, so lithe and graceful, present the viewer with a pleasant conundrum: where does ornament end and figure begin? Are these lines, or birds—and what does this imply about other lines? The visual riddle continues on the other side, with the rays on the bottom linking the two sides, the middle register occupied by vertical sigmas and rosettes, and on the rim, spiked spirals that evoke the water birds. Are they purely decorative ornament? Without seeing the other side of the vase, the answer likely would be affirmative, but after considering the water birds, it is difficult not to turn the vase back around and see the spiked spirals as birds, or as potential birds, and to question the category of ornament altogether. As the epigram on Nestor's cup offered a surprising conclusion that compelled the listener or reader to revise his interpretations of the opening line, so, too, the kantharos ultimately compels a constant reappraisal of what the drinker thinks the vase represents.

While the size, shape, and imagery of these two kantharoi seem well suited for a symposium, their find context unfortunately does not allow a firm conclusion about their function. Both kantharoi were located in road fill that contained much redeposited votive material.[36] Their size, and the thickness of the walls, however, do not preclude use in a sympotic context prior to deposition at a sanctuary, or in commensal practices at the sanctuary itself.[37] There were many occasions for feasting at a sanctuary, and it also was not uncommon to dedicate a vase at a sanctuary that was previously used elsewhere.

While these two kantharoi traded on a subtle interplay of ornament, other vases might showcase a surfeit of ornament that could awe, enchant, and delight, providing visual *euphrosyne* and distinguishing their user's taste. Like the Levantine bowls, they could enthrall participants as they deployed new ornamental forms to

Figure 6.6. Protoattic kotyle (see Figure 1.4). Athens, Agora P 7023. Photo courtesy of the American School of Classical Studies at Athens: Agora Excavations.

Figure 6.7. Protocorinthian kotyle. Athens, Agora P 7143. Illustration by Piet de Jong. Photo courtesy of the American School of Classical Studies at Athens: Agora Excavations.

shape objects of admiration and contemplation. A kotyle, for example, was lavishly painted with a variety of unusual ornamental combinations set in multiple panels (Figure 6.6 and Figure 1.4).[38] The hooked rays vary slightly, providing visual variety, and the panels of decoration are not centered, compelling the user to turn the vase to look at each. The alternating direction of the hooked rays on the base and waves on the lip promotes oscillation, transforming the waves into the frothy surface of an undulating sea. These maritime references recall the frequent comparison in later literary sources of the symposium with a journey at sea, a simile probably already current in the seventh century.[39] Participants were like the crew of a ship, bound together on a common journey led by a symposiarch. Under the influence of alcohol, the room might even feel like it was moving. The shape of the kotyle invites comparison with Protocorinthian pottery and establishes a competitive contrast with these more sober kotylai, which were well known in Athens and from which the vase clearly derives yet so visibly departs, such as figure 6.7.[40] Both kotylai (Figures 6.6–6.7) were found in a well at least 16.95 m deep at the eastern edge of Kolonos Agoraios.[41] The material, which seems to have been thrown in at one time, dates primarily to the first half of the seventh century, but is heterogeneous. Terra-cotta figurines and at least ninety small unglazed cups point to a votive origin for some of the material, but the presence of household wares suggests there were nonvotive origins for some of the material, too.[42] The imagery on the kotyle in figure 6.6 makes a sympotic context attractive. Unable to grasp the decorative scheme with one glance, the user was encouraged to put the ornament in motion, turning it in his hand, tracing the variety of curves and loops deployed in an innovative and unexpected manner.

From the same deposit came a second drinking vessel that also invokes the metaphor of the symposium as sea voyage and, like the kantharoi, manipulates the boundary between ornament and figure (Figure 6.8).[43] The shape is archaicizing: a deep

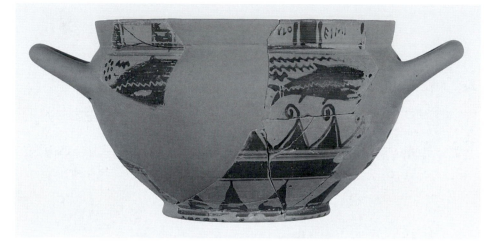

Figure 6.8. Protoattic skyphos with dipinto. Athens, Agora P 7014. Photo courtesy of the American School of Classical Studies at Athens: Agora Excavations.

skyphos with offset lip close in form to Late Geometric shapes and already well out of style in the mid-seventh century. Rays articulate the bottom of the cup, then a solid band, hooked rays, fish among zigzags and rosettes, and on the lip triglyphs. The reverse of the vase is too poorly preserved to identify the scene. Fish are possible but not certain. On the obverse, within the triglyphs, the remains of a dipinto are preserved, stating the ownership of the vase: "of ——ylos" (genitive case) followed by "I am," or "I belong to ——ylos."

We will return to the dipinto below; for now, it is the decoration that merits our attention, in particular, the way in which the hooked rays under the fish serve to signify water or waves rather than mere decoration. Juxtaposed with upright rays at the base, they offer a delightful contrast and, like the pairing on the kantharos in figure 6.5, urge the viewer to move between modes of seeing and interpretation to consider how lines could hold varying semantic weight. The painted zigzags themselves oscillate between ornament and figure. On other cups, they provide ornamental structure to the surface of the vase; here, above the fish, they contribute to the depiction of a watery atmosphere. The user touched the representations of liquid with his hands and felt the actual liquid drink with his lips. The imagery, made on commission (as the dipinto suggests), is as complex and ambitious as the epigram on Nestor's cup.

MYTHS AND COMMUNITIES OF VIEWERS

The seventh century saw not only a sophisticated interplay of figure and ornament but also the appearance of myths. While there were a few potential mythical representations in eighth-century vase-painting, it is only in the seventh century that unambiguous myths appear.[44] They opened a new world of figural possibilities, with

Figure 6.9. Protoattic oinochoe, name-vase of the Ram Jug Painter, from the sanctuary of Apollo on Aigina. View from the top. Aigina, Archaeological Museum K 566. Photo courtesy of the Deutsches Archäologisches Institut, Athens (Tsimas, DAI-NM-2612).

implications for users as individuals and as members of groups in a sympotic context. By offering prompts and props for storytelling, for discussion of the heroic past, and for tales about the broader Mediterranean world, they contributed to an ambience of culture and sophistication and solicited collective discussion. Mythical images did not merely represent taste; they demanded a response and the formation of subjectivity. As Luca Giuliani puts it: "Confronted with narrative images, the recipients could no longer sustain a merely passive attitude; they were called to action. Suddenly and unexpectedly it became possible—indeed necessary—to talk about images, to tell the stories that images related to."[45] Giuliani downplays the function of ornament, such as we saw on the vases described above, but correctly identifies the ways in which objects with myths could prompt and channel dialogue, particularly in a sympotic setting, where people saw vases in motion and engaged in conversation.

The scene of Odysseus escaping from Polyphemus's cave on the Ram Jug oinochoe shows how mythical subject matter could be apt for the symposium context, in several ways (Figure 6.9).[46] The story hinges on wine, for the hero only manages to escape because the cyclops was drunk. Much like later depictions of Centaurs popular on sympotic vessels, the myth of Polyphemus raises concerns about proper drinking behavior. But unlike other representations of the myth, Polyphemus is nowhere to be seen, and this specific part of the scene, with Odysseus and his men clinging to the underside of rams, seems like a slightly ridiculous moment to depict, picturing the shrewd hero in a decidedly awkward position. There is no visible threat from which Odysseus escapes—unless it is the symposiasts themselves, the wine drinkers picking up the oinochoe, who are transformed into potential cyclopes, not only through their drinking, but through their tactile engagement with the vase. They feel its surface as they decant the wine, acting like Polyphemus grasping for Odysseus. Drinkers looking on the image and handling the vase were invited to evaluate how they would act in the symposium and reflect on who they might become.

Like Nestor's cup, the oinochoe uses humor to surprise and delight. To get the joke, the users had to know the broader stories, especially those parts that were not depicted on the vases themselves. To understand the implications of the inscription on Nestor's cup, one needed to know how Nestor's cup appeared in epic; to appreciate the visual play on the Ram Jug, one needed to know about Polyphemus, even though he did not appear in the painting. The literate, skilled observer would understand the implications of the image by drawing on his or her knowledge of oral poetry.[47]

Writing accompanying figural content clarified or expanded on the subject matter, narrowing the range of interpretations and at the same time referencing wider semantic fields. A good example is a stand in Berlin with what at first seems to be a generic male procession (Figure 6.10).[48] But there is a dipinto, "Menelas," next to one of the figures. This single name, made before the vase was fired, transforms the generic representation into a specific mythical story, implicating texts and creating a reading event for a community of viewers. For the readers, the image became more narrow, more specific. At the same time, it became more expansive, alluding to a broader world of myth.

The significance of Menelas here may not have been quickly discernible, but subject to debate. Armed with iconographic encyclopedias, scholars still cannot agree on the precise narrative moment of this image. Perhaps it is Menelaus among Helen's suitors.[49] Only a reader could access the subject of the figural scene and identify one of the figures, while the drinking group together needed to debate its meaning, with individuals holding different points of view.

Along similar lines, the neck of an amphora from the agora bears a dipinto that Immerwahr restores as Νυκτοπαιδίας, "children of Night," written behind a bearded siren (Figure 6.11).[50] Was it a reference to the furies? An inside story, an epithet, or an allusion that only a select group could grasp?[51] The dipinto was an invitation to a conversation. Reading was not necessarily restricted to an elite audience, but it did open the possibility of varying levels of comprehension and interpretation.[52] It entailed close looking, access to knowledge, and discussion apt to a sympotic context.

The Ram Jug and the Menelaus Stand were found on Aigina (the jug in the sanctuary of Apollo, the stand from the necropolis) and possibly were not made for an Attic audience. But they nevertheless show the possibilities that the Protoattic style afforded, with objects made for contexts in which behavior and personality were

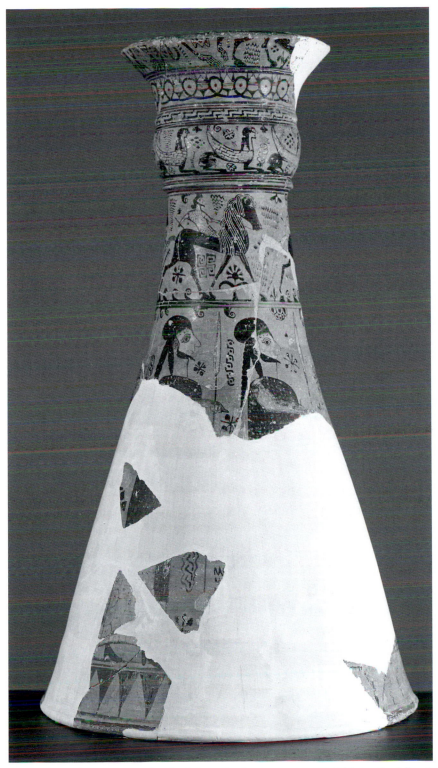

Figure 6.10. Protoattic stand with dipinto (the beginning is just visible to the right of the rightmost man's hand), from the necropolis at Aigina, attributed to the Polyphemus Painter. Berlin, Staatliche Museen, Antikensammlung A 42. Photo bpk Bildagentur / Antikensammlung, Staatliche Museen, Berlin / Art Resource, NY.

the object of scrutiny and performance. While there was enmity between Athens and Aigina in the seventh century, we might imagine that there were still interpersonal ties that could facilitate the exchange of goods, or sufficient Aiginetan demand to import some Protoattic vases.[53] The Ram Jug is particularly international in style, its shape close to East Greek and Cycladic models, its decoration revealing Cycladic and Corinthian links. Using such a vase may have invoked these different horizons. If Nestor's cup offers an inscription, and only an inscription, that testifies to the complex social dynamics of feasting, by the seventh century the style and imagery of a Protoattic vase also could engage with the drinking ritual and shape its participants as individuals and as a group.

ENTERING THE GROUP THROUGH WRITING

As we have seen, objects and their decoration facilitated and shaped the participation of individuals in the group ritual. They enabled drinking and inflected that experience through imagery. At the same time, this drinking took place in groups, and objects made possible the performance of the ritual as a collective practice that constituted a group. Vases were extensions of the individual, letting him join in the group, and they also acted as the glue that bound the group together. Writing added an interesting dimension to this individual/group dynamic mediated by interaction with material culture. We have looked at writing accompanying myths; more often, it appeared alone. For example, let us consider again the skyphos of ——ylos (Figure 6.8). His name was added before firing, probably at the bequest of ——ylos himself (but possibly by someone else, as an intended gift) and does not refer to the subject matter of the vase. Why include his name? Surely this was not a simple claim to ownership and a precaution against potential loss or confusion. He could not have feared that such a unique vessel might be misplaced at a symposium, or that someone would inadvertently take his cup. The name instead attests to pride in this distinctive object and serves to closely associate ——ylos with the object. With a name, the dipinto places ——ylos visibly into the symposium space and inserts him into the group dynamic. It is most clearly and manifestly *his* cup, and all seeing the cup in the room, nestled in his hand or circulating through their own, would see his name. They might also speak his name as they read it, giving him a sonic presence.

Figure 6.11. Protoattic fragment with a dipinto. Athens, Agora P 13323. Photo courtesy of the American School of Classical Studies at Athens: Agora Excavations.

In fact, if they read the dipinto aloud, they would make the cup speak, for it is the cup that declares, "I am [the cup] of ——ylos."[54] Unlike Nestor's cup and another cup we will look at in a moment, it leaves out a word for defining itself (i.e., "cup") and only uses the first person of the verb "to be" and the genitive of the owner's name, thereby emphasizing ——ylos rather than the object. The name is placed off center, so that when the drinker held the cup in two hands and put his lips to the rim, the words emerged out of the side of his mouth. In the symposium room, the cup, ——ylos, and other drinkers performed his presence through speech acts that joined him to the group and helped the group coalesce.

Other cups in the agora with names on them could enable a similar dynamic to unfold, although they usually do not accompany such sophisticated imagery. It is revealing that of thirteen name graffiti from the seventh century that Henry Immerwahr cataloged from the agora, all but two are on individual drinking vessels (cups, mugs, skyphoi).[55] Evidently in Attica a drinking vase was a suitable place for a name, an object on and through which to place oneself into commensal activity.[56] Moreover, the conspicuous location of the names is significant. Although a study of graffiti in the agora found that the vast majority of inscribed open vases had writing on the underside (73 percent),[57] where a name might be construed as a simple declaration of ownership, all the names specifically on drinking cups from the seventh century were prominently scratched onto the main body. This placement made them visible to those using the cup or to those elsewhere in the room, and the name asserted a person's presence and participation. Some illustrative examples will elucidate the dynamics and also allow a discussion of specific contexts.

The skyphos in Figure 6.12 claims, "I am the cup of Tharrias"[58] (Θαρ<ρ>ίο εἰμὶ ποτέριον). (The cup is broken at the right of the inscription, so the words may have continued.) In the inscription, the name comes first, the cup last, separated by "I am." The placement of the words below a band and the slight arc that they form help them stand out. They were inscribed in the soft clay prior to firing, intentionally added by potter or patron and not an afterthought. The cup was found in fill placed over the Geometric retaining wall of the Late Geometric Tholos cemetery. Among the items in the fill were two seventh-century skyphoi, the wall fragment of a Protoattic or Corinthian small open vessel, and a seventh-century octopus amphora.[59] None of these objects would be out of place in a symposium. In addition, there is a tantalizing amphora sherd in the deposit inscribed either with two names or, as Rodney Young proposed, with some form of τρυπάω ("to pierce or bore, perhaps here to broach") and κώμο- (relating to κῶμος, a revel), which he understood as "an exhortation by a reveller to his companions to broach a new vessel of wine."[60] Young thought the material may have come from the nearby cemetery because of the completeness of several of the vases, which is possible, but given the sympotic qualities of the assemblage, they may have originated from commensal activities that took place in a nearby seventh-century structure.[61] This building

Figure 6.12. Inscribed skyphos, 7th century. Athens, Agora P 4663. Photo courtesy of the American School of Classical Studies at Athens: Agora Excavations.

Figure 6.13. Inscribed mug, 7th century. Athens, Agora P 10151. Photo courtesy of the American School of Classical Studies at Athens: Agora Excavations.

(max. L. 30.50 m, max. p.W. ca. 6 m), adjacent to the Late Geometric cemetery, was founded circa 700 and destroyed in the third quarter of the seventh century. Disturbed by later activity, little architecture has survived to interpret. The few remains consisted of one room in the west with a hard-packed earth floor and three open rooms or yards in the east with a sand and gravel floor, the westernmost with a kiln, and the middle with traces of a basin for the preparation of clay.[62] Unfortunately, there is not enough evidence to securely label the complex a house-workshop let alone to confidently associate the cup of Tharrias with drinking activity that took place there, but it remains a possibility.

On a simple, black-glaze, one-handled mug, the retrograde name of "——atichos" (——ατιχος), in either the genitive or nominative case, prominently stands out scratched into the dark slip (Figure 6.13).[63] It is placed at the part of the body where the wall starts to transition toward the flaring lip. The user holding his cup in his right hand would face the inscription.

The cup was found among debris dumped into a well.[64] Although some of the material in the well, especially the terra-cotta figurines, seem to come from a sanctuary (likely the Eleusinion), there is no reason to imagine that all the material originally stemmed from a votive context. The cook ware and coarse ware in the deposit either come from a different, more domestic context or indicate that the preparation and storage of food took place alongside the votive activity.

Another name appears scratched deeply into the black slip of a one-handled cup (known as a Phaleron cup): "of Philon" (Φίλονος, Figure 6.14).[65] It was found in a well 7.55 m deep along with potters' debris, and Eva Brann and John Papadopoulos associate the material with the same workshop that produced potter debris

(test pieces and discards) in a
nearby circular pit and irregular
cutting (both identified as deposit
S 17:2).[66] As so often, however, the
well did not exclusively include
potters' debris. There were also
household wares and mended
vases.[67] From the well itself, no material was votive, and some of the
cups, mixing, and serving vessels
could relate to sympotic activity
(e.g., Figure 4.41, from S 17:2). A
fragment of a worked tortoise shell,
which Brann proposed may have
been part of a musical instrument, is
particularly suggestive of the type of
ambience in which the cup of
Philon may have circulated.[68] If
the cup was held in the right hand,
the inscription faced away from the
drinker, toward the room. While the
cup of Philon shows someone ex-
pressing and asserting himself in a
setting of convivial drinking, another fragment from this deposit
reflects the type of conversation that
could take place across an object.
Inscribed just below the lip on a
cup fragment are the words "the
boy is lewd" or "the boy is hateful"
(μισετος ho πα[ῖς, with the translation depending on whether the ac-
cent is on the iota or the omicron,

Figure 6.14. Inscribed Phaleron-type cup, 7th century. Athens,
Agora P 26420. Photo courtesy of the American School of
Classical Studies at Athens: Agora Excavations.

Figure 6.15. Inscribed cup fragment, 7th century. Athens, Agora
P 26452. Photo courtesy of the American School of Classical
Studies at Athens: Agora Excavations.

Figure 6.15).[69] In either case, it inverts the more common declaration on later vases
that a boy is beautiful (καλός).

We can look to cups found on Mount Hymettos for further examples of the types
of conversations that could take place on and through objects. The shapes themselves are simple, nonelite objects.[70] Some preserve words that could relate to
their votive use, but others have drinking and erotic inscriptions, and they evidently were reused for dedication. One example is a cup with a multiword inscription (Figure 6.16).[71] The inscription is written retrograde in one hand in large letters
across the surface of the vase, the deep marks standing out against the monochrome

Figure 6.16. Inscribed "Phaleron cup," 7th century. Athens, National Museum 16092. Photo N. T. Arrington. Copyright © Hellenic Ministry of Culture and Sports / Archaeological Receipts Fund.

black, the variation in size of the letters (from 6 mm to 16 mm) adding visual interest. It starts under the lip, near the handle. The restoration is unclear: "Nikodemos son of (?) Ph[——] is a bugger. Leofrades eri," with the last three letters erased (Νι[κό]δεμος Φ[——]ίδες καταπύγον. Λεό[φρα]δες [[ερι]]). Most interesting here is the word clearly readable, centrally placed under the white band, which seems to read, "a bugger." Although the object was found in a votive deposit, it obviously had an earlier and more complex life, the vituperative inscription representing the type of banter, criticism, rivalry, and insult that could occur at a drinking event that entailed sex. The erasure may have been a mistake, or reflect the ways in which the vase was manipulated during or after a symposium.

Another inscription from Mount Hymettos that evokes a sympotic context is preserved in two lines in retrograde on a Phaleron cup.[72] The letters of the first line are large and prominent on the surface of the vase, while those on the second line are not inscribed as deep, and they could be two different inscriptions, perhaps even the traces of a conversation that took place across an object. Only portions of the first line are readable, but it clearly includes a declaration of love for a man or a woman ([——]εμ' ἀ⟨ν⟩δρὸ[ς μ]ά[λιστ]α φιλεῖ τε[——/——]αταχ[——]ε.αρα). We might imagine someone scratching the first line on the vase and letting someone else read it as it circulated through the group and another person scratching the second line. Obviously there are many possibilities. The point is that like Nestor's cup the vase was a medium for people to write and read individually and together.

There are more examples,[73] and with all these inscriptions, we see how drinking cups could be three-dimensional surfaces in a symposium setting. The inscriptions not only reflected the type of talk we imagine, on the basis of later sources, took place during these drinking events, but as material manifestations of speech they participated in the articulation and expression of the individual, his place in the group, and the group itself. They were visible words to be seen, read, and performed, adding to *euphrosyne*, and creating bonds formed through imagery, names, jest, and even insult. As objects they allowed people to participate in the drinking and interact meaningfully with one another.

Many of the drinking groups may have been composed of elites. As Węcowski describes, someone could use participation in a symposium as a means to move from the margins to the "inside" group with political power. The symposium might also provide an escape from political life, a reaction against the development of a community of citizens, as Murray and Brisart argue. But so, too, may groups of drinkers have been bound by ties other than politics or status. Gender may have been the operative feature of one group, or kinship, or membership in a cult group, or proximity of the participants' residences to one another. The simple cups and the type of dynamics outlined here suggest that using vases to interact in drinking was not restricted by rank.

DRINKING AND THE ORIENT

Examining ornament, myths, and writing has not required recourse to an "Orient," neither did the iconography, shapes, styles, or words we have seen so far make any specific connections to Near Eastern cultures. Take again, for example, the cup of ——ylos (Figure 6.8). For all its sophistication, it can hardly be classed as an Orientalizing vase. There is nothing about the shape or the decoration that gestures toward a Levantine culture. Instead, it shows an affinity to the previous Geometric style, with the reelaborated Geometric motifs making visual puns to partake of the exploration of figure and ornament rampant in Protoattic. The even more lavish kotyle in figure 6.6 also makes few concessions to any "Orient." The shape is Corinthian, the walls so thin they may have been thrown by an immigrant Corinthian potter, and the ornament finds its closest parallels in Mycenaean and Corinthian art. The drinking shape of the kantharos that we considered in some detail also has no Near Eastern connection but instead a more local history (Figures 6.4–6.5). Finally, while myths provided a venue for both elaborate decoration and sophisticated discussion, they were Hellenic. Ultimate origins of some of the myths may have been located to the east, but it is difficult to imagine that the majority of users would have thought of the stories as anything but indigenous, and some of them, such as Odysseus's adventures with Polyphemus, took place in the west.[74]

But obviously Near Eastern cultures had some role to play in commensal activity in Attica. They are most closely associated with the practice of reclining while drinking, attested from the eighth century in Syrian and Cypro-Phoenician art and in a biblical reference (Amos 6:4),[75] and prevalent in later Archaic and Classical Greek art. The question is when and why this practice started in Greece. Reclining is absent from Homer, and on Attic Late Geometric vases of the Rattle Player Group, people still drink seated. In searching for an eighth-century date, Matthäus was only able to point to two miniature, fragmentary, poorly dated votive shields from the Idaean cave. Węcowski's suggestion that the iconography on these shields had a local and ritual significance seems more likely.[76] Reclining is only explicitly depicted in the late seventh century (in Corinth), around the same time that a few fragments of poetry may refer to drinking while reclined.[77] The couches depicted for reclining are a new type of furniture on mainland Greece, with East Greek origins.[78] While establishing a chronology for Greek reclining is admittedly fraught since Protoarchaic painters rarely depicted symposia themselves and since poets cannot be expected to systematically describe how people were drinking, the appearance of reclining in ceramics and poems in the late seventh century does seem to reflect a chronological reality. It seems most likely that reclining was a late seventh-century addition to practices of commensal drinking that were already taking place in Attica. Reclining was a way to elaborate the symposium. So like the development of the Protoattic style traced in cemeteries (chapter 4), the trajectory of the symposium entailed a process of appropriation and transformation. Since the consumption of wine was relatively ubiquitous, elite groups were compelled to constantly draw on new sources to make the ritual more distinctive. Reclining was one way to transform the event.

It is possible to be more specific about where this habit came from than reverting to a vague Orient. Recall that for scholars the broad designation "Orientalizing" has been used to indicate generic Near Eastern elements that for ancient consumers, too, were vague. The "Orientalizing" object so transformed its models that it became distinctively Greek yet with just enough Near Eastern flavor to give it an exotic taste for Greek users. But this is not what we see happening in the symposium. Around the same time as reclining began, in the late seventh century, references specifically to Lydia start to abound in sympotic literature. We hear of Lydian headbands and foot coverings, and Kritias wrote of Lydian cups or bowls in the symposium.[79] Poets frequently made an association between the Lydian customs of drinking and luxury, such as when Xenophanes famously claimed that the Colossians learned *habrosyne* from the Lydians.[80] The writers are clear: Lydianizing took place in the late seventh century. Lydia was a source for customs and attitudes associated with a leisurely elite, and those drawing on the source were perfectly aware of the move that they were making. This is an important change. While we

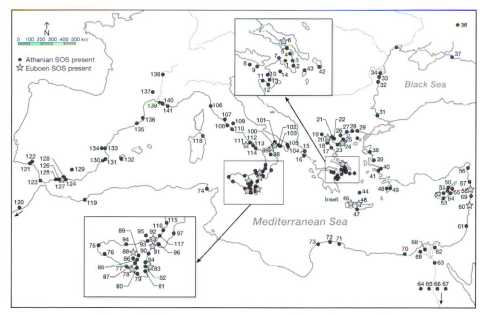

Figure 6.17. Distribution of SOS amphoras (mid-8th to early 6th century) in the Mediterranean. Compare Figure 3.1. Map by Catherine Pratt. From Pratt 2015, reproduced with permission. Numbers refer to her catalog.

were not able to find clear elements of Orientalizing in the early seventh-century symposia, in the later seventh and then the sixth centuries, the references are present, specific, and charged.[81] The ongoing elaboration of the diacritical feast would continue, and in the later sixth century, symposiasts clothed themselves in Lydian, Scythian, and/or Persian garb.

Access to Lydia likely was mediated through contact with the elite of Sardis, through political alliances, through the circulation of poets, poetry, music, and instruments, and through cross-cultural contact in those Greek *poleis* under Lydian control by the mid-sixth century.[82] Connections with Asia Minor are evident in trade, too, with the changing distribution patterns of Attic SOS amphoras revealing. Whereas none of the early type of amphoras, of the mid-eighth to mid-seventh century, reached Anatolia, the later type, from the mid-seventh century to the early sixth century, did extend to Asia Minor (Figures 3.1, 6.17). The fight to establish a toehold at Sigeion was also part of changing Attic connections in the Mediterranean. In the late seventh century, Lydia was a new horizon.[83]

CULT AND SUBJECTIVITY

We can broaden our investigation of the formation and expression of subjectivity in connection with objects and elucidate the types of groups that people formed in seventh-century Attica by turning to another source of evidence: cult. Like the symposium, cult activity operated at individual and collective levels and was facilitated by objects. But it offers more contexts and assemblages for analysis, which will allow us to consider several different aspects of self and personhood, such as gender, kinship, profession, and membership in a regional or political community. It also allows us to integrate ceramics with other types of material culture.

First, some preliminary words are necessary about the sanctuary record in seventh-century Attica. In contrast to the mortuary record, the sanctuary evidence demonstrates an increase in the number of sacred sites from the eighth into the seventh century and, in many cases, an increase in activity.[84] The boom was not accompanied by major building programs such as other communities in Greece experienced, and prominent temples, as far as we can tell, were neither an essential nor widespread aspect of cult in Attica. Instead, much religious activity was located outside of communities. Most common were mountain sanctuaries on peaks and hillsides, where worship typically focused on Zeus. Also present, but in smaller numbers, were cave shrines and sanctuaries in plains, on the coast, and in Athens itself. During cult activity at all these sites, rituals were accompanied by objects. People dedicated vases and figurines in great number, followed in popularity by other terra-cotta objects, such as plaques and votive shields. The Protoattic style was one component of a broader spectrum of cult activities. In the following sections, I will consider how individuals may have shaped their sense of self during cult activity, explore which types of actors were involved, and discuss what types of communities were formed. I will investigate the particular place of Athens in the broader Attic landscape. Then, I will examine what role eastern imports may have played in sanctuaries.

THE FORMATION OF SUBJECTIVITY AND COMMUNITY THROUGH RITUAL PRACTICE

Cult sites typically had a ritual focus, an altar and/or a statue, that helped people orient themselves toward the divinity. Much archaeological study of cult, or potential cult, has examined how this focusing effect manifested in the material culture.[85] But the process of supplication and worship was not unidirectional. While it might seem that the siting and arrangement of a cult served to channel people toward the supernatural, the act of visiting a sanctuary was of course more reciprocal and more introspective. In such acts of worship as asking for rain, giving thanks for a rich harvest, or marking a rite of passage, people declared their own mortality and their dependence on supernatural help.[86] To ask for aid was to realize one needed it; to give thanks for an event was to relive one's experience of that event. These are important steps in the formation and expression of subjectivity.

The act of devotion also was directed horizontally. Many rituals took place in the company of other suppliants, and often with outside observers in mind. Scholars have noted that in the seventh century, display moved from the cemetery to the sanctuary as grave goods decreased in number and sanctuaries rose.[87] In Attica, however, many of the objects were relatively humble. The plain cups that frequently were dedicated, for example, were poor substitutes for the sumptuous grave goods that engaged in status competition in the Late Geometric period (Figure 6.18).[88] Cult activities evidently were open to a wide group of people, and status competition was not always the ultimate aim, yet they still took place for the eyes of gods and men alike.

The objects involved in cult served to enable and highlight the ritual act. Prayers were accompanied by such object-mediated actions as dedicating a figurine in thanks, or pouring a libation and depositing the cup during a supplication. As in the symposium or the funeral, these objects became extensions of people and their bodies. When people left objects, they left a trace of their ritual activity in the sanctuary. And through these dedications, which filled sanctuaries, people made themselves continually present. Particularly clear are those occasions when people wrote on votives their names and the name of the god to whom they were dedicating, transforming the object into a materialized prayer.[89] For example, on a skyphos from Mount Hymettos, the graffito seems to read, "I belong to ('I am of') Zeus. —— as wrote me" ([τõ Δι]òς εἰμί. [——]ας δὲ μ' ἔγραφ[σε]ν).[90] The words make the object speak, and the vase declares its transfer from a mortal hand to Zeus. It also enunciates the name of the person who inscribed the letters, making him or her forever present. Likewise, dedications of inscribed cups once used in symposia were closely intertwined with the person who dedicated them and were repurposed to make a compelling and embodied prayer intimately linked to the dedicator (Figure 6.16).

As far as we can tell, most dedications were from individuals rather than groups. When names are inscribed, they are from individuals, as graffiti on vases from Parnes, Pani, and especially Hymettos indicate.[91] We are far from the corporate dedications well known in the later Greek world and particularly characteristic of Panhellenic sanctuaries. We also learn that Attic sanctuaries were not exclusively for people from Attica. At Parnes, Boiotian vases and Boiotian script suggest a wider group.

Even though many of the cult sites were located away from settlement centers and not explicitly linked to Athens, the process of worship could shape peoples' subjectivity as members of a group with regional, social, professional, or gender affiliations. At a site like Parnes, local regional identity may have been the common tie that bound dedicators together. At mountain sanctuaries, the sense of subjectivity may have been formed in relation to a community of like-minded shepherds. Zeus, probably as a weather god, was certainly worshipped on Parnes and Hymettos, and probably also at many other mountain sanctuaries. The primary audience for most of these mountain sanctuaries probably were the farmers and herders from the surrounding region who, regardless of their mother tongue, formed a cult community. The dedication of miniature shields found in the agora and also on Kiapha Thiti (Figures 6.19–6.20) could relate to one's participation in hoplite warfare.[92] Those who dedicated such shields asserted one salient part of their personhood and

Figure 6.18. "Phaleron cup" dedicated on Mount Hymettos, 7th century. New York, Metropolitan Museum of Art 30.118.47. Gift of the Greek Government, 1930.

Figure 6.19. Miniature terra-cotta votive shield, 7th century. Athens, Agora T 183. Illustration by Piet de Jong. Photo courtesy of the American School of Classical Studies at Athens: Agora Excavations.

Figure 6.20. Interior of a miniature terra-cotta votive shield, 7th century. Athens, Agora T 245. Photo courtesy of the American School of Classical Studies at Athens: Agora Excavations.

identity, and the act of dedicating along with others fostered a sense of collective purpose and belonging. There were other types of groups as well. *Phratriai* were organizations with religious affiliations and possibly regional associations that may have had a bearing on worship. Other cults focused on rites of passage for girls and/or boys, particularly at sanctuaries for Artemis, located at Mounichia, Brauron, and Loutsa.[93] Rites of passage that once were more private, or at least more restricted to the family circle, assumed an increasingly public dimension at these developing sanctuaries.[94] The Sanctuary of the Nymphs in Athens is an important example of this process, where from around the mid-seventh century brides dedicated in especially great number the loutrophoroi they used for baths or miniature substitutes (Figures 6.21–6.22, Plate 16).[95] The role of gender in rituals is also evident in a festival like the Thesmophoria, exclusively for women, which sharpened male/female distinctions and forged a sense of belonging to a corporate group based on gender.

As the variety of these communities of practice shows, community should not necessarily be conceived in political terms, and certainly not political in the sense of the well-defined Classical *polis*. But seventh-century cult activities could provide anchors and points of stability for settlement regions, as d'Onofrio has emphasized, and be a catalyst in the ongoing process of *polis* formation.[96] She underscores that even though much cult activity occurred outside of settled political communities, the peripheral location does not imply a disconnect between cult and community but rather a different spatial configuration of settlement in the Protoarchaic period. Even when local settlement patterns were unstable, the location of cult for people in a broader region could remain fixed. Josine Blok has gone further and argued that participating in religious rites, festivals, and duties helped make one a citizen.[97] The Acropolis, which might be considered a type of peak sanctuary, may offer a model for how settlement and cult could interact.[98]

How to fit the settlement of Athens into this regional picture is indeed a difficult question. It is possible that Athens in the seventh century was emerging as a major cult center with a poliadic deity. D'Onofrio and Doronzio have argued that the region of the Classical agora became a center for communal and cultic activity over the course of the seventh century.[99] They feel that scholars have downplayed or neglected the votive material from this area. There are obvious implications for our conception of the development of the region of Attica, where demes eventually were dependent on Athens, and the material should be handled with care. In support of a poliadic deity, d'Onofrio relies on her questionable interpretation that one figurine represents Athena with a spear, but it actually shows a bearded charioteer or warrior.[100] And Laughy has argued that the votive deposits that d'Onofrio associates with several religious structures in the agora actually result from widescale filling activity and ultimately originated in or near the Eleusinion.[101] Despite such objections, there is still quite a bit of votive activity in the area of the agora, even if it only stems from one sanctuary. By the end of the seventh century, some open space had developed, which could indicate the emergence of a communal center.

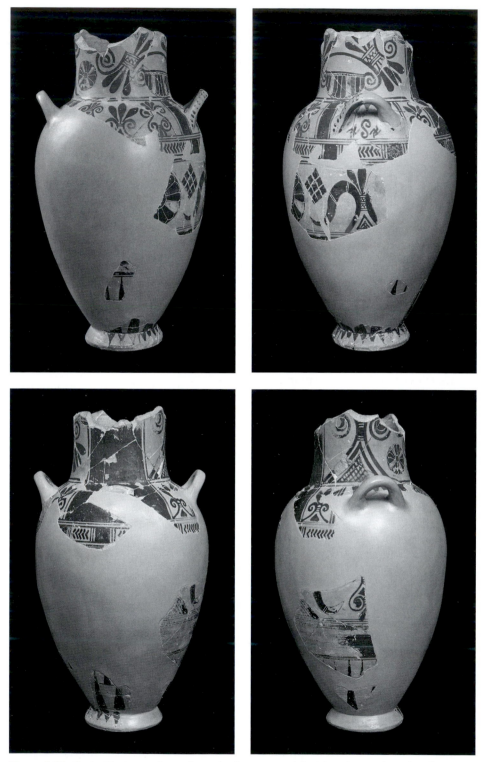

Figure 6.21. Protoattic loutrophoros from the Sanctuary of the Nymphs, attributed to the Group of Protomelian and Melian Inspiration. Acropolis Museum, Fetichie Tzami NA-57-Aα 456. Photo Yiannis Koulelis © Acropolis Museum, 2020.

The evidence from the Acropolis may form a more compelling case for the increasing cultic stature of Athens within Attica. Bronze tripods began to be dedicated in the eighth century and stand out in terms of numbers and material in Attica. Nowhere else in Attica are these lavish offerings so visible, and they may testify to the cult's regional importance.[102] Further support comes from the literary reports that when Cylon attempted to become a tyrant in Athens, he seized the Acropolis, evidently deemed a locus of power. The reason may have been merely topographical, but it is significant that when Cylon failed, he took refuge on the Acropolis at an altar in a temple or sanctuary with a cult statue.[103] The site may already have been considered the religious heart of the region.

The Eleusinian Mysteries also elucidate how sanctuaries could form an important component to the development of Athens as the major *polis* within its region. We have already

Figure 6.22. Late Protoattic loutrophoros from the Sanctuary of the Nymphs. Acropolis Museum, Fetiche Tjami Na-57-Aa-189. Photo Yiannis Koulelis © Acropolis Museum, 2018.

seen some of the evidence for votive activity stemming from the site of the Eleusinion in the later agora. At Eleusis itself, ritual activity in the sanctuary of Demeter began in the early seventh century, or possibly the Late Geometric period.[104] By the period of Solon at the latest, the two sanctuaries were ritually connected, forming an important link between Athens and its hinterland.[105] If the sanctuaries to Demeter at Eleusis and Athens were connected in some way over the course of the seventh century, as seems probable, then we have a significant example of cult both shaping a sense of belonging to Athens/Attica and asserting *polis* control over Attic sanctuaries.[106] There are other possible candidates for such a dynamic. For example, Thucydides reports that when Cylon seized the Acropolis, all Athenians were in the country celebrating the festival of the Diasia to Zeus Meilichios (Thuc. 1.12.6), marking another occasion when people came together in groups and moved from within the city to the outlying territory. Ritual links between Athens and Sounion and Athens and Mount Hymettos are also possible.[107]

Kin were one of the groups whose membership could be shaped through cult activity, and family belonging formed an important component of peoples' subjectivity. The power and influence of families in this context of emerging communal religious activity underwent significant changes, as they were both limited and enhanced by the changes. Some private, or semiprivate, rituals, particularly the maturation rites, became increasingly public, testifying to the dynamics by which a community of citizens would eventually become the Late Archaic and Classical *polis*. As the community grew in size and cohesion, it increasingly asserted influence over private life, taking control of previously more private rituals. At the same time, the presence of these cults in the public sphere showed familial life extending outward. By marking life passages in a sanctuary, such as the Sanctuary of the Nymphs, family members helped the community consolidate. Familial life seeped into the cultic sphere; the two were intertwined and coevolved. A dedication in the Sanctuary of the Nymphs could have a double valence, reinforcing not only the community but also family structures. Moreover, Michael Laughy has described how the management and oversight of cult activities provided a venue for maintaining family power.[108] Even in later periods, much cult activity was in the hands of families.

One might well ask what is unique to vases in the cultic contexts mentioned here and their individual-group dynamics. Much of what I have described could be possible through interaction with other forms of material culture, such as figurines. Vases, however, are the most common dedication in sanctuaries, for good reasons. Pots were particularly fitting for deposition because they could be used in a range of bodily acts of worship, especially pouring a libation. Moreover, unlike a figurine or other votive object made specifically for cult use, vases were more closely entwined with their user. They might have long, complex biographies, like a symposium cup dedicated on Mount Hymettos. And finally, vases were relatively common and inexpensive and accessible to a variety of social groups.

THE DEMANDS OF CULT

Near Eastern imports sometimes were dedicated at Attic sanctuaries. Sounion offers the best example of this phenomenon. Located on the southeast coast of Attica, it was a natural stopping point for ships heading from the Mediterranean to sites like Aigina, Phaleron, or Corinth. In addition to the pottery, figurines, and votive plaques typical of other Attic sanctuaries, Sounion saw the dedication of Egyptian and Egyptianizing figurines and amulets, metalwork including a Levantine warrior god, scarabs from Rhodes and the Nile delta, Levantine or North Syrian Lyre-Player seals, and other gems and seals.[109] The coastal location of the sanctuary and the possible non-Attic origin of itinerant dedicants may have something to do with the imports. Other sites, too, have imports, albeit in much lower numbers. At Brauron, which is poorly published, we nevertheless hear of a wide variety of dedicated goods, including gems. At inland Pallini, dedications included a ring with pseudo-hieroglyphs.[110] The ritual activity at these sanctuaries evidently could be performed and enhanced with the types of imports and objects that give the Orientalizing period its name.

But such dedications are a very small component of cult activity in Attica. They were absent from most cult sites. Consider Eleusis. The imports in the Middle Geometric "Tomb of Isis" might lead one to expect a wide range of later imports, like Sounion witnessed, and an opening toward the Levant in the seventh century.[111] The location of the site on the edge of Attica and near the sea would also suggest a high level of connectivity. But there are actually few seventh-century imports or "Orientalizing" goods. Instead, it is the amount of Argive monochrome that stands out in comparison to other cult sites in Attica.[112] The mountain sanctuaries have an even more limited material record. Vases predominate, and they are never imitations of Near Eastern imports. Complex as well as relatively plain pottery was used. Corinthian pottery, too, appears frequently in Attic sanctuaries. At Parnes, Protocorinthian aryballoi and alabastra dominate the votive assemblage and even outnumber Attic vases.[113] At Kithairon, too, the pottery was mostly Protocorinthian and Corinthian,[114] and pottery from Corinth has been documented at other sites, such as Kiapha Thiti and Profitis Ilias, even when few other objects were dedicated.[115] Clearly Near Eastern artifacts and an Orientalizing style were not the default mechanisms for honoring the gods, communicating with the supernatural, making connections to a community, and forming subjectivity. What this suggests is the capacity of plain pottery to be used meaningfully in ritual acts that connected mortals to the gods and to one another.

Pottery could also provide a surface on which to imagine the supernatural world and how to engage with it. With the proliferation of cult sites, and in the context of massive political and social developments, people came to see the world of the gods, their own world, and themselves differently, in a process that was both manifest in and enabled by the Protoattic style.[116] With its wide range of iconography and ornament and its openness to multiple horizons, it was a fitting style for this period of cultural change. Sphinxes, winged bulls, and gorgons strutting across vases, and vegetal ornaments including the sacred tree, opened windows to other worlds. Bronze Age and Geometric references evoked the past. The agora goddess, for example, redeploys Bronze Age iconography in a fearsome epiphanic figure wrapped in sumptuous clothing, framed by snakes, and emerging from the physical matrix of the plaque (Figure 5.8). The experimentation characteristic of the Protoattic style and the free and fluid approach to the vases's surface made this type of religious object possible.

If we return to Sounion and look specifically at vase-painting, the lack of correlation between imports and Protoattic is striking. The only hand of a painter that has been identified belongs to the Analatos Painter, but he did not work on a vase. Instead, he decorated a votive plaque with a ship (Figure 6.23), with no Near Eastern connections.[117] The subject matter of the votive plaque was a fitting dedication for a sanctuary located by the sea and was probably custom made.[118] This instance draws attention to the constraints cultic contexts placed on what one could or should dedicate; not all was possible. Sanctuaries and their cult activity made specific ritual demands that artists strove to meet (see also chapter 5). People visited a sanctuary of Zeus for one reason, of Artemis for another, and so on, and the different sites elicited different forms of material engagement. The Protocorinthian

Figure 6.23. Votive plaque from Sounion, attributed to the Analatos Painter. Athens, National Museum 14935. Photo Eleftherios Galanopoulos. Copyright © Hellenic Ministry of Culture and Sports / Archaeological Receipts Fund.

pottery that dominates some assemblages, mainly aryballoi and alabastra, was probably purchased in part because of their contents, likely unguents. At Parnes, many were pierced at the bottom or burned, a result of their use in a performative act at this site. At other sanctuaries, cult elicited a different type of vessel, and different uses, although we can rarely recover these functions in the archaeological record. For example, at Mounichia, seventh-century vases consisted mainly of standed kraters;[119] maybe they contained food offerings. At the Sanctuary of the Nymphs in Athens, loutrophoroi dominate the assemblage, a shape that was a new creation in the Protoattic period and associated with the bridal bath. Participants in cult activities therefore engaged in a process of personal expression and also social conformity through their interaction with vases. They used objects, primarily vases, in response to ritual needs, social custom, and taste. People did not take tripods to Parnes, and they did not burn aryballoi on the Acropolis. They still had some choice in what they did and how, but the range of options was not limitless, and in following ritual norms, they helped communities of practice cohere.

THE VASE IN HAND

Vases with riffs on the figure-ornament relationship, with myths, and with writing, vases that were stunningly complex and also downright plain in their decoration, allowed people from a range of social backgrounds to participate in drinking rituals that fostered group membership. In this ritual, people performed their identity, inserted their names into a group, and shared cups. They scrutinized images, debated myths, bantered over verse, and placed decoration into motion as they passed cups from hand to hand. Through their activity, enabled and colored by material culture, they inserted themselves into a group, and they helped that group form. Some of these groups may have been elite, but in others, the ties that bound may have been more closely related to other aspects of personhood, such as geographical location, kinship, or gender, as the cult activity suggests. In such a context, there was space for an increasing search for distinction among the rich and a steady rise, in some circles, in ostentation and refinement, with Lydia ultimately a source for inspiration. But it is misleading to see the symposium exclusively through an Orientalizing paradigm. In cult activity, too, we have seen how participation in individual and group activities mediated by objects contributed to the social and political formation of Attica, with space for a variety of actors. Sanctuary and votive activity rose markedly in the seventh century in Attica. The Acropolis began to stand out as a central place of worship, while other sanctuaries like Eleusis helped knit the landscape together. Painting operated alongside other votive objects to enable people to express their relationship to the gods and to each other, all the while forming their own sense of subjectivity and identity, including a nascent Athenian identity. Worship demanded conformity with ritual norms and demands and also left room for independent practice as people made themselves present in a cultic space through votives and expressed their gender, age, profession, or regional belonging. There were festivals specifically for women, clusters of votives closely tied to hoplites, and practices that brought rites of passage into the public eye. There were cult settings that attracted people from nearby and others that drew them from afar. Pots helped people engage in sanctuary activities, to make themselves present, to cross geographic and temporal horizons, and to imagine new possibilities. Vases in hand and in mind, people in the symposium and the sanctuary worked through who they were and their relation to one another and to the gods.

CHAPTER 7

Back to Phaleron

RECAP

In this book, the framework of the margins offered a reorientation of Attica in the seventh century. Historiography revealed how aesthetic tastes and intellectual trends, along with the need to classify and organize material, created a corpus and a period with far-reaching implications. The scholarly turns to consumption, quantitative analysis, spatial analysis, and contextual archaeologies have uncritically used a canon and a period label, fostering an Orientalizing paradigm in which the elite and the east are the main agents of change. We need to go back to Phaleron, in more ways than one.

The number and variety of burials in the seventh century (more precisely, as mentioned in chapter 1, the late eighth to late seventh century, the time conventionally known as the Orientalizing period in Attica) and the range of ways in which material culture was deployed in them spoke against social limitations on funerals, coherent ranking, and any consistent language of status display. Graves with very low investment of labor and graves located in an enormous cemetery alongside burials of social deviants showed that marginalized people could use Protoattic pottery. Indeed, the Phaleron cemetery suggested under what circumstances the style may have emerged in the first place. A marginalized, multicultural port settlement may have been the very place that a new style could develop, from which it was appropriated by the elite. Yet an elite never seemed to agree on how to use Protoattic to assert and maintain status. The formal and iconographic properties of the style were unstable and disruptive, and dissent always remained a distinct possibility. The absence of cultural hegemony along with evidence for horizontal and vertical mobility, in which the Protoattic style participated, helped explain the social conflict that emerged at the end of the seventh century, and to which Solon responded.

By suspending acceptance of an Orientalizing phenomenon or revolution, it was possible to look beyond status at a broader, richer array of ways in which people used seventh-century pottery to engage with one another and rituals, to construct subjectivity, and to form communities. This was not to deny the role of status in the production and consumption of goods in the seventh century but to resist the narrow interpretive moves that the Orientalizing paradigm posits, to recover a greater range of types and uses of material culture, and to look more closely at the interaction between pottery and people as communities formed. Near Eastern imports and local bronzes, such as the cauldrons dedicated on the Acropolis, may have offered overt ways to use "Orientalizing" for status display in the traditional understanding of the word, but imports did not increase notably in the seventh century compared to the eighth century, and straightforward imitations of Near Eastern objects were rare. When we looked closely at a variety of contexts for the consumption of ceramics—the most abundant surviving evidence for how people and material culture interacted—those contexts that fit the Orientalizing paradigm neatly, such as the funeral trenches in the Kerameikos, were rare. They expose the degree to which practice was necessary to make latent Levantine aspects of the style cohere. This notion of performance coincided with Duplouy's insights on how status constantly needed to be reasserted, although he focused too narrowly on the elite without enough regard for material culture that cannot simply be dismissed as derivative. Cook ware and coarse ware could meaningfully connect tomb and home at multiple social levels, and simple Protoattic fine ware allowed mourners to engage with mortuary rites, to participate in drinking events, and to worship the gods. Through practice, they cohered as a group in terms not restricted to citizenship.

A closer assessment of the geographical connections of Protoattic showed that the style interacted with multiple horizons, not just the eastern one. And the eastern geographical connection explicit in the word Orientalizing, on closer analysis, was not particularly pronounced in the style, iconography, or use of the vases until the late seventh century, when it should be termed Lydianizing. At that time, Athenians connected with the shores of Asia Minor and were well aware of the cultural references that they were making. Earlier, those Near Eastern elements that do appear could reach the Protoattic style through surprising sources, as a consideration of historical context and network models suggested: a place like Attica could connect to the Near East in unexpected, nonlinear ways. The region was situated in a marginal location, not yet on the main trading routes, and with its main city, Athens, positioned for ease of access to the region rather than the sea. At the meso-scale, Panhellenic and other sanctuaries offered important nodes of connection. There was engagement with the broader Mediterranean through the mediation of places such as Aigina, Euboia, Megara, Corinth, and Crete.

Aspects of the Protoattic style suggested the presence of Cycladic and Corinthian immigrants at work, and the Corinthian dimension of Protoattic was so strong that much Attic Orientalizing might more accurately be designated Corinthianizing. In terms of long-distance connections, I argued that the role of the west has been underplayed in scholarship that has accepted the geographical assumptions of Orientalizing terminology and that continues to operate under a spell of diffusion. Trade, artisan mobility, and sustained cross-cultural interaction were more pronounced to the west than to the east, and notions of the exotic were as western as they were eastern in orientation.

Marginality as a framework allowed us to reconsider geography and status. It let us look at the individual in society and his and her connections through material culture to larger social groups. With a close examination of peoples' interactions with objects, we could see some individual experiences with material culture, thereby disaggregating the developing *polis* into its smaller constituent parts. We started by looking at how artists were able to develop and express subjectivity through objects, techniques, and markets. So, too, users, such as the mourner in a cemetery, the drinker at a symposium, or the supplicant in a sanctuary. Vases as props, extensions, interfaces, and substitutes of the body allowed self-reflection, participation in rituals, and consolidation of groups. As multifunctional objects with potentially complex lives, pots were uniquely able to facilitate and inflect practice. People using them could cross horizons by bringing the home to the grave, evoking Mediterranean connections, or alluding to a Bronze Age past.

In discussing the interaction of people with pottery, I used the terminology of subjectivity rather than identity to highlight mutability and to underscore the constitution of aspects of personhood through relations with others and objects. This terminology also encouraged discussion of multiple types of subjectivity rather than focusing on political forms of personhood. The continuing development of the city-state (rather than a single moment when a *polis* was born, or a seventh-century retreat), certainly had an impact on the development of Protoattic, as settlement patterns changed, new markets opened, and new vectors for power and authority appeared. But objects and their contexts showed a number of different aspects of personhood that could emerge at different times and places. Subjectivities, for example, could relate to smaller regional communities, to religious organizations, to gender, or to occupations. Artists were a compelling example of people who are left out of discussions that focus on citizenship, yet in the seventh century their "personalities" appeared as never before. They expressed subjectivities through personal styles, encounters with objects and media and artists, responses to patrons and contexts, and experimentations with ornament and technique. Other people developed and expressed subjectivities as they looked at and used vases in civic and communal settings, participating in group actions while distinguishing themselves within those groups.

BEYOND ATTICA AND THE SEVENTH CENTURY

This book has focused on Athens and Attica in order to provide detail on historiography, contexts, and artists, and because there are aspects of Protoattic pottery that make it distinctive in the early Mediterranean world. But it is worth asking which arguments in the book are applicable beyond Attica, and which are relevant before and after the seventh century. I hope that some readers could detect many of the parallels as well as the divergences with other regions and periods, and I do not want to make a list that goes through every point in the book, but it might be helpful to discuss some of the most relevant.

While some research has sought to recover nonelite *experiences*, I have tried to argue that it is possible to look at the role of the marginalized in cultural development and to treat them as potential agents of change. One reason I have focused on Protoattic is that chronologies and contexts offered the opportunity to look just about as closely as we can in the early first millennium at how style and practice were deployed at different social scales. From a comparative perspective, some contexts and objects seem subelite, such as the Phaleron cemetery when compared to the Kerameikos, or a plain cup when compared to an elaborately decorated kantharos. Rather than just pursue these examples, I have tried to draw attention to weaknesses of current oppositional, structuralist approaches and to create an interpretive space that can accommodate margins as places both real and perceived. Artists, immigrants, and multicultural communities emerged as catalysts for change, and artistic forms were developed at the social margins only to be usurped and appropriated at the top of society, especially in the cemetery and in the symposium. If this model holds for "Orientalizing," usually considered the elite style par excellence, then it might be more widely applicable to Greek art. The search for distinction may more often involve an elaboration of cultural forms and the gradual creation of a distinct cultural sphere rather than the invention (at the top) of completely new traditions. The hypothesis would need to be tested on more regions, with a close look at styles and contexts. It is unlikely, however, that other regions could offer such a stunning historiographic turn as the elimination of the term "Phaleron Ware" from scholarship, followed many decades later by the highly publicized excavation and rediscovery of the subelite cemetery.

Like Attica, every region in Greece had a distinctive way of connecting to Mediterranean networks. Some nodes were widely accessible, such as prominent sanctuaries and ports. But different regions experienced connectivity in different ways. Crete, Lakonia, Euboia, Corinth, and Rhodes (to take just a few examples) were all part of an interconnected Mediterranean world in the seventh century, but their relationships cannot be conceived in terms of "Greece and the Near East" or "Greece and the Aegean." Each had a unique geographical location as well as different resources and social and political structures. This view coincides with research on the fragmentation of the Mediterranean and also nuances some of the perhaps overly optimistic ideas about a global Mediterranean world. I am not advocating for returning to isolationism or a model of diffusion but for recognizing that the process of incorporation into the Mediterranean currents was sometimes slow, with a high degree of variability. Regional styles in the seventh-century Mediterranean were pronounced, and they merit scrutiny as such.

Judging from the Attic material, I think we need to be much more cautious about how we think that Greek objects and their supposed Orientalizing styles connected to other areas and to the values that those areas might have had for ancient users. For many Greeks, like the Athenians, the west could be as much if not more a source of the unknown as the east, antiquity as much a source of fascination as the Phoenicians. Only a close study of the material culture of a time and place will be able to show the extent to which a region's style was Orientalizing in the way that scholars have used the term.

Objects have played an important role in discussions of connectivity, but in Attica and elsewhere there was considerable horizontal mobility of persons, too. I have underlined in particular the role for moving artists, both within Attica and to and from Attica. One advantage to stylistic analysis has been to find hints of Athenian artists working in Italy and of Cycladic artists working in Athens and strong connections between Corinth and Attica that probably entailed immigration. This degree of artist mobility quite likely was also present in other regions of Greece. Following the dissolution of the Bronze Age palaces, artists were not linked to strong states or to closed patronage systems.[1] Political disruptions and war probably compelled some Near Eastern artists to move, too. Moving in antiquity was a risky but not impossible endeavor and an important component to cultural change, particularly when the movers were artists who brought their own cultural conceptions in addition to technical skills. They conformed to some extent to new markets and societies while also transforming their new world.

The ways in which artists developed subjectivity across their objects and markets is applicable to regions other than Attica, although there are some distinctive features of Protoattic that make this mode of analysis more apropos. In particular, Attica had an unusual combination of a lack of strong markets (internal and external), a variety of techniques, and a freehand style that indexed the body at work. Compared to other regions, there seems to be a higher degree of experimentation in Attic vase-painting. More hands have been identified, for example, than in Cycladic painting. Some other wares, like Corinthian and East Greek, seem to have been made with an export market in mind, where customers expected to receive a certain type of product, leading to a higher degree of standardization.

Social instability in Attica that related to a rise in demography, to social mobility (horizontal and vertical), and to developing political institutions was shared by some but not all regions of Greece. One difference is that many other regions experienced tyranny, leading to stronger state structures and more fixed notions of status. The top and bottom of society became much clearer in these political contexts. Athens is relatively exceptional in not having a tyrant until the Peisistratus, and the failure of Cylon's coup is notable. Objects, I have argued, participated in this instability, but not merely as reflections of status. They interacted and mediated between and among people and sites, allowing participation in various communities, engagement with mourning rituals, the formation of subjectivity, and the expression of dissent. This model of how objects worked is obviously applicable to other places and times, too. Also, the notion that objects could function as sites and nodes, conveying new ways to represent and imagine the world, is applicable beyond Protoattic and the seventh century.

The distinctive aesthetics of the Attic seventh-century style, however, merits our attention. I have provided copious illustrations, including maligned and "ugly" vases, to highlight the appearance of art that disrupts classicizing conventions. But transitions in and out of the style were not abrupt. The latest Geometric pottery, particularly the work of the Workshop of Athens 894, clearly paves the way for the Protoattic style. At the other end, an artist like the Nessos Painter bridges both Protoattic and black-figure. Drawing a clear line between early black-figure and Protoattic is in fact extremely difficult. Black-figure is really a technique, while Protoattic is a style. Primarily produced in the sixth century, the technique of black-figure nevertheless appeared as early as circa 640.[2] Cook included much black-figure in his Late Protoattic category, whereas Beazley claimed the Painter of the Piraeus Amphora and the Nessos Painter for his Late Archaic black-figure style.[3] Given these gradual transitions, it is possible to overemphasize the distinctive aspects of Protoattic. And yet compare mid-seventh- with either mid-eighth- or mid-sixth-century vases and there is a significant difference in appearance.

Did the sociopolitical structure change along with style? Certainly it had changed by the early sixth century, when Solon instituted a number of important reforms. One of the most significant was shifting the qualifications of office from wealth and birth to just wealth. In the process, he divided citizens into classes based on wealth.[4] As a result, there was a more fixed social order and clearer rules for the determination of status. While it would be convenient to put Solon and the end of Protoattic at the same moment, they obviously do not neatly coincide. This is, in part, because art and politics rarely evolve lockstep. Solon responded to processes probably taking place over decades, and the transition into black-figure was gradual. We might speak, however, of a broad interrelation of a change in style with changes in society and connectivity. Protoattic was becoming less heterogeneous as the society was becoming more fixed into what scholars designate elite and nonelite, *agathoi* and *kakoi*, or insiders and outsiders.

In terms of connectivity, there were also important developments in the late seventh century. Athens came into military conflict over the island of Salamis.

Even more significant was its conflict with Mytilene over Sigeion in the Troad, positioned for good access to the Black Sea and Anatolia. Both are signs of greater Attic engagement with the Mediterranean, which could not have happened overnight.[5] Lydian elements start to enter the symposium in the late seventh century, too.

In the early sixth century, the place of Attica in the Mediterranean had changed considerably, and the production and consumption of black-figure played a part. Attic black-figure vases, at first closely related to Corinthian pottery, took form as a distinct style and found a market overseas, along with SOS amphoras, now traded much more widely.[6] In sharp contrast to the limited circulation of Proto-attic pottery, more than half of the vessels that survive from the early black-figure painter the Gorgon Painter and his circle were found outside of Attica. And some black-figure shapes, like the lekanis, were made primarily for export. The development of a market and an export industry is also evident in the concentration of some painters on specific shapes. The primary places of export were Naukratis, Samos, and some coastal sites in Asia Minor. These were areas not yet cornered by Corinth, and it is possible that the wares were carried by East Greeks.[7] The possible role for intermediaries, however, does not minimize the extent to which Attica was increasingly engaging in Mediterranean currents. The region was stepping out onto a stage that could be considered global. Connections with and influence at the meso-scale increased, too, as Attica was able to take advantage of its geographical location between Corinth and the Peloponnese to the west and Boiotia, Euboia, and Thessaly to the north. As cities in these regions developed in size and importance, Athens became a prominent node in a mainland Greek network.[8]

Black-figure not only found export markets and eventually became an industry, produced at a vast scale and for a wide audience, but also the technique itself demanded a different approach to the vase and curtailed some of the possibilities for heterarchy and subjectivity that we saw in chapters 4–6. While Protoattic departed from Geometric in emphasizing the painterly over the linear, the hand over the multiple brush and the wheel, black-figure marked a return to the linear. The technique was characterized by the rejection of outline, the presence of silhouette, the application of added red and white, and, most importantly, the use of incision. Applied with a sharp tool, the incised lines were of a uniform shape and size. The technique revived the mechanical idiom that had characterized Geometric. It entailed a regular, repeated, predictable stroke. It indexed the tool, not the hand. The technique coincided with a decrease in the representation of fluid motion on the vases and a reduction in the variety of ornament, which moved out of the figural field to the edges of the frame. Such uniformity and predictability were probably an advantage for markets, as standardization could contribute to increased output and to more widely recognizable types conducive to an export market. Vase-painting became "sober" once again.

Figure 7.1. View of the excavations at the Stavros Niarchos Foundation Cultural Center in 2019. Photo N. T. Arrington.

THE FUTURE OF PHALERON

It would be refreshing if Protoattic were once again called Phaleron Ware, but that is too much to expect. More pressing than terminology is the fate of the cemetery. According to Greek law, during construction of the Stavros Niarchos Foundation Cultural Center, the foundation only had to finance the excavation of antiquities that were going to be damaged.[9] This might seem reasonable, but under these guidelines, the center's extensive gardens placed on deep fill laid *on top* of the cemetery were not considered to pose a threat to the underlying remains. So only about one-fifth of the cemetery affected by the construction of the center ultimately was excavated, on opposite sides of the garden.[10] These two regions alone produced almost two thousand burials (not just seventh century in date). Thousands more dead, and the ceramics that accompany them, are located in the area between the excavation zones, under the gardens, and possibly farther away to the east.[11] Construction may not have physically damaged this part of the Phaleron cemetery, but it has sealed it for the foreseeable future.[12]

People walking in the lush and fragrant gardens funded by a shipping magnate have no idea that they tread above the unexcavated dead. The remains are not discussed in any of the center's signage and have no role to play in its identity as a cultural center.[13] Meanwhile, along the edge of the property, a fence surrounds the excavation of the mass graves, discovered in 2016, but in 2020 still inaccessible to the public (Figure 7.1). What to do about these remains has provoked considerable debate. Cover them up? Remove them? Conservation has been a nightmare, and in 2020 government archaeologists lamented the poor state of preservation, noting that considerable damage already had occurred.[14] The latest plan is to remove the bones of the mass burials and then to return them to the site and to build a museum that will be accessible to the public.[15] Reports are that the architect of the Center, Renzo Piano, may design it, and that it will include one upper space or structure with information on the finds and a second lower space or structure for viewing.[16] The language that has been used, however, is very revealing about the intended place of the past in the center's programming: the building should be "subtle" (διακριτικά),[17] and there will be limits on circulation in the museum and age restrictions.[18] It seems that the center's leaders do not want the dead to disrupt the way that people enjoy the center's spaces, or a museum to distract too much from its other activities. I can't help but wonder if the story wouldn't be different if a funeral trench (Opferrinne) had been found, or maybe something with a few more vases, or something a bit richer. The excavator, meanwhile, hopes the site will tell a very specific story. She doesn't want something macabre, she explains, but for the bones to illuminate a period of time that was critical for the development, ultimately, of Athenian democracy.[19] This interpretive move integrates the anonymous dead of the seventh century with a much more celebrated and known period of Athenian history. It may not be entirely inaccurate. Initial reports are that the bones from the mass burials belonged to people in good health, maybe to members of the elite involved in social conflict—perhaps, the excavator suggested, even to those who participated in Cylon's coup.[20] But it is troubling that the seventh century might be framed primarily in terms of a teleological progression toward democracy, that Protoarchaic could be made Classical again, and that the opportunity would be lost to show the battered remains of bodies, from the mass grave as well as from other burials. A museum could showcase the presence of the subelite in ancient Greece and the violence that people in the past suffered, and it might dare to put subtlety aside. The conversation over what to do about these dead will continue for some years, but I fear the Phaleron cemetery, and its numerous dead, will return once again to the margins: to the margins of the center's site, and to the margins of history. There they won't distract too much from the opera and library to the south, from the Parthenon that shines in the distance to the north, and from the stories that we tell about Greeks and Classical Greek democracy.

Table 1

Protoattic Burials

This table gathers the published data on burials that are coterminous with the production of Protoattic pottery, from the late eighth to the late seventh century. I exclude graves that contain only Late Geometric or Early Corinthian pottery. The graves are organized in alphabetical order according to findspot, without chronological subdivision, because I am not always confident in the dates that are assigned to Protoattic pottery.

I include material from museums when there is a reported Attic mortuary provenance.

The age categories should be interpreted with some flexibility. "Child" includes infants; "adults" includes juveniles.

When the burial is a jar burial (*enchytrismos*), the vessel type is listed first under "contents." When known, the placement of grave offerings (e.g., inside an inhumation jar) is specified.

ABBREVIATIONS (see also p. 253)

AA = *Archäologischer Anzeiger*
Agora VIII = Brann 1962
AM = *Mitteilungen des Deutschen Archäologischen Instituts, Athenische Abteilung*
att. = attributed
Coldstream = Coldstream 1968 [2008]
Cook = Cook 1934–35
Coulié = Coulié 2013
EPA = Early Protoattic
EPC = Early Protocorinthian
Kerameikos XVII = Knigge, Ursula. 2005. *Der Bau Z. Kerameikos XVII*. Munich: Hermer.
LPA = Late Protoattic
Neeft = Neeft 1987
PC = Protocorinthian
Rocco = Rocco 2008
W = Workshop

Location	Area	Burial Type	Age	Finds	Bibliography
Sagariou Street, Grave 1	Acharnai	inhumation in jar	child	pithos (burial jar); oinochoe, PC pyxis, two kotylai	https://chronique.efa.gr; ID 4851
Agora N 11:1	Agora	inhumation in cist	child (10-year-old girl)	oinochoe (P 22412), jug (P 22413), two 3-handled cups (P 22414, P 22415)	Brann 1960, 413–14, pl. 88; *Agora* VIII, 129; Coldstream 84
Agora Q 17:6	Agora	inhumation in jar	child (1-month-old)	pithos (burial jar, P 25787) closed by base of a bowl (P 25788); outside: oino-choe (P 25790), aryballos (P 25791), Phaleron cup (P 4963), skyphos (P 25792)	Brann 1960, 414–16, fig. 8, pls. 92–93; *Agora* VIII, 37–38, 54, 130, nos. 58, 65, 191, pls. 4, 10; Coldstream 84
Agora, Archaic Cemetery	Agora	unknown	unknown	fragment of closed pot (P 16991), att. to the Horse P or early Polyphemus P	Young 1951, 86, no. J, pl. 37c; *Agora* VIII, 94–95, no. 558, pl. 35; Rocco 140, no. Po 2
Agora, Archaic Cemetery	Agora	unknown	unknown	fragment of stand (P 16989)	Young 1951, 86, no. K, pl. 37d; *Agora* VIII, 85, no. 479, pl. 29
Agora, Archaic Cemetery	Agora	unknown	unknown	neck of oinochoe att. to the Passas P (P 16993)	Young 1951, 86, no. L, pl. 37e; *Agora* VIII, 80, no. 432, pl. 26; Rocco 77, no. Pa 5
Agora, Tholos Cemetery	Agora	unknown	unknown	oinochoe att. to the Ram Jug P or his W (P 4611)	Young 1939, 106–9, no. B1, figs. 74–75; *Agora* VIII, 37, nos. 53, 543, pls. 33, 44; Rocco 150, no. BAr 6
Agora, Tholos Cemetery	Agora	unknown	unknown	hydria? (P 6469), att. to the Group of the Thebes Louterion	Young 1939, 109–11, figs. 76–77; Rocco 119, no. LT 2, pl. 18.4
Agora, Tholos Grave V, G 12:5	Agora	inhumation in jar	child	hydria (burial jar, P 4614); inside: cup (P 4616), sky-phos (P 4615)	Young 1939, 26–28, figs. 14–15; *Agora* VIII, 127
Agora, Tholos Grave VI, G 12:10	Agora	inhumation in jar	child	amphora (burial jar, P 4768); outside and under neck: cup (P 4786), plate (P 4767), oinochoe (P 4785), aryballos(?); upright by neck: coarseware pitcher (P 4769)	Young 1939, 28–31, figs. 16–18; *Agora* VIII, 127
Aigaleos	Agora	inhumation in jar	child	pithos burial; inside: mug (P 24298), two cups (P 24299, P 24300), bronze bracelet	*AJA* 64 (1960) 71–72, pl. 15.1–4
Kavalas and Papanikoli Streets	Aigaleos	unknown	unknown	sherds of an unspecified EPA vase from disturbed grave	*ArchDelt* 19 (1964) 70

Table 1 • 229

Location	Area	Burial Type	Age	Finds	Bibliography
Analatos	Analatos	unknown	unknown	hydria (Athens NM 313) att. to the Analatos P	Böhlau 1887, 34, pl. 3; Cook 166, pls. 38b, 39; Rocco 28, no. An 11, pl. 1.4; Coulié 196, fig. 189; here, fig. 2.6
Anavyssos	Anavyssos	unknown	unknown	one to three PC kotylai	PAE 1911, 120, figs. 15–17
Anavyssos (plot of Xatziantonios)	Anavyssos	inhumation in jar	child	oinochoe	ArchDelt 39 (1984), 43–44, pl. 11a
Anavyssos (plot of Xatziantonios)	Anavyssos	inhumation in jar	child		ArchDelt 39 (1984), 43–44
Anavyssos (plot of Xatziantonios)	Anavyssos	inhumation in jar	child		ArchDelt 39 (1984), 43–44
Anavyssos (plot of Xatziantonios)	Anavyssos	inhumation in jar	child		ArchDelt 39 (1984), 43–44
Anavyssos (plot of Xatziantonios)	Anavyssos	primary cremation	adult		ArchDelt 39 (1984), 43–44
Anavyssos	Anavyssos	unknown	unknown	krater att. to the Mesogeia P (Athens NM VS 497)	Cook 188–89, 191, pl. 51c; Rocco 39, no. Me 25
Anavyssos, Tomb 22	Anayvssos	unknown	unknown	handmade aryballos	Kourou 1987, 42, no. 33; here, fig. 3.4
Academy	Athens (Other)	unknown	unknown		PAE 1960, 318
Academy	Athens (Other)	secondary cremation	child	two oinochoe, skyphos	ArchDelt 17 (1961–62), 21, pl. 21a
Achilleos 4	Athens (Other)	inhumation in jar	child	SOS amphora (burial jar); skyphos	ArchDelt 29 (1973–74), 123–24, pl. 97a
Agiou Dimitriou 20	Athens (Other)	unknown	unknown	at least one Protoattic sherd in area of an earlier Geometric grave	ArchDelt 19 (1964) 54–55, pl. 50β
Aristonikou 4	Athens (Other)	primary cremation	adult	pit with two standed bowls and some burnt bones, att. to the W of Analatos P	ArchDelt 29 (1973–74), 85, pls. 73d–e; Rocco 30, nos. BAn 10–11; Doronzio 2018, 233, fig. 3
Athens	Athens (Other)	unknown	unknown	two standed bowls att. to the Vulture P (NY MMA 10.210.4, 10.210.5), amphora att. to Würzburg Group (NY MMA 210.8)	CVA Metropolitan Museum of Art 5, 56–63, pls. 31–37; Rocco 60–61, nos. Av 8, Av 9, Wü 3; here, fig. 4.20
Athens	Athens (Other)	unknown	unknown	kotyle krater att. to the Group of Opferplatz α/IV (Karlsruhe 1892.C2678)	Hackl 1907, 99, no. 1, fig. 12; Rocco 44, no. Op α 6

Location	Area	Burial Type	Age	Finds	Bibliography
Athens	Athens (Other)	unknown	unknown	amphora att. to the Group of the Buffalo Krateriskos, EPC kotyle (Frankfurt VF β 231ab)	*CVA* Frankfurt am Main 1, 15–17, pls. 10.5–6, 13.1; Rocco 107, no. KB 1, pl. 15.5
Athens, Dipylon	Athens (Other)	unknown	unknown	krater att. to the Pernice P (La Haye 2007, 2005)	*CVA* La Haye 2, III Hd, pls. 4, 5–6; S. Morris 1984, 87, n. 196; Rocco 156–57, no. Per 4
Athens, Dipylon	Athens (Other)	unknown	unknown	standed bowl att. to the W of the Analatos P (Athens NM 752)	Rocco 30, no. BAn 12
Athens, Dipylon	Athens (Other)	unknown	unknown	krater fragments (The Hague 2005, 2007)	*CVA* La Haye 2, 6, pls. 4.5, 6
Athens, Dipylon	Athens (Other)	unknown	unknown	oinochoe att. to the Group of the Standed Bowl of Buffalo (Toulouse 26086)	Stackelberg 1837, pl. 9; Karouzou 1979; Rocco 108, no. KB 5; here, fig. 2.1
Ermou 90	Athens (Other)	unknown	unknown	sherds of 7th cen. include a small oinochoe	*ArchDelt* 30 (1975) 20–21
Kriezi 23–24 (drain), Grave IV	Athens (Other)	inhumation in jar	child	amphora with inscription (burial jar)	*AAA* 1 (1968) 24–26, 29, figs. 12–13
Kynosarges	Athens (Other)	unknown	unknown	three amphoras (incl. Athens NM 14497), two cups, kantharos, three oinochoai, EPA aryballos att. to the W of the Würzburg group, zoomorphic vessel, phiale	Smith 1902; Coldstream 2003, 335–38, fig. 1, pls. 42–44, nos. K15–16, K20–22, K25–28, K44, K79; Rocco 61, 180, nos. BWü 7, Kyn 1, pls. 27.3–5 ; Coulié 217, fig. 214; Doronzio 2018, 233–39, Table 1, fig. 16; here, fig. 2.15
Meïntani 12–14	Athens (Other)	inhumation in pit	unknown	two standed bowls att. to the Vulture P and the Würzburg Group, two oinochoai, handmade jug, bowl	*ArchDelt* 19 (1964) 58–60, pls. 54β–γ, 55; Rocco 49, n. 249; Doronzio 2018, 279, fig. 33
Mitrodorou and Geminou K.10	Athens (Other)	primary cremation	adult		*ArchDelt* 33 (1978) 24
Olympieion	Athens (Other)	unknown	unknown	amphora or hydria att. to the Analatos P	Brann 1959, pl. 44, no. 1; Rocco 27, no. An 6, pl. 1.5; Doronzio 2018, 214, table 1
Peiraios Street	Athens (Other)	unknown	unknown	amphora (Athens NM 1002) att. to the Nessos P	BAPD 300025; Coulié 219, fig. 216; here, fig. 2.11

Table 1 ▪ **231**

Location	Area	Burial Type	Age	Finds	Bibliography
Peiraios street (1893)	Athens (Other)	unknown	unknown	krater, name-vase of the Pernice P (Athens NM 801)	*AM* 20 (1895) 121–26, pl. 3.2; Cook 193–94, fig. 9; S. Morris 1992, 86–88; Rocco 156, no. Per 3, pl. 24.2; Coulié 214, fig. 210
Peiraios street (1893) Grave VIII	Athens (Other)	inhumation in pit	unknown	two standed bowls (one, inv. 746, att. to the Analatos P), skyphos, plate, footed cup, kalathos, two lidded kraters	*AM* 18 (1893) 115–17, pls. VII–VIII; Rocco 15, 29, 223, no. An 32
Peiraios street (1893) Grave XIX	Athens (Other)	inhumation in jar	adult	pithos (burial jar, NM 807)	*AM* 18 (1893) 133–34, fig. 30, pl. VII
Peiraios street 57 Grave XVIII	Athens (Other)	inhumation in jar	child	amphora (burial jar, A 4956) att. to the Passas P; oinochoe, kalathos	*ArchDelt* 23 (1968) 79–84, fig. 34, pl. 45; Rocco 67, 77, no. Pa 3, pls. 9.2, 9.5
Peiraios street drain excavation	Athens (Other)	unknown	unknown	hydria (A 1916) att. to the W of the Polyphemos P	*ArchDelt* 17 (1961–62) 22–23, pl. 25; Rocco 131, 141, no. BPo 2, pl. 20.3
Peiraios street drain excavation	Athens (Other)	unknown	unknown	amphora	*ArchDelt* 17 (1961–62) 22–23, pl. 26
Sapfous 10–12, Grave XIV	Athens (Other)	inhumation in jar	child	amphora (burial jar); olpe, one-handled cup, skyphos	*ArchDelt* 23 (1968) 89–92
Sapfous 10–12, Grave XVII	Athens (Other)	inhumation in jar	child	pitcher (burial jar); bowl, one-handled cup, oinochoe attributed to the W of the N P	*ArchDelt* 23 (1968) 89–92, pl 50g; Rocco 66, no. BN 3
Themistokleous 4, Pyre 2	Athens (Other)	primary cremation	adult	PA sherds	*ArchDelt* 42 (1987) 65
Themistokleous 4, Pyre 7	Athens (Other)	primary cremation	adult	PA sherds	*ArchDelt* 42 (1987) 65
Themistokleous 4, Pyre 9	Athens (Other)	primary cremation	adult	PA sherds	*ArchDelt* 42 (1987) 65
Themistokleous 4, Pyre 10	Athens (Other)	primary cremation	adult	aryballos (Corinthian?)	*ArchDelt* 42 (1987) 65
Themistokleous 4, Pyre 13	Athens (Other)	primary cremation	adult	PA sherds	*ArchDelt* 42 (1987) 65
Themistokleous 4, Pyre 14	Athens (Other)	primary cremation	adult	PA sherds	*ArchDelt* 42 (1987) 65

Location	Area	Burial Type	Age	Finds	Bibliography
Mainz, "Grabfund"	Athens (Other)	unknown	unknown	five dinoi att. to the Analatos, Mesogeia, Passas, and/or N Ps (153–58)	*CVA* Mainz University 1, 8–31, pls. 8–26; Hampe 1960; Kistler 1998, 202–3; Rocco 28, 39, 77–78, nos. An 19–20, Me 18, Pa 6–8, BPa 16; Coulié 194, fig. 188; here, fig. 5.4
Chalandri E I 1	Chalandri	primary cremation	adult	associated with a trench with kotyle (K 739), lidded skyphos (K 740), standed bowl (K 741)	Pologiorgi 2003–9, 182–84, 186–87, figs. 57–62
Chalandri E I 2	Chalandri	primary cremation	adult	pyxis (K742α), kotyle (K742β)	Pologiorgi 2003–9, 182, 187–88, figs. 57, 63–64
Chalandri E I 3	Chalandri	primary cremation	adult		Pologiorgi 2003–9, 188
Chalandri E I 6	Chalandri	primary cremation	adult	kotyle (K 717)	Pologiorgi 2003–9, 190–91, fig. 67
Chalandri E II 1	Chalandri	inhumation in jar	child	pitcher (burial jar, K 700); outside: oinochoe (K 702), three cups (K 701, K 703, K 704), handmade oinochoe (K 731), jug (K 705)	Pologiorgi 2003–9, 193–98, figs. 68–77
Chalandri E II 4	Chalandri	inhumation in jar	child	pitcher (burial jar, K 723α); outside: plate (K 723β), two cups (K 716, K 720), jug (K 721)	Pologiorgi 2003–9, 204–6, figs. 92–96
Draphi	Draphi	unknown	unknown	two oinochoai and one lid (att. to the Agora Group)	*BCH* 82 (1958) 680–81, 683, figs. 18, 23; Rocco 171–72, nos. AG 3–4, 15
Draphi	Draphi	unknown	unknown	ceramics including oinochoe, krateriskos, and thymiaterion from at least one unspecified burial	*BCH* 81 (1957) 518
Eleusis	Eleusis	inhumation in cist	unknown	EPC kotyle	Skias 1898, 79, pl. 2.11
Eleusis	Eleusis	unknown	unknown	open vessel	Skias 1912, 5, fig. 3
Eleusis	Eleusis	inhumation in jar (double)	child	amphora att. to the P of Amphora Acropolis 345 (burial jar, inv. 935); inside: EPC kyathos, kotyle, two incised aryballoi, two small oinochoai, two small skyphoi, one-handled cup	Skias 1898, 91, pl. 3.2 (and the two kotylai are compared to pls. 2.11, 12); Rocco 92, no. Acr 3, pl. 13.1; here, fig. 5.2
Eleusis	Eleusis	unknown	unknown	vase att. to the Analatos P (Eleusis inv. 1078 or 1089)	Cook pl. 40; Skias 1912, 5, fig. 2; Rocco 29, no. An 33

Table 1 ▪ 233

Location	Area	Burial Type	Age	Finds	Bibliography
Eleusis	Eleusis	inhumation in pit	unknown	handmade lekythos (665) and one unknown vessel	Skias 1898, 106, fig. 26; Kourou 1987, 42, no. 37; Kourou 1988, 320, fig. 4
Eleusis 62	Eleusis	inhumation in jar	child	kotyle attributed to the W of the Passas P (inv. 882), one EPC aryballos, eight other vases	*ArchDelt* 1912, 32, 34, 36–37; Rocco 2008, 68, 73, 78, no. BPa 24
Eleusis VI	Eleusis	secondary cremation	child	amphora att. to the Group of the Wild Style (cremation urn), LG shallow bowl closing mouth	Skias 1912, 32–33, 39, fig. 14; Rocco 101, no. W 5
Eleusis Γ6	Eleusis	inhumation in jar	child (10–12 years old)	amphora by the Polyphemus P (burial jar); inside: handmade aryballos	Mylonas 1975, Vol. 1, 91–92, Vol. 3, pl. Γ, figs. 222–24; Rocco 140, no. P4; here, figs. 1.9, 4.1–4.3, 5.22
Eleusis Γ17	Eleusis	inhumation in jar	child	pithos (burial jar); inside: PC aryballos and kotyle	Mylonas 1975, Vol. 1, 114–15, Vol. 3, pl. Γ, fig. 243
Eleusis Δ7	Eleusis	inhumation in jar	child	amphora (burial jar); outside: handmade lekythos	Mylonas 1975, Vol. 1, 181–82, Vol. 3, pls. Δ, 277α, β, δ; Kourou 1987, 42, no. 41
Eleusis Z9	Eleusis	inhumation in jar	child	amphora (burial jar)	Mylonas 1975, Vol. 1, 251–52, Vol. 3, pls. Z, 306
Eleusis Z10	Eleusis	inhumation in jar	child	amphora (burial jar)	Mylonas 1975, Vol. 1, 251–53, Vol. 3, pls. Z, 306–7
Eleusis Z12	Eleusis	inhumation in jar	child	amphora (burial jar); inside: PC pyxis	Mylonas 1975, Vol. 1, 253–54, Vol. 3, pls. Z, 208, 425
Elliniko (Old Airport)	Elliniko	unknown	unknown	unspecified number of 7th-cen. graves	*AR* 50 (2003–4), 8
Hymettos	Hymettos	inhumation in jar	child	amphora att. to the Group of the Wild Style (burial jar; Berlin F 56); inside: oinochoe (Berlin F 57) att. to Group of the Wild Style	*CVA* Berlin 1, pls. 43–45; Rocco 208, 101, nos. W 2, 10; Coulié 189, fig. 183; here, fig. 2.4
Kallithea "Tomb 1"	Kallithea	unknown	unknown	PC amphora, cup, two shallow bowls, standed bowl, vase in form of hut, three EPC aryballoi, PC pyxis, figurine of mule carrying pithoi, enthroned female figurine	Callipolitis-Feytmans 1963, 412–30, figs. 7–17
Kallithea Tomb IV	Kallithea	inhumation in pit	adult	two standed bowls (inv. 1106, 1107)	Callipolitis-Feytmans 1963, 404–7, 411, figs. 1–2, 6

Location	Area	Burial Type	Age	Finds	Bibliography
Kallithea Tomb V	Kallithea	inhumation in pit	adult	two standed bowls (inv. 1109, 1110)	Callipolitis-Feytmans 1963, 407–9, 411, figs. 3, 6
Kallithea Tomb VI	Kallithea	inhumation in pit	adult	two standed bowls (inv. 1111, 1112), inv. 1111 att. to the W of the Analatos P	Callipolitis-Feytmans 1963, 409–12, figs. 4–6; Coldstream 84; Rocco 15, 30, 223, no. BAn 9
Kalyvia Kouvara	Kalyvia Kouvara	unknown	unknown	hydria att. to the Mesogeia P (Athens NM VS 67)	Cook 177, pl. 44; Rocco 38–39, no. Me 10; Coulié 203, fig. 195; here, fig. 5.11
Kalyvia Kouvara, "The Vlastos Assemblage"	Kalyvia Kouvara	unknown	unknown	hydria att. to the Mesogeia P (Athens NM VS 179), two standed bowls (Athens NM VS 534, Athens NM 18497) att. to the Mesogeia P and the W of the Mesogeia P, EPC kotyle	Cook 177, pls. 45, 46a; Brokaw 1963, 71, fig. 34.2, 5; Rocco 39-40, nos. Me 11, Me 30, BMe 11, pls. 4.3, 4.5
Kerameikos	Kerameikos	inhumation in jar	child	pithos (burial jar)	*ArchDelt* 19 (1964), 41
Kerameikos 169 assemblage	Kerameikos	primary cremation	adult	Material from fill, not necessarily originally associated with the grave. PC olpe (4307), PC aryballoi (4308, 4309), PC bowl (4324), oinochoe (4310) att. to the P of Opferrinne ζ/XIV, three footed cups (4312–16, 4326) att to the P of Opferrinne ζ/XIV, kotyle (4311) att. to the P of Opferrinne ζ/XIV, three standed bowls (4317–18, 4321, 4322) att. to the P of Opferrinne ζ/XIV, two lids (4319, 4320) att. to the P of Opferrinne ζ/XIV, stand (4325) att. to the P of Opferrinne ζ/XIV, footed plate (4323) att. to the P of Opferrinne ζ/XIV, kotyle krater (4327), pithos fragments (4328)	von Freytag 1975, 58–71, figs. 6–13, pls. 16–19; Rocco 183–86, nos. Op ζ 2, 5, 7–8, 13–16, 18, 20–21; Kistler 1998, 206–8; Doronzio 2018, 98–99, figs. 81–83, Table 13
Kerameikos hS 68	Kerameikos	inhumation in jar	child	amphora (burial jar, 8967); inside: olpe, cup, bowl (all receive inv. 8708)	*AM* 81 (1966) 12, pls. 15.1, 16.3–5, 17.6
Kerameikos hS 70	Kerameikos	inhumation in jar	child	amphora (burial jar, 8979); inside: olpe, oinochoe, two skyphoi, one kotyle (all receive inv. 8726)	*AM* 81 (1966) 12–13, pls. 17.5, 17.7
Kerameikos HT 1	Kerameikos	inhumation in jar	child	pithos (burial jar, 5232)	*Kerameikos* XVII, 106, no. 4, pl. 41

Table 1 ▪ 235

Location	Area	Burial Type	Age	Finds	Bibliography
Kerameikos HT 5	Kerameikos	inhumation in jar	child	hydria (burial jar, 11252); two cups (5229, 5230), PC pyxis (5228)	*Kerameikos* XVII, 106, 108, no. 5, pl. 40
Kerameikos HT 6	Kerameikos	inhumation in jar	child	pithos (burial jar, 6106); shallow bowl (6107), five cups (6108, 6115, 6117–6119), feeder (6113), three oinochoai (6110, 6111, 6116), pyxis (6114), aryballos (6109), PC pyxis (6112)	*AA* 1984, 32–35; *Kerameikos* XVII, 104–5, 107, no. 3, figs. 13–14, pls. 42–43; Doronzio 2018, 122, fig. 106
Kerameikos HT 7	Kerameikos	inhumation in jar	child	amphora (burial jar, 4841); skyphos (4842), cup (4843), oinochoe (4844)	*Kerameikos* XVII, 104, no. 2, pl. 41
Kerameikos LZB I	Kerameikos	inhumation in jar	child	PC aryballos (4282), pyxis (4285), louterion on stand (4278, 4279) att. to the Group of Kerameikos Tomb LZB, oinochoe (4280) att. to the Group of Kerameikos Tomb LZB, bowl (4281) att. to the Group of Kerameikos Tomb LZB, feeder (4286) att. to the Group of Kerameikos Tomb LZB, two cups (4289, 4288), trefoil mouth cup (4287) att. to the Group of Kerameikos Tomb LZB, two model granaries (4283, 4284), iron wedge (M 301)	von Freytag 1975, 76–81, figs. 15–16, pls. 22–23; Rocco 179, nos. K 1–6; Doronzio 2018, 82–83, table 8; here, fig. 5.3
Kerameikos V-63	Kerameikos	inhumation in shaft	child	two standed bowls (303, 304), 303. att. to the Group of the Buffalo Krateriskos, one cup (305)	Kübler 1954, 254, pls. 10, 100, 127; Rocco 108, no. KB 9; Doronzio 2018, 79, fig. 37
Kerameikos V-68	Kerameikos	inhumation in jar	child	pitcher (burial jar, 355) covered with amphora base (1146); cup (354)	Kübler 1954, 256, pls. 106, 149, 155
Kerameikos V-98 (=Rb 6Λ)	Kerameikos	inhumation	unknown	two standed bowls att to the Analtos P (inv. 301, 302), kotyle, hand-made hydria	Kübler 1954, 271, no. 98, pls. 126, 132, 155; Rocco 28, nos. An 26–27; Doronzio 2018, 110, fig. 92
Kerameikos V-99	Kerameikos	inhumation in shaft	child	two kotylai, oinochoe, PC aryballos	Kübler 1954, 271, Beil. 4.1, pls. 82, 132, 139; here, fig. 4.34
Kerameikos V-100	Kerameikos	inhumation in jar	child	amphora (burial jar); kotyle, oinochoe, cup	Kübler 1954, 272, Beil. 4.1, pls. 81, 106, 132; here, fig. 4.35
Kerameikos VI-2	Kerameikos	primary cremation	adult	associated with mound A	Kübler 1959, 13–14, Beil. 1–2, pl. 47
Kerameikos VI-3	Kerameikos	primary cremation	adult	associated with mound B	Kübler 1959, 14, Beil. 1–3, pls. 38, 45–46

Location	Area	Burial Type	Age	Finds	Bibliography
Kerameikos VI-4	Kerameikos	primary cremation	adult	associated with Opferplatz α and Mound Γ. From the Opferplatz: PC oinochoe (1267), PC kotyle (1273), two PC lidded pyxides (1268, 1269), PC pyxis (uninv.), two PC aryballoi (uninv.), three lidded lekanides (1151, 1155, 1158) att. to the Group of Opferplatz α/IV, two koytlai (1152,1270) att. to the Group of Opferplatz α/IV, amphora or jug base (1271) att. to the Group of Opferplatz α/IV, oinochoe (1154) att. to the Group of Opferplatz α/IV, two standed cups (1153, 1275) att. to the Group of Opferplatz α/IV, two lids (1272, 1367), horse figurine (1156), chariot? figurine (1274), amphora (1157), sherds of three footed cups att. to the Group of Opferplatz α/IV	Kübler 1959, 14–15, 126–31, Beil. 1, 3–4, pls. 47, 57–59, 67; Kübler 1970, 416–27, figs. 47–48, pls. 4–9, 104; Kistler 1998, 203–6; Rocco 44, nos. Op α 3–4, 8–17; Doronzio 2018, 80–82, fig. 38, table 7; here, fig. 3.20
Kerameikos VI-5	Kerameikos	primary cremation	adult	associated with mound Δ	Kübler 1959, 15–16, Beil. 1, 4–5, pl. 47
Kerameikos VI-6	Kerameikos	primary cremation	adult	associated with mound E	Kübler 1959, 16, Beil. 1, 5–6, pls. 47–49
Kerameikos VI-7	Kerameikos	primary cremation	adult	associated with mound Z	Kübler 1959, 16–17, Beil. 1, 5, 6, pls. 47–49
Kerameikos VI-8	Kerameikos	primary cremation	adult	associated with mound H. PC kotyle (1355), handmade hydria (1356)	Kübler 1959, 17–18, 131, fig. 1, Beil. 1, 6–7, pls. 47, 60; Kübler 1970, 427, pls. 104, 128; Doronzio 2018, 86, fig. 59
Kerameikos VI-9	Kerameikos	inhumation in shaft	adult	associated with Opferrinne β and mound Θ. From the Opferrinne: PC aryballos (78), PC lidded lekanis (1278), three lidded lekanides (75, 76, uninv.) att. to the KMG Group, five tankards (73, 80, 1279, 1280, uninv.) att. to the KMG Group, two kotyle kraters (1361, uninv.) att. to the KMG Group, plate (74) att. to the P of Opferrinne β/IX, kotyle (134) att. to the P of Opferrinne β/IX, three oinochoai (77, 79, 1281), 79 att. to the P of Opferrinne β/IX, 1281 att. to the KMG Group. From the mound: kotyle krater (98) att. to the Oresteia P	Kübler 1959, 18–21, 131–33, Fig. 1, Beil. 1, 7–9, pls. 4–12, 22–26, 38–46, 60, 67; Kübler 1970, 427–48, pls. 10–29; Kistler 1998, 185–88; Rocco 155, 164, 168, nos. Or 1, KMG 3, 8–17, Op β 1–3; Coulié 214–16, figs. 211–13; Doronzio 2018, 85–86, fig. 58, table 9; here, fig. 3.31

Table 1 • 237

Location	Area	Burial Type	Age	Finds	Bibliography
Kerameikos VI-10	Kerameikos	inhumation in jar	child	pithos (burial urn, 1370); inside: amphora (92); outside: four cups (93, 94, 95, 96), two standed bowls (89, 90) att. to the Group of Kerameikos Tomb LZB, pyxis (91)	Kübler 1959, 21, fig. 2, Beil. 1, 8–9, pls. 11–12, 22–23; Kübler 1970, 448–53, pls. 30–31, 105; Rocco 170, nos. K 11–12
Kerameikos VI-11	Kerameikos	primary cremation	adult	associated with Opferrinne γ, Opferplatz δ, Mound I. Opferrinne: six standed bowls (136–38 att. to the P of Opferrinne γ II, 147, 148, 150 att. to the P of Opferrinne γ I), kotyle (139) att. to the P of Opferrinne γ II, oinochoe (140) att. to the P of Opferrinne γ I, two lidded pyxides (142, 143) attributed to the P of Opferrinne γ I, oinochoe (149) atttributed to the P of Opferrinne γ I, four thymiateria (141, 144, 145, 146) att. to the P of Opferrinne γ I. Mound: Attic kotyle krater (153) att. to the P of Opferrinne γ II. Opferplatz: oinochoe (163) att. to the P of Opferrinne γ II	Kübler 1959, 22–24, fig. 2, Beil. 1, 8–11, pls. 2–6, 12, 14–16, 18–19, 21–26; Kübler 1970, 453–73, pls. 32–60; Rocco 179–80, nos. Op γ II 1–5, 11, 196, nos. Op γ I 1–11; Kistler 1998, 188–90; Doronzio 2018, 88–92, figs. 60–61, table 10; here, figs. 3.8, 4.16, 4.38
Kerameikos VI-12	Kerameikos	primary cremation	adult	associated with Opferrinne ε, Erdmal a. Opferrinne: PC kotyle (97).	Kübler 1959, 24–26, 133–34, fig. 3, Beil. 1, 10–11, 13, pls. 21–35, 37–38, 61; Kistler 1998, 192–93
Kerameikos VI-13	Kerameikos	primary cremation	adult	associated with Opferrinne ζ, Opferplätze η, θ, mound K. Opferrinne: standed bowl (50) att. to the Agora Group, two footed cups (51, 52) att. to the P of Opferplatz ζ/XIV, kotyle (53) att. to the P of Opferplatz ζ/XIV, oinochoe (54) att. to the P of Opferplatz ζ/XIV, lid (55) att. to the P of Opferplatz ζ/XIV, three footed kraters (56, 57, 58) att. to the P of Opferplatz ζ/XIV, footed plate (59) att. to the P of Opferplatz ζ/XIV	Kübler 1959, 27–30, Beil. 1, 11–16, pls. 2–4, 6–12, 14–17, 19–24, 26, 41–43, fig. 5; Kübler 1970, 474–81, pls. 62–71; Kistler 1998, 191–92; Rocco 172, 183–86, nos. AG 14, Op ζ 1, 3–4, 6, 11–12, 17, 19; Doronzio 2018, 97, figs. 79–80, pl. 12; here, fig. 2.16
Kerameikos VI-14	Kerameikos	primary cremation	adult	associated with Opferrinne ι, mound Λ. Material from the Opferrinne may be within Kerameikos assemblage 169	Kübler 1959, 30–32, fig. 6, Beil. 1, 14–15, 17, pls. 21–29, 31–35, 37–40, 42–44; Kistler 1998, 193–94
Kerameikos VI-15	Kerameikos	inhumation in shaft	child	PC pyxis (963), three kotylai (964, 966, 967), oinochoe (969), alabastron (965), handmade jug (968)	Kübler 1959, 32, 135–39, fig. 7, Beil. 1, 37, pls. 47, 61–62

Location	Area	Burial Type	Age	Finds	Bibliography
Kerameikos VI-16	Kerameikos	inhumation in shaft	child		Kübler 1959, 32–33, fig. 7, Beil. 1, 16–17
Kerameikos VI-17	Kerameikos	inhumation in shaft	child		Kübler 1959, 33, fig. 7, Beil. 1–2, 17–18, pls. 35–36
Kerameikos VI-18	Kerameikos	primary cremation	adult	associated with Opferrinne κ, mound M. Grave: standed bowls (1276, 1277) att. to the Group of Kerameikos 18/XIX. Opferrinne: PC oinochoe, kotyle, and six aryballoi (no inv. numbers)	Kübler 1959, 33–35, 139–40, fig. 7, Beil. 1, 16–18, pls. 40–43, 68; Kübler 1970, 482–84, pls. 72–73; Kistler 1998, 194–95; Rocco 79, nos. C 3–4; Doronzio 2018, 99, fig. 84
Kerameikos VI-19	Kerameikos	primary cremation	adult	associated with Opferrinne λ, Erdmal c	Kübler 1959, 36–37, fig. 8, Beil. 1, 16–18, pls. 4–7, 9–10, 12
Kerameikos VI-20	Kerameikos	primary cremation	adult	associated with Opferrinne μ, mound N, Opferplatz ν. Grave: incised pithos. Opferrinne: PC kotyle (67), olpe (68). Mound: krater (152)	Kübler 1959, 37–39, 140–42, fig. 9, Beil. 1, 18–19, 22, pls. 14–24, 26, 63–64; Kübler 1970, 485, pls. 74–75; here, fig. 4.13
Kerameikos VI-21	Kerameikos	primary cremation	adult	associated with Erdmal d. PC oinochoe (1358)	Kübler 1959, 39–40, 142–43, fig. 10, Beil. 1, 18, 20, 22, pls. 30–35, 37, 39, 64
Kerameikos VI-22 (=V-68)	Kerameikos	inhumation in jar	child	handmade jug (burial urn, 355), covered with base of amphora (1146); outside: cup (354)	Kübler 1954, 68, pls. 106, 149, 155; Kübler 1959, 41, fig. 10, Beil. 1, 18, pls. 4–6
Kerameikos VI-23	Kerameikos	primary cremation	adult	associated with Opferrinne ξ, Grabbau e. Opferrinne: PC oinochoe (69), two kotylai (70, 71), cup (72)	Kübler 1959, 41–43, 143–45, fig. 11, Beil. 1, 20–24, pls. 2–12, 14–17, 20, 22–24, 41, 64–65; Kübler 1970, 486–88
Kerameikos VI-27	Kerameikos	primary cremation	adult	associated with Opferrinne σ, Grabbau i, Opferplatz τ. From Opferrinne: PC transitional sherds	Kübler 1959, 47–49, fig. 15, Beil. 1, 27–29, pls. 21–29, 31, 35
Kerameikos VI-28	Kerameikos	primary cremation	adult	associated with mound Ξ	Kübler 1959, 49–50, Beil. 1, 37–38
Kerameikos VI-33	Kerameikos	inhumation in shaft	adult	associated with Opferrinne υ, mound Π. Inside: Attic aryballos (60), sherds of the foot of a bowl. Mound: krater (129)	Kübler 1959, 51–53, fig. 16, Beil. 1, 30–32, pls. 7–12, 20–26, 28, 41–43; Kübler 1970, 491–92, pls. 77–79
Kerameikos VI-38	Kerameikos	primary cremation	adult	associated with Grabbau o, Brandgrab 39. Inside: handmade jug (1150), plate (uninv.; fragments were also found in the fill of the structure)	Kübler 1959, 58–60, figs. 21–22, Beil. 1, 37–38, pls. 48–49; Kübler 1970, 493–94, pls. 92, 105
Kerameikos VI-52	Kerameikos	inhumation in shaft	child	Corinthian kotyle (1359), oinochoe (1360)	Kübler 1959, 71, 148, Beil. 1, pls. 55, 65; Kübler 1970, 504, pl. 103

Table 1 ▪ **239**

Location	Area	Burial Type	Age	Finds	Bibliography
Kerameikos VI-62	Kerameikos	secondary cremation for 3	adult	three undecorated bronze vessels and two decorated bronze bowls (M 139–43); two PC oinochoai (82, 83), PC aryballos (87), three oinochoai (81, 84, 88), 81 att. to the Group of the Wild Style, two cups (86, 1369), handmade jug (85)	Kübler 1959, 75–76, 148–49; Kübler 1970, 509–12; Neeft 386, no. 163; Rocco 101–2, no. W 19; d'Onofrio 2017, 267–78; Doronzio 2018, 115, figs. 101–2; here, fig. 3.29
Kerameikos VI-63	Kerameikos	primary cremation	adult	pithos and krater fragments (132)	Kübler 1959, 76–77, Beil. 43; Kübler 1970, 512, pl. 92
Kerameikos VI-74 (=XII-4, Rb 13A)	Kerameikos	inhumation in shaft	adult	bronze plate, kotyle, three bowls, handles with bird finials, strips from tripod or belt (M 133–38)	Kübler 1959, 79; Knigge 1980, 77, figs. 1, 7, pl. 18.2; d'Onofrio 2017, 267–78; Doronzio 2018, 111–14, figs. 94–100
Kerameikos VI-I (=V-67)	Kerameikos	inhumation? in shaft	unknown	PC standed bowl (661), standed bowl (660)	Kübler 1954, 256, Beil. 2, pls. 13, 127; Kübler 1959, 13, 124–26, Beil. 1–2, pls. 44–45, 56; Kübler 1970, 416; Coldstream 84; Doronzio 2018, 79, fig. 37
Kerameikos XII-3 (=Rb 16)	Kerameikos	inhumation	unknown		Knigge 1980, 77, figs. 1, 7
Kerameikos XII-5 (=Rb 13B)	Kerameikos	inhumation	adult		Knigge 1980, 77, figs. 1, 7
Kerameikos XII-6 (=Rb 5)	Kerameikos	inhumation in shaft	adult		Knigge 1980, 61-63, 77, figs. 1, 7
Kerameikos XII-7 (=Rb 8)	Kerameikos	primary cremation	adult	PC aryballos (4215), Cor. juglet (no inv). Associated with horse burial Kerameikos XII-8, Rb 9	Knigge 1980, 78, figs. 1, 7, pls. 19.1–2; Doronzio 2018, 118–19
Kerameikos XII-9 (=Rb 15)	Kerameikos	primary cremation	adult		Knigge 1980, 78, figs. 1, 7, pl. 19.1, pl. 19.2
Kerameikos XII-10 (=Rb 15A, VI-71)	Kerameikos	primary cremation	adult		Knigge 1980, 78, figs. 1, 7, pl. 12.2
Kerameikos XII-10 (=Rb 15B, VI-70)	Kerameikos	primary cremation	adult		Knigge 1980, 78, figs. 1, 7, pl. 12.2
Kerameikos XII-10 (=Rb 15C, VI-72)	Kerameikos	primary cremation	adult		Knigge 1980, 78, figs. 1, 7, pl. 12.2
Kerameikos, north of Sacred Way	Kerameikos	primary cremation	adult	cup, oinochoe, olpe	AA 1964, 434, 441–42, fig. 28
Kerameikos, north of Sacred Way	Kerameikos	inhumation in jar	child	amphora (burial jar, 2718) att. to the Group of the Wild Style; kotyle, cup, olpe, aryballos, oinochoe. Over the burial, an ivory head	AA 1964, 434-35, 441–42, fig. 29; Rocco 101, no. W 7; Doronzio 2018, 63, fig. 9; here, fig. 4.17

Location	Area	Burial Type	Age	Finds	Bibliography
Kerameikos, north of Sacred Way	Kerameikos	inhumation in jar	child	pithos (burial jar); outside: cup, pyxis, coarse jug.	*AA* 1964, 435, 443–44, fig. 30; Rocco 170, no. K 15
Kerameikos, north of Sacred Way	Kerameikos	primary cremation	adult	five skyphoi, two kotylai, five plates, Corinthian olpe, louterion with stand, pyxis	*AA* 1964, 435, 445–46, fig. 31
Kerameikos, north of Sacred Way	Kerameikos	primary cremation	adult	oinochoe (2894) att. to the Group of the Wild Style, in grave under Grabbau A	*AA* 1964, 435–36, 447–48, fig. 32; Rocco 101, no. W 11
Kerameikos Station, Tomb 101	Kerameikos Station	unknown	unknown	head of a figurine (E 1039. E7)	Parlama and Stampolidis 2000, 276, fig. 248; Doronzio 2018, 61, fig. 7
Kerameikos Station, Tomb 152	Kerameikos Station	inhumation in jar	child	amphora (Geometric?, burial urn); outside: oinochoe (A 15335), lidded pyxis (A 15340), feeder (A 15337), footed cup (A 15343), three cups (A 15341, A 15342, A 15359), bowl (A 15336)	Parlama and Stampolidis 2000, 284–88, figs. 263–70; Doronzio 2018, 61, fig. 6
Kerameikos Station, Tomb 191	Kerameikos Station	inhumation in jar	child	oinochoe (A 15345), olpe (A 15348), aryballos (A 15349), feeder (A 15346), lidded lekanis (A 15353), phiale (A 15344), kotyle (A 15347), seven cups (A 15360, A 15350, A 15359, A 15356, A 15354, A 15358, A 15357)	Parlama and Stampolidis 2000, 276–84, figs. 249–62
Kerameikos Station, Tomb 239	Kerameikos Station	inhumation in jar	child	amphora (Geometric?, burial urn); outside: oinochoe (A 15379), PC pyxis (A 15382), lidded lekanis (A 15380), lekanis (A 15381), kotyle (A 15383)	Parlama and Stampolidis 2000, 288–90, figs. 271–75
Sokratous and Acharnon Streets	Kifissia	primary cremation	adult	lid (K 111), hydria (K 112) att. to the W of the Mesogeia P, standed bowl (K 113) att. to the W of the Mesogeia P	Rocco 40, nos. BMe 5, BMe 12; Skilarnti 2011, 681–82, 700–701, figs. 13–16, 21
Sokratous and Acharnon Streets	Kifissia	primary cremation	adult	unspecified number of 7th-cen pyres	Skilarnti 2009, 598
Koropi	Koropi	unknown	unknown	LG-Early Archaic sherds reported from a cemetery	https://chronique.efa.gr; ID 2277
Skaleza, T3	Marathon	inhumation in cist	unknown	LG-EPA sherds	*ArchDelt* 35 (1980) 84
Skaleza, T5	Marathon	inhumation in cist	unknown	LG-EPA sherds	*ArchDelt* 35 (1980) 84
Merenda	Merenda	unknown	unknown	skyphos (1743)	Xagorari-Gleissner 2005, 84, no. 223, fig. 22a
Merenda	Merenda	unknown	unknown	cup (1879)	Xagorari-Gleissner 2005, 86, no. 233, fig. 29c

Table 1 ▪ 241

Location	Area	Burial Type	Age	Finds	Bibliography
Merenda	Merenda	unknown	unknown	oinochoe (334, 1388, 1395)	Xagorari-Gleissner 2005, 87, no. 237, fig. 3d
Merenda	Merenda	unknown	unknown	closed vase (325)	Xagorari-Gleissner 2005, 87, no. 241, fig. 37a
Merenda	Merenda	unknown	unknown	oinochoe (1232) att. to the Analatos P	Xagorari-Gleissner 2005, 24, 79, no. 200, figs. 5a, 41b
Merenda	Merenda	unknown	unknown	standed bowl (1572) att. to the Analatos P	Xagorari-Gleissner 2005, 24, 85, no. 227, pl. 15b, fig. 27a; Rocco 28–29, no. An 28
Merenda	Merenda	unknown	unknown	amphora	*ArchDelt* 25 (1970) 129
Merenda	Merenda	unknown	unknown	Cycladic relief pithos	Kontoleon 1969, 217, n. 9; *ArchDelt* 25 (1970) 129
Merenda "Grave 5"	Merenda	unknown	unknown	standed bowl (1609) att. to the Analatos P, closed vase (1326)	Xagorari-Gleissner 2005, 30, 43–45, nos. 28, 31, figs. 27b, 35g; Rocco 29, no. An 29
Merenda Grave 11	Merenda	unknown	unknown	horse figurine (483)	Xagorari-Gleissner 2005, 49, no. 64
Merenda Grave 17	Merenda	unknown	unknown	oinochoe (1603), open vase (1463), a further 45 sherds. Near grave: closed vases (355, 356, 367, 372), a further 23 sherds	Xagorari-Gleissner 2005, 60–61, nos. 113, 115–17, figs. 7, 34d, 34g, 34i, pl. 9C
Merenda Grave 4	Merenda	unknown	unknown	oinochoe (1610), EPC aryballos (160), handmade jug (1740), closed vases (924, 925), 15 sherds	Xagorari-Gleissner 2005, 42–43, figs. 6c, 32f, 35a, 35g, pls. 7d, 8d
Oinoe Jar Burial α	Oinoe	inhumation in jar	child	amphora (burial jar, K. 1282) att. to the Group of "Protomelian" and "Melian" Inspiration; PC kotyle (K. 1252)	Arapogianni 1985, 210–11, 214, fig. 2, pls. 86b, 87b, 87g; Rocco 93, 226, no. Ml 1, pl. 13.6
Oinoe Jar Burial β	Oinoe	inhumation in jar	child	pithos (burial jar, K. 1281); inside: cup (K. 1253), oinochoe (K. 1254), skyphos (K. 1255)	Arapogianni 1985, 210–11, 214–15, fig. 2, pls. 88–89
Oinoe Jar Burial δ	Oinoe	inhumation in jar	child	pithos (burial jar); horse figurine (M. 587)	Arapogianni 1985, 210–11, 216, fig. 2
Oinoe Jar Burial ε	Oinoe	inhumation in jar	child	pithos (burial jar, K. 1280); inside: PC oinochoe (K. 1259), cup (K. 1260), LPC ayballos (K. 1261), LPC lidded lekanis (K. 1262), bronze ring, steatite spindle whorl (M 588)	Arapogianni 1985, 210–11, 216–17, fig. 2, pl. 91

Location	Area	Burial Type	Age	Finds	Bibliography
Oinoe Jar Burial στ	Oinoe	inhumation in jar	child		Arapogianni 1985, 210–11, 217–18, fig. 2, pl. 92
Oinoe Pyre 10	Oinoe	primary cremation	adult	oinochoe (K. 1270)	Arapogianni 1985, 210–12, fig. 2, pls. 85b, 87d
Oinoe Pyre 9	Oinoe	primary cremation	adult	ceramics from the late 7th century	Arapogianni 1985, 210–12, fig. 2
Olympos	Olympos	funerary plaque	unknown	funerary plaque (NY MMA 14.146.3a)	Richter 1942, 83–84, figs. 4, 6; Boardman 1955, 58, no. 1; here, fig. 4.14
Olympos	Olympos	funerary plaque	unknown	funerary plaque (NY MMA 14.146.3b)	Richter 1942, 83–84, figs. 4–5; Boardman 1955, 58, no. 1; here, fig. 4.15
Palaia Kokkinia Pot Burial 1	Palaia Kokkinia	inhumation in jar	child	cooking jug (burial jar, ΜΠ 16517), sealed by reused krater(?) base; outside: lid (ΜΠ 16518), oinochoe (ΜΠ 15832), pyxis (ΜΠ 15833), three cups (ΜΠ 15837–39), PC pyxis (ΜΠ 15834)	Arrington, Spyropoulos, and Brellas 2021, 237–41; here, fig. 4.5
Palaia Kokkinia Pot Burial 2	Palaia Kokkinia	inhumation in jar	child (2.5–3.5 year old)	amphora (burial jar); outside: two oinochoai (ΜΠ 15852, ΜΠ 15846), two stands (ΜΠ 14257, ΜΠ 14258), louterion (ΜΠ 14260), Transitional aryballos (ΜΠ 15835); inside: stand (ΜΠ 14259), louterion (ΜΠ 14261), cups (ΜΠ 15829, ΜΠ 15853), Transitional aryballos (ΜΠ 15830)	Arrington, Spyropoulos, and Brellas; 2021, 241–49; here, figs. 4.28, 4.30, 5.5
Palaia Kokkinia Pot Burial 3	Palaia Kokkinia	inhumation in jar	child	amphora (burial jar)	Arrington, Spyropoulos, and Brellas 2021, 249
Palaia Kokkinia Pyre 1	Palaia Kokkinia	primary cremation	adult	two horse and rider figurines (ΜΠ 15843–44)	Arrington, Spyropoulos, and Brellas 2021, 249–50; here, figs. 4.6, 4.26
Palaia Kokkinia Pyre 2	Palaia Kokkinia	primary cremation	adult		Arrington, Spyropoulos, and Brellas 2021, 251
Palaia Kokkinia Pyre 3	Palaia Kokkinia	primary cremation	adult		Arrington, Spyropoulos, and Brellas 2021, 251
Palaia Phokaia	Palaia Phokaia	primary cremation	adult	lid att. to the Group of Opferplatz α/IV	*ArchDelt* 42 (1987) 96–97, pl. 49β; Rocco 44, no. Op α 19
Palaia Phokaia	Palaia Phokaia	primary cremation	adult	lid from one of the burials (unspecified), att. to the Group of Opferplatz α/IV	*ArchDelt* 42 (1987) 96–97; Rocco 44, no. Op α 19, pl. 5.3

Table 1 ▪ 243

Location	Area	Burial Type	Age	Finds	Bibliography
Palaia Phokaia	Palaia Phokaia	primary cremation	adult		*ArchDelt 42* (1987) 96–97
Palaia Phokaia	Palaia Phokaia	primary cremation	adult		*ArchDelt 42* (1987) 96–97
Palaia Phokaia	Palaia Phokaia	primary cremation	adult		*ArchDelt 42* (1987) 96–97
Palaia Phokaia	Palaia Phokaia	primary cremation	adult		*ArchDelt 42* (1987) 96–97
Palaia Phokaia	Palaia Phokaia	primary cremation	adult		*ArchDelt 42* (1987) 96–97
Phaleron	Phaleron	unknown	unknown	oinochoe (4505)	*CVA* La Haye II, III Hb, 6, pl. 4.3
Phaleron	Phaleron	unknown, jar burials, primary cremations	adult	68 graves from the Kourouniotis excavation in 1911, insufficiently published to provide any statistics	Kourouniotis 1911
Phaleron	Phaleron	mass inhumation	adult	18 men with chains	Pelekidis 1916, 25, 49–64; here, figs. 4.8–4.9
Phaleron	Phaleron	mass inhumation	adult	one of three trenches with a total of 78–79 men, some in chains	https://chronique.efa.gr/?kroute=report&id=6141
Phaleron	Phaleron	mass inhumation	adult	one of three trenches with a total of 78–79 men, some in chains	https://chronique.efa.gr/?kroute=report&id=6141
Phaleron	Phaleron	mass inhumation	adult	one of three trenches with a total of 78–79 men, some in chains	https://chronique.efa.gr/?kroute=report&id=6141
Phaleron	Phaleron	unknown	unknown	oinochoe (Athens NM 551) att. to the Group of Kerameikos 18/XIX	Dumont 1869; Rocco 79, no. C 1; Coulié 189, fig. 182
Phaleron	Phaleron	unknown	unknown	amphora (Athens NM 222) att. to the Group of the Wild Style	Couve 1893; Rocco; here, figs. 1.1, 4.40, 101, no. W 1, pl. 14.1; here, figs. 1.1, 4.40
Phaleron	Phaleron	unknown	unknown	oinochoe (London BM 1865.7–20.1) att. to the W of the Passas P	Böhlau 1887, 48, fig. 8; Rocco 77, no. BPa 3, pl. 10.2; here, fig. 2.13
Phaleron	Phaleron	unknown	unknown	oinochoe (Oxford 1887.4304) att. to the Agora Group	Rocco 171, no. AG 2
Phaleron	Phaleron	unknown	unknown	oinochoe (London BM 1865.7-20.6) att. to the W of the Checkerboard P	Rocco 116, no. BS 3
Phaleron	Phaleron	unknown	unknown	oinochoe (London BM 1865.7-20.2) att. to the W of the Checkerboard P	Rocco 116, no. BS 2

Location	Area	Burial Type	Age	Finds	Bibliography
Phaleron	Phaleron	unknown	unknown	pyxis (Athens NM 2491) att. to the Group of Kerameikos 18/XIX	Böhlau 1887, 46–47, figs. 6–7; Rocco 79, no. C 2
Phaleron	Phaleron	unknown	unknown	oinochoe (Boston MFA 27187) att. to the Group of the Ortiz Krater	Rocco 88, no. O 1
Phaleron	Phaleron	unknown	unknown	standed cup (London BM 1865.7-20.10) att. to the Group of the Schliemann Krater and the Vari Loutrophoros	Rocco 123, no. SV 9
Phaleron	Phaleron	unknown	unknown	oinochoe (London BM 1865.7-20.4) att. to the Group of the Wild Style	Rocco 101, no. W 17
Phaleron	Phaleron	unknown	unknown	oinochoe (London BM 1865.7-20.3) att. to the Group of the Wild Style	Rocco 101, no. W 17
Phaleron	Phaleron	unknown	unknown	ovoid krater (Dunedin, Otago Museum E 28.87) att. to the Group of the Wild Style	CVA New Zealand 1, pl. 2.1–4; Rocco 102, no. W 29
Phaleron	Phaleron	unknown	unknown	oinochoe (Athens NM 322) att. to the P of the Burgon Krater	Böhlau 1887, 52, fig. 14; Rocco 160, no. B 2; here, fig. 5.1
Phaleron	Phaleron	unknown	unknown	tankard (London BM 1865.7–20.7) att. to the P of the Boston Amphora	Böhlau 1887, 50, figs. 9–10; Rocco 62, no. Bo 2; here, fig. 2.7
Phaleron	Phaleron	unknown	unknown	amphora (Athens NM 15958, 15983, 15994) att. to the Passas P	Kourouniotis 1911, 249–50, figs. 11–15; Cook pl. 48; Rocco 77, no. Pa 2
Phaleron	Phaleron	unknown	unknown	oinochoe (London BM 1865.7-20.1) att. to the W of the Passas P	Böhlau 1887, 48, fig. 8; Rocco 77, no. BPa 3, pl. 10.2
Phaleron	Phaleron	unknown	unknown	oinochoe (Athens NM 309) att. to the W of the Passas P	Rocco 77, no. BPa 6
Phaleron	Phaleron	unknown	unknown	oinochoe (Athens NM 306) att. to the W of the Passas P	Böhlau 1887, 46, fig. 4; Rocco 78, no. BPa 8
Phaleron	Phaleron	unknown	unknown	oinochoe (Athens NM 307) att. to the W of the Passas P	Rocco 78, no. BPa 10
Phaleron	Phaleron	unknown	unknown	oinochoe (Athens NM 308) att. to the W of the Passas P	Rocco 78, no. BPa 11; here, fig. 4.25
Phaleron	Phaleron	unknown	unknown	oinochoe (London BM 1865.7-20.9) att. to the W of the Passas P	Rocco 78, no. BPa 13
Phaleron	Phaleron	unknown	unknown	stand (Athens NM 3823) att. to the W of the Passas P	Kourouniotis 1911, 250, fig. 14; Rocco 78, no. BPa 19

Table 1 ▪ 245

Location	Area	Burial Type	Age	Finds	Bibliography
Phaleron	Phaleron	unknown	unknown	179 vases from the 1863 excavation of G. Bournias, including Protoattic material	Keramopoullos 1923, 5–6
Phaleron	Phaleron	unknown	unknown	oinochoe "from Phaleron?" (Ashmolean 1887.3402)	*CVA* Oxford Ashmolean 4, 11, pls. 28.7–8; here, fig. 4.23
Phaleron	Phaleron	unknown	unknown	oinochoe (The Hague 4504), from Phaleron, bought in England 1928	*CVA* La Haye 2, 6, pl. 4.3
Phaleron	Phaleron	unknown	unknown	oinochoe (Ashmolean 1887.3403), possibly by the Vulture P	*CVA* Oxford Ashmolean 4, 10, pls. 27.10–11
Phaleron 3a	Phaleron	primary cremation	adult	PC aryballoi, PC kotylai, standed bowl (Athens NM 863) att. to the W of the Würzburg Group	Pelekidis 1916, 17, no. 13, 37–38, no. 51, 47, fig. 51; Rocco 61, no. BWü 10
Phaleron 4	Phaleron	inhumation in jar	child	amphora (burial jar)	Pelekidis 1916, 19, no. 34, 28 no. 6
Phaleron 10	Phaleron	inhumation in jar	child	hydria (burial jar); outside: two cups, skyphos	Young 1942, 30
Phaleron 11	Phaleron	inhumation in jar	child	incised pithos (burial jar); inside: three cups, PC oinochoe, oinochoe, four PC aryballoi, two PC kotylai, PC pyxis (all receive inv. Athens NM 14953)	Young 1942, 32–33, figs. 12–13; Neeft, 41, IX, no. 15, 54, XXII, no. B 2, 105, LIII, no. C 1, 112, LV, no. B 1; here, fig. 4.21
Phaleron 14a	Phaleron	primary cremation	adult	standed bowl	Pelekidis 1916, 17, no. 25
Phaleron 16	Phaleron	inhumation in jar	child	amphora (burial jar); outside: skyphos, kalathos, cup	Young 1942, 43, fig. 28
Phaleron 18	Phaleron	inhumation in jar	child	amphora (burial jar, 15294) att. to the Group of the Wild Style; outside: cup, PC aryballos, PC pyxis (all other objects apart from amphora receive inv. Athens NM 14955)	Young 1942, 35–36, figs. 17–18; Neeft, LXVIII, no. B 2; Rocco 101, no. W 8, pl. 14.2
Phaleron 18A	Phaleron	inhumation in jar	child	hydria (burial urn); inside: cup, pyxis, oinochoe (all receive inv. Athens NM 14056)	Young 1942, 42–43, fig. 27
Phaleron 19	Phaleron	inhumation in jar	child	amphora (burial jar); inside: three cups, jug-aryballos, oinochoe, PC kotyle, Attic kotyle; outside: two oinochoai att. to the W of the Würzburg Group, three PC kotylai, kotyle, skyphos, PC aryballos (all receive inv. Athens NM 14957)	Young 1942, 27–28, fig. 4; Neeft, 108, III, no. E 1; Rocco 61, nos. BWü 3–4; here, fig. 1.6

Location	Area	Burial Type	Age	Finds	Bibliography
Phaleron 25	Phaleron	inhumation in jar	child	amphora (burial jar) covered by a louterion; inside: cup, kotyle, PC aryballos, two jug-aryballoi one att. to the Group of the Wild Style (all receive inv. Athens NM 14958)	Young 1942, 33–35, fig. 15; Neeft, 101, XLIX, no. 5; Rocco 102, no. W 22
Phaleron 27	Phaleron	inhumation in jar	child	amphora, probably Corinthian (burial jar); inside: two cups, PC kotyle, PC aryballos, PC pyxis, Attic kotyle, aryballos, oinochoe (all receive inv. Athens NM 14959)	Young 1942, 28–30, figs. 6–7; Neeft, 53, XXI, no. A 4; here, fig. 3.19
Phaleron 29	Phaleron	inhumation in jar	child	incised pithos (bural jar) with a louterion covering the mouth; oinochoe, cup, PC aryballos, skyphos, louterion att. to the Group of the Wild Style	Young 1942, 30–32, figs. 10–12; Neeft, 91, XXXVI, no. C 3; Rocco 102, no. W 39
Phaleron 32	Phaleron	inhumation in jar	child	pithos (burial jar); inside: cup, PC kotyle, PC pyxis, amphoriskos, pyxis, oinochoe att. to the Group of the Wild Style (all receive inv. Athens NM 14960)	Young 1942, 39, fig. 21; Rocco 101, no. W 14
Phaleron 34	Phaleron	primary cremation	adult	outside: two oinochoai, skyphos	Pelekidis 1916, p. 18, no. 29
Phaleron 34	Phaleron	primary cremation	adult	cup, two oinochoai (all receive inv. Athens NM 14962)	Young 1942, 35, fig. 16
Phaleron 37	Phaleron	inhumation in jar	child	pithos (burial jar); two cups, pyxis, two PC aryballoi, oinochoe (all receive inv. Athens NM 14963)	Young 1942, 33, fig. 14; Neeft, 114, LVI, no. B 5
Phaleron 40	Phaleron	primary cremation	adult	standed bowl	Pelekidis 1916, 18, no. 30, 48, fig. 52.1
Phaleron 41	Phaleron	primary cremation	adult	standed bowl	Pelekidis 1916, 17, no. 20, 48, fig. 52.2
Phaleron 42	Phaleron	primary cremation	adult	PC kotyle, PC aryballos, other PC sherds	Pelekidis 1916, 17, no. 21, 32, no. 18, 38, nos. 54–55
Phaleron 46	Phaleron	inhumation in jar	child	amphora (burial jar)	Pelekidis 1916, 20, no. 51, and 28, no. 6
Phaleron 47	Phaleron	inhumation in jar	child	amphora (burial jar); inside: PC kotyle, PC aryballos, oinochoe; outside: oinochoe, cup (all receive inv. Athens NM 14964)	Pelekidis 1916, 21, no. 52, 27, fig. 11, 32, fig. 22.1, 37, fig. 33.3, 42, fig. 43.2; Neeft, 38, IV, no. 3

Table 1 ▪ 247

Location	Area	Burial Type	Age	Finds	Bibliography
Phaleron 48	Phaleron	inhumation in jar	child	incised pithos (burial jar); inside: three tankards including two att. to the Group of the Wild Style, three cups, two oinochoai including one att. to the Group of the Wild Style, PC kotyle, Attic kotyle, pyxis, six PC aryballoi (all receive inv. Athens NM 14965)	Cook 202; Young 1942, 36–38, fig. 19; Neeft, 56, XXI–XXII, no E 4, 91, XXXVI, nos. A 4–5, 98, XLV, no. A 2, 99, XLVI, no. D 3, 122 LXI, no. C 4; Rocco 101, no. W 12, 104, nos. W 44–45; here, fig. 4.22
Phaleron 50	Phaleron	inhumation in jar	child	pithos (burial jar); three cups, two PC kotylai, skyphos, oinochoe (all receive inv. Athens NM 14966)	Young 1942, 40–42, fig. 25
Phaleron 54	Phaleron	primary cremation	adult	two pyres, one with PC oinochoe and aryballos	Pelekidis 1916, 17, no. 24
Phaleron 56	Phaleron	inhumation in jar	child	cup, two skyphoi (all receive inv. Athens NM 14967)	Young 1942, 28, fig. 5
Phaleron 58	Phaleron	inhumation in jar	child	amphora (burial jar)	Alexandropoulou 2019, pl. 75.2
Phaleron 62	Phaleron	inhumation in jar	child	amphora (burial jar); outside: two cups, pyxis, oinochoe att. to the Group of the Wild Style (all receive inv. Athens NM 14969)	Young 1942, 38–39, fig. 20; Rocco 101, no. W 13
Phaleron 64	Phaleron	inhumation in jar	child	pithos (burial jar); inside: PC pyxis, PC aryballos, skyphos, oinochoe, cup	Pelekidis 1916, 22, no. 64, 36, fig. 30, 38, no. 56, 43, fig. 45.8, 46, fig. 46.2
Phaleron 65	Phaleron	inhumation in jar	child	amphora (burial jar); inside: oinochoe, PC oinochoe	Pelekidis 1916, 22, no. 65, 28 fig. 13
Phaleron 70	Phaleron	inhumation in jar	child	amphora (burial jar); two cups, oinochoe	Young 1942, 30
Phaleron 71	Phaleron	inhumation in jar	child	amphora (burial jar); outside: two cups, three PC pyxides, oinochoe (all receive inv. Athens NM 14971)	Young 1942, 39–40, fig. 22
Phaleron 74	Phaleron	inhumation in jar	child	amphora (burial jar); bowl, cup, PC pyxis	Young 1942, 40, fig. 23
Phaleron 78	Phaleron	inhumation in jar	child	pithos (burial jar); inside: PC pyxis, oinochoe	Young 1942, 40, fig. 24
Phaleron 80	Phaleron	inhumation in jar	child	pithos (burial jar); outside: two cups, skyphos, two PC kotylai, oinochoe	Pelekidis 1916, 21, no. 54
Phaleron 83	Phaleron	inhumation in jar	child	amphora (burial jar); inside: PC aryballos, PC kotyle, two cups, jug-aryballos, standed bowl, oinochoe	Young 1942, 25–26, fig. 3; Neeft, 41, IX, no. a

Location	Area	Burial Type	Age	Finds	Bibliography
Phaleron 432	Phaleron	inhumation in pit	child	louterion on stand, standed bowl, standed cup, amphoriskos, oinochoe, grain silo, horse and rider figurine, pack animal figurine, two PC aryballoi, PC kotyle	Alexandropoulou 2019, pl. 78.1
Phaleron 578	Phaleron	inhumation in pit	adult	standed bowl, PC kotyle	Alexandropoulou 2019, pl. 72.2
Phaleron 657	Phaleron	primary cremation	unknown	imitation of a grain silo	Alexandopoulou 2019, pl. 73.1
Phaleron 773	Phaleron	inhumation in jar	child	amphora (burial jar)	Alexandropoulou 2019, pl. 73.2
Pikermi	Pikermi	unknown	unknown	fragment of a Cyladic(?) pithos with Antilochos	*AAA* 4 (1971) 75–76
Piraeus	Piraeus	unknown	unknown	amphora att. to the Piraeus P (Athens NM 353)	Couve 1897; BAPD 300012; here, fig. 1.11
Spata	Spata	unknown	unknown	amphora, aryballos, from a grave in a tumulus	*ArchDelt* 6 (1920–21) 133
Spata	Spata	unknown	unknown	"Orientalizing" vases reported from the Mazareïka area	*ArchDelt* 6 (1920–21) 133
Spata	Spata	unknown	unknown	kotyle krater (Athens NM VS 188) att. to the Checkerboard P	Cook 188; Rocco 116, no. S 5, pl. 17.1; here, fig. 5.18
Spata, "The Vlastos Assemblage"	Spata	unknown	unknown	hydria (Athens NM VS 63) att. to the Mesogeia P, kotyle (VS 169) att. to the W of the Mesogeia P, both allegedly from same grave	Cook pls. 46b–c; Cook 1947, 147, fig. 6b; Brokaw 1963, 71, pl. 34.3, 6; Rocco 39–40, nos. Me 12, BMe 13, pl. 4.2
Tavros, Pyre XIX	Tavros	primary cremation	adult	Corinthian kotyle (AK 3524)	Skilarnti 1975, 68, 107–8, 115, figs. 2, 212–13, pl. 38η
Tavros, Pyre XX	Tavros	primary cremation	adult	Corinthian pyxis (AK 3525), Corinthian oinochoe (AK 3406), two standed bowls (AK 3526, 3527) att. to the Group of Kerameikos Tomb LZB	Skilarnti 1975, 68, 108–13, 116, 122–49, figs. 2, 14–15, pls. 41–45; Rocco 170, nos. K13–K14
Thorikos	Thorikos	unknown	unknown	oinochoe att. to the Group of the Vari Oinochoai (65.1ba)	*Thorikos* 1965, 28, fig. 30; Rocco 124, no. V 4
Thorikos, South Cemetery, T. 4	Thorikos	inhumation in jar	child	cup (63.79), oinochoe	*Thorikos* 1963, 57
Thorikos, South Cemetery, T. 5	Thorikos	inhumation in jar	child	cup (63.85)	*Thorikos* 1963, 58
Thorikos, South Cemetery, T. 7	Thorikos	inhumation in jar	child	PC pyxis (63.66), oinochoe	*Thorikos* 1963, 54–55, figs. 35–36

Table 1 ■ 249

Location	Area	Burial Type	Age	Finds	Bibliography
Thorikos, South Cemetery, T. 8	Thorikos	inhumation in jar	child	PC pyxis (63.58), cup	*Thorikos* 1963, 54–55, figs. 33–34
Thorikos, South Cemetery, T. 10	Thorikos	inhumation in jar	child	pithos (burial jar, 63.1063); PC aryballos (63.62), bowl (63.63), oinochoe (63.64)	*Thorikos* 1963, 52–53, figs. 26–30
Thorikos, South Cemetery, T. 11	Thorikos	inhumation in jar	child	oinochoe (63.54), bowl (63.53)	*Thorikos* 1963, 58
Thorikos, South Cemetery, T. 12	Thorikos	inhumation in jar	child	amphora (burial jar, 63.82), cup (63.83)	*Thorikos* 1963, 56–57, figs. 39–40
Thorikos, South Cemetery, T. 15	Thorikos	inhumation in jar	child	two cups (including 63.88)	*Thorikos* 1963, 57
Thorikos, South Cemetery, T. 16	Thorikos	inhumation in jar	child	cup	*Thorikos* 1963, 57
Thorikos, South Cemetery, T. 17	Thorikos	inhumation in jar	child	PC aryballos (63.47), skyphos (63.46), cup (63.48)	*Thorikos* 1963, 54, figs. 31–32
Thorikos, West Cemetery, T. 13	Thorikos	inhumation in jar	child	burial jar; six vases including oinochoe (64.364), bronze bracelet	*Thorikos* 1964, 35, fig. 24.
Thorikos, West Cemetery, T. 101	Thorikos	inhumation in jar	child	pithos (burial jar); outside: three cups (66.222, 66.223, 66.224), two oinochoai (66.219, 66.220), aryballos (66.221)	*Thorikos* 1966/67, 99–101, figs 105–14
Thorikos, West Cemetery, T. 109	Thorikos	inhumation in jar	child	pithos (burial jar, 71.1401); inside: lidded pyxis (71.1402), cup (71.1403)	*Thorikos* 1972/1976, 117–19, figs. 67–68
Thorikos, West Cemetery, T. 111	Thorikos	inhumation in jar	child	pithos (burial jar, 71.1404); inside: pitcher (71.1405), cup (T71.1406), skyphos (71.1407)	*Thorikos* 1972/1976, 113–15, figs. 63–64
Thorikos, West Cemetery, T. 112	Thorikos	inhumation in jar	child	pitcher (burial jar, 71.1408); under: pyxis lid (71.1409)	*Thorikos* 1972/1976, 115–17, figs. 65–66
Thorikos, West Cemetery, T. 113	Thorikos	inhumation in jar	child	pithos (burial jar, 71.1410); outside: feeder (71.1411), oinochoe (71.1412), aryballos (71.1413), three cups (71.1414–16)	*Thorikos* 1972/1976, 107–11, figs. 59–61
Thorikos, West Cemetery, T. 125	Thorikos	inhumation in pit	adult	hydria att. to the Würzburg P (71.1443), EPC kotyle (71.1444), PC skyphos (71.1445), aryballos (71.1446), juglet (71.1447)	*Thorikos* 1972/1976, 120–25, figs. 69–70, 72–73; Rocco 61, no. Wü 6, pl. 7.2
Thorikos, West Cemetery, T. 126	Thorikos	inhumation in jar	child	amphora (burial jar, 71.1432) covered by an amphora fragment (71/1433); oustide: cup (71.1434), oinochoe (71.1435), handmade lekythos (71.1436)	*Thorikos* 1972/1976, 88–93, figs. 48-49; Kourou 1987, 45, no. 50

Location	Area	Burial Type	Age	Finds	Bibliography
Thorikos, West Cemetery, T. 128	Thorikos	inhumation in jar	child	pithos (burial jar, 71.1437); outside: cooking jug (71.1438), oinochoe (71.1439), handmade aryballos (71.1440), kantharos (71.1441), cup (71.1442)	*Thorikos* 1972/1976, 93–98, figs. 50–52 p. 96, no. 23, fig. 52; Kourou 1987, 42, no. 32
Thorikos, West Cemetery, T. 151	Thorikos	inhumation in jar	child	pitcher (burial jar, 75.2001); inside: cup (75.2003)	*Thorikos* 1972/1976, 111–12, fig. 62
Thorikos, West Cemetery, T. 203	Thorikos	inhumation in jar	child	pithos (burial jar, 75.2018); outside, near mouth: handmade lekythos (75.2010), olpe (75.2013), skyphos (75.2011), cup (75.2012); near foot: handmade lekythos (75.2014), oinochoe (75.2015), skyphos (75.2016), cup (75.2017)	*Thorikos* 1977/1982, 96–102, figs. 127–46; here, fig. 4.29
Thorikos, West Cemetery, T. 209	Thorikos	inhumation in cist	unknown	oinochoe (75.2043), PC kotyle (75.2044), standed cup (75.2045), lid att. to the Group of the Vari Oinochoai (75.2046), two cups (75.2047-8), shallow bowl, PC aryballos (TC 75.2050)	*Thorikos* 1977/1982, 79–83, figs. 76–90; Rocco 124, no. V 5
Trachones A 30.1	Trachones	secondary cremation	adult	ovoid krater (burial jar, Tr 303); outside: standed bowl (Tr 305), two oinochoai (Tr 308, Tr 304), tankard (Tr 306), two PC aryballoi (Tr 309, Tr 310), PC kotyle (Tr 307), bronze ring	Geroulanos 1973, 34–35, pls. 13, 18; Neeft 41, IX, nos. 11, 39, VI, no. 3; Steinhauer 2001, 89, fig. 109
Trachones A 8	Trachones	secondary cremation	adult	pithos (burial jar, Tr 63); inside: PC aryballos (Tr 58), aryballos (Tr 59); outside: oinochoe (Tr 60), tankard (Tr 62), cup (Tr 60)	Geroulanos 1973, 28–29, pls. 12.4, 20; Neeft 91, XXXVI, no. 7
Trachones A 12	Trachones	secondary cremation	adult	pithos (burial jar, Tr 75) closed with sherds of amphora (Tr 74) att. to the Vulture P; inside: two PC aryballoi (Tr 69, Tr 70); outside: two plates (Tr 71, Tr 72), tankard (Tr 73)	Geroulanos 1973, 29–30, pl. 12.3, pl. 19; Rocco 60, no. Av 1, pl. 6.6; Neeft 91, XXXVI, no. 3; Neeft 92, XXXII, no. 7
Vari	Vari	unknown	unknown	lidded lekanis (att. to the Group of the Wild Style, Munich 7615), acquired in 1928; lidded lekanis (att. to the Group of the Wild Style, Munich 7616), acquired in 1928	*CVA* Munich 3, 32, pl. 134.4–7; Rocco 103, nos. W 48–49
Vari	Vari	unknown	unknown	standed bowl attributed to the circle of the Vulture-Würzburg Group (Berlin 31053), formerly coll. Von Massow, bought 1926/27	*CVA* Berlin 10, 80–81, pls. 41, 42.1–2

Table 1 ▪ 251

Location	Area	Burial Type	Age	Finds	Bibliography
Vari, E Cemetery	Vari	unknown	unknown	sherds including EPA reported, including krater att. to the W of the Würzburg Group	*ArchDelt* 20 (1965) pl. 87; Rocco 61, no. BWü 8
Vari, E Cemetery, T1	Vari	primary cremation	adult	amphora (burial jar); olpe, two phialai, one-handled cup, Corinthian kotyle, Corinthian pyxis, dinos with plastic heads	Kallipoliti 1963, 116, 118–20, figs. 1, 4–5, pl. 48; Callipolitis-Feytmans 1985, 45–47, figs. 18–19
Vari, E Cemetery, T2	Vari	primary cremation	adult	oinochoe, att. to the Group of the Oinochoai of Vari, two cups, one att. to the Group of the Wild Style, standed cup att. to the Group of the Schliemann Krater and the Vari Loutrophoros, loutrophoros att. to the Group of the Schliemann Krater and the Vari Loutrophoros, gaming table (Athens NM 26665) att. to the Group of the Schliemann Krater and the Vari Loutrophoros), die	Kallipoliti 1963, 116, 120–24, figs.1, 6, pls. 49–55; Callipolitis-Feytmans 1985, 31–43, figs. 1–13; Rocco 103, 123–24, nos. W 46, V 1, SV 1, SV 8, SV 10, pl. 19.1
Vari, E Cemetery, T7	Vari	primary cremation	adult	aryballos, cup	Kallipoliti 1963, 124–26, pl. 56
Vari, E Cemetery, T8	Vari	primary cremation	adult	aryballos, cup	Kallipoliti 1963, 124–26, pl. 56
Vari, E Cemetery, T15	Vari	primary cremation	adult	oinochoe, ovoid krater	Kallipoliti 1963, 116, 127–28, fig. 1, pls. 43b, 58b, 59a–b; Callipolitis-Feytmans 1985, 42–43, fig. 14
Vari, E Cemetery, T16	Vari	primary cremation	adult	amphora and second amphora or hydria from same hand as the krater in T15	Kallipoliti 1963, 116, 128–29, fig. 1, pls. 43b, 58b, 59g–d, 60a, g; Callipolitis-Feytmans 1985, 44–45, figs. 15–17
Vari, E Cemetery, T53g	Vari	inhumation in jar	child	incised pithos (burial jar); outside: cup	*ArchDelt* 20 (1965), 114, fig. 5, pls. 79d, ζ
Vari, E Cemetery, T61	Vari	inhumation in jar	child	amphora (burial jar); lekanis, PC kotyle	*ArchDelt* 20 (1965), 114, pl. 79b; Callipolitis-Feytmans 1984, 35–36, fig. 8
Vari, N Cemetery, burial under tumulus 1?	Vari	inhumation in shaft	adult	LPA vases (unburnt) possibly associated with an adult inhumation under Tumulus I	Karouzou 1963; Alexandridou 2012, 4–10

Location	Area	Burial Type	Age	Finds	Bibliography
Vari, N Cemetery, grave 27	Vari	primary cremation	adult	associated with an offering place over burials 27–33. Offering place: many Corinthian oil vessels, mostly aryballoi and alabastra; oinochoe, standed dinos with plastic mourners on rim (Athens NM 19159a), two stands (19156, 19157) att. to the P of Opferrinne ζ/XIV, louterion, tankard, two phialai, skyphos, cup, lekanis, two askoi with animals carrying vessels (19165, 19190), pyxides, dog figurine, horse and rider figurine, three terracotta chariot wheels, three terracotta shields, ekphora figurine (26747) att. to the P of Opferrinne ζ/XIV.	Rocco 186, nos. Op ζ 9–10, 22, pl. 28.5; Coulié 221, fig. 218; Alexandridou 2012, 33–37, figs. 19–21; Alexandridou 2017, 284–86; here, fig. 4.27
Vari, N Cemetery, grave 28	Vari	primary cremation	adult	associated with an offering place; see entry for grave 27	Alexandridou 2012, 33–35; Alexandridou 2017, 284–86
Vari, N Cemetery, grave 29	Vari	primary cremation	adult	associated with an offering place; see entry for grave 27; aryballos	Alexandridou 2012, 33–35; Alexandridou 2017, 284–86
Vari, N Cemetery, grave 30	Vari	primary cremation	adult	associated with an offering place; see entry for grave 27; aryballos	Alexandridou 2012, 33–35; Alexandridou 2017, 284–86
Vari, N Cemetery, grave 31	Vari	primary cremation	adult	associated with an offering place; see entry for grave 27	Alexandridou 2012, 33–35; Alexandridou 2017, 284–86
Vari, N Cemetery, grave 32	Vari	inhumation in jar	child		Alexandridou 2012, 33–35; Alexandridou 2017, 284–86
Vari, N Cemetery, grave 33	Vari	inhumation in pit	adult	associated with an offering place; see entry for grave 27	Alexandridou 2012, 33–35; Alexandridou 2017, 284–86
Vari, N Cemetery, jar burial 1	Vari	inhumation in jar	child	PC pyxis	Alexandridou 2012, 10–13
Vari, N Cemetery, jar burial 3	Vari	inhumation in jar	child	cup	Alexandridou 2012, 10–13
Vari, N Cemetery, jar burial 7	Vari	inhumation in jar	child	amphora (burial urn)	Alexandridou 2012, 10–13
Vourva	Vourva	unknown	unknown	kotyle krater from an offering trench (I) (Athens NM 993) att. to the P of Berlin A 34, along with later objects	Staïs 1890a, 1890b; Cook 199, pl. 55e; Coulié 190, fig. 185; Alexandridou 2015, 131; here, fig. 2.12

Abbreviations

Ancient authors are abbreviated according to the *Oxford Classical Dictionary*, 4th ed., 2012, edited by Simon Hornblower and Antony Spawforth, Oxford: Oxford University Press.

AAA	*Archaiologika analekta ex Athēnōn*
ABV	Beazley, John Davidson. 1956. *Attic Black-Figure Vase-Painters.* Oxford: Clarendon Press.
AR	*Archaeological Reports*
ArchDelt	*Archaiologikon Deltion*
ARV²	Beazley, John Davidson. 1963. *Attic Red-Figure Vase-Painters*, 2nd ed. Oxford: Clarendon Press
BAPD	Beazley Archive Pottery Database (https://www.beazley.ox.ac.uk /pottery/default.htm)
BCH	*Bulletin de correspondence hellénique*
CEG	Hansen, Petrus Allanus. 1983–1989. *Carmina epigraphica Graeca.* Berlin: de Gruyter.
CVA	*Corpus Vasorum Antiquorum*
DNO	Kansteiner, Sascha, et al., eds. 2014. *Der Neue Overbeck (DNO): Die Antiken Schriftquellen Zu Den Bildenden Künsten Der Griechen.* Berlin: de Gruyter.
Ergon	*To Ergon tes Archaiologikes Etaireias*
FGrH	*Die Fragmente der griechischen Historiker*
MonAnt	*Monumenti antichi*
NSc	*Notizie degli scavi di antichità*
Para	Beazley, John Davidson. *1971. Paralipomena: Additions to Attic Black-Figure Vase-Painters and to Attic Red-Figure Vase-Painters.* Oxford: Clarendon Press.
PAE	*Praktika tēs en Athēnais Archaiologikēs Hetairias*

Perachora   *Perachora: The Sanctuaries of Hera Akraia and Limenia. Excavations of the British School of Archaeology at Athens, 1930–1933.* Oxford: Clarendon Press.

ThesCRA   *Thesaurus Cultus et Rituum Antiquorum*

Thorikos   *Thorikos.* Gent: Comité des fouilles belges en Grèce

Notes

CHAPTER 1 THE MARGINS

1   Daremberg and Saglio 1877–1919, vol. 5, 639; Burr 1933, 633; Cook 1934–35, 188; Cook 1997, 65. Athens, National Museum 222: Couve 1893; *CVA* Athens 2, plate 5; Collignon and Couve 1904, 9, no. 469, plate XX; Rocco 2006, 36–37, plate 4.1–2; Rocco 2008, 101, no. W 1.

2   Burr 1933, 633; Robertson 1953, 185.

3   Throughout this book, I use "seventh century" as a convenient terminology for the time period that coincides with Protoattic, even though Protoattic was made in the late eighth century and stopped circa 610. Agora P 5062: Young 1939, 82–83, no. XVII 14; Brann 1962, 61, no. 265. Paris, Musée du Louvre E 874: BAPD 300035; *ABV* 8.1, 679; *Para* 6; Beazley 1986, 15–16, plates 14, 15.1.

4   Lagogianni-Georgakarakou 2018. It is also interesting to note that the Acropolis Museum has only one Protoattic object on display, despite the abundant Protoattic finds from the area.

5   Burr 1933, 633; Young 1939, 230; Brann 1962, 28; Cook 1997, 65.

6   Agora P 7023: Young 1939, 149–50, C 31, figs. 104–5; Brann 1962, 51, no. 165, plate 9; Papadopoulos 2007, 146–47, no. 57, fig. 135; Coulié 2013, 199, fig. 190.

7   New York, Metropolitan Museum of Art 11.210.1, allegedly from Smyrna (Richter 1912, 371): Richter 1912; *CVA* Metropolitan Museum of Art 5, plates 42–44; Rocco 2008, 128, no. NY 1; Coulié 2013, 209, fig. 203.

8   Horden and Purcell 2000; Abulafia 2011; Broodbank 2013; Hodos 2017; Manning 2018.

9   Horden and Purcell 2000.

10   I add "micro" because the Mediterranean itself may also be considered a region.

11   The emphasis on history "of" is developed in Horden and Purcell 2000. For the changing approach to art in the Mediterranean, contrast Boardman 1999 with Broodbank 2013.

12   I am thinking in particular of Horden and Purcell 2000; Abulafia 2011; the edited volume with Hodos 2017; and Manning 2018.

13   Brisart 2011.

14   Morris 1987; Doronzio 2018; Dimitriadou 2019.

15   On the dominant role of the elite in Early Iron Age cultural change, see, e.g., Pallottino 1965; Arafat and Morgan 1989, 336; Matthäus 1993; Raaflaub 2004; Langdon 2008, 119; Duplouy 2009; Brisart 2011; Broodbank 2013, 519; Kistler, Krieg, and Reichenbach 2015. On the elite in later periods, see, e.g., Filser 2017.

16   Discussion of colonization is starting to take into account the nonelite: Zuchtriegel 2018.

17   Athens, National Museum 14957; Pelekidis 1916, 39, no. 65, fig. 37; Friis Johansen 1923, 39, 52, n. 7; Young 1942, 27–28, fig. 4; Kübler 1970, 61, 173, 613, nos. 256–57; *Perachora* II, 128, n. 2; Brokaw 1964, 53, figs. 11–12; Dierichs 1981, 89, 90, 97, no. AV 12; Rocco 2008, 50, 51, 53, 61, no. BWü 3, plate 8.2.

18   Morris 1987; Duplouy 2006.

19   I am selectively drawing on the work of Antonio Gramsci; see Bocock 1986.

20 Said 1978.

21 E.g., Prost et al. 2010, 256–57; Brisart 2011; Haug 2012; Morgan 2016. See also the comments in Gunter 2009, 51–57. And for the idea that Greeks improved whatever they borrowed, see Pl. *Epinomis* 987d. I addressed how these perceptions have influenced interpretations of Lefkandi, an early example of "Orientalizing" in Greece, in Arrington 2015b.

22 On the "Orientalizing" style in art, see Poulsen 1912; Akurgal 1968; Moscati and Grassi 1988; S. P. Morris 1992; Karageorghis and Stampolidis 1998; Stampolidis, Kanta, and Karetsou 1998; Boardman 1999, 35–159; Uehlinger 2000; Whitley 2001, 102–33; Stampolidis 2003b; Braun-Holzinger and Rehm 2005; Gunter 2009; Hasserodt 2009; Papalexandrou 2010; Brisart 2011; Coulié 2013; Aruz, Graff, and Rakic 2014; Gunter 2014; Gunter 2016; Whitley 2019a.

23 On "Orientalizing" in art, see n. 22, above. On "Orientalizing" and other aspects of culture, see Mazzarino 1947; Dunbabin 1957; Carter 1972; Burkert 1992; Faraone 1992; Kopcke and Tokumaru 1992; Matthäus 1993; West 1997; Kistler 1998; Boardman 1999; Karetsou, Andreadaki-Vlazaki, and Papadakis 2000; Burkert 2004; Suter and Uehlinger 2005; Riva and Vella 2006b; Karageorghis and Kouka 2009; López-Ruiz 2010; Brisart 2011, 43–46; Louden 2011.

24 On this problem, see also Martin 2017, 7, 34–35, 73–96.

25 See also the description of the cultures in Greek culture in Dougherty and Kurke 2003.

26 S. Morris 1992, 130. Fantalkin 2006 has adopted a very different position from Morris and argued that the late eighth and seventh centuries actually represent a "Great Divide" in relations between Greece and the Near East.

27 S. Morris 1992. On Greece and Asia in the fifth century, see also Hall 1989; Miller 1997.

28 Horden and Purcell 2000; Abulafia 2011; Broodbank 2013; Manning 2018.

29 Hodos 2017 surveys the literature.

30 E.g., Sherratt and Sherratt 1993; Sherratt 2017.

31 Kistler 2012; de Angelis 2013; Dommelen 2017.

32 Hodos 2006; Hodos 2009; Hodos 2010.

33 See Shaw 2001 and Morris 2003 for cogent critiques, and Horden and Purcell 2020 for a series of responses.

34 Manning 2018 discusses the move away from Moses Finley's emphasis on status.

35 See also Morris 2003; de Angelis 2013. In the other direction, for emphasis on *koinai*, see Handberg and Gadolou 2017.

36 As Nino Luraghi once remarked to me, there was not one single "Orientalizing package."

37 Gunter 2009; Gunter 2016. For a critique of Lanfranchi's views of Greek contact with the Neo-Assyrians, on which Gunter relies, see Fantalkin 2006, 201.

38 Huelva: González de Canales, Serrano, and Llompart 2006; González de Canales 2018. Carthage: Docter et al. 2005; Nijboer 2005. Cautious evaluation of the evidence: Gilboa 2013. On the problem of Early Iron Age chronology, see further chapter 3. On Phoenicians in the Mediterranean, see the essays in López-Ruiz and Doak 2019.

39 Shrine: Shaw and Shaw 2000; Gilboa 2013, 325. Eleftherna: Stampolidis 2003a, 221–24; Stampolidis 2004, 238, no. 257.

40 Calvet 1980.

41 Smith 2009.

42 Kourou 2019a.

43 *AR* 50 (2004) 39–40; *AR* 51 (2004–5) 50–52; *AR* 52 (2005–6) 62–63; *AR* 53 (2006–7), 38–40; *AR* 54 (2007–8) 51–54; Lemos 2007; *AR* 55 (2008–9) 47–49; Lemos 2012, 22–24.

44 *BCH* "Chronique des fouilles en ligne" 5058; Bessios, Tzifopoulos, and Kotsonas 2012.

45 Kiderlen et al. 2016.

46 Stager 2003; Nantet 2010; Rouillard 2010, 150; Aruz, Graff, and Rakic 2014, 230–43. See also the reports of shipwrecks found around the Fourni islands, near Samos: http://news .nationalgeographic.com/2015/11/151103-greek-shipwreck-find-trading-route/.

47 Brixhe 2004; DeVries, Sams, and Voigt 2005; Voigt 2005. Contra: Muscarella 2003; Keenan 2004.

48 Moscati and Grassi 1988; Stampolidis, Kanta, and Karetsou 1998; Karetsou, Andreadaki-Vlazaki, and Papadakis 2000; Stampolidis 2003b; Aruz, Graff, and Rakic 2014.

49 Étienne 2010; Charalambidou and Morgan 2017.

50 Xagorari-Gleissner 2005; Palaiokrassa-Kopitsa and Vivliodetis 2015.

51 Rocco 2008; Haug 2012; Doronzio 2018; Dimitriadou 2019.

52 On the "Orientalizing paradigm," see Arrington forthcoming.

53 But for criticism of the labels of Protogeometric and Geometric art applied to periods, see Fitton 1995, 250.

54 Purcell 2006, 26.

55 For pointed criticism of the term, see also Croissant 2010, and along similar lines Coulié 2013, 107. In defense, see esp. Osborne 2006b; Brisart 2011, 51–58. For problems applying it to Crete, see Kotsonas 2013, 238. On the historiography of the term, see chapter 2.

56 Winckelmann 1764 [2006]. The literature on style is vast. I have found the following discussions particularly helpful: Schapiro 1962 [1994]; Plog 1983; Sauerländer 1983; Dietler and Herbich 1989; Conkey 1990; Conkey and Hastorf 1990; Davis 1990; Layton 1991, 150–92; Hegmon 1992; Shanks and Tilley 1992, 137–71; Dietler and Herbich 1994a; Dietler and Herbich 1994b; Carr and Neitzel 1995; Dietler and Herbich 1998; Ginzburg 1998; Neer 2005; Conkey 2006.

57 Wölfflin 1929 [1932]; Riegl 1966 [2004].

58 In the field of ancient art, however, see most recently Feldman 2014.

59 See the overviews in Hodder 1982; Plog 1983; Dietler and Herbich 1989; Dietler and Herbich 1989; Shanks and Tilley 1992, 137–71; Dietler and Herbich 1994a; Dietler and Herbich 1994b; Dietler and Herbich 1998.

60 Wollheim 1995, 33–39; Boast 1997.

61 On the relational aspect of stylistic analysis: Davis 1990, 21; Bagley 2015, 24–27.

62 On this critical methodological move, see Davis 1990, 19.

63 Drawing on Davis 1990, 19; Winter 1998, 56; Neer 2010. Dietler and Herbich 1998, 244: "although material culture participates in processes of *signification* . . . it is not primarily a system of *communication* like language."

64 Poulsen 1912; Akurgal 1968; Boardman 1999.

65 Jones 1997, 15–26; Trigger 2006, 217–23.

66 E.g., Whitley 1994b; Morris 1997; Gunter 2009; Brisart 2011.

67 On ideology, e.g., Crielaard 2015.

68 On art as a tool, see esp. Brisart 2011.

69 For this approach, see also Dietler and Herbich 1994a; Dietler and Herbich 1994b; Dietler and Herbich 1998.

70 Efforts at rapprochement: Whitley 1991; Neer 2005; Neer 2010, 6–11; Feldman 2014.

71 Thuc. 2.15.2–6; Plut. *Thes.* 24; van Gelder 1991; Parker 1996, 10–17. For *synoikismos* as an invention of the historical era, see S. Morris 1992, 338–39; Papadopoulos 2003, 314–15. For a relatively conventional survey of the historical sources, see Stahl and Walter 2009. For a recent survey of Athens and Attica from the Bronze Age into the Iron Age, see Alexandridou 2019.

72 Osborne 2019. A dominant center, of course, does not mean a depopulated landscape. Thucydides (2.15.1) reports that in the fifth century, Athenians still were living predominantly in the countryside, to a greater extent than other regions in Greece.

73 Osborne 2019, 145. Houby-Nielsen 2009 emphasizes the ability of Attic settlements to connect to the outside world.

74 Scholl 2006. See further 215–16, above.

75 The link between burials and demographics has been justly criticized (esp. I. Morris 1987). However, in the Late Geometric period, several types of data suggest that the population rose. Against a population explosion, see, however, Scheidel 2003.

76 For Near Eastern influences of Geometric art, see Coldstream 1977 [2003], 358–66.

77 See further chapter 3 on the import record.

78 Osborne 1989 and d'Onofrio 1997 are fundamental for the archaeology of seventh-century Attica. On settlement patterns, see Mersch 1996; Mersch 1997.

79 D'Onofrio 1997 argues that the role of these sanctuaries was not peripheral.

80 See further chapter 3.

81 Camp 1979, with Snodgrass 1983; Dunbabin 1936; Morris 1984, 107–15; Morris 1987.

82 Osborne 1989, 300.

83 Doronzio 2018; Dimitriadou 2019. On the gradual infilling of the landscape, see Bintliff 1990.

84 Ma 2016 reviews the historiography and explains some of the consequences and contradictions from a shift from emphases on institutions to individuals. He argues that state institutions were in place in the Protogeometric period, and that by the seventh century, there were public goods and a sufficient political body to allow for individual performances. For continuity across the Bronze Age–Early Iron Age transition, see Papadopoulos 2017, 973–84. For a view that the *polis* was not yet in existence in the seventh century, see Manville 1992, 55–91. Many earlier scholars espousing a period of invention put it in the Early Iron Age: Snodgrass 1977; Polignac 1984; Morris 1987, 171–210. Duplouy 2018b provides an extensive and thoughtful historiography of the frameworks for interpreting the *polis*. For a deconstruction of the historical category of the *polis*, see Vlassopoulos 2007. For a history of states beyond the *polis*, see Morgan 2003.

85 Papadopoulos 2003, 314; Papadopoulos 2017, 981 (with an emphasis on the Acropolis); Dimitriadou 2019, 140–42.

86 [Arist.] *Ath. Pol.* 3.1, 3.6.

87 Parian Marble fr. 32.

88 [Arist.] *Ath. Pol.* 3.6; but cf. Plut. *Vit. Sol.* 19.

89 [Arist.] *Ath. Pol.* 3.4; Rhodes 1992, 102–3.

90 Hdt. 5.71; [Arist.] *Ath. Pol.* 8.3; *Poll.* 8.108.

91 Ismard 2010; Duplouy 2011; Blok 2014; Blok 2018; Duplouy 2018a; Ismard 2018; Duplouy 2019a; Duplouy 2019b.

92 Ismard 2010; Ismard 2018.

93 On *orgeones*, see Parker 1996, 28; Ustinova 1996.

94 On the law code, see Stroud 1968; Fornara 1977, 15–16; Gagarin 1981; Meiggs and Lewis 1988, 264–67; Welwei 1992, 138–46; Osborne and Rhodes 2017, 504–11. On the *phylai* and *phratriai*, see further Hedrick 1991; Welwei 1992, 77, 114, 116–23. On the date of Drakon, see Leão and Rhodes 2015, 2.

95 Agora P 23883: Brann 1962, 33, no. 23, plate 2.

96 Hdt. 5.82–88.

97 Solon frs. 1–3; Plut. *Vit. Sol.* 8–10, 12; [Arist.] *Ath. Pol.* 17.2.

98 Alc. 428 (Loeb); Hdt. 5.94–95; Strabo 13.1.38–39; Diog. Laert 1.74. See further Eijnde 2019, 59–60.

99 Hdt. 5.71; Thuc. 1.126.3–127.1; [Arist.] *Ath. Pol.* 1, frag. 8; Paus. 1.28.1; Plut. *Thes.* 12; Plut. *Vit. Sol.* 12; Schol. Ar. *Eq.* 445; Harris-Cline 1999.

100 On the date, see Leão and Rhodes 2015, 3. For other views, see Lévy 1978; Flament 2007.

101 Thuc. 1.126.7.

102 [Arist.] *Ath. Pol.* 5.1.

103 See Bintliff 2006; Forsdyke 2006, 334–40.

104 Stanton 1990, 34–85; Welwei 1992, 150–206; Foxhall 1997; Mulke 2002; Leão and Rhodes 2015. It is possible that he did not make these class divisions, but only the highest, and assigned the others new functions. For this view, see Rhodes 2006. For skepticism on the property classes, see Raaflaub 2006.

105 The term "Protoattic" was first used, in French ("proto-attique"), by Couve 1893 not Smith 1902, as often claimed. See further the historiography in chapter 2. The most important treatments of Protoattic are: Böhlau 1887; Pfuhl 1923, 121–27; Burr 1933; Cook 1934–35; *CVA* Berlin 1 (Richard Eilmann and Kurt Gebauer, 1938); Young 1939; Cook 1947; Kübler 1950; Mylonas 1957; Hampe 1960; Brann 1962; Karouzou 1963; Morris 1984; Whitley 1994b; Petrocheilos 1996; Cook 1997, 63–70; Rocco 2008; Coulié 2013, 188–222; Alexandridou 2015.

106 For a convenient and widely adopted chronological chart, see Cook 1934–35, 205. Following Cook, e.g., Cook 1947, 151–54; Brann 1961a, 95; Brann 1962, 307; Coulié 2013, 188. Young 1942 dated the transition about a generation later but subsequently signaled that he would revise his

dating scheme: Davison 1961, 127, n. 2. Kübler (1954, 1959, 1970) favored a higher dating, which has been roundly criticized, e.g., Knigge and Walter-Karydi 1974.

107 Cook 1934–35, 169–72.

108 Cook 1997, 42.

109 Rombos 1988, 388.

110 Brann 1962, 19.

111 On the Polyphemus Amphora, see further chapter 4 and chapter 5.

112 Haugh 2012 surveys the changes in subject matter.

113 Rome, Museo Nazionale Etrusco di Villa Giulia 61566: Colonna 1976, 233, no. 77/16, plate 49b; Canciani and Hase 1979, 36–37, no. 16, plates 12.2–13; Markoe 1985, 191–92, no. E3; Markoe 1992–93, 22, plate 7; Aruz, Graff, and Rakic 2013, 266, fig. 4.12.

114 Brisart 2011 excluded sub-Geometric from his definition of Protoattic, and Whitley 1994b similarly associated Protoattic only with an Orientalizing style.

115 Vierneisel 1964, 434–35, 441–42, fig. 29; Rocco 2008, 101, no. W 7; Doronzio 2018, 63, fig. 9.

116 Examples of other assemblages with so-called Orientalizing and sub-Geometric vases found together are: Parlama and Stampolidis 2000, 284–88, figs. 263–70; Doronzio 2018, 61, fig. 6—Parlama and Stampolidis 2000, 276–84, figs. 249–62—*CVA* Germany 2, Berlin 1, plates 43–45; Rocco 2008, 101, nos. W 2 and W 10—Vierneisel 1964, 435, 443–44, fig. 30; Rocco 2008, 170, no. K 15—von Freytag 1975, 76–81, figs. 15–16, plates 22–23; Rocco 2008, 179, nos. K 1, 2, 3, 4, 5, 6; Doronzio 2018, 82–83, table 8—Pelekidis 1916, 20, no. 44, 30, fig. 18, 33, no. 22, 37, fig. 35.2; Young 1942, 30–32, figs. 10–12—*Thorikos* 1977/1982, 79–83, figs. 76–90; Rocco 2008, 124, no. V 5.

117 Athens, National Museum 353: BAPD 300012; Couve 1897; *ABV* 2; *Para* 1.

118 Brokaw 1963. For the middle period of Protoattic, Opferrinne β in the Kerameikos is critical (see table 1).

119 For the problems in differentiating Late Protoattic and early black-figure, see Alexandridou 2011, 3–4; Coulié 2013, 195. See further chapter 7.

120 Arrington, Spyropoulos, and Brellas 2021.

121 A possible fragmentary signature survives on a votive plaque attributed to the Analatos Painter, but not enough to reconstruct a name, and it might instead be the name of the dedicator. See further Chapter 5, n. 16.

122 Notable imports include a Cycladic relief pithos from Merenda with the representation of a Minotaur (Simantoni-Bournia 2004, 85–86, plate 42, fig. 103), and a possible Cycladic pottery fragment from Pikermi (*AAA* 4 [1971] 75–76).

123 Coulié 2013, 193.

CHAPTER 2 FROM PHALERON WARE TO EXOTICA

1 Bernal 1987–2006; Bernal 2001. For critiques, see, e.g., Lefkowitz and Rogers 1996.

2 Said 1978; Marchand 1996, 188–227; Marchand 2009. On Said's exclusion of Germany, see esp. Marchand 2009, xviii–xxvi.

3 Bohrer 2003.

4 Gunter 2014, 50–79.

5 See also the interesting discussion of the historiography of Greek–Near Eastern relations in the study of Homer, examined in Burkert 1991a.

6 Other historiographies of Protoattic are: Morris 1984, 2–20; Coulié 2013, 188–91; Alexandridou 2015, 125–31. For a historiography of Greek pottery, see Cook 1997, 275–311. I treat some of the issues in this chapter in Arrington forthcoming.

7 I. Morris 2000, 77–106; Kotsonas 2016.

8 On the display of sculpture, see Vout 2018, 149, 157.

9 On the notion of an enduring Orientalizing paradigm, see Arrington forthcoming.

10 Jahn 1854, 21 lamented how little was known about vases found in Greece, with no systematic excavations or comprehensive reports from the field.

11 Stackelberg 1837, plate 9. Toulouse 26086: Audiat 1954; Kübler 1970, 625–26, no. 316; Karouzou 1979; Landes and Laurens 1988, 81, 90, no. 47; Rocco 2008, 108, no. KB 5. Karouzou first noticed the connection of the vase in Toulouse with the illustration in Stackelberg, but to my knowledge no one has identified this oinochoe as the first illustrated Protoattic vase. The tall foot, long neck, and birds recall Italic and Euboian vases, but Rocco attributes it to a Protoattic painter, the Group of the Buffalo Krateriskos.

12 Birch 1858, 257, no. 123. London, British Museum 1842.7–28.827: Rocco 2008, 160, no. B 1; Coulié 2013, 188, fig. 181. The vase was accessioned in 1842, but museum records indicate that it was acquired in Athens in 1813. I thank Sarah Norvell for her research on this object.

13 Dumont 1869. Athens, National Museum 304: Rocco 2008, 79, no. C 1; Coulié 2013, 189, fig. 182.

14 On the geology of the area, see Fragkopoulou 2015, 133.

15 Kourouniotis 1911, 246.

16 Furtwängler 1880, 46–47. On the historiography of Athenian Geometric, see Siebert 2010; Papadopoulos 2017, 28–29.

17 Furtwängler 1880. Berlin, Staatliche Museen, Antikensammlung F 56: *CVA* Berlin 1, plates 43.1–2, 44.1–2; Rocco 2008, 101, no. W 2; Coulié 2013, 189, fig. 183. The oinochoe is Berlin F 57: *CVA* Berlin 1, plate 45.1; Rocco 2008, 101, no. W 10.

18 Furtwängler 1882. Berlin, Staatliche Museen, Antikensammlung F 1682: Coulié 2013, 189, fig. 184; *ABV* 5.4; *Para* 2.8.

19 Furtwängler 1882, 206.

20 Benndorf 1883, 104–6, plates 54.1, 54.2.

21 Collignon 1886, 15–16.

22 In Böhlau 1898, he further clarifies routes of transmission, with roles for Aeolian and Euboian ware (esp. 117).

23 Athens, National Museum 313: Cook 1934–35, plates 38b, 39; Rocco 2008, 28, no. An 11; Coulié 2013, 196, fig. 189.

24 London, British Museum 1865.7–20.7: Böhlau 1887, 50, figs. 9–10; Rocco 2008, 62, no. Bo 2.

25 For example, the influential Caylus et al. 1752.

26 Hom. *Od.* 4.617.

27 Pliny *HN* 35.15–16.

28 See esp. Larsen 1996.

29 Esp. Said 1978.

30 Bohrer 2003, 13, 54–60.

31 Bohrer 2003. Current perceptions of Orientalism have been built predominantly on the reception of the Orient in France and England, yet German scholars played a fundamental role in classical archaeology: see Marchand 2009, xviii–xxvi.

32 Creuzer 1810–12; Baur 1824–25; Gruppe 1887. See also the "Pan–Babylonists": Marchand 1996, 220–27; Marchand 2009, 236–49. For early views on Phoenician movement in the Mediterranean, see Movers 1841–56.

33 Müller 1847–48, vol. 2, 523–37; Müller 1852; Brunn 1856; Reinach 1893; Beloch 1894. See also Marchand 1996, 43–48, 110–11. It is possible to overemphasize (as Bernal 1987–2006, 308–16 does) the influence of Müller, whose work was criticized in his own time. Even Brunn concedes foreign influence on Greek art, e.g., Brunn 1868. But he retorts: "Aber ist darum die griechische Kunst aus der asiatischen geradezu abzuleiten? ist sie eine Tochter derselben? Ich antworte mit Entscheidenheit: nein!" (7) In Brunn 1893, he is at pains to downdate (from the Bronze Age) Phoenician involvement in the Mediterranean and deny the presence of colonies, but he does not dispute the presence of Phoenician traders in the eighth century.

34 Layard 1903, 187.

35 Witte 1865, 3.

36 Semper 1863, 139–40, n. 1.

37 Riegl 1893 [1992]; Marchand 2009, 400–403. This does not imply that Riegl valued Greek and Near Eastern art equally: e.g., Riegl 1893 [1992], 83.

38 Riva and Vella 2006a, 4–10.

39 Brunn 1868, 12, 14–15.

40 Birch 1858, 251.

41 On Panionism, see Cook 1997, 295–97. For nineteenth- and early twentieth-century views of
    Ionia, see Hogarth 1909, esp. 7–23. In later work, such as that of Conze, Dorians became
    associated with the more indigenous aspects of Hellenic art.

42 Rhodes: Salzmann 1875. Cyprus: Cesnola 1877 (quickly reprinted and also translated into
    German); Ohnefalsch-Richter 1893 (promptly translated into English); Myres and Ohnefalsch-
    Richter 1899. Note Cesnola 1877, 1–2: "In recent years it has been argued with great show of
    reason that the Greeks had also learned from the Phoenicians what has been called the
    alphabet of art, that is a knowledge of the technical processes of such industrial arts as
    weaving, embroidery, pottery, metal-working, and wood-carving." Cyprus is often left out of
    narratives of nineteenth-century archaeology, which is surprising. The island demonstrated an
    intermingling of Phoenicians and Greeks; the publication of its discoveries were aimed at
    scholars and laymen alike, with translations in German and in English; and many objects went
    with Cesnola to the Metropolitan Museum of Art. Thera: Gaertringen 1899–1909, esp. volume 2;
    Dragendorff 1903.

43 Gerhard 1831.

44 Kramer 1837, 46–47.

45 Jahn 1854, 145–46. He used "orientalisirend" and "orientalisch" to characterize a very small
    number of figures in vase-paintings: 146, 200, 206.

46 Salzmann 1875.

47 Burgon 1847, 283.

48 Birch 1858, 257.

49 Witte 1865, 37–40.

50 Witte 1863, 265–67: "On donne le nom de vases de style asiatique ou oriental à une classe
    très-nombreuse de vases enrichis de peintures plus ou moins compliquées.... Quelques
    archéologues leur donnent le nom de vases corinthiens, parce qu'on a trouvé quantité de petits
    vases de cette nature dans les tombeaux, aux environs de Corinthe. Mais aujourd'hui qu'un
    grand nombre de localités du continent grec, des îles, des côtes de l'Asie, de la Sicile et de l'Italie
    ont fourni des vases tout à fait pareils, il semble qu'on doit abandonner cette dénomination et y
    substituer une dénomination plus générale. On leur a donné aussi le nom de *vases phéniciens*,
    gréco-phéniciens ou *pseudo-phéniciens*. Nous préférons celui de *vases de style asiatique ou
    oriental*" (italics original).

51 E.g., see the use of "Oriental" in Smith 1884, 176, where one today would expect "Orientalizing."

52 Kramer 1837, 46–72.

53 Burgon 1847; Birch 1858, 252–57. The isolation of Geometric was already evident in Burgon 1847,
    but had escaped most scholars' notice: see Cook 1997, 284.

54 Cook 1997, 279.

55 Poulsen 1905, 10; Cook 1997, 284; Siebert 2010, 300.

56 E.g., Furtwängler 1880, 19.

57 Conze 1870, 526.

58 Conze 1870, 520–23.

59 Conze 1870, 523. The alternative term "asiatisierend" can still be found in some later authors,
    such as Lau 1877.

60 Conze 1870, 532.

61 See also the discussion in Cook 1997, 289.

62 Fitton 1995, 31, 100.

63 Fitton 1995, 104–7.

64 Greek prehistory was not at first acknowledged as Greek. Voutsaki 2002 describes and analyzes
    the process.

65 Riegl 1893 [1992], 117.

66 Furtwängler 1880, 7, 42.

67 Furtwängler 1880, 7, 43.

68 Furtwängler 1880, 19.

69 Furtwängler and Loeschcke 1886, x. Milchhöfer 1883 recognized foreign influences on Bronze Age art but emphasized the Aryan components and the native (Pelasgian) nature of the earliest Greek art.

70 Similarly, in a later publication, he wrote, "Alle ostgriechischen orientalisierenden Stile knüpfen an die mykenische Periode an" (Böhlau 1898, 118).

71 Böhlau 1887, 60.

72 Müller 1852, 374–76.

73 Müller and Oesterley 1832–56, vol. 1, 3, 14, plates 3, 19.

74 Rayet and Collignon 1888, 42–44.

75 Dumont and Chaplain 1888, 93–104.

76 Athens, National Museum 1002: BAPD 300025; *ABV* 4.1, 679; *Para* 2.6; *ArchDelt* 6 (1890), 4–5, 30–31; Staïs and Wolters 1891; Coulié 2013, 219, fig. 216.

77 Athens, National Museum 993: *ArchDelt* 5 (1890), 10–12; Staïs 1890, 323–24, plate 10; Coulié 2013, 190, fig. 185.

78 London, British Museum 1865.7–20.1: Böhlau 1887, 48, fig. 8; Moore 2003, 29, fig. 32; Rocco 2008, 77, no. BPa 3, plate 10.2; Coulié 2013, 206, fig. 200.

79 Pallat 1897.

80 Athens, National Museum 353: BA 300012; *ABV* 2; *Para* 1; Couve 1897.

81 Athens, National Museum 27967α–στ (and Oxford, Ashmolean 1948.282): Waldstein et al. 1902, esp. 161–64, plate 67; Rocco 2008, 46, no. Arg 1. See Waldstein et al. 1902 for a drawing of all the fragments.

82 Athens, National Museum 14497: Smith 1902; Rocco 2008, 180, no. Kyn 1; Coulié 2013, 217, fig. 214; Doronzio 2018, 237, fig. 16.

83 E.g., Eleusis uninventoried: Skias 1912; Rocco 2008, 101, no. W 5.

84 Graef et al. 1925, vol. 1, 34–41.

85 Burr 1933; Kübler 1959, 1–2.

86 Munich, Antikensammlungen 6077: Hackl 1907; Cook 1934–35, 173, 205, plate 41; *CVA* Munich 3, 29–30, plates 130–131.1; Rocco 2008, 28, no. An 18, plate 1.6; Coulié 2013, 201, fig. 193.

87 S. Morris 1984, 5–8.

88 Cambridge, Fitzwilliam Museum inv. 7/25: *CVA* Cambridge 1, plate 2.7; Rocco 2008, 116, no. Cam 1. For other publications of early finds and acquisitions, see also *CVA* Pays-Bas 2, La Haye 2, III H, plate 4, and the publication of vases from Athens: Collignon and Couve 1902, 96–100, 112–16; Collignon and Couve 1904, plates 17, 19, 20.

89 Hackl 1907, 98–99; Richter 1912, 383; Burr 1933, 626–27.

90 Smith 1902 is claimed in S. Morris 1984, 3; Coulié 2013, 190; Alexandridou 2015, 125. For bibliography on the vase, see Chapter 1, n. 1, above.

91 E.g., Richter 1912, 370.

92 E.g., Hackl 1907; Herford 1919.

93 Graef et al. 1925, 40–41. On the historiography of Late Protoattic / early black-figure, see Alexandridou 2011, 1–5.

94 Brunn 1893, 131–35.

95 Perrot and Chipiez 1882–1914, vol. 9 (1911), 308, fig. 152, 672, fig. 366.

96 Daremberg and Saglio 1877–1919, vol. 5, 639. Generally, Daremberg and Saglio 1877–1919, vol. 5, 639–40, and cf. vol. 4, 1029, fig. 6054. The pottery is designated as "attique-orientalisant." Later Protoattic is classed as "attique-primitif," and the Nessos vase is illustrated (640, fig. 7290).

97 Nicole 1926 contains no discussion of Athens and no image of Protoattic, although he writes that Corinthian Orientalizing artists follow Athenian precedent (16–17).

98 Brunn 1893, 135 (with direct reference to Böhlau), 145.

99 Buschor 1913, 41–42.

100 Pfuhl 1923, 121.

101 Contrast with the willingness of Dumont and Chaplain in 1888 to spot Orientalizing, beginning in the Myceanean period and visible in Geometric pottery as well (e.g., 90, 131, 161–62).

102 Buschor 1913, 31; Pfuhl 1923, 122.

103 Pfuhl 1923, 121–22.

104 Friis Johansen 1923.

105 Friis Johansen 1923, 63.

106 Hanfmann 1953, esp. 15–19, arguing that Ionia was provincial until the mid-seventh century.

107 Friis Johansen 1923, 64–66. On the role of Crete in the development of sculpture, see Löwy 1909, 1911.

108 Payne 1931, ix, 5–6, 53.

109 Payne 1931, viii, 10.

110 Payne 1931, 53–54.

111 Burr 1933, 634.

112 Furtwängler 1880, 46–47; Furtwängler 1881; Furtwängler 1882; Smith 1884, 176; Dumont and Chaplain 1888, 101–3; Collignon 1902, 96–100; Collignon 1904, plate 17; Hackl 1907, 98–99; Herford 1919.

113 Pfuhl 1923, 125.

114 One could also add that Pottier 1926 provides a discussion of the relationship between "art industriel" and "grand art" through thirty-three illustrated vases, none of them Protoattic, but illustrates a Protoattic vase (classified as Geometric but now associated with the Analatos Painter) as a representative example of the amphora shape (42–43, plate 9, no. 4).

115 Boardman 2001, 34–35. His handbook on early Greek vase-painting is more comprehensive, with three vases from Phaleron (Boardman 1998, 102, 104, figs. 198–99, 205).

116 Neer 2012, 107.

117 Stansbury-O'Donnell 2015, 144.

118 Gunter 2009, 65, 75.

119 Coulié 2013 is a notable exception, illustrating a wide range of Protoattic vases, including those from Phaleron, in large part because of her attention to historiography.

120 Böhlau 1887, 65–66.

121 Early manifestations of this paradigm can be found in Rayet and Collignon 1888, 41–42.

122 Daremberg and Saglio 1877–1919, vol. 5, p. 639.

123 Quoted in Larsen 1996, 103.

124 Richter 1917, xv.

125 Cook 1934–35, 171.

126 Cook 1934–35, 184–85, 188.

127 Beazley 1986, 4, emphasis added.

128 Beazley 1986, 12, emphasis added.

129 Robertson 1953, 185.

130 Rumpf 1953, 23–38.

131 On Beazley, see Arrington 2017, with bibliography.

132 Whitley 1997. See also Neer 1997.

133 Beazley's method also met resistance, from the very beginning: Rouet 2001. Followers include Payne 1931; Haspels 1936.

134 Cook 1934–35, and also Cook 1947.

135 Sheedy 1992, 12, n. 6 citing a letter from Cook.

136 Cook 1947, 142. On the Analatos Painter: Cook 1934–35, 172–76; Hampe 1960, 30–35, 77–78; Davison 1961, 51–52; Brann 1962, 18–20; Coldstream 1968 [2008], 63–64; Sheedy 1990; Denoyelle 1996; Rocco 2008, 13–30; Coulié 2013, 199–202; S. Morris 2014, 101–2.

137 E.g., Davison 1961, 51; Coulié 2013, 195.

138 Denoyelle 1996, 72.

139 Hood 1982, 47.

140 See Cook 1947, 143: "The Potter's Quarter in Athens . . . seems at the beginning of the Orientalising phase to have contained no more than three flourishing workshops which attracted the higher class of customers by producing a range of expensive vases for grave and cult turned out in the progressive style. The leader of this style was the painter of the Analatos hydria. In imitation of him the workshop of the Mesogeia Painter turned out a range of vases for

purchasers who demanded the Orientalising fashion in pottery but were satisfied with inferior craftsmanship. The third of these workshops was that of the Vulture Painter."

141 Cook 1971, 175–76.
142 On these painters, see Rocco 2008, 60–61, 67–78, 107–8.
143 Richter 1912, 379–80.
144 Burr 1933, 633.
145 It is also worth noting that excavations at Al Mina, first published in 1938 (Woolley 1938a, 1938b) suggested that Greeks could take the initiative in the Orientalizing phenomenon.
146 E.g., Hampe 1960; Hood 1982; Sheedy 1990; Denoyelle 1996; Moore 2003.
147 *CVA* Berlin 1 (Richard Eilmann and Kurt Gebauer, 1938).
148 Kraiker 1951; Mylonas 1957; Karouzou 1963.
149 Cook 1962, 822.
150 Beazley himself treated high- and low-quality Archaic and Classical Attic pottery, and his method does not necessarily exclude "bad" art.
151 Cook 1934–35, 166, n. 1.
152 Young 1942, 23.
153 Young 1942, 54.
154 Diepolder 1947.
155 Kübler 1959, Kübler 1970. Critical review: Knigge and Walter-Karydi 1974.
156 Kübler 1950.
157 Evans 1912; Fitton 1995, 134.
158 Hawes and Hawes 1911, 2.
159 Fitton 1995, 117. Cf. the Orient as an alternative to the study of the classical world in Germany: Marchand 2009, 213–14.
160 Kübler 1950; Morris 1984; Kübler 1970; Rocco 2008.
161 For the historiography of find contexts, see also Alexandridou 2015, 127–31.
162 Morris 1987. See also Morris 2000, 155–91.
163 E.g., d'Agostino and d'Onofrio 1993 and Papadopoulos 1993.
164 E.g., Houby-Nielsen 1992; Houby-Nielsen 1995; Kistler 1998.
165 Whitley 1994b.
166 Whitley 1994b, 52.
167 Whitley 1994b, 57. On social rationing, see also Whitley 1991, 8.
168 See 20–23, above.
169 I. Morris 1997, 9, n. 1.
170 E.g., I. Morris 2000, 184: "The orientalizing movement was a class phenomenon."
171 For example, Duplouy 2019a rejects the formulation of *agathoi* and *kakoi* but accepts the relationship between "formal burial" and citizenship and develops an interpretation of "insiders" and "outsiders."
172 D'Onofrio 2007–8, 437–41; Doronzio 2018, 5; Dimitriadou 2019.
173 Alexandridou 2009; Alexandridou 2017.
174 I. Morris 1997.
175 Osborne 1989, 309–13.
176 Osborne 1989, 318–21. See also Osborne 1988, for an interpretation of Protoattic painting that reverts neither to connoisseurship nor to quantitative analysis.
177 "Osborne's . . . approach is still largely that of the art historian, who, for the most part, is reluctant to consider the mucky details of context and deposition" (65). The quotation is in reference to Osborne 1988.
178 In many ways, S. Morris 1992 inaugurated this approach.
179 Brisart 2011, 56–58.
180 Brisart 2011, 138.
181 Brisart 2011, 139. On Protoattic, Brisart 2011, 136–49.
182 Brisart 2011, 55–56. See also Haug 2012 for an example of a relatively recent work that repeats conventional views of Orientalizing (e.g., 490).

183 Brisart 2011, 146–49.

184 Brisart 2011, 145.

185 E.g., Osborne 1988, 1–6; Osborne 1989, 312–13.

186 Cook 1997, 329, first published in 1960. Specifically, he criticizes the application of the term "Phaleron" to a style. For a recent study of Phaleron pottery, see now Fragkopoulou and Zosi 2017.

CHAPTER 3 THE PLACE OF ATHENS IN THE MEDITERRANEAN

1   West 1997, 1. Pallottino 1965 offers a classic discussion of Orientalizing as diffusion.

2   Botto 2017. The chapter, however, is more methodologically sophisticated than the title implies.

3   Aruz, Graff, and Rakic 2014.

4   E.g., Broodbank 2013, 517; Osborne 1998, 43: "At every turn, the art of seventh-century Greece stares you in the face, and its stare is the inscrutable stare of the east." Catherine Pratt drew my attention to this apt quotation. Bowersock 2005 notes the east–west orientation, and that north and south were the cultural outliers for many ancient observers. Kotsonas 2019 also notes the *ex oriente lux* paradigm perpetuated by museum exhibitions.

5   On networks, see Granovetter 1973; Granovetter 1983; Brughmans 2010; Knappett 2011; Malkin 2011; Rost 2011; Brughmans and Poblome 2015; Knappett 2017; Scott 2017; Yang, Keller, and Zheng 2017; Peeples 2019.

6   See Knappett 2017 for how networks as a method and globalization as a framework together can productively inform analysis.

7   Pratt 2015.

8   Horden and Purcell 2000, 141.

9   Osborne 2019, 143.

10   See 25, above. Rocco 2008, 215; Coulié 2013, 191–93.

11   See, e.g., Burkert 1992; S. Morris 1992; West 1997; Burkert 2004.

12   For recent surveys of the Near East and Egypt, see Manolova 2019 and Kelder 2019.

13   The material consists of three Egyptian faience lions from a Dipylon tomb that also contained ivory female figurines probably made in Greece (Brückner and Pernice 1893, 131; Perrot 1895, 282, figs. 13–16); a scarab (Phoenician, Rhodian, or Egyptian) and a Phoenician glass bead from the same cemetery; an Egyptian (?) scarab and Phoenician glass bead from the Kerameikos; a third scarab, perhaps Phoenician or Egyptian, from agora grave E 19:3; and a spindle whorl from an eighth-century well deposit, with an impression from a similar scarab. For a survey of the evidence, with further references, see Skon-Jedele 1994, 10–73. For Near Eastern imports to Greece, see Braun-Holzinger and Rehm 2005; Hölbl 2005, 114–23. For connections in the Middle Bronze Age, see Kourou 2019b.

14   Athens, National Museum 6709 (bull head protome): de Ridder 1896, 189, no. 518, fig. 164; Herrmann 1966, 125 n. 34, 129; Scholl 2006, 155, no. 105—Athens, National Museum 617 (Assyrian bird attachment): Herrmann 1966, 58, 70—Athens, National Museum 6686: de Ridder 1896, 186, no. 512, fig. 159; Herrmann 1966, 155, no. 12—Athens, National Museum 6663: Herrmann 1966, 155, no. 31—Athens, National Museum 7037 (Cypro-Phoenician bowl): de Ridder 1896, 72, no. 218; Markoe 1985, 203–4, no. G2; Scholl 2006, 110–11, 160, no. 136.

15   Coldstream 1968 [2008], 361.

16   Hanfmann 1962; Theodoropoulou-Polychroniadis 2015, 88–89, 226, no. 216.

17   Laughy 2010, 242–44; Theodoropoulou-Polychroniadis 2015, 74–78, 212–13, 273–80.

18   Bowls: Kerameikos M133, M134, M140 (M139 from the same grave as M140 is Greek); d'Onofrio 2017, 271–72, figs. 24.24–26. Belt: Kerameikos M138; d'Onofrio 2017, 276–77, figs. 24.39–40. Figurine: Freytag 1964, 434–35, 441–42, fig. 29; Doronzio 2018, 63, fig. 9. Candelabrum: Athens, National Museum 6720; de Ridder 1896, 131, no. 403; Scholl 2006, 159, no. 131; Doronzio 2018, 39, fig. 26. Ivory figurine: Athens, National Museum 6532; Perrot 1895, 294, fig. 17; Scholl 2006, 110, 161, no. 139. Harpokrates: de Ridder 1896, 280–81, no. 756, fig. 264; Skon-Jedele 1994, 58–59,

no. 0001. There are an additional three Egyptian faience objects that may have been imported in the seventh century but that lack good contexts: Skon-Jedele 1994, 32–33.

19   Athens, National Museum 6666, 6516, 6499: Scholl 2006, 157, no. 118, 159, no. 129, 165, no. 167. A literary source that may be relevant is the story that a certain Epimenides came from Crete (Phaistos) to Athens in the early sixth century to ceremonially purify the city following the slaughter of Cylon's followers, the exile of the Alcmaeonidae, and the disinterring of graves (Bernabé 2007, 105–68). This report might indicate some level of connection with that island back in the seventh century.

20   On Sounion, see Skon-Jedele 1994, 135–89; Theodoropoulou-Polychroniadis 2015, esp. 74–78, 273–80. Some of the amulets are Egyptian, but the majority were made on Rhodes, which may also have been the source of the Egyptian imports. For a role for Aiginetans at Sounion, see S. Morris 1992, 96–100, 107–17.

21   For surveys of Greeks in the Levant, see Waldbaum 1994; Haider 1996, 60–95; Boardman 1999a, 35–109; Niemeier 2001; Boardman 2006, 510–23; Hodos 2006, 25–88.

22   On which, see, e.g., Papadopoulos 1997; Waldbaum 1997.

23   For a more generous view of mercenary activity in the Levant, see Luraghi 2006.

24   On Al Mina, see Boardman 1990; Papadopoulos 1997; Boardman 1999a, 39–51, 270–72; Boardman 1999b; Kearsley 1999; Boardman 2002; Pamir and Nishiyama 2002; Luke 2003; Niemeyer 2004; Yener 2005; Boardman 2006; Niemeyer 2006.

25   For more sites with possible material evidence of mercenaries, see Wenning 2001, 260.

26   On the literary evidence mentioned in this paragraph, see Kuhrt 2002.

27   Similarly, Wenning 2001, 257.

28   For the sources on mercenary activity in Egypt, see Haider 2001. On Carians in Egypt, see esp. Vittmann 2003, 155–79. For Greek-Egyptian relations, see esp. Haider 1996, 95–113; Boardman 1999a, 111–59; Vittmann 2003, 194–235; Boardman 2006, 524–31; Villing and Schlotzhauer 2006; Villing 2013; Spier, Potts, and Cole 2018.

29   Hdt. 2.152–54; Diod. 1.66.12–67.2. See also Polyainos *Strategica* 7.3. See Williams and Villing 2006, with earlier bibliography.

30   Novotny and Jeffers 2018, 238. For the relationship between Psammetichos and Gyges, see Haider 1988, 164–75.

31   Luraghi estimates the mercenaries numbered in the tens of thousands (Luraghi 2006, 25), which seems too high.

32   Diod. 1.67.8–9.

33   On Naukratis, see Hdt. 2.178; Möller 2000; Höckmann and Kreikenbom 2001; Villing and Schlotzhauer 2006; Schlotzhauer and Weber 2012; Fantalkin 2014. On possible trade dynamics, see Wilson and Gilbert 2007, 260–65.

34   Hdt. 2.179.

35   Weber 2007, 303–4.

36   Höckmann and Vitmann 2005, 97–98.

37   Höckmann and Vitmann 2005, 100. See also the cuboid statue dedicated by Pa-di-shehdedit: Höckmann and Vitmann 2005, 488–89, no. 41.

38   Schlotzhauer and Weber 2012, 15.

39   Fantalkin 2006, 201–2. His view can be contrasted with a more conventional narrative of deepening Near East–Greek relations in Brisart 2011, 38–43.

40   Sørensen 1988, 14, 17; Luke 2003, 42–44. See also the discussion in Kourou 2019a.

41   Luke 2003, 32–35.

42   Pratt 2015; Pratt 2016.

43   Ahlberg-Cornell 1967; Ahlberg-Cornell 1971a; Ahlberg-Cornell 1971b; Rombos 1988; Hiller 2006; Mikrakis 2015.

44   Borell 1978. Athens, National Museum 784, from Dipylon Grave VII, between Samouil Street and Plateia Eleftherias: Brückner and Pernice 1893, 111–15; Coldstream 1968 [2008], 60, no. 48; Kübler 1970, 583, no. 93; Carter 1972, 46–48, plate 11b–c; Borell 1978, 8–9, no. 24, plate 20; Rombos 1988, 244–45, 291–92, 460–61, no. 202; Langdon 2008, 170, fig. 3.21; Coulié 2013, 93,

fig. 66; Aruz, Graff, and Rakic 2014, 259, fig. 4.7. Edinburgh 1956.422: BAPD 9011856; *CVA* Edinburgh, plate 3.3–4; Borell 1978, 40, no. 13, plates 8–9.

45 Ohly 1953.

46 Agora P 4611: Young 1939, 107, no. B 1, fig. 74; Brann 1962, 93, no. 543, plates 4, 33, 44; Papadopoulos 2007, 136, fig. 127A; Rocco 2008, 150, no. BAr 6.

47 Barclay 2013.

48 Boulder, Colorado, University Museum 22317: Rocco 2008, 61, no. BWü 1.

49 New York, Metropolitan Museum of Art 74.51.965: *CVA* The Metropolitan Museum of Art 5, 79–84, plates 46–49. An example from Pithekoussai: Ischia 238649.

50 On Phaleron oinochoai, see Petrocheilos 1996. Kerameikos 138: Kübler 1970, 469–70, plates 56–57.1.

51 For example, the horse trappings dedicated at Samos and Eretria (Aruz, Graff, and Rakic 2014, 296–97, nos. 165–66) or the statue dedicated by Pedon near Priene (Boardman 1999a, 281, fig. 324; Vittmann 2003, 205, fig. 103; Höckmann and Vittmann 2005, 100, fig. 2).

52 Pratt 2015, 221–24.

53 See d'Agostino 2006 and Greco 2006 for overviews of Greek colonization. See also Osborne 1998; Yntema 2000; Fischer-Hansen, Nielsen, and Ampolo 2004a; Fischer-Hansen, Nielsen, and Ampolo 2004b; and Osborne 2016, with Malkin 2016.

54 Ephoros *FGrH* 70 F 137. Contrast Thuc. 6.3.1. See further Kourou 1998, 167–68; Donnellan 2014, 47–50.

55 Pontecagnano: Kourou 2005, 504; d'Agostino and Gastaldi 2016, 165. Cumae: Johannowsky 1983, 99, plate VIII. Capua: Melandri 2011, 307–8, 58A2, plate 2-XL; Melandri and Sirano 2016, 216, fig. 8. Veii: Descoeudres and Kearsley 1983, 36, n. 12, fig. 28. Tarquinia: Bruni 1994, 297–98, plates 2a–b, 3.4. Jug: *NSc* 1967, 245, fig. 96; Descoeudres and Kearsley 1983, 8–39, no. 16; Sgubini 2001, 109, no. I.G.6.11. Pyxis: Cook 1934–35, 204, n. 5; Szilágyi 2005, 39, n. 1. For Attic Middle Geometric finds even farther west, at Huelva and Málaga, see Kourou 2019a, 87; Kourou 2019b. For Attic Middle Geometric amphoras at Gela and Fusco, see Kourou 2019a, 88. Kourou 2008a and 2008b offer good overviews.

56 Syracuse: Tréziny 1979, 12, no. 3, plates I and VII; Coldstream 1968 [2008], 78, no. 33; Denoyelle and Iozzo 2009, 44, fig. 31. Pithekoussai: Coldstream 1995, 265–66, no. 111, plate 32b. Canale: Blakeway 1932, 179, fig. 6b; Åkerström 1943, 41–44, fig. 12.2 (made in Calabria); Coldstream 1968 [2008], 79, no. 40; Stampolidis 2003b, 330, no. 285 (related to workshop); Giuliano 2005, 64–65, figs. 1–3 (made at Locri); Denoyelle and Iozzo 2009 41, n. 39. On Naxian (Sicilian) connections with Athens, see Coldstream 2004.

57 Åkerström 1943, 38, 43–44, no. Can. 21, plate 8.8; Mercuri 2004, 27, no. 17, 64–70, figs. 9.1, 10.1, 11.1 (emphasizing Euboian parallels); Martelli 2008, 7, 19, fig. 80 (made by an immigrant from Athens or the Cyclades).

58 Tréziny 1979; Tréziny 1980; Denoyelle and Iozzo 2009, 44–45.

59 Syracuse 44090: *NSc* 6 (1925) 316–17, fig. 69 (where it is considered Argive). I thank Nota Kourou for discussing the fragment with me.

60 Jucker 1982, plate 12; Isler 1983, 28–29, 41; Kleibrink 2001, 51, fig. 8; Giuliano 2005, 66, figs. 4–5; van der Wielen-van Ommeren, Mekacher, and Christiansen 2006, 21–22, 69, figs. 4–5, 30; Martelli 2008, 10, figs. 40–42; Denoyelle and Iozzo 2009, 41–42, fig. 23.

61 Attema 2008; Jacobsen, Handberg, and Mittica 2008–9; Handberg and Jacobsen 2011. Further on the excavation: Kleibrink 2000; Kleibrink, Jacobsen, and Handberg 2004; Guggisberg 2016.

62 Dion. Hal. *Ant. Rom.* 3.46.3–5; Strabo 5.2.2, 8.6.20; Pliny *HN* 35.152; *DNO* 104–5, no. 189.

63 Pliny *HN* 7.205; *DNO* 341, no. 432. Pausanias records that a Eucheir was the teacher of Klearchos of Rhegion and a pupil of the otherwise unattested Lakedaimonians Syadras and Chartas (Paus. 6.4.4; *DNO* 211–12, no. 306). On the Pliny passages, see further Rouveret 1990, 319–20.

64 Orlandini 1988; Orlandini 1991; Orlandini 1998; Denoyelle and Iozzo 2009, 50–51; Denti 2013; Denti and Villette 2013; Denti 2015; Denti 2016; Savelli 2016; Denti 2018a; Denti 2018b. See also Carter 2006 for the wider region.

65 Metaponto 298.978.9: Orlandini 1988, 6–14, plate 2; Denoyelle 1996, 82–85, plate 19; Pugliese Carratelli 1996, 666, no. 26; Denti 1999, 211, fig. 3; Giuliano 2005, 67–68, figs. 8–14; Rocco 2008, 119, no. LT 8; Denoyelle and Iozzo 2009, 51, fig. 44, plate V; Denti 2013, 79, 93, fig. 7; Morris 2014, 98, fig. 4; Denti 2018b, 50, fig. 9.

66 Denti 2018b, however, argues for a Cycladic origin for the artist (56–57). But see also 58: "there may have been a community of 'mixed' Greek potters, including representatives of these schools [Greek East, Attica, Corinth], in activity at the same time and in the same space. Or, conversely, one can imagine a Cycladic workshop in which some painters decided . . . to reproduce certain elements typical of other schools' stock imagery."

67 Martelli 1984 and Martelli 2008 are important for drawing attention to Greek influences on Italian painting prior to Aristonothos and for advocating for the role of regions other than Euboia, although in some cases she seems to overstate the case.

68 Szilágyi 1985, 623; Martelli 2008, 11–16; Boitani, Neri, and Biagi 2010; Boitani et al. 2014; Drago et al. 2014.

69 Szilágyi 2005, 31, fig. 14; Budapest *CVA* 2, 161, plate 2; Martelli 2008, 11, figs. 44–48.

70 Painter of the Cranes: Dik 1980; Dik 1981a; Szilágyi 1985, 627; Martelli 1987a, 17; Martelli 1987b; Martelli 2001, 7–16; Michetti 2009. Heptachord Painter: Szilágyi 1985, 623–26; Martelli 1987a, 18; Martelli 2001, 2–7. Cerveteri 105391: Martelli 1987a, 86, fig. 33; Martelli 1987b, 3–4, figs. 5–9. Figure 3.15: Dik 1980, 72, fig. 34; Martelli 1984, 3–4, figs. 1–5; Martelli 1987a, 90–91, fig. 37; Martelli 2001, 2, fig. 1.

71 Schweitzer 1955; Martelli 1987a, 93, fig. 40; Denoyelle and Iozzo 2009, 56–58, plate 4; Harari 2014. Schweitzer surmised Aristonothos was an Athenian who worked in Syracuse before immigrating to Etruria. Martelli thought Cycladic elements may have come through exposure to artists working at Sicilian Naxos (Martelli 1984, 13).

72 Blakeway 1935, with all quotations from 129. See also Blakeway 1932–33. One could add a fifth category: ceramics made by second-generation Greeks, for example, painters who emigrated from Pithekoussai or Cumae to Etruria.

73 E.g., d'Agostino 1996b; Torelli 1996; d'Agostino 1999d, 82; Paoletti and Perna 2002; Vanzetti 2002; d'Agostino 2006, 206; Burgers and Crielaard 2007; d'Agostino 2010, 77–78; Greco 2014, 62–63; Kreindler 2015; Procelli 2016, 204; Quondam 2016.

74 Matthäus 2000b; Camporeale 2004c, 78–80; d'Agostino 2006, 208; Naso 2010, 184–85.

75 Dunbabin 1948, 226–27.

76 A consistent problem is that the "Greek" and "colonial" material is presented separately. For example, see the lack of overlap between Denoyelle and Iozzo 2009 and Coulié 2013.

77 Similarly, Denoyelle and Iozzo 2009, 33, 47. Vallet and Villard 1964 argue that colonial production at Megara Hyblaia was too heterogeneous to be a style (199). Denti provides the most penetrating analysis and defense of "colonial style": Denti 1999; Denti 2000, esp. 781–86, 836–39; Denti 2018b, 57.

78 Louvre CA 3837: Devambez and Villard 1979; Denoyelle and Iozzo 2009, 61, figs. 64–65. Syracuse 13893: Denoyelle and Iozzo 2009, 55, figs. 53–54. For surveys of colonial ware, see Villard 1981; d'Agostino 1982; Rouveret 1990, 322–25; Maruggi 1996; Semeraro 1996; Denoyelle and Iozzo 2009, 33–65.

79 Similarly, Mermati 2012a, 233.

80 Antonaccio 1995, 104–9; Deoudi 1999, 30–33, 103–5; Boehringer 2001, 48–54; Boardman 2003, 59; *ThesCRA* II, 135, no. 3.

81 Antonaccio 1995, 109–12; Deoudi 1999, 30–33, 105–6; Boehringer 2001, 54–59; *ThesCRA* II, 135, no. 5.

82 Antonaccio 1995, 118 (discussing the wrong vase); Deoudi 1999, 102; Boehringer 2001, 59.

83 Shear 1940, 292; Brann 1960, 412; Papadopoulos 2017, 230–36, 453–56, 459–66.

84 Antonaccio 1995, 121.

85 On burial markers, see Papadopoulos 2017, 576.

86 Papadopoulos 2017, 45. And cf. 233: "There is increasing evidence that Early Iron Age tombs in the area of the later Athenian Agora were intentionally located in the same cemeteries as Mycenaean tombs, and sometimes in direct relationship to individual Mycenaean tombs."

87 For the possibility of hero worship at Sounion, too tenuous to include here, see Antonaccio 1995, 166–69; Deoudi 1999, 113–15; Boehringer 2001, 64–66; Boardman 2003, 65; *ThesCRA* II, 139, no. 22.

88 Travlos 1971, 42; Antonaccio 1995, 187–91; Mazarakis Ainian 1997, 140–43, 150–54; Deoudi 1999, 66–67; Mazarakis Ainian 1999, 16; Boehringer 2001, 77 n. 3; Laughy 2010, 267–70; *ThesCRA* II 136, no. 10, 139, no. 20; Mazarakis Ainian and Alexandridou 2011.

89 Alexandridou 2018, 31–40.

90 Burr 1933; Antonaccio 1995, 122–25; Deoudi 1999, 68–70; Boehringer 2001, 68–72; d'Onofrio 2001, 277–91; Laughy 2010, 255–64; van den Eijnde and Laughy 2017; Papadopoulos 2017, 118–23, 220–29; Alexandridou 2018, 41–42.

91 Antonaccio 1995, 112–17; Deoudi 1999, 102–3; Boehringer 2001, 63–64; Boardman 2003, 62; Laughy 2010, 265–67; *ThesCRA* II, 135, no. 4. Compare Hdt. 9.27.3; Paus 1.39.2; Plut. *Vit. Thes.* 29.4–5.

92 Coldstream 1977 [2003], 351; Antonaccio 1995, 115.

93 Antonaccio 1995, 190–91; Deoudi 1999, 71–72; Mazarakis-Ainian 1999, 29–32; Boehringer 2001, 60–64; Laughy 2010, 265–67; Alexandridou 2018, 46.

94 Young 1939, 115–16, 194.

95 Brann 1961a, 125.

96 Brann 1962, 43, 54. Outside of Attica, the clearest example of revival are the Island Gems, which employ the amygdaloid and lentoid shapes of Bronze Age gemstones, and occasionally the iconography.

97 Benson 1970. For parallels, see also Hiller 1991; Hiller 2006. More cautious: Cavanagh and Mee 1995.

98 Kantor 1945/1999, 795–98 provides a cogent critique of the connections between Helladic and Orientalizing art. On Crete: Matthäus 2000a; Kourou 2011.

99 There was no need for Geometric images to depict epic, or a specific epic past, for them to assume a heroic coloring.

100 For example, there are only two fragments of Etruscan bucchero reported in Brann 1962 (106).

101 On networks, see Granovetter 1973; Granovetter 1983; Brughmans 2010; Knappett 2011; Malkin 2011; Rost 2011; Brughmans and Poblome 2015; Knappett 2017; Scott 2017; Yang, Keller and Zheng 2017; Peeples 2019.

102 On Italian dedications in Greek sanctuaries, see Baitinger 2015–16; Naso 2016; Naso 2017. On sanctuaries as networks, see, e.g., Kistler, Krieg, and Reichenbach 2015. For Athenian participation in the Olympic games, see Kyle 1987, nos. A 40, 50, 53, 60, 68.

103 On the passage, Naso 2017, 1682–83.

104 See also Knappett 2011. For the ways in which objects can participate in and shape the social, see Latour 2005, 63–86.

105 On the importance of Corinth, see already Coldstream 1977 [2003]: "Around 700 B.C., when the 'Orientalizing' Protoattic style was just beginning, it seems that the Athenians no longer had any direct access to oriental models; new ideas could reach them only at second hand, either through the more progressive vase-painting of Corinth, or through adaptations of oriental cauldrons made by other Greeks" (133). For an interesting but difficult interpretation of the Protocorinthian style, see Shanks 1999.

106 Brann 1962, 28. Further on the impact of Corinthian art and artists on Athens: Dunbabin 1950; Papadopoulos 2009.

107 Young 1942, 28–29.

108 Kübler 1959, 14–15, 126–31; Kübler 1970, 416–27.

109 Tübingen O.Z. 247 = 7447: Kübler 1954, 153–55, figs. 2–3; Kübler 1970, 75, 79–81, 83, 102, 123–26, 275, 294, 605, no. 216; *CVA* Tübingen 2, 39, fig. 23, plate 25.4–6; Rombos 1988, 192, 194. Munich, Antikensammlungen, missing (ex. Collezione Arndt): Friis Johansen 1923, 174, fig. 117; Buschor

1940, 23–24, fig. 25; Kübler 1954, 148–49, 155; Kübler 1970, 68, 87, 140, 605, no. 215; Rocco 2008, 78, no. BPa 18, plate 10.6. Munich, Antikensammlungen V.I. 761: Sieveking and Hackl 1912, 77, fig. 79, plate 28; Friis Johansen 1923, 174, fig. 117; Bakalakis 1961–62, 78, n. 2, plate 29; Kübler 1954, 149, 155; Kübler 1970, 68, 87, 605, no. 215; Neeft 1987, 65, n. 187, no. 9. Thessaloniki, Aristotle University, Cast Museum, uninventoried: Bakalakis 1961–62; *CVA* Thessaloniki, Aristotle University, Cast Museum, 28, fig. 10, plate 11, nos. 1–2; Rocco 2008, 56, 89, no. E5. Eleusis 882: BAPD 901906; Skias 1912, 32, 34, 36–37; Cook 1934–35, 183, fig. 6, 203; Coldstream 1968 [2008], 85; Kübler 1970, 593, no. 153; Rocco 2008, 68, 73, 78, no. BPa 24.

110 Papadopoulos 2003, 222–24; Papadopoulos 2009.

111 Athens, National Museum 2378: Friis Johansen 1923, 174, fig. 118.

112 Croissant 2010, 335: "L'enjeu n'était pas, en d'autres termes, de paraître 'plus exotique,' mais d'affirmer son originalité en donnant d'un motif déjà utilisé par d'autres Grecs une version nouvelle, particulièrement séduisante ou spectaculaire du point de vue formel." Croissant argues that Greek artisans, in a process of gradual stylistic development and in an atmosphere of competition and emulation among workshops, dipped into the repertoire of foreign objects to make works more seductive and spectacular. See also Coulié 2013, 107. Croissant's skepticism toward the typical interpretations of Orientalizing is salutary. However, he entirely neglects literary references to Near Eastern cultures and treats the evolution of style as uniform. His analysis cannot explain why not all pottery in Greece "Orientalizes."

113 Contrast Kistler, Krieg, and Reichenbach 2015.

114 Bibliography on these chronological issues is extensive: see, e.g., González de Canales, Serrano, and Llompart 2006; Sagona 2008; Bernardini 2016; Botto 2016. On the Phoenicians, see now the essays in Doak and López-Ruiz 2019. On western Phoenician establishments, see Aubet 1993. For Phoenicians in Iberia, see Dietler and López-Ruiz 2009. Some progress in resolving chronological conundrums may be solved not by changing Geometric pottery dates but by acknowledging the early movement of Levantine goods: see esp. Nijboer 2016, 36. Designating this phenomenon proto-Orientalizing, however, should be avoided, for it risks precluding local agency (d'Agostino 2010, 79).

115 See the balanced assessment in Gilboa 2013.

116 Sciacca 2010, 51, 58; Bartolini 2016, 144; Bernardini 2016, 13, 17, 25; Botto 2016.

117 Martelli 1991; Hölbl 2005, 123–26; Botto 2008a; Botto 2008b, 157–62; Nijboer 2008, 433–40; Pace 2008; Naso 2010, 185; Sciacca 2010, 45–51; Naso 2012, 185; Pace 2014; Melandri and Sirano 2016; Nijboer 2016; Botto 2017.

118 For the earliest Greek imports, see esp. Coldstream 2001; Kourou 2005; also Guzzo 2016. For a view that "pre-colonial" contacts with Greece were extensive, see Delpino 1989.

119 Dempster 1723–24 (published many years after writing). On the origins of the Etruscans, see Hdt. 1.94; Thuc. 4.109; Camporeale 2016, 72; Becker 2016; Ulf 2017.

120 On the princely tombs, see Holloway 1994, 156–64; d'Agostino 1999d; Bartolini et al. 2000; Sannibale 2014; Sannibale 2016. On the manipulation of foreign goods to suit local needs, see Feldman 2016.

121 On the Bernardini tomb, see Curtis 1919; Canciani and von Hase 1976; Colonna 1976, plates 44–56; Sannibale 2014.

122 Rome, Villa Giulia 61553, 61545, 61565: Aruz, Graff, and Rakic 2014, 319, 322, nos. 188–89, 192, with further bibliography. On Etruscan "Orientalizing," see also Pallottino 1965; Strøm 1971; Rathje 1979; Geppert 2006; Rathje 2010; Sannibale 2014; Menichetti 2017.

123 Von Hase 1995, 277–78; Aigner-Foresti 2000; Geppert 2006, 4–5; Nijboer 2008, 434–35; Sannibale 2013, 115.

124 Rathje 1983; Rathje 1988, 83–84.

125 Curtis 1919, 15; Markoe 1985, 127–48, esp. 138, 144, 146–48; Rathje 1986; Markoe 1992–93; Camporeale 2004b, 43–45; Dore 2003; Pace 2008, 101–2; Sciacca 2010; Sciacca 2015; Naso 2012; Botto 2017, 600–605.

126 On Pithekoussai, see esp. Buchner 1982; Ridgway 1992; Coldstream 1995; Coldstream 1998; d'Agostino 1999c; Hussein 2009; Carafa 2011; Mermati 2012b, 298–99; Nizzo 2016; Esposito 2018. Connections with Carthage: Docter and Niemeyer 1994; Ridgway 2000a; Ridgway 2000b.

127 For a seventh-century date for the *Iliad*, see West 1995; West 2011, 15–19. Nestor's cup (see chapter 6) still seems to me to support an eighth-century date for the Homeric epics.

128 On this point, see also Schwabl 1961, esp. 9, 13, 28–29.

129 Hall 1989, 19–55. But see Mackie 1996; Patzek 1996a; Patzek 1996b.

130 E.g., Homer *Il.* 9.379–384, 11.19–28.

131 On the Phoenicians in Homer, see esp. Winter 1995.

132 Homer *Od.* 3.286–302, 4.78–92, 4.120–32, 4.227–32, 4.611–19.

133 Homer *Od.* 13.256–86, 14.199–359, 17.415–44.

134 Thuc. 4.24.6, 6.2.1. On the geography of the *Odyssey*, see Bérard 1927–29; Wikén 1937, 30–36; Dickie 1995; Wolf 2009. Nakassis 2004 locates some of his wanderings in the east. On geography as a literary genre, see Romm 1992.

135 Homer *Od.* 10.25–26.

136 Homer *Od.* 5.55, 5.100–101.

137 Homer *Od.* 5.269–77.

138 Hesiod *Theog.* 1011–16; West 1971, 433: "it cannot be proved later than our *Odyssey*, but is likely enough to be so." On *nostoi*: Malkin 1998; Skinner 2012, 125–28.

139 For the influence of Near Eastern cultures on the form and content of Homer, see Burkert 1991a, 163–66, 169–74; Morris 1997; West 1997, 334–437.

140 Hdt. 4.152.

141 On Tarshish and Tartessos, see López-Ruiz 2009.

142 For the constitutive role of colonization in the west on the formation of the *polis* in Greece, see Malkin 1994; Malkin 2011.

143 Botto 2017, 596–98.

144 On the Cumae Group, see Friis Johansen 1923, 20–21; Payne 1931, 8–9; Heurtley and Robertson 1948, 33; Dunbabin and Roberston 1953, 174–75; Amyx 1988, 19–20; Denoyelle and Iozzo 2009, 48–49; Coulié 2013, 112, 133.

145 Naples 128199: *MonAnt* 22 (1913), 393, fig. 146; Payne 1931, 9, fig. 4; Cook 1997, plate 8c; Boardman 1998, fig. 167 (as inv. 128193).

146 Dik 1981b. Francesca Mermati argues that the Cumae Group designation is too broad. She defines an Ischia-Cumae-Tarquinia group, which she wants to restrict to those oinochoai with fish or snakes (Mermati 2007, 317–35; Mermati 2012a, 148). Similarly, Cuozzo 2003, 54–55. For more expansive conceptions, see, e.g., Denoyelle and Iozzo 2009, 49: "Ce côté fantastique des éléments figurés, très proches de ceux de la céramique corinthienne, mais avec un traitement du décor difficile à situer dans la sphère proprement corinthienne, ainsi que, du point de vue technique, l'usage limité des incisions, constituent les traits distinctifs du style de la céramique figurée de Cumes." Tarquinia RC 2102: *CVA* Tarquinia 3, 11, plate 5.1–2 (attributed to the Bocchoris Workshop)—Pithekoussai 168828: Buchner and Ridgway 1993, 701 Sp 3/1, plate 242; Denoyelle and Iozzo 2009, 47, fig. 36; Mermati 2012a, Scheda A 184.

147 Mermati 2009–12, 104.

148 Kerameikos 81: Kübler 1970, 509–10, no. 122, plate 1.

149 Callipolitis-Feytmans 1963, 421–25, no. 7 (no. 1083), figs. 12–13.

150 See Chapter 1, n. 113, above.

151 New York, Metropolitan Museum of Art, 21.88.18: Cook 1934–35, 184–85, plate 50; Moore 2003, 7, 15–23, 26, 28, 32–35, figs. 3–9, plate 1; *CVA* The Metropolitan Museum of Art 5, 66–69, plates 39–41; Rocco 2008, 77, no. Pa 1. Kerameikos 73: Kübler 1970, 428–30, no. 20, plates 10–11.

152 Cogan and Tadmor 1977, 68; Novotny and Jeffers 2018, 41. See also Prism A, which claims that none of the kings before Assurbanipal had heard of Lydia, "a remote place" (Novotny and Jeffers 2018, 237).

153 On the mobility of artists, see further chapter 5.

CHAPTER 4 INTERACTION AT THE GRAVE

1   Mylonas 1957; Mylonas 1975, vol. 1, 91–92, vol. 3, plate Γ, figs. 222–24; Rocco 2008, 140, no. P4.

2   Grethlein 2018, 77–85 is the latest example of a treatment of the object that ignores context.

3   For cultural biographies of vases, see, e.g., Langdon 2001; Papadopoulos and Smithson 2002; Verdan 2015; Charalambidou 2018.

4   On this type of monochromatic vase, see Kourou 1987; Kourou 1988; Kokkou-Vyridi 1999, 69. Specifically on the object accompanying the Polyphemus Amphora, see Kourou 1987, 42, no. 40.

5   I. Morris 1987, e.g., 105. Important critical reviews include d'Agostino and d'Onofrio 1993 and Papadopoulos 1993.

6   Whitley 1991, 8; Whitley 1994b.

7   Whitley adduces as an ethnographic parallel tribal groups in Nuristan (Afghanistan) (Whitley 1994b, 59; see also Whitley 1991, 192–93), but elders there closely monitored the consumption and display of goods and symbols, and objects across ranks maintained formal similarity with varying degrees of elaboration. For example, the number of bells on a bowl or iron bars on a table indicated rank at a feast. There is no parallel in seventh-century Athens and Attica either for consistent symbols of rank or for any authority that could enforce display.

8   See Chapter 1, n. 83, above.

9   See also 58, above.

10 I. Morris 1987, 222–33; Whitley 1994b, 68–70; d'Onofrio 1997, 79–84. Doronzio 2018, 59 provides a link to her very informative database, but it focuses on the Kerameikos. Kakavoyianni and Petrocheilos 2020 appeared shortly before this book went to press. I discuss some of the graves below, but I have not been able to completely address their findings nor add the data to my graphs, charts, and table 1. See further n. 44, below.

11 Consider, for example, Rocco's reworking of Cook's tripartite chronological scheme (Rocco 2008, 11–12), or the problems of dating sub-Geometric graves.

12 I thank Sarah Norvell for her assistance with this research.

13 Unfortunately, osteological data for determining age are rarely available and a categorization more precise than "infants and young children" not possible. In Classical Athens, at age three an individual was considered no longer a baby and participated in the Choes festival for the first time, and Papadopoulos sees some evidence in the agora that two and a half to three years marked a difference in mortuary treatment in the Early Iron Age (see Papadopoulos 2017, 658–59). The osteological study at Palaia Kokkinia showed that the deceased in a seventh-century funeral urn was two and a half to three and a half years old (Arrington, Spyropoulos, and Brellas 2021). It would seem that the upper age date could only go so far, since corpses had to fit into the funeral urns, so five to six years old may represent an upper limit for the inhumation in a jar of a "young child." The dead in the large Polyphemus Amphora, however, was reported to be ten to twelve years old.

14 Mylonas 1957, 4–5.

15 But Alexandridou 2016 rightly emphasizes the unprecedented variability in this period, and cremation, usually secondary, did persist.

16 Shallow pits for primary cremations are well-attested in Athens and Attica, e.g., Pelekidis 1916, 17–18; Kallipoliti 1964, 118–24; Skilarnti 1975, 107, 115; Karagiorga-Stathakopoulou 1978; Arapogianni 1985.

17 Kübler 1959, 22.

18 Doronzio 2018, 55–162, writing about the Kerameikos, also emphasizes variety.

19 Agora N 11:1; Brann 1960, 413–14, plate 88; Brann 1962, 129; Coldstream 1968 [2008], 84.

20 Children: Kerameikos graves V-63, VI-15, VI-16, VI-17, and LZB. Kübler 1954, 254, plates 10, 100, 127; Rocco 2008, 108, no. KB 9—Kübler 1959, 32–33, 135–39, fig. 7, plates 35–36, 47, 61–62, Beil. 1–2, 16–18, 37—von Freytag 1975, 76–81, figs. 15–16, plates 22–23; Rocco 2008, 179 nos. K 1, 2, 3, 4, 5, 6; Doronzio 2018, 82–84, table 1. Adults: Kerameikos VI-9, VI-74 = XII-4 and Rb 13 A, XI-5 = Rb 13 B, Kerameikos XII-6 = RB 5. Kübler 1959, 18–21, 131–33, fig. 1, plates 4–12,

22–26, 38–46, 60, 67, Beil. 1, 7–9; Kübler 1970, 427–48, plates 10–29; Kistler 1998, 185–88; Rocco 2008, 155, no. Or 1, 164, nos. KMG 3 and 8–1, 168, nos. Op β 1–3—Kübler 1959, 79; Knigge 1980, 77, figs. 1, 7, plate 18.2—Knigge 1980, 77, figs. 1, 7—Knigge 1980, 61–63, 77, figs. 1, 7.

21 Callipolitis-Feytmans 1963.

22 *Thorikos* 1977/1982, 79–83, figs. 76–90; Rocco 2008, 124, no. V 5.

23 E.g., Kübler 1959, 30–32, 51–53, fig. 16, plates 7–12, 20–26, 28, 41–43, Beil. 1; Kübler 1970, 491–92, plates 77–79.

24 Athens, National Museum 807: Brückner and Pernice 1893, 133–34, fig. 30.

25 Grave VI: Skias 1912, 32–33, 39, fig. 14; Rocco 2008, 101, no. W 5.

26 Kübler 1959, 75–76, 148–49; Kübler 1970, 509–12; Rocco 2008, 101–2, no. W 19; d'Onofrio 2017, 268–71; Doronzio 2018, 115, figs. 101–2.

27 Trachones A 8, A 12, A 30.1: Geroulanos 1973, 28–29, plates 12.4, 20; Neeft 1987, 91, List XXXVI, no. 7—Geroulanos 1973, 29–30, plates 12.3, 19; Neeft 1987, 91, List XXXVI, no. 3, 92, List XXXII, no. 7; Rocco 2008, 60, no. Av 1, plate 6.6—Geroulanos 1973, 34–35, plates 13, 18; Neeft 1987, 41, List IX, nos. 11 and 39, List VI, no. 3; Steinhauer 2001, 89, fig. 109.

28 Pelekidis 1916, 25, 49–64; Keramopoullos 1923; Karali and Tsaliki 2011.

29 On the excavation, see Archaeology in Greece Online Report ID 6141 https://chronique.efa.gr/ ?kroute=report&id=6141; Alexandropoulou 2018; Alexandropoulou 2019; Chryssoulaki 2019; Ingvarsson and Bäckström 2019. On the date of the grave, see Alexandroupoulou 2019, 265, n. 50. On the cemetery, see also Fragkopoulou 2019.

30 In Ingvarsson and Bäckström 2019, Chryssoulaki conjectures that it was hidden in a boot (11).

31 www.kathimerini.gr/856663/article/politismos/polh/oi-80-desmwtes-elkoyn-episthmones. On the health of the bodies, see also Chryssoulaki 2019, 113, without making a connection to Cylon; Ingvarsson and Bäckström 2019.

32 Ingvarsson and Bäckström 2019, 61–73.

33 Ingvarsson and Bäckström 2019, 78.

34 Ingvarsson and Bäckström 2019, 79.

35 Mounds θ, I, L, N, Π, P: Kübler 1959, 21, 24, 31, 39, 53, 66.

36 Kübler 1959, 89–90. For mud brick structures at Phaleron, see Alexandropoulou 2019, 266–67.

37 *ArchDelt* 39 (1984), 43–45; *ArchDelt* 42 (1987), 96–97.

38 Skias 1912, 32–33, 39.

39 Alexandropoulou 2019, 263; Chryssoulaki 2019, 111–13.

40 Arapogianni 1985, 207.

41 Kerameikos Grave 169: von Freytag 1975.

42 New York, Metropolitan Museum of Art 14.146.3a, 14.146.3b, allegedly from Olympos: Boardman 1955, 58, no. 1; Richter 1942, 83–84, figs. 4–6.

43 On the funeral trenches, see esp. Kistler 1998; Alexandridou 2015; Doronzio 2018, 154–57. See also Junker 2018, for a comparison with the potlatch ceremony.

44 Trenches at Chalandri (Pologiorgi 2003–9, 182–84) and Palaia Phokaia (*ArchDelt* 42 [1987] 96–97; Alexandridou 2015, 138; Kakavoyianni and Petrocheilos 2020, 271–72, 285) have started to enter the literature as Opferrinnen (e.g., Alexandridou 2016, 335; Doronzio 2018, 148), but I am dubious. At Chalandri, a trench next to and above the primary cremation of an adult was preserved for 1.15 m. The walls of the trench were burnt and the burnt remains of three vessels were in and around it. But there were no signs of post holes, mud bricks were only located at one end of the trench, and burning seems to have concentrated near the other end. This seems to be a different ritual, more in line with an offering place (Opferplatz) or ceremonial pyre than the formalized Opferrinne of the Kerameikos. The situation at Palaia Phokaia (ancient Anavyssos) is also unclear. Three primary cremations were accompanied by trenches of some sort. Grave 5 (Kakavoyianni and Petrocheilos 2020, 29–30) is a primary cremation in a pit, next to which is a trench with partial burning. The only two cataloged finds, however, are from the cremation pit, not from the trench. Grave 6 (Kakavoyianni and Petrocheilos 2020, 31–37) is a primary cremation in a pit 2.10 m long, and outside of it there are two trenches, but without any mention of burning. Seven Protoattic vases and four Early Protocorinthian vases are cataloged,

but it is not clear where they were deposited. In the primary cremation pit itself were found the bones of an infant, which is odd for a few reasons. Cremations of infants were very rare, and the frail bones would not be likely to survive a cremation fire. The size of the pit also seems more fitting for an adult cremation. Grave 8 also is curious (Kakavoyianni and Petrocheilos 2020, 37–53). A primary cremation pit 1.80 m long had a trench next to it. A pit 0.50 × 0.3 × 0.12 m was dug *into* this trench, and it contained the bones of a small child and over a dozen Protoattic vases and figurines. No finds are reported from the cremation pit or the trench itself. All of this evidence, only recently published in full, merits close consideration, but it does not seem to be a straightforward case of Opferrinnen close in form and practice to the Kerameikos. The evidence at a third site, Vari, is also difficult to evaluate because of the looting of the graves and the incomplete and often incoherent publication. The material associated with the trench is overwhelmingly black-figure, with only one Protoattic vase. Alexandridou (2012, 2015, 2017) provides the most cogent presentation of the evidence and argues for the use of the offering trench over a period of time.

45 But see also Papadopoulos 2017, 609–17, discussing "simple pyres." Following Evelyn Smithson, he suggests that some of the pits may have been cut into the earth after cremation, which would explain some of the absence of evidence for in situ burning.

46 Offering place outside of mounds: Kübler 1959, 92.

47 Conversely, pyres that were primary cremations may be misconstrued in scholarship as ceremonial. Republishing pottery from Phaleron, Young maintained that the pyres there contained no bones and instead were used in connection with jar burials (Young 1942, 24, n. 8). But in this cemetery, in fact, only one jar burial (undated) was in close proximity to a pyre, which did contain bones (Pelekidis 1916, 20 [Grave 11]). Ian Morris classified Phaleron as a large cemetery for children, but including pyres yields many adult burials there as well, not to mention the mass burials.

48 Vierneisel 1964, 434–35, 441–42, fig. 29; Rocco 2008, 101, no. W 7; Doronzio 2018, 63, fig. 9.

49 Jar burials α, γ, δ, στ, η, and κ: Arapogianni 1985, 214–20.

50 Grave VI: Skias 1912, 32–33, 39, fig. 14.

51 Grave Δ7: Mylonas 1975, vol. 1, 181–82, vol. 3, plates Δ, 277α, β, δ. Near graves Z9 and Z10: Mylonas 1975, vol. 1, 271.

52 Grave T. 45: Pelekidis 1916, 16–17.

53 Morris 1987, 22; Houby-Nielsen 1992; Houby-Nielsen 1995; Houby-Nielsen 1996, esp. 44; Alexandridou 2009, 497; Duplouy, Mariaud, Polignac 2010, 287; Brisart 2011, 136–49; Haug 2012, 556; Alexandridou 2015, 121–22. Even the excellent discussion in Doronzio 2018 of the variety of burials in Athens in the seventh century only treats the Kerameikos.

54 See n. 44, above.

55 Kistler 1998, 9; Doronzio 2018, 162.

56 Alexandropoulou 2019, plate 74.

57 I. Morris 1987, 22. See also the criticism of this view in Alexandropoulou 2019.

58 I. Morris 1987, 219.

59 Arapogianni 1985.

60 "Report of the Managing Committee for Session 1895–1896," *Annual of the British School at Athens* 2 (1895–96): 8, 22–25. For more recent work at the site, see Archaeology in Greece Online (https://chronique.efa.gr), Report IDs 2136, 2137, 5332, 6116. For a synopsis of excavation in the area, see Doronzio 2018, 229–47.

61 Smith 1902.

62 Droop 1905–6; Coldstream 2003.

63 Philadelpheus 1920–21, 131.

64 See Alexandridou 2017a, with further bibliography.

65 For bibliography on the piece, see Rocco 2008, 28, no. An 11.

66 *Ergon* 1960, 30–37; *Bulletin de correspondance héllenique* 85 (1961) 626–30; *Ergon* 1961, 37–38.

67 Xagorari-Gleissner 2005, 42–43 (Grave 4), 43–45 ("Grave 5"), 60–61 (Grave 17), 49, no. 64, 79, no. 200, 84, no. 223, 85, no. 227, 86, no. 233, 87, nos. 237, 241.

68 *AAA* 1 (1968), 31–35 (31 for the Protoattic reference); *ArchDelt* 25 (1970) 127–29 (129 for the amphora reference). See also Vivliodetis 2007, 167–69.

69 Keramopoullos 1923, 5–6. Some of these vases seem to have gone to the British Museum (e.g., Figures 2.7, 2.13) in 1865: Smith 1884, 176; Böhlau 1887, 47, n. 15; Chryssoulaki 2019, 104.

70 Kourouniotis 1911, 246. Keramopoullos 1923, 5, n. 1, attributes the damage to Bournias's excavations, but it seems from the early reports he records that there was indeed other looting.

71 See n. 29, above.

72 Ingvarsson and Bäckström 2019, 8.

73 *CVA* New York, Metropolitan Museum of Art 5, 56–63, plates 31–37; Rocco 2008, 60–61, nos. Av 8, Av 9.

74 *ArchDelt* 29 (1973–74), 85, plates 73d–e; I. Morris 1987, 230, no. 61; Rocco 2008, 30, nos. BAn 10–11.

75 *ArchDelt* 19 (1964), 58–60.

76 Callipolitis-Feytmans 1963, 404–12 (Tombs IV–VI); Coldstream 1968 [2008], 84.

77 On the sensory experiences of cremation, see Williams 2004; Williams 2015; Sørensen and Bille 2015.

78 On the shallow topsoil, see Mylonas 1975, vol. 1, 6.

79 Young 1951, 78, 86.

80 Brann 1959b. Doronzio 2018, 213–15 speculates that the material came from a sanctuary, but the chariot scene on one of the vases is more appropriate for a grave, and Brann, who worked on the material and had also published sanctuary finds, deemed that the vases came from a cemetery.

81 Houby-Nielsen argues that much of the variation may be due to changing attitudes to age and gender: "Social hierarchies are difficult to reconstruct, since 'poor' burial does not necessarily represent a low-status person in daily life, but a person of a certain age and gender role which it was not thought important to manifest in a burial context" (Houby-Nielsen 1995, 145). In Houby-Nielsen 1992, she interprets the variation at the Kerameikos through changes in the ideology within an elite group.

82 I. Morris 1987, 95–96.

83 Kourou 1988 discusses the possible contents of so-called Argive monochrome ware, noting the type's appearance in sanctuaries of Hera or Demeter and its association with vegetation and with chthonic deities. She suggests it may have contained a sedative, perhaps opium.

84 For a phiale, see Parlama and Stampolidis 2000, 279, no. 254.

85 Athens, National Museum 14965: Young 1942, 36, no. 48.3, fig. 19; Rocco 2008, 101 no. W 12. Oxford, Ashmolean 1887.3402: *CVA* Oxford, Ashmolean Museum 4, 11, plates 28.7–8. Athens, National Museum 307: Rocco 2008, 78, no. BPa 10.

86 Piraeus 15843: Arrington, Spyropoulos, and Brellas 2021. Athens, National Museum 26747: Xagorari 1996, 80, no. 17, plate 14; Rocco 2008, 186, no. Op ζ 22; Coulié 2013, 221, fig. 218.

87 Surveys of the various interpretations of the ritual can also be found in Kistler 1998, 20–30; Alexandridou 2015, 139–41. For an attempt to look at Phaleron Ware, but with a different approach than I adopt, see Fragkopoulou and Zosi 2017.

88 Hampe 1960, 71–75.

89 d'Onofrio 1993, esp. 148–50.

90 Houby-Nielsen 1992; Houby-Nielsen 1995; Houby-Nielsen 1996.

91 Whitley 1994b, esp. 52.

92 Whitley 1991, 8; Whitley 1994a, 217–18, 222–26.

93 Kistler 1998, 41–42, 49.

94 See esp. Alexandridou 2009; Alexandridou 2015, 142–43.

95 Brisart 2011, 146–49.

96 See the critiques in Dietler and Herbich 1998; Knappett 2005; Boivin 2008, 1–29, 82–128.

97 Perhaps most famously Gell 1998. See also Osborne and Tanner 2007.

98 Warnier 2001; Warnier 2006 (quotation from 187). See also Knappett, Malafouris, and Tomkins 2010. On style and practice, see also Feldman 2014.

99 Knappett 2005, 85–106, 113–16, 143–56.

100 For the funeral banquet at the grave in the Late Geometric period, see Young 1939, 112. On the *perideipnon*, see Garland 1985, 38–41, 146. Small animals and shells were placed on the platforms in the offering trenches: Kübler 1959, 83–84; Doronzio 2018, 138–40, tables 17–19. For meals at the tomb, see also d'Onofrio 1993, 148–50. For a horse burial in the Kerameikos, see Kerameikos XII-8 = Rb 9, Knigge 1980, 78 and Doronzio 2018, 118–19, and for horses at Phaleron (undated), Alexandropoulou 2019, 268.

101 See Garland 1985, 38–41, 104–05, 146, 166, for the occasions for rituals at the tomb, including the Genesia and Nemesia festivals. See also Parker 2005, 470, 476.

102 Arrington, Spyropoulos, and Brellas 2021.

103 *Thorikos* 1977/1982, 96–102, figs. 127–46.

104 More oinochoai have been attributed to Protoattic hands than any other shape apart from amphoras (according to data I compiled from Rocco 2008), and since so many oinochoai are sub-Geometric, the numbers are underreported.

105 See also the study of Early Bronze Age burials in Ireland and Britain in Brück 2004, downplaying claims of social status in the mortuary record and looking at how material culture fostered interpersonal connections.

106 For the impact of the *polis* on social communities, see Brisart 2011; Alexandridou 2016.

107 So, too, some of the decorated vases. A fine ware louterion from Thebes has many ancient repairs, suggesting that by the time it was used, it had accrued layers of meaning for the mourners and was a prized personal possession. Athens, National Museum 238: Böhlau 1887, 34, plate 4; Cook 1934–35, 174, plate 42b; Rocco 2008, 119, no. LT 9; Coulié 2013, 191, fig. 186. Rocco 2008, 206, says that it had a cemetery context, but a sanctuary context was probably also possible. There are also ancient repairs on the standed bowl attributed to the Polyphemus Painter (Figure 6.10, Rocco 2008, 206).

108 Ian Hodder's notion of entanglement may be useful here, with multiple threads connecting people, objects, practices, and sites: Hodder 2011; Hodder 2012.

109 Zeitlin 1996, 65; Ebbinghaus 2005; Steiner 2013.

110 See Zeitlin 1996, 65.

111 Rotroff 2015, 182.

112 Piraeus 14260: Arrington, Spyropoulos, and Brellas 2021. See also Kerameikos Tomb LZB: von Freytag 1975, 76–81, figs. 15–16, plates 22–23; Rocco 2008, 179, nos. K 1, 2, 3, 4, 5, 6; Doronzio 2018, 82–83, table 8.

113 Kübler 1954, 242, plates 13, 33, 76, 99, 120; Coldstream 1968 [2008], 74.

114 Kübler 1954, 242–43, plates 81, 88, 107, 108, 121, 145.

115 Kübler 1954, 240–42, plates 79, 132–34, 136–38; Kistler 1998, 180–83; Doronzio 2018, 74–75.

116 Kübler 1954, 271, plates 82, 132, 139; Doronzio 2018, 78.

117 Kübler 1954, 272, plates 81, 106, 132; Doronzio 2018, 78.

118 E.g., Hurwit 1985, 125.

119 It might be useful to think of the community as stratified rather than ranked. See further Whitley 1991 and Whitley 2019b.

120 Similarly Whitley 1994b, 60.

121 Brisart 2010.

122 Donlan 1980, 49–64; Murray 1980, 80; Murray 1983; Murray 1991; Kistler 1998, 65–77. On changes in subject matter, see also Haug 2012.

123 Raaflaub 1997 (with further bibliography on the topic) argues that the hoplite phalanx underwent a long and gradual development, with a formalization and perfection circa 650, within the context of the development of the *polis*.

124 For arguments that debate took place only within elite, see Foxhall 1997, or Morris's notion of the middling (I. Morris 2000, 155–91).

125 For urbanization and its impact on the landscape, see d'Onofrio 2017, 261; Doronzio 2018; Dimitriadou 2019.

126 Morris 1987, 94. For some of the problems (and proposed solutions) to identifying and
      analyzing the elite, particularly in the Classical period, see Ober 1989, 11–17. For the (changing)
      ancient terminology to designate the elite, see Fouchard 2010.

127 Van Wees and Fisher 2015; Duplouy 2006; Duplouy, Mariaud, and Polignac 2010; Duplouy 2015.
      Benedetto Bravo's work on the instability of the *aristoi* is also relevant; Węcowski 2014, 23–25
      provides a cogent summary. See also the criticism of aristocracy and the elite in Ulf 2001, who
      sees the *polis* as prerequisite. And Donlan 1980 has seen an evolving aristocratic ideal as a
      defensive and increasingly self-conscious attempt to prove superiority and impose values. For a
      historiography, see also Giangulio 2016.

128 Duplouy 2011. See also Duplouy 2018a; Duplouy 2019b.

129 Prost 2010 provides some intellectual context for Duplouy 2009 and argues that he overem-
      phasizes individual mobility at the expense of efforts in the late seventh century to define
      groups. Ma 2016 provides an excellent analysis of the ways in which an elitist-
      entrepreneurial-individual model emerged in scholarship in response to conventional
      narratives of state formation and also highlights some of its shortcomings. As for the term
      Eupatridai, which first occurs in the late sixth century but is used to describe seventh-
      century social structure, Duplouy 2003 argues that, rather than a synonym for *eugeneis*, it
      has greater resonance with a place and political system (the *patris*) than a father. He relates it
      to the antityrannical sentiments and the philosophical preoccupations of fifth-century
      thinkers rather than to the existence of noble lineage. See also Fouchard 2010, 368–79.
      Contrast Pierrot 2015, who maintains the conventional view. Further on lineage and social
      structure, and on the related problem of the *genos*: Calhoun 1934; Bourriot 1976; Roussel
      1976; Lambert 1999. Laughy 2010 argues compellingly that individuals and families retained
      a prominent role in founding, sponsoring, and enacting festivals and sanctuaries during the
      process of *polis* formation.

130 [Arist.] *Ath. Pol.* 3.

131 On the Cylonian affair, see Chapter 1, above.

132 For scholarship on the poor in ancient Greece, including problems of definition, see Osborne
      2006a; Morch 2012; Galbois and Rougier-Blanc 2014; Werlings 2014. Discussion tends to
      privilege texts (e.g., Ndoye 2010).

133 Thgn. 315–18: πολλοί τοι πλουτοῦσι κακοί, ἀγαθοὶ δὲ πένονται· / ἀλλ' ἡμεῖς τούτοις οὐ
      διαμειψόμεθατῆς / τῆς ἀρετῆς τὸν πλοῦτον, ἐπεὶ τὸ μὲν ἔμπεδον αἰεί, / χρήματα δ' ἀνθρώπων
      ἄλλοτε ἄλλος ἔχει.

134 E.g. Thgn. 1059–62, 1109–14.

135 Solon fr. 15 (Loeb), l. 4: χρήματα δ' ἀνθρώπων ἄλλοτε ἄλλος ἔχει.

136 Thgn. 173–78.

137 Tyrtaios fr. 10 (Loeb); Mimnermos fr. 2 (Loeb).

138 For the poor becoming rich, see also, in addition to the passages below, Anacreon Fr. 388.

139 Archil. fr. 130 (Loeb).

140 Semon. fr. 1, ll. 6–10 (Loeb), trans. D. E. Gerber: ἐλπὶς δὲ πάντας κἀπιπειθείη τρέφει / ἄπρηκτον
      ὁρμαίνοντας· οἱ μὲν ἡμέρην / μένουσιν ἐλθεῖν, οἱ δ' ἐτέων περιτροπάς· / νέωτα δ' οὐδεὶς ὅστις
      οὐ δοκεῖ βροτῶν / πλούτῳ τε κἀγαθοῖσιν ἵξεσθαι φίλος.

141 Solon fr. 13, ll. 41–43 (Loeb), trans. D. E. Gerber: εἰ δέ τις ἀχρήμων, πενίης δέ μιν ἔργα βιᾶται, /
      κτήσεσθαι πάντως χρήματα πολλὰ δοκεῖ. / σπεύδει δ' ἄλλοθεν ἄλλος.

142 Cf. Thgn. 179–80, advising Cyrnus to search over land and sea to escape poverty.

143 Arist. *Pol.* 2.1274a.15–21; Arist. [*Ath. Pol.*] 7.3–4; Leão and Rhodes 2015, 127–29. Van Wees and
      Fisher 2015, 10 dispute this view of an emergent "class," but this requires rather untenable
      readings of Theognis and downplays the role of commercial enterprise and the consequences of
      hoplite warfare, which may not have been an invention of the seventh century but does become
      more central to communities at this time.

144 Solon fr. 36 (Loeb); [Arist.] *Ath. Pol.* 5; Plut. *Vit. Sol.* 13.

145 Dem. 43.62–63; Cic. *Leg.* 2.59, 63–66; Plut. *Vit. Sol.* 21.5–7. Leão and Rhodes 2015, 116–21 gather
      and discuss the sources.

146 On the prototypes, see Amiran 1970, plate 92, nos. 5, 8; Bikai 1978, 36; Nuñez 1997, 316–20, 365, figs. 179, 250; Taloni 2015. For the Phaleron jugs in Attica, see Petrocheilos 1996.

147 Illustrated: d'Agostino 1977, 20–23, no. L 66, fig. 20, plate 19. For the products from Tarquinia and Caere, see also Taloni 2015, 126.

148 In such a model, the elite distinguished themselves from the nonelite through their taste, and the nonelite imitated their superiors, who subsequently had to evolve new forms of distinction to separate themselves from the masses. It was an endless cycle, complicated by competition within the elite for distinction. For this type of model, see Simmel 1904 [1957]; Bourdieu 1984, and cf. Morris 1987, 16, fig. 4. On the dominant role of the elite in Early Iron Age cultural change, see, e.g., Arafat and Morgan 1989, 336; Matthäus 1993; Raaflaub 2004; Langdon 2008, 119; Broodbank 2013, 519; Kistler, Krieg, and Reichenbach 2015; Bohen 2017. On the sociology of elite distinction, see Daloz 2010. Brumfiel 1992 situates the focus on the elite in archaeology within the ecosystem approach and advocates greater attention to social negotiation, including subelite. For the Roman context, Wallace-Hadrill 2008 challenges the top-down model of cultural change and argues for a realignment of identities and construction of power within Roman society. But it was not strictly a bottom-up process, either: "the elite is challenged by groups immediately below and outside the elite, which successfully establish their claim to belong to a redefined elite" (36).

149 The most recent and extensive discussion of conspicuous consumption and the elite, focusing on the later Archaic and Classical periods, is Filser 2017.

150 Kistler 1998, 185–88.

151 See Chapter 2, n. 146, above.

152 Early Protoattic vases by painters other than the Analatos Painter with evidence for external dating: Merenda 1610: Xagorari-Gleissner 2005, 42, no. 18, plate 7d. Athens, National Museum VS 179: Cook 1934–35, 176–78, 203, plates 45, 46a; Cook 1947, 141–42; Brokaw 1963, 71, fig. 34.2, 5; Tölle-Kastenbein 1964, 22, no. 57, plate 19; Coldstream 1968 [2008], 85; Fittschen 1969, 95, no. R 11; Kübler 1970, 23, 26, 32 n. 21, 42, 49, 53, 64, 89–90, 103–6, 114–15, 241 n. 299, 294–97, 599 no. 188; Rombos 1988, 62, 252, 349; Rocco 2008, 31–32, 34, 37, 39, no. Me 11, plate 4.3, 5. Athens, National Museum VS 534: Cook 1934–35, 203; Cook 1947, 142, fig. 3; Kübler 1970, 60, 103–4, 106, 166, 295, 602 no. 203; Burke 1974, 65; Schiffler 1976, 244, no. A 11; Rocco 2008, 39, no. Me 30. Athens, National Museum 18497: Cook 1934–35, 203; Cook 1947, 142 n. 1; Rocco 2008, 40, no. BMe 11. Thorikos TC 71.1443: *Thorikos* 8 (1972/1976), 120–25, no. 56, figs. 69–70, 72–73; Rocco 2008, 61, no. Wü 6, plate 7.2. Frankfurt am Main, VF β 231a: *CVA* Frankfurt am Main 1, 15, plate 10.5–6; Coldstream 1968 [2008], 85; Kübler 1970, 49, 108–9, 123, 635, no. 365; Rocco 2008, 107, no. KB 1, plate 15.5. Eleusis 935: Skias 1898, 91; Friis Johansen 1923, 40; Cook 1934–35, 185; Coldstream 1968 [2008], 85; Kübler 1970, 611, no. 247; Rocco 2008, 92, no. Acr 3, plate 13.1. Athens, National Museum VS 63: Cook 1934–35, 176–78, 203, plate 46b–c; Cook 1947, 141–42; Brokaw 1963, 71, plate 34.3, 6; Kübler 1950, 10, plate 11; Coldstream 1968 [2008], 85; Kübler 1970, 23–24, 75, 79, 82, 88–90, 103, 106, 114, 123, 128, 132, 135, 137, 145 n. 6, 257–59, 294, 296–97, 306, 600, no. 191; Rombos 1988, 191, 252; Rocco 2008, 26, n. 122, 33, 36–38, 39, no. Me 12, plate 4.2. Athens, National Museum 14957: Pelekidis 1916, 39, no. 65, fig. 37; Friis Johansen 1923, 39, 52, n. 7; Young 1942, 27–28, fig. 4; Kübler 1970, 61, 173, 613, nos. 256–57; *Perachora* II, 128, n. 2; Brokaw 1964, 53, figs. 11–12; Dierichs 1981, 89, 90, 97, no. AV 12; Neeft 1987, 108, LIII, no. E 1; Rocco 2008, 50, 51, 53, 61, no. BWü 3, plate 8.2. Athens, National Museum 14957 (distinct from the preceding entry; all items from the Phaleron grave received the same inventory number): Pelekidis 1916, 39, no. 65, fig. 37; Friis Johansen 1923, 39, 52, n. 7; Young 1942, 27–28, fig. 4; Kübler 1970, 61, 173, 613, nos. 256–57; *Perachora* II, 128, n.2; Brokaw 1964, 53, figs. 11–12; Dierichs 1981, 89, 90, 97, no. AV 13; Neeft 1987, 108, LIII, no. E 1; Rocco 2008, 50, 51, 53, 61, no. BWü 4.

153 On the resilience, resourcefulness, and creativity of the poor, see the reading of Harvey and Reed 1996 of Oscar Lewis's subculture of poverty thesis (Lewis 1968, with further references).

154 On mercenaries as nonelite, see Luraghi 2006.

155 Schapiro 1962 [1994], 62.

156 Schapiro 1962 [1994], 62.

157 Kerameikos 149: Kübler 1970, 456–59, plates 38–42; Rocco 2008, 196, no. Op γI 4, plate 30.1.
158 Kistler 1998.
159 Halnon 2002. For trickle-up processes, see also Daloz 2010, 148–49.
160 https://media.daimler.com/marsMediaSite/en/instance/ko/Mercedes-Benz-Vans-expands
      -product-range-Mercedes-Benz-Concept-X-CLASS--First-outlook-on-the-new-pickup-bearing
      -the-three-pointed-star.xhtml?oid=14171033. Accessed February 13, 2019.
161 Morris 1996b; Morris 1998, 26–27, 30; Morris 2000, 155–91.
162 Morris 1987, 41.
163 Athens, National Museum 551: Dumont 1869; Dumont 1888, 101, fig. 37; Böhlau 1887, 46–47, figs.
      6–7; Rocco 2008, 79, no. C 1; Coulié 2013, 189, fig. 182.
164 See Chapter 1, n. 1, above.
165 Cook 1934–35, 185.
166 Agora P 26556: Brann 1962, 89, no. 512, plate 31; Papadopoulos 2003, 169.

CHAPTER 5 ARTISTS AND THEIR STYLES

1   Rocco 2008.
2   On Beazley and his method, see Arrington 2017, with further bibliography.
3   Cook 1962.
4   E.g., Whitley 1997; Whitley 2018.
5   Athens, National Museum 322: Böhlau 1887, 52, fig. 14; Rocco 2008, 160, no. B 2.
6   Similarly, Neer 1997, 26 asks why some pots assert the importance of their makers; why and
      how some have an "author-effect."
7   See also the analysis in Sapirstein 2013; Sapirstein 2014. Coulié 2015 has revisited the hands in
      the workshop of the Dipylon Master.
8   Coldstream 1968 [2008], 29–90.
9   Rocco 2008.
10   Archaeological Museum of Eleusis, 935: Rocco 2008, 92, no. Acr 3.
11   Kerameikos 4278: von Freytag 1975, 79, no. 4, plates 22.3, 23.2, 23.5; Rocco 2008, 170, no. K 2.
12   Rocco 2008, 11–12.
13   Rocco 2008, 221–22.
14   Pithekoussai 239083: Pugliese Carratelli 1996, 666, no. 22; Coldstream 2000, 94, fig. 7;
      Denoyelle and Iozzo 2009, 10, 37–38, plate III; Mermati 2012a, 198–99. Signatures appear on
      Greek vases for the first time in the latest eighth and seventh century, on objects from Naxos,
      Thera, Chios, Ithaka, Ischia, Etruria, Selinunte, Pithekoussai, Old Smyrna, and Selinunte.
      See the corpus in Wachter 2001.
15   Rocco 2008, 200. There are some exceptions, e.g., the Group of Opferplatz α/IV: Rocco 2008,
      41–44.
16   I exclude from this discussion a tantalizing dipinto on a votive plaque attributed to the
      Analatos Painter from the sanctuary of Apollo at Aigina, which reads "sonos epist." Cook
      translated it as a claim by an artist with a name ending "sonos" to have made the piece
      "skillfully/expertly" (*epistamenos*), but it is much more likely to be a dedicatory inscription
      rather than an artist signature. Athens, National Museum 18772: BAPD 9016848; Cook 1971,
      175; Immerwahr 1990, 9, no. 9; Rocco 2008, 29, no. An 49.
17   Signatures on Greek vases from later periods served multiple functions, including commercial,
      agonistic, and self-reflective (Villard 2002; Osborne 2010; Giuliani 2013, 89–130; Hurwit 2015;
      Bolmarcich and Muskett 2017; Hurwit 2017).
18   It is also possible that he was the potter, but the close integration of the dipinto with the
      ambitious scene makes it more likely he was the painter.
19   Hedreen 2016, 59–100.
20   Archaeologists employ the related but not identical term "personhood" much more often than
      "subjectivity." I prefer the lens of "subjectivity" because it seems more mutable and because it

invites attention to intersubjectivity. For a synopsis of the archaeological approaches to personhood, see Fowler 2004; Fowler 2016.

21 When signatures are preserved, it is evident that the majority of Greek vase-painters were men. But this cannot exclude the presence of women in the production of vases; Murray, Chorghay, and MacPherson 2020 draw together ethnographic parallels. They see men taking over the production of vases starting in the late eighth century.

22 Mainz, Sammlung der Universität 153–58: *CVA* Mainz, Universität 1, 18–31, plates 8–26; Hampe 1960; Kistler 1998, 202–3; Moore 2003; Rocco 2008, 16, 28, 39, 77–78, nos. An 19, An 20, Me 18, Pa 6, Pa 7, Pa 8, BPa 16; Coulié 2013, 194, fig. 188.

23 Von Freytag 1975, 76–81, figs. 15–16, plates 22–23; Rocco 2008, 179, nos. K 1–6; Doronzio 2018, 82–83, table 8.

24 Kübler 1959, 22–24, plates 2–6, 12, 14–16, 18–19, 21–26, fig. 2, Beil. 1, 8, 9–11; Kübler 1970, 453–73, plates 32–60; Rocco 2008, 179–80, 196, nos. Op γ II 1–5, 11, Op γ I 1–11; Kistler 1998, 188–90; Doronzio 2018, 88–92, figs. 60–61, table 10.

25 Kübler 1959, 18–21, 131–33, plates 4–12, 22–26, 38–46, 60, 67, fig. 1, Beil. 1, 7, 8, 9; Kübler 1970, 427–48, plates 10–29; Kistler 1998, 185–88; Rocco 2008, 155, 164, 168, nos. Or 1, KMG 3, 8–17, Op β 1–3; Coulié 2013, 214–16, figs. 211–13; Doronzio 2018, 85–86, fig. 58, table 9.

26 Agora P 22550: Brann 1962, 93, no. 544, plate 33; Rocco 2008, 150, no. BAr 3, plate 23.1.

27 On this group, see Rocco 2008, 95–103.

28 Coulié 2013, 219.

29 Morris 2014, 97–98, emphasizing the role of rituals in causing artisan mobility. Aravantinos 2009, 238, fig. 379; Morris 2014, 100, fig. 5; Aravantinos 2017, 227, fig. 21.9.

30 Jena V 96: *CVA* Jena 1, 30, plates 4–7. Heidelberg 60/4: *CVA* Heidelberg 3, 47, plate 111.8.

31 On the Aiginetan contexts of Protoattic pottery, see S. Morris 1984.

32 Papadopoulos 2003, 222–24; Papadopoulos 2009.

33 Rocco 2008, 199–200, 203, 204, 219–20.

34 Berlin A 42 (Immerwahr 1990, 9, no. 10); Athens, National Museum 1002 and Berlin 1682, both attributed to the Nessos Painter (Immerwahr 1990, 20, nos. 55, 57).

35 Papadopoulos 2003, 143–86. On this deposit, see also 202–3, above.

36 Papadopoulos 2003, 126–43. On this deposit, see also 201–2, above.

37 Athens, National Museum 26747: Xagorari 1996, 80, no. 17, plate 14; Rocco 2008, 186, no. Op ζ 22; Coulié 2013, 221, fig. 218.

38 Agora T 175: Burr 1933, 604–5, no. 280, figs. 72–73; Brann 1962, 87, no. 493, plate 30; Papadopoulos 2007, 149, no. 59, fig. 138; Rocco 2008, 151, no. BAr 13; Doronzio 2018, 186, fig. 19; Laughy 2018, 667–73. Attempts to identify the deity seem too speculative.

39 Rocco 2008, 203.

40 See also the shield devices on the name-vase of the Passas Painter: Moore 2003, 25–27, figs. 18–29.

41 Boston, Museum of Fine Arts 03.782: Rocco 2008, 62, no. Bo 1.

42 See also the Painter of the Munich Stand 8936: Rocco 2008, 80–82.

43 Hes. *Op.* 25. Croissant 2010 offers an important interpretation on the role of internal emulation in artistic developments of the seventh century.

44 Haug 2015.

45 Athens, National Museum VS 67: Cook 1934–35, 77, plate 44; Rocco 2008, 38–39, no. Me 10, plate 4.1; Coulié 2013, 203, fig. 195.

46 Paris, Musée du Louvre CA 1960: *CVA* Louvre 18, 20, plate 27; Rocco 2008, 29, no. BAn 2.

47 Athens, National Museum 17762: *CVA* Athens 2, 3, plates 1–2; Rocco 2008, 123, no. SV 3, plate 18.6–7.

48 For discussion of the representational possibilities of ornament, see Kraiker 1954; Boardman 1983; Hurwit 1992; Himmelmann 2005; Haug 2015 (with Arrington 2016); Dietrich and Squire 2018.

49 On the aesthetics of the maeander, see Himmelmann 1962.

50 Kantor 1945/1999, 805–46 on the relation of Greek ornament to Near Eastern art. On the sacred tree, see also Kourou 2001.

51 Rocco 2008, 12.

52 Boardman 1960; Papadopoulos, Vedder, and Schreiber 1998.

53 Corinth KP 182: *Corinth* XV.3, 247, no. 1361, plate 57; Papadopoulos, Vedder, and Schreiber 1998, 513, fig. 2.

54 Athens, National Museum 1294: Böhlau 1887, 51, fig. 11; Rocco 2008, 103, no. W 47.

55 Athens, National Museum VS 188: Walter-Karydi 1997, 387, fig. 7; Rocco 2008, 116, no S 5, plate 17.1.

56 Berlin, Staatliche Museen, Antikensammlung A 39: *CVA* Berlin, Antiquarium 1, 21, plate 24.2–3; Rocco 2008, 116, no. S 6, plate 17.3–4.

57 Agora P 531: Burr 1933, 589, no. 201, fig. 52; Brann 1962, 87, no. 493, plate 30; Doronzio 2018, 183, fig. 16.

CHAPTER 6 DRINKING AND WORSHIPPING TOGETHER

1 Brussels, Musées royaux d'art et d'histoire, A717: BAPD 200102.

2 Hedreen 2016.

3 Hedreen 2016, 22–58. Murray 2017, 143–48 critiques the view that potters and painters were necessarily excluded from symposia. For Neer, whether or not artisans actually participated in banquets, "such mingling was *ideologically* impossible" (Neer 2002, 91). For a sympotic assemblage with perhaps less sophisticated imagery, see Lynch 2011.

4 Osborne 2007.

5 New York, Metropolitan Museum of Art 74.51.4554: Markoe 1985, 177–79, 256–59, no. Cy8.

6 Feldman 2014, 111–37.

7 The writing is difficult to make out in the photograph.

8 The secondary literature on the inscription is enormous. A selection would include *CEG* I 454; Jeffery 1961 [1990], 294, no. 378; Meiggs and Lewis 1988, 1–2; Powell 1991, 166–67, 183–86; Murray 1994; Węcowski 2014, 127–41. The translation here is Powell 1989, 338. On the cup and workshop, see Coldstream 1968 [2008], 277–79, 479. On the tomb, see Buchner and Ridgway 1993, 212–23; Nizzo 2007, 33–36; Ridgway 2009, 445–46.

9 West 1994 and Faraone 1996 see instead magic at work.

10 On *euphrosyne* and the symposium, see Murray 2005 [2018].

11 For the aesthetics of text in the Geometric period, see Binek 2017.

12 Bessios, Yannis, and Kotsonas 2012; Węcowski 2017. Scholars such as Fehr 1971 and Dentzer 1982 once leaned on iconography—i.e., the representations of symposia—and placed its introduction in the late seventh century, but this view is less prevalent today.

13 Murray 1990; Murray 1994; Murray 2016.

14 Matthäus 1999a; Matthäus 1999b. For the connection of Greek commensal rituals with the Near East, see also Carter 1997. Nijboer 2013 argues for a gradual incorporation of *marzeah* rituals and equipment from the Early Iron Age if not the Late Bronze Age. Burkert 1991, however, notes "more contrasts than parallels" with Near Eastern practices (8). For the *marzeah*, see further Martin 2018.

15 Węcowski 2010–12; Węcowski 2014. Kathryn Topper (2009, 2012) also advocates for indigenous origins to the symposium in Athens, although she is mainly concerned with perceptions in the sixth and fifth century of the origins of the ritual.

16 Węcowski 2014, 304.

17 Dietler 2001, productively deployed by Węcowski 2010–12; Węcowski 2014. Cf. Kistler and Ulf 2005. Eijnde 2018a, 16 and Lynch 2018 instead underline how the symposium promoted the equality of its members, in distinction to many types of feasts.

18 Dietler 2001, 85.

19 Dietler 2001, 85–88.

20 Murray 1983; Murray 1994; I. Morris 2000, 178–85. For critiques, see esp. Hammer 2004; Kistler 2004; Rabinowitz 2004, 171–77; Corner 2005, e.g., 469.

21 Węcowski 2014, esp. 74–78. In a model that is still more a complement than a sharp contrast to Murray, Rabinowitz 2004 maintains that the ritual channeled and controlled elite competition among members of a group riddled by tension and anxiety over power, wealth, and status. Similarly, Brisart 2011, 166–73 sees the symposium as a "mode de reconnaissance sociale" and a theater for internal rivalries.

22 Corner 2005; Corner 2010.

23 Murray 2017, 140.

24 Murray 2017, 141.

25 On reading events not necessarily associated with the elite, see Baird and Taylor 2010, 11.

26 Ridgway 1992, 77, where it is called a "prosperous middle-class community" and distinguished from the elite on Euboia and the Italian mainland.

27 Schmitt Pantel 1992 drew attention to the variety of drinking practices in the city and to public drinking during religious events. On dining at temples, see also Bergquist 1990. Burkert 1991, 18 suggests that dining on couches was introduced via ritual feasts at sanctuaries rather than symposia. Eijnde 2018b argues for a transfer of meat consumption in the seventh century to sanctuaries and drinking to domestic contexts. The evidence may be too limited to make such a sweeping claim.

28 On the kantharos shape, see Young 1939, 204; Brann 1962, 51–52; Coldstream 1968 [2008] 23, 48, 86–87; Węcowski 2014, 287–88.

29 Lissarrague 1990 first discussed at length the interaction of drinking vessels and their symposium context. See also Neer 2002; Lynch 2011; Gagné 2016. Węcowski 2014, 85–97 discusses the movements of cups in the symposium and adduces the primary sources. Murray 2015b feels that Węcowski overstates the case but concedes that at least during toasts a cup could circulate.

30 Papadopoulos 1996; Papadopoulos 2003. Similarly, Dimitriadou 2019.

31 D'Onofrio 1997, 67–68; d'Onofrio 2007–8; Doronzio 2018.

32 Étienne 2004, 31–33 agrees that the space of the agora was cleared over the course of the seventh century, and he relates it to a process of synoikism, but unlike d'Onofrio and Doronzio, he downplays the role for cult. Dimitriadou 2019 sees the process taking place over the course of the seventh century and onward.

33 On habitation in the area of the later agora, see also Monaco 2012.

34 Agora P 530: Burr 1933, 589, no. 200, fig. 51; Brann 1962, 87, no. 497, plate 30.

35 Agora P 579: Burr 1933, 589–92, no. 204, figs. 55–56; Papadopoulos 2007, 116–17, fig. 113D.

36 Laughy 2018 offers a valuable a reassessment of the votive deposit over the Late Geometric Oval Building, with the find context of our kantharoi specified on 644. Laughy's presentation of the material as fill renders d'Onofrio's (2001, 292–316) view of in situ votive activity untenable. More cautious than d'Onofrio 2001 is Doronzio 2018, 176–89.

37 With their handles, P 530 is 11.3 cm tall, P 579 is 14.4 cm tall. D'Onofrio 2001, 292–316, notes the preponderance of drinking vessels in the deposit.

38 See Chapter 1, n. 6, above.

39 For the symposium and sea, see Slater 1976; Lissarrague 1990, 107–22; Corner 2010. For nautical imagery in later poetry, see, e.g., Bacchyl. 13, 17; Pind. *Pyth*. 4.

40 Agora P 7143: Young 1939, 143–44, 149, C 8, figs. 101, 104; Papadopoulos 2007, 146–47, no. 57, fig. 135.

41 Deposit D 11:5: Young 1939, 139–94; Brann 1962, 125; d'Onofrio 2007–8, 453, no. 5; Doronzio 2018, 198–99.

42 Young excludes graves as an origin for the material because there were not enough bones found in the deposit: Young 1939, 139.

43 Agora P 7014: Young 1939, 151, C 39, fig. 107; Brann 1962, 47, 89, nos. 132, 511, plates 8, 31; Rocco 2008, 172, no. AG 13.

44 On myths in vase-painting, see Snodgrass 1998; Hurwit 2011; Giuliani 2013.

45 Giuliani 2013, 87. Giuliani relates the emergence of narrative to the "stylistic upheavals" of the seventh century.

46 Archaeological Museum of Aigina K 566: Morris 1984, 4, 51–53, 123, no. 4, plate 10; Rocco 2008, 149, no. Ar 2, plate 21.4; Coulié 2013, 192, fig. 87.

47 Other myths probably circulated as folk tales; see, e.g., Cook 1983.

48 Berlin, Staatliche Museen, Antikensammlung A 42: *CVA* Berlin 1, 24–25, plates 31–33; Morris 1984, 5–6, 41–43, 122, no. 9, plate 7; Immerwahr 1990, 9, no. 10; Wachter 2001, 26; Rocco 2008, 140–41, no. Po 12, plate 20.5–6.

49 Giuliani 2013, 97–98. Ferrari 1987, on the other hand, argues that the vase represents a chorus singing a poem.

50 Agora P 13323: Brann 1962, 97, no. 577, plates 37, 44; Immerwahr 1990, 10, no. 16; Rocco 2013.

51 Other Protoattic vases with possible mythical dipinti are a large krater from Aigina with Ag[amemnon] or Al[exandros] (Athens, National Museum 2226: Immerwahr 1990, 10, no. 15) and a fragment from the Acropolis with Ἀντένο[ρ] (Antenor), which could be a mythical reference or the name of the vase-painter or dedicator (Acropolis 368: Immerwahr 1990, 9, no. 11; Rocco 2008, 143, 150, no. Ar 9, plate 22.6; Doronzio 2018, 32).

52 On different levels of literacy, different types of reading events, and written text as an image and a visual sign, see Baird and Taylor 2010.

53 For Aiginetan production of Protoattic pottery, see Morris 1984. Contra: Walter-Karydi 1997; Coulié 2013, 191.

54 On speaking objects, see Whitley 2017, 74–75, 82–90.

55 Immerwahr 1990, 11–12.

56 The pattern does not seem to hold for Corinth and Euboia, for which Wachter 2001 does not record any inscribed cups of the seventh century.

57 Lang 1976, 28.

58 Agora P 4663: Young 1939, 124–26, B 55, figs. 89–90; Lang 1976, 30, F 3, plate 11; Immerwahr 1990, 11, no. 19; Papadopoulos 2007, 129, no. 48, fig. 122.

59 Agora P 4659: P 6466, P 6464, P 641; Young 1939, 106, 123–26.

60 Agora P 4664: Young 1939, 126, no. B 56, figs. 88, 144; Lang 1976, 17, D 4 (reading instead two names).

61 "Building A": Thompson 1940, 3–8; Brann 1962, 110; Doronzio 2018, 165–75.

62 On the kiln, see esp. Papadopoulos 2003, 126–43.

63 Agora P 10151: Brann 1962, 54, no. 194, fig. 1, plate 10; Lang 1976, 30, F 1, plate 11; Immerwahr 1990, 11, no. 27; Doronzio 2018, 194, fig. 28.

64 Well T 19:3. On the deposit, see Brann 1962, 131.

65 Agora P 26420: Brann 1961b, 377, S 17, fig. 1, plate 87; Lang 1976, 30, F 2; Immerwahr 1990, 11, no. 20.

66 For the deposits, see Brann 1961b, 374–79; Brann 1962, 110–11, 131; Papadopoulos 2003, 143–87.

67 For the mending evidence, see Papadopoulos 2003, 187, n. 131.

68 For the fragment, see Brann 1961b, 375.

69 Agora P 26452: Brann 1961b, 377, S 18, fig. 1; Lang 1976, 12, no. C 1; Immerwahr 1990, 11, no. 21.

70 See Polignac 1995, 96–97 on the status of the dedicants.

71 Athens, National Museum 16092: Blegen 1934, 10–12, fig. 1, plate 1; Jeffery 1961 [1990], 69, 401, no. 3b, plate 1; Langdon 1976, 22, no. 36.

72 Athens, National Museum 16091: Blegen 1934, 12, fig. 2, plate 2; Jeffery 1961 [1990], 69, 401, no. 3a, plate 1; Langdon 1976, 23, no. 50.

73 Including a skyphos declaring that someone or something is "virile" or "grim" (βλοσ[υρός]; Langdon 1976, 23, no. 51, fig. 9, plate 6) and a cup urging "drink this up" (πρόπινε τενδί; Young 1940, 8, no. 12, fig. 11; Langdon 1976, 23, no. 49, fig. 9, plate 6).

74 While some myths can be traced back ultimately to Near Eastern sources, there is little doubt that someone looking at the depictions of the myths would have considered them to be "their" myths.

75 Matthäus 1999a, 256–57 surveys the evidence.

76 Węcowski 2014, 143–48.

77 Alkman fr. 19 (Page). Slightly earlier, Kallinos fr. 1 (West) and Archilochos fr. 2 (West) may refer to reclining. On these passages, see Murray 1994, 48, 52–54; Węcowski 2014, 160–66.

78 Baughan 2013, 74–76, who also surveys other perspectives.

79 Alkman 1.68; Sappho 39 (Loeb); Kritias fr. 6 (West).

80 Xenophanes fr. 3.

81 Several scholars have spoken of Lydian "accelerators" to the custom of reclining at the symposium (Franklin 2008, 197, followed by Baughan 2013, 223). Węcowski 2014, 189 speaks of the banquet in the late seventh century Orientalizing *à la lydiennne*. On the role of Lydians in transmitting a culture of *habrosyne*, see Kurke 1992.

82 On music, see Franklin 2008.

83 Miller 1991, with further references. See also Miller 1997, 153–87; Neer 2002, 19–22.

84 Osborne 1989, 308. Polignac 1995; d'Onofrio 1997; Baumer 2004, 12–30; and Laughy 2010, 210–53, survey the evidence for cult. For distribution maps, see in particular Polignac 1995, 78, fig. 1 and d'Onofrio 1997, 66, fig. 2. For a table of cult sites with their dates of activity, see d'Onofrio 1995, 60, fig. 2. For a synopsis of religious life in the seventh century, see Parker 1996, 26–28, and on the emergence of votive practices in Attica, see Eijnde 2018b. In providing bibliographic references for cult sites in the discussion below, I mention the most recent publications and the key corpora, where more bibliography may be found.

85 See, e.g., the influential Renfrew 1985.

86 On the connection of mountain sanctuaries to weather gods, see Langdon 1976, 79–95, and on reciprocity, Parker 1998.

87 Snodgrass 1980, 52–54.

88 New York, Metropolitan Museum of Art 30.118.47: *CVA* Metropolitan Museum of Art 5, 49–50, plate 27.9. The vase belongs to a collection from the sanctuary on Mount Hymettos that the Greek government gifted to the Metropolitan Museum of Art in 1930: see *CVA* Metropolitan Museum of Art 5, 33.

89 For the dedication of a vessel inscribed with the name of a woman, see Palaiokrassa-Kopitsa and Vivliodetis 2015, 159.

90 Langdon 1976, 20, no. 29, fig. 8, plate 4.

91 Parnes: Palaiokrassa-Kopitsa and Vivliodetis 2015. Pani: d'Onofrio 1997, 82, no. 54; Laughy 2010, 250. Hymettos: Langdon 1976; d'Onofrio 1997, 18, no. 15; Baumer 2004, 90–91, no. Att 11; Laughy 2010, 229–23; Doronzio 2018, 218–21.

92 Kiapha Thiti: d'Onofrio 1997, 81, no. 39; Christiansen 1996/2000; Baumer 2004, 101–2, no. Att 34; Laughy 2010, 236–37. Agora T 183: Burr 1933, 610, no. 283, fig. 75; Papadopoulos 2007, 150–51, no. 60, fig. 139A. Agora T 245: Burr 1933, 611, no. 284, fig. 77; Doronzio 2018, 208, fig. 34. The Protoattic votives in the agora appear in several deposits, and their origins are disputed. Laughy 2018 argues plausibly that they ultimately stem from worship in the Demeter sanctuary (the Eleusinion).

93 Mounichia: Palaiokrassa-Kopitsa and Vivliodetis 2015; Palaiokrassa-Kopitsa 2017. Brauron: d'Onofrio 1997, 84, no. 79; Mitsopoulos-Leon 2009; Laughy 2010, 245–48. Loutsa: Baumer 2004, 92, no. Att 15; Laughy 2010, 249; Kalogeropoulos 2013.

94 Palaiokrassa-Kopitsa 2017, 248–49.

95 Doronzio 2018, 255–64 provides the most recent overview of the complex and fragmentary evidence. See also Kyrkou 1997; Mösch-Klingele 2010, 33–34. Fetiche Tjami Na-57-Aa-456: Kyrkou 1997, 426–27, no. 3, figs. 6–7, color plate 2b; Rocco 2008, 93, no. Ml 2, plate 13.3–4; Coulié 2013, 222, fig. 219. Fetiche Tjami Na-57-Aa-189: Brouskari 1974, 98; Oakley and Sinos 1993, 5, n. 6, where it is called the earliest representation of a wedding; Winkler 1999, 26, no. LH 17, plate 1; Rocco 2015, 70, 94, fig. 2b; Doronzio 2018, 260, fig. 14. On the ideological value of marriage in developing *poleis*, see Langdon 2008, 287.

96 D'Onofrio 1995; d'Onofrio 1997. The importance of religion for the development of the city-state could be traced back to Fustel de Coulanges and François de Polignac.

97 Blok 2014. See also Blok 2018; Duplouy 2019a, 70–93; 2019b, 211.

98 At rural Lathouriza, too, cult and stable settlement seem closely integrated. On Lathouriza, where the remains have received multiple interpretations, see Lauter 1985; Osborne 1989, 307–8; d'Onofrio 1997, 84, no. 73; Baumer 2004, 105–7; Laughy 2010, 233–36.

99   See also 192, above. Doronzio 2018 proposes multiple cult locations in Athens: in the region of
      the Olympieion (216–27), near the Kynosarges necropolis (233–47), and on the south slope of
      the Acropolis near Rovertou Galli and Parthenonos Streets (254).

100 D'Onofrio 2001, 299–300, on Agora T 194. Contrast Burr 1933, 615, no. 297, fig. 82; Laughy 2018,
      644.

101 Laughy 2018.

102 Scholl 2006, 76–79; Doronzio 2018, 51.

103 For the sacred topography of the city cf. *Il.* 2.546–51.

104 Binder 1998. See also Kokkou-Vyridi 1999; Lippolis 2006, 145–58; Laughy 2010, 210–13. On the
      proerosia, which has been used to argue for a mid-eighth-century date for the Mysteries,
      see Mylonas 1961, 7 and the doubt expressed in Binder 1998, 136. For the Bronze Age period
      of the sanctuary, see Cosmopoulos 2014. Thucydides (2.15.1) reports that the Eleusinians
      waged war against Erechtheus of Athens. According to Pausanias (1.38.3), after the war, they
      retained management of the Mysteries but were otherwise subservient to Athens. For further
      primary references, see Miles 1998, 1, n. 2, and for discussion, see also Hornblower 1991,
      260–61.

105 On the Solonian legislation, see Mylonas 1961, 63–64.

106 But for a different perspective, see Rönnberg 2020.

107 De Polignac 1995, 94 also argues for an important Athens-Sounion link, and Doronzio 2018,
      218–21 sees a ritual connection between Athens and Mount Hymettos. Parker 1996, 25, argues
      for a critical role for Athens in the establishment of countryside cults.

108 Laughy 2010. Although Polignac 1995 notes that many of the Attic sanctuaries decline in the
      sixth as cults in Athens start to dominate.

109 Laughy 2010, 242–44; Theodoropoulou-Polychroniadis 2015.

110 Brauron: see n. 93, above. Pallini: Laughy 2010, 245.

111 On the tomb, see Coldstream 1977 [2003], 79.

112 Kokkou-Vyridi 1999, 69–72.

113 Palaiokrassa-Kopitsa and Vivliodetis 2015.

114 Laughy 2010, 253.

115 Kiapha Thiti: see n. 92, above. Profitis Ilias: Langdon 1976, 104; Laughy 2010, 239.

116 Cf. Osborne 1989, 318: "the scenes of Protoattic pottery . . . ask questions about what the world
      might be, about whether the order of the world as it is the proper and necessary order. The
      viewer is challenged to match his actual world to the possible world, the mythical world, the
      animal world, which the artist presents to him."

117 Athens, National Museum 14935: Cook 1934–35, 173, plate 40b; Rocco 2008, no. An 48, plate 2.2;
      Theodoropoulou-Polychroniadis 2015, 64–66, no. 147.

118 It is also possible that the site honored a hero: see Chapter 3, n. 87, above.

119 Palaiokrassa-Kopitsa 2017, 248.

CHAPTER 7 BACK TO PHALERON

1   Although on Demaratus, see 76, above.

2   Hünnekens 1987.

3   Cook 1934–35; Beazley 1986. An earlier figure difficult to place is the Painter of Opferrinne β/
     IX, who works with incision but is not considered a black-figure artist because of the lack of
     added white and purple (Rocco 2008, 166).

4   It is possible that he did not make these class divisions, but only the highest, and he assigned
     the others new functions. For this view, see Rhodes 2006. For skepticism on the property
     classes, see Raaflaub 2006.

5   On these naval conflicts, see 18, above.

6   See Alexandridou 2011, 104–8 on the market.

7   Alexandridou 2011, 105.

8 If Athens participated with Thessalians and Sikyonians in the First Sacred War against Delphi, it would be a sign that this mainland network was well developed. The veracity of the conflict, however, is disputed. See the doubts most recently expressed in Londey 2015.

9 "Ξεθάβονται ή θάβονται ξανά οι Δεσμώτες του Φαλήρου;" March 9, 2017, www.protothema.gr /greece/article/660844/-xethavodai-i-thavodai-xana-oi-desmotes-tou-falirou/.

10 Chryssoulaki 2019, 103, fig. 2.

11 Ingvarsson and Bäckström 2019, 8.

12 "Ξεθάβονται ή θάβονται ξανά οι Δεσμώτες του Φαλήρου;" March 9, 2017, www.protothema.gr /greece/article/660844/-xethavodai-i-thavodai-xana-oi-desmotes-tou-falirou/, for a critical discussion of the situation.

13 The only mention I could find of the cemetery is a short appearance on its website: www.snfcc .org/kpisn/h-periohi. Archaeology is notably absent from plans and tours of the site itself, with the exception of the fencing around the part where work is still occurring.

14 "Σε πολύ κακή κατάσταση οι Δεσμώτες του Φαλήρου' δηλώνει η Λ. Μενδώνη: Ζητά αναπομπή στο ΚΑΣ," January 22, 2020, www.kathimerini.gr/1061435/article/epikairothta/ellada/se-poly -kakh-katastash-oi-desmwtes-toy-falhroy-dhlwnei-h-l-mendwnh-zhta-anapomph-sto-kas; "Οι Δεσμώτες του Φαλήρου επιστρέφουν στο ΚΑΣ," January 23, 2020, www.kathimerini.gr /1061539/article/politismos/eikastika/oi-desmwtes-toy-falhroy-epistrefoyn-sto-kas.

15 "KAS Green-Lights Shelter for Ancient Mass Grave in Faliro, South of Athens," June 11, 2019, www.ekathimerini.com/241454/article/ekathimerini/life/kas-green-lights-shelter-for-ancient -mass-grave-in-faliro-south-of-athens; "'Σηκώνονται' οι Δεσμώτες του Φαλήρου με απόφαση του ΚΑΣ," February 6, 2020, www.kathimerini.gr/1063455/article/politismos/eikastika /shkwnontai-oi-desmwtes-toy-falhroy-me-apofash-toy-kas; "Το ΚΑΣ ενέκρινε τη μέθοδο απόσπασης των 'Δεσμωτών,'" May 5, 2020, www.kathimerini.gr/1079087/article/epikairothta /ellada/to-kas-enekrine-th-me8odo-apospashs-twn-desmwtwn.

16 "Μουσείο για τους 'δεσμώτες' του Φαλήρου σχεδιάζεται με δωρεά του Ιδρύματος Σ. Νιάρχος," November 25, 2019, www.kathimerini.gr/895108/article/epikairothta/ellada/moyseio-gia-toys -desmwtes-toy-falhroy-sxediazetai-me-dwrea-toy-idrymatos-s-niarxos-fwto; "Μουσείο 'χωρίς μπάλα', αλλά με Ρέντσο Πιάνο," July 24, 2020, www.kathimerini.gr/1088984/article/politismos /eikastika/moyseio-xwris-mpala-alla-me-rentso-piano.

17 "Προστασία και ανάδειξη για τους 'Δεσμώτες' του Φαλήρου," June 12, 2019, www.avgi.gr/article /10966/9954469/prostasia-kai-anadeixe-gia-tous-desmotes-tou-phalerou.

18 "Μουσείο 'χωρίς μπάλα', αλλά με Ρέντσο Πιάνο," July 24, 2020, www.kathimerini.gr/1088984 /article/politismos/eikastika/moyseio-xwris-mpala-alla-me-rentso-piano.

19 Stella Chryssoulaki, "Μουσείο για τους 'δεσμώτες' του Φαλήρου σχεδιάζεται με δωρεά του Ιδρύματος Σ. Νιάρχος," November 25, 2019, www.kathimerini.gr/society/895108/moyseio-gia -toys-desmotes-toy-faliroy-schediazetai-me-dorea-toy-idrymatos-s-niarchos-foto/.

20 www.kathimerini.gr/856663/article/politismos/polh/oi-80-desmwtes-elkoyn-episthmones. On the health of the bodies, see also Chryssoulaki 2019, 113, without making a connection to Cylon, and Ingvarsson and Bäckström 2019.

Bibliography

Abulafia, David. 2011. *The Great Sea: A Human History of the Mediterranean*. London: Allen Lane.

Ahlberg-Cornell, Gudrun. 1967. "A Late Geometric Grave-Scene Influenced by North Syrian Art." *Opuscula Atheniensia* 7:177–86.

———. 1971a. *Fighting on Land and Sea in Greek Geometric Art*. Stockholm: Lund.

———. 1971b. *Prothesis and Ekphora in Greek Geometric Art*. Stockholm: Paul Åström.

Aigner-Foresti, Luciana. 2000. "Orientalische Elemente im Etruskischen Königtum." In *Akten des Kolloquiums zum Thema der Orient und Etrurien zum Phänomen des "Orientalisierens" im westlichen Mittelmeerraum (10.-6. Jh. v. Chr.)*, edited by Friedhelm Prayon and Wolfgang Röllig, 275–86. Pisa: Istituti editoriali e poligrafici internazionali.

Åkerström, Åke. 1943. *Der geometrische Stil in Italien: Archäologische Grundlagen der frühesten historischen Zeit Italiens*. Leipzig: O. Harrassowitz.

Akurgal, Ekrem. 1968. *The Art of Greece: Its Origins in the Mediterranean and Near East*. New York: Crown.

Alexandridou, Alexandra. 2008. "Athens versus Attika: Local Variations in Funerary Practices during the Late Seventh and Early Sixth century BC." In *Essays in Classical Archaeology for Eleni Hatzivassiliou 1977–2007*, edited by Donna C. Kurtz, 65–69. Oxford: Archaeopress.

———. 2009. "Offering Trenches and Funerary Ceremonies in the Attic Countryside: The Evidence from the North Necropolis of Vari." In *From Artemis to Diana: The Goddess of Man and Beast*, edited by Tobias Fischer-Hansen and Birte Poulsen, 497–522. Copenhagen: Museum Tusculanum.

———. 2011. *The Early Black-Figured Pottery of Attika in Context (ca. 630–570 BCE)*. Leiden: Brill.

———. 2012. "The North Necropolis of Vari Revisited." *Archaiologikon Deltion A, Meletes* 151:1–73.

———. 2015. "Shedding Light on Mortuary Practices in Early Archaic Attica: The Case of the Offering Trenches." In *Classical Archaeology in Context: Theory and Practice in Excavation in the Greek World*, edited by Donald C. Haggis and Carla M. Antonaccio, 121–47. Berlin: de Gruyter.

———. 2016. "Funerary Variability in Late Eighth-Century B.C.E. Attica (Late Geometric II)." *American Journal of Archaeology* 120:333–60.

———. 2017. "Special Burial Treatment for the 'Heroized' Dead in the Attic Countryside: The Case of the Elite Cemetery of Vari." In *Interpreting the Seventh Century BC: Tradition and Innovation*, edited by Xenia Charalambidou and Catherine Morgan, 281–92. Oxford: Archeopress.

———. 2018. "Feasting in Early Iron Age Attika: The Evidence from the Site of the Academy." In *Feasting and Polis Institutions*, edited by Floris van den Eijnde, Josine H. Blok, and Rolf Strootman, 38–59. Leiden: Brill.

———. 2019. "Athens and Attica." In *A Companion to the Archaeology of Early Greece and the Mediterranean*, edited by Antonis Kotsonas and Irene Lemos, 743–62. Hoboken, NJ: John Wiley and Sons.

Alexandropoulou, Anna. 2018. "Ein protoattisches Kraterfragment aus Phaleron." In *Festschrift für Heide Froning*, edited by Taner Korkut and Britta Özen-Kleine, 1-8. Istanbul: E. Yayinlari.

———. 2019. "Die Kindergräber in Phaleron (Attika)." In *Griechische Nekropolen: Neue Forschungen und Funde*, edited by Heide Freilinghaus, Jutta Stroszeck, and Panos Valavanis, 261–85. Möhnesee, Germany: Bibliopolis.

Amiran, Ruth. 1970. *Ancient Pottery of the Holy Land: From Its Beginnings in the Neolithic Period to the End of the Iron Age*. New Brunswick, NJ: Rutgers University Press.

Amyx, Darrell A. 1953. "Review of Kübler 1950." *American Journal of Archaeology* 57:294–95.

———. 1988. *Corinthian Vase-Painting of the Archaic Period*. Berkeley: University of California Press.

Antonaccio, Carla Maria. 1995. *An Archaeology of Ancestors: Tomb Cult and Hero Cult in Early Greece*. Lanham, MD: Rowman and Littlefield.

Arafat, Karim, and Catherine Morgan. 1989. "Pots and Potters in Athens and Corinth: A Review." *Oxford Journal of Archaeology* 8:311–46.

Arapogianni, Xeni. 1985. "Νεκροταφείο του 7ου και 6ου αι. π.Χ. στην Οινόη Μαραθώνος." *Archaiologikon Deltion A, Meletes* 40:207–28.

Aravantinos, Vassilis L. 2009. "Thebes." In *Archaeology: Euboea and Central Greece*, edited by Andreas G. Vlachopoulos, 234–47. Athens: Melissa Publishing House.

———. 2017. "The Sanctuaries of Herakles and Apollo Ismenios at Thebes: New Evidence." In *Interpreting the Seventh Century BC: Tradition and Innovation*, edited by Xenia Charalambidou and Catherine Morgan, 221–30. Oxford: Archaeopress.

Arrington, Nathan T. 2015a. *Ashes, Images, and Memories: The Presence of the War Dead in Fifth-Century Athens*. New York: Oxford University Press.

———. 2015b. "Talismanic Practice at Lefkandi: Trinkets, Burials, and Belief in the Early Iron Age." *Cambridge Classical Journal* December:1–30.

———. 2016. Review of Haug 2016. *Bryn Mawr Classical Review*, 2016.11.35.

———. 2017. "Connoisseurship, Vases, and Greek Art and Archaeology." In *The Berlin Painter and His World: Athenian Vase-Painting in the Early Fifth Century B.C.*, edited by J. Michael Padgett, 21–39. New Haven, CT: Yale University Press.

———. Forthcoming. "The Persistence of Orientalizing." *Ancient West and East*.

Arrington, Nathan T., Georgios Spyropoulos, and Demetrios J. Brellas. 2021. "Glimpses of the Invisible Dead: A 7th-Century B.C. Burial Plot in Northern Piraeus." *Hesperia: The Journal of the American School of Classical Studies at Athens* 90:233–79.

Aruz, Joan, Sarah B. Graff, and Yelena Rakic, eds. 2014. *Assyria to Iberia at the Dawn of the Classical Age*. New York: Metropolitan Museum of Art.

Attema, Peter. 2008. "Conflict of Coexistence? Remarks on Indigenous Settlement and Greek Colonization in the Foothills and Hinterland of the Sibaritide (Northern Calabria, Italy)." In *Meetings of Cultures in the Black Sea Region: Between Conflict and Coexistence*, edited by Pia Guldager Bilde and Jane Hjarl Petersen, 69–99. Aarhus, Denmark: Aarhus University Press.

Aubet, María Eugenia. 1993. *The Phoenicians and the West: Politics, Colonies, and Trade*. Cambridge: Cambridge University Press.

Audiat, Jean. 1954. "Un vase protoattique inédit au Musée de Toulouse." *Revue des Études Anciennes* 56:5–14.

Bagley, Robert W. 2015. *Gombrich among the Egyptians, and Other Essays in the History of Art*. Seattle: Marquand Books.

Baird, J. A., and Claire Taylor. 2010. "Ancient Graffiti in Context: Introduction." In *Ancient Graffiti in Context*, edited by J. A. Baird and Claire Taylor, 1–19. New York: Routledge.

Baitinger, Holger. 2015–16. "Votive Gifts from Sicily and Southern Italy in Olympia and Other Greek Sanctuaries." *Archaeological Reports* 62:111–24.

Bakalakis, Georgios. 1961–62. "Πρωτοαττικός ἀρύβαλλος." *Archaiologikon Deltion* 17:77–82.

Barclay, Alison E. 2013. "Influence, Inspiration, or Innovation? The Importance of Contexts in the Study of Iconography: The Case of the Mistress of Animals in 7th-Century Greece." In *Regionalism and Globalism in Antiquity: Exploring Their Limits*, edited by Franco de Angelis, 143–75. Leuven, Belgium: Peeters.

Bartolini, Gilda. 2016. "Le comunità tirreniche all'alba della Magna Grecia." In *Contexts of Early Colonization*, edited by Lieve Donnellan, Valentino Nizzo, and Gert-Jan Burgers, 141–52. Rome: Palombi Editori.

Bartolini, Gilda, Valeria Acconcia, and Silvia ten Kortenaar. 2014. "Le service du vin en Étrurie méridionale à l'époque orientalisante." In *Les potiers d'Etrurie et leur monde: Contacts, échanges, transferts*, edited by Laura Ambrosini and Vincent Jolivet, 51–67. Paris: Colin.

Baughan, Elizabeth P. 2013. *Couched in Death: Klinai and Identity in Anatolia and Beyond*. Madison: University of Wisconsin Press.

Baumer, Lorenz E. 2004. *Kult im Kleinen: Ländliche Heiligtümer spätarchaischer bis hellenistischer Zeit. Attika - Arkadien - Argolis - Kynouria*. Rahden/Westf.: Verlag Marie Leidorf.

Baur, Ferdinand Christian. 1824–25. *Symbolik und Mythologie: Oder, die Naturreligion des Altertums*. Stuttgart: Metzler.

Beazley, John Davidson. 1986. *The Development of Attic Black-Figure*. Berkeley: University of California Press.

Becker, Marshall J. 2016. "Etruscan Skeletal Biology and Etruscan Origins." In *A Companion to the Etruscans*, edited by Sinclair Bell and Alexandra A. Carpino, 181–202. Malden, MA: Wiley-Blackwell.

Beloch, J. 1894. "Die Phoeniker am aegäischen Meer." *Rheinisches Museum* 49:111–32.

Benndorf, Otto. 1883. *Griechische und sicilische vasenbilder*. Berlin: I. Guttentag.

Benson, J. L. 1970. *Horse, Bird, and Man: The Origins of Greek Paintings*. Amherst: University of Massachusetts Press.

———. 1983. "Corinthian Kotyle Workshops." *Hesperia: The Journal of the American School of Classical Studies at Athens* 52:311–26.

———. 1986. "An Early Protocorinthian Workshop and the Sources of Its Motifs." *Bulletin antieke beschaving* 61:1–20.

Bérard, Victor. 1927–29. *Les navigations d'Ulysse*. Paris: A. Colin.

Bergquist, Birgitta. 1990. "Sympotic Space: A Functional Aspect of Greek Dining-Rooms." In *Sympotica: A Symposium on the Symposion*, edited by Oswyn Murray, 37–65. Oxford: Clarendon.

Bernabé, Albertus. 2007. *Poetarum epicorum Graecorum: Testimonia et fragmenta, Pars II, Fasc. 3*. Berlin: de Gruyter.

Bernal, Martin. 1987–2006. *Black Athena: The Afroasiatic Roots of Classical Civilization*. London: Free Association Books.

———. 2001. *Black Athena Writes Back: Martin Bernal Responds to His Critics*. Durham, NC: Duke University Press.

Bernardini, Paolo. 2016. "I Fenici sulle rotte dell'Occidente nel IX sec. a.C. Cronologie, incontri, strategie." *Cartagine. Studi e Ricerche* 1.

Bessios, Matthaios, Yannis Tzifopoulos, and Antonis Kotsonas. 2012. *Methone I: Inscriptions, Graffiti, and Trademarks on Geometric and Archaic Pottery from the "Ypogeio."* Thessaloniki: Centre for the Greek Language.

Bikai, Patricia Maynor. 1978. *The Pottery of Tyre*. Warminster: Aris and Phillips.

Binder, Judith. 1998. "The Early History of the Demeter and Kore Sanctuary at Eleusis." In *Ancient Greek Cult Practice from the Archaeological Evidence*, edited by Robin Hägg, 131–39. Stockholm: Paul Åström.

Binek, Natasha M. 2017. "The Dipylon Oinochoe Graffito: Text or Decoration?" *Hesperia: The Journal of the American School of Classical Studies at Athens* 86:423–42.

Bintliff, John. 1994. "Territorial Behaviour and the Natural History of the Greek Polis." In *Stuttgarter Kolloquium zur Historischen Geographie des Altertums* 4, edited by Eckart Olshausen and Holger Sonnabend, 207–49. Amsterdam: A. M. Hakkert.

———. 2006. "Solon's Reforms: An Archaeological Perspective." In *Solon of Athens: New Historical and Philological Approaches*, edited by Josine H. Blok and André P.M.H. Lardinois, 321–33. Leiden: Brill.

Birch, Samuel. 1858. *History of Ancient Pottery*. London: J. Murray.

Blakeway, Alan. 1932–33. "Prolegomena to the Study of Greek Commerce with Italy, Sicily, and France in the Eighth and Seventh Centuries B.C." *Annual of the British School at Athens* 33:170–208.

———. 1935. "'Demaratus': A Study in Some Aspects of the Earliest Hellenisation of Latium and Etruria." *Journal of Roman Studies* 25:129–49.

Blegen, Carl W. 1934. "Inscriptions on Geometric Pottery from Hymettos." *American Journal of Archaeology* 38:10–28.

Blok, Josine. 2014. "A 'Covenant' between Gods and Men: *Hiera kai Hosia* and the Greek Polis." In *The City in the Classical and Post-Classical World: Changing Contexts of Power and Identity*, edited by Claudia Rapp and H. A. Drake, 14–37. Cambridge: Cambridge University Press.

———. 2018. "Retracing Steps: Finding Ways into Archaic Greek Citizenship." In *Defining Citizenship in Archaic Greece*, edited by Alain Duplouy and Roger W. Brock, 79–101. Oxford: Oxford University Press.

Boardman, John. 1955. "Painted Funerary Plaques." *Annual of the British School at Athens* 50:51–66.

———. 1960. "The Multiple Brush." *Antiquity* 60:85–89.

———. 1965. "Tarsus, Al Mina, and Greek Chronology." *Journal of Hellenic Studies* 85:5–15.

———. 1983. "Symbol and Story in Geometric Art." In *Ancient Greek Art and Iconography*, edited by Warren G. Moon, 15–36. Madison: University of Wisconsin Press.

———. 1990. "Al Mina and History." *Oxford Journal of Archaeology* 9:169–90.

———. 1998. *Early Greek Vase Painting: 11th–6th Centuries BC*. New York: Thames and Hudson.

———. 1999. *The Greeks Overseas: Their Early Colonies and Trade*. 4th ed. London: Thames and Hudson.

———. 2001. *The History of Greek Vases: Potters, Painters, and Pictures*. New York: Thames and Hudson.

———. 2002. "Al Mina: The Study of a Site." *Ancient West and East* 1:315–31.

———. 2003. *The Archaeology of Nostalgia: How the Greeks Re-created Their Mythical Past*. London: Thames and Hudson.

———. 2006. "Al Mina: Notes and Queries." *Ancient West and East* 4:278–91.

Boast, Robin. 1997. "A Small Company of Actors: A Critique of Style." *Journal of Material Culture* 2:173–98.

Bocock, Robert. *Hegemony*. London: Tavistock Publications.

Boehringer, David. 2001. *Heroenkulte in Griechenland von der geometrischen bis zur klassischen Zeit: Attika, Argolis, Messenien*. Berlin: Akademie Verlag.

Bohen, Barbara. 2017. *Kratos and Krater: Reconstructing an Athenian Protohistory*. Oxford: Archeopress.

Böhlau, Johannes. 1887. "Frühattische Vasen." *Jahrbuch des kaiserlich deutschen archäologischen Instituts*:3–66.

———. 1898. *Aus ionischen und italienischen Nekropolen: Ausgrabungen und Untersuchungen zur Geschichte der nachmykenischen griechischen Kunst*. Leipzig: Teubner.

Bohrer, Frederick Nathaniel. 2003. *Orientalism and Visual Culture: Imagining Mesopotamia in Nineteenth-Century Europe*. Cambridge: Cambridge University Press.

Boitani, Francesca, Folco Biagi, and Sara Neri. 2014. "Amphores de table étrusco-géométriques d'époque orientalisante à Véies." In *Les potiers d'Etrurie et leur monde: Contacts, échanges, transferts*, edited by Laura Ambrosini and Vincent Jolivet, 69–80. Paris: Colin.

Boitani, Francesca, Sara Neri, and Folco Biagi. 2010. "Riflessi della ceramica geometrica nella più antica pittura funeraria veiente." *Bolletino di Archaeologia on-line* F / F7 / 3:20–27.

Boivin, Nicole. 2008. *Material Cultures, Material Minds: The Impact of Things on Human Thought, Society, and Evolution*. Cambridge: Cambridge University Press.

Bolmarcich, Sarah, and Georgina Muskett. 2017. "Artists' Signatures on Archaic Greek Vases from Athens." In *Artists and Artistic Production in Ancient Greece*, edited by Kristen Seaman and Peter Schultz, 154–76. Cambridge: Cambridge University Press.

Borell, Brigitte. 1978. *Attisch Geometrische Schalen: Eine spätgeometrische Keramikgattung und ihre Beziehungen zum Orient*. Mainz am Rhein: von Zabern.

Botto, Massimo. 2007. "I rapporti fra la Sardegna e le coste medio-tirreniche della penisola Italiana: La prima metà del I millennio A.C." In *Etruschi greci fenici e cartaginesi nel mediterraneo centrale*, edited by Giuseppe M. Della Fina, 75–136. Rome: Quasar.

———. 2008a. "Le più antiche presenze fenicie nell'Italia meridionale." *Rivista di Studi Fenici* 36:157–79.

———. 2008b. "I primi contatti fra i Fenici e le popolazioni dell'Italia peninsulare." In *Contacto cultural entre el Mediterráneo y el Atlántico (siglos XII–VIII ane)*, edited by Sebastián Celestino Pérez, Núria Rafel Fontanals, and Xosé-Lois Armada Pita, 123–48. Madrid: Consejo superior de investigaciones científicas.

———. 2016. "The Phoenicians in the Central-West Mediterranean and Atlantic between 'Precolonization' and the 'First Colonization.'" In *Contexts of Early Colonization*, edited by Lieve Donnellan, Valentino Nizzo, and Gert-Jan Burgers, 289–309. Rome: Palombi Editori.

———. 2017. "The Diffusion of Near Eastern Cultures." In *Etruscology*, edited by Alessandro Naso, 581–616. Berlin: de Gruyter.

Bourdieu, Pierre. 1984. *Distinction: A Social Critique of the Judgement of Taste*. Cambridge, MA: Harvard University Press.

Bourriot, Félix. 1976. *Recherches sur la nature du génos: Étude d'histoire sociale Athénienne*. Lille, France: Université Lille III.

Bowersock, Glen W. 2005. "The East-West Orientation of Mediterranean Studies and the Meaning of North and South in Antiquity." In *Rethinking the Mediterranean*, edited by W. V. Harris, 167–78. Oxford: Oxford University Press.

Brann, Eva. 1959a. "An Early Protoattic Hydria." *American Journal of Archaeology* 63:178–79.

———. 1959b. "Seventh Century Sherds from the Olympieion Area." *Hesperia: The Journal of the American School of Classical Studies at Athens* 28:251–52.

———. 1960. "Late Geometric Grave Groups from the Athenian Agora." *Hesperia: The Journal of the American School of Classical Studies at Athens* 29:402–16.

——. 1961a. "Late Geometric Well Groups from the Athenian Agora." *Hesperia: The Journal of the American School of Classical Studies at Athens* 30:93–146.

——. 1961b. "Protoattic Well Groups from the Athenian Agora." *Hesperia: The Journal of the American School of Classical Studies at Athens* 30:305–79.

——. 1962. *Agora 8: Late Geometric and Protoattic Pottery, Mid 8th to Late 7th Century B.C.* Princeton, NJ: American School of Classical Studies at Athens.

Braun-Holzinger, Eva A., and Ellen Rehm. 2005. *Orientalischer Import in Griechenland im frühen 1. Jahrtausend v. Chr.* Münster: Ugarit-Verlag.

Brisart, Thomas. 2011. *Un art citoyen: Recherches sur l'orientalisation des artisanats en Grèce proto-archaïque.* Brussels: Académie royale de Belgique, Classe des lettres.

Brixhe, Claude. 2004. "Nouvelle chronologie anatolienne et date d'élaboration des alphabets grec et phrygien." *Comptes rendus des séances de l'Académie des Inscriptions et Belles-Lettres* 148:271–89.

Brokaw, Clotilda. 1963. "Concurrent Styles in Late Geometric and Early Protoattic Vase Painting." *Mitteilungen des Deutschen Archäologischen Instituts, Athenische Abteilung* 78:63–73.

——. 1964. "The Dating of the Protocorinthian Kotyle." In *Essays in Memory of Karl Lehmann,* edited by Lucy Freeman Sandler, 49–54. New York: Institute of Fine Arts.

Broodbank, Cyprian. 2013. *The Making of the Middle Sea: A History of the Mediterranean from the Beginning to the Emergence of the Classical World.* London: Thames and Hudson.

Brouskari, Maria S. 1974. *Musée de l'acropole: Catalogue descriptive.* Athens: Édition de la banque commerciale de grèce.

Brück, Joanna. 2004. "Material Metaphors: The Relational Construction of Identity in Early Bronze Age Burials in Ireland and Britain." *Journal of Social Archaeology* 4:307–33.

Brückner, Alfred, and Erich Pernice. 1893. "Ein Attischer Friedhof." *Mitteilungen des Deutschen Archäologischen Instituts, Athenische Abteilung* 18:73–191.

Brughmans, Tom. 2010. "Connecting the Dots: Towards Archaeological Network Analysis." *Oxford Journal of Archaeology* 29:277–303.

Brughmans, Tom, and Jeroen Poblome. 2015. "Pots in Space: An Exploratory and Geographical Network Analysis of Roman Pottery Distribution." In *New Worlds from Old Texts: Revisiting Ancient Space and Place,* edited by Elton Barker, Stefan Bouzarovski, Christopher Pelling, and Leif Isaksen, 255–80. Oxford: Oxford University Press.

Bruins, Hendrik J., Albert J. Nijboer, and Johannes van der Plicht. 2011. "Iron Age Mediterranean Chronology: A Rejoinder." *Radiocarbon* 53:199–220.

Brumfiel, Elizabeth M. 1992. "Breaking and Entering the Ecosystem—Gender, Class, and Faction Steal the Show." *American Anthropologist* 94:551–67.

Bruni, Stefano. 1994. "Prima di Demarato: Nuovi dati sulla presenza di ceramiche greche e di tipo greco a Tarquinia durante la prima età orientalizzante." In *La presenza etrusca nella Campania meridionale,* edited by Patrizia Gastaldi and Guglielmo Maetzke, 293–328. Florence: L. S. Olschki.

Brunn, Heinrich. 1856. "Über die Grundverschiedenheit im Bildungsprincip der griechischen und ägyptischen Kunst." *Rheinisches Museum für Philologie* 10:153–66.

——. 1868. *Die Kunst bei Homer und ihr Verhältniss zu den Anfängen der griechischen Kunstgesechichte.* Munich: Verlag der k. Akademie.

——. 1893. *Griechische Kunstgeschichte. Erstes Buch. Die Anfänge und die älteste decorative Kunst.* Munich: Verlagsanstalt für Kunst und Wissenschaft.

Buchner, Giorgio. 1953–54. "Figürlich bemalte spätgeometrische vasen aus Pithekussai und Kyme." *Mitteilungen des Deutschen Archäologischen Instituts, Römische Abteilung* 60–61:37–55.

——. 1979. "Early Orientalizing: Aspects of the Euboean Connection." In *Italy before the Romans: The Iron Age, Orientalizing, and Etruscan periods,* edited by David Ridgway and Francesca R. Ridgway, 129–44. New York: Academic Press.

——. 1982. "Die Beziehungen zwischen der euböischen Kolonie Pithekoussai auf der Insel Ischia und dem nordwestsemitischen Mittelmeerraum in der zweiten Hälfte des 8. Jhs. v. Chr." In *Phönizier im Westen,* edited by Hans Georg Niemeyer, 277–306. Mainz am Rhein: Philipp von Zabern.

Buchner, Giorgio, and David Ridgway. 1993. *Pithekoussai.* Rome: G. Bretschneider.

Burgers, Gert-Jan, and Jan Paul Crielaard. 2007. "Greek Colonists and Indigenous Populations at L'Amastuola, Southern Italy." *Bulletin antieke beschaving* 82:77–114.

Burgon, Thomas. 1847. "An Attempt to Point Out the Vases of Greek Proper Which Belong to the Heroic and Homeric Ages." *Transactions of the Royal Society of Literature* 2:258–96.

Burkert, Walter. 1991a. "Homerstudien und Orient." In *Zweihundert Jahre Homer-Forschung: Rückblick und Ausblick,* edited by Joachim Latacz, 155–81. Stuttgart: B. G. Teubner.

———. 1991b. "Oriental Symposia: Contrasts and Parallels." In *Dining in a Classical Context*, edited by William J. Slater, 7–24. Ann Arbor: University of Michigan Press.

———. 1992. *The Orientalizing Revolution: Near Eastern Influence on Greek Culture in the Early Archaic Age*. Cambridge, MA: Harvard University Press.

———. 2004. *Babylon, Memphis, Persepolis: Eastern Contexts of Greek Culture*. Cambridge, MA: Harvard University Press.

Burr, Dorothy. 1933. "A Geometric House and a Proto-Attic Votive Deposit." *Hesperia: The Journal of the American School of Classical Studies at Athens* 2:542–640.

Buschor, Ernst. 1913. *Griechische Vasenmalerei*. Munich: R. Piper.

Byvanck, A. W. 1937. "Untersuchungen zur Chronologie der Funde in Italien aus dem VIII. und VII. vorchristlichen Jahrhundert." *Mnemosyne* 4:181–225.

Calhoun, George M. 1934. "Classes and Masses in Homer." *Classical Philology* 29:192–208, 301–16.

Callipolitis-Feytmans, Denise. 1963. "Tombes de Callithéa en Attique." *Bulletin de correspondance hellénique* 87:404–30.

———. 1965. *Les louteria attiques*. Athens: Direction des antiquités et des anastyloses.

Calvet, Y. 1980. "Sur certains rites funéraires à Salamine de Chypre." In *Salamine de Chypre: Histoire et archéologie; état des recherches*, edited by Marguerite Yon, 115–20. Paris: Éditions du Centre National de la Recherche Scientifique.

Camp, John McK. 1979. "A Drought in the Late Eighth Century B.C." *Hesperia: The Journal of the American School of Classical Studies at Athens* 48:397–411.

Camporeale, Giovannangelo, ed. 2004a. *The Etruscans Outside Etruria*. Los Angeles: J. Paul Getty Museum.

Camporeale, Giovannangelo. 2004b. "Etruscan Civilization." In *The Etruscans Outside Etruria*, edited by Giovannangelo Camporeale, 12–77. Los Angeles: J. Paul Getty Museum.

———. 2004c. "The Etruscans in the Mediterranean." In *The Etruscans Outside Etruria*, edited by Giovannangelo Camporeale, 78–101. Los Angeles: J. Paul Getty Museum.

———. 2016. "The Etruscans and the Mediterranean." In *A Companion to the Etruscans*, edited by Sinclair Bell and Alexandra A. Carpino, 67–86. Malden, MA: Wiley-Blackwell.

Canciani, Fulvio, and Friedrich-Wilhelm von Hase. 1979. *La tomba Bernardini di Palestrina*. Rome: Consiglio nazionale delle ricerche.

Carafa, Paolo. 2011. "Fenici a Pitecusa." *Rivista di Studi Fenici* 36:181–204.

Carr, Christopher, and Jill E. Neitzel. 1995. *Style, Society, and Person: Archaeological and Ethnological Perspectives*. New York: Plenum Press.

Carter, Jane B. 1997. "Thiasos and Marzeah: Ancestor Cult in the Age of Homer." In *New Light on a Dark Age: Exploring the Culture of Geometric Greece*, edited by Susan Langdon, 72–112. Columbia: University of Missouri Press.

Carter, John. 1972. "The Beginning of Narrative Art in the Greek Geometric Period." *Annual of the British School at Athens* 67:25–58.

Carter, Joseph Coleman. 2006. *Discovering the Greek Countryside at Metaponto*. Ann Arbor: University of Michigan Press.

Cavanagh, William, and Christopher Mee. 1995. "Mourning Before and After the Dark Age." In *Klados: Essays in Honour of J. N. Coldstream*, edited by Christine Morris, 45–61. London: Bulletin of the Institute of Classical Studies.

Caylus, Anne Claude Philippe. 1752. *Recueil d'antiquités égyptiennes, étrusques, grecques et romaines*. Paris: Desaint and Saillant.

Cesnola, Luigi Palma di. 1877. *Cyprus: Its Ancient Cities, Tombs, and Temples; A Narrative of Researches and Excavations during Ten Years' Residence in That Island*. 3rd ed. New York: Harper and Brothers.

Charalambidou, Xenia. 2018. "On the Style and Cultural Biography of Euboean and Euboean-Related Amphorae: (Re)visiting Material Evidence from the Hygeionomeion Cemetery at the Spanou Plot in Eretria." *Antike Kunst* 61:3–15.

Charalambidou, Xenia, and Catherine Morgan, eds. 2017. *Interpreting the Seventh Century BC: Tradition and Innovation*. Oxford: Archeopress.

Christiansen, Jette. 1996/2000. *Kiapha Thiti: Ergebnisse der Ausgrabungen III.1*. Marburger Winckelmann-Programm.

Chryssoulaki, Stella. 2019. "The Excavations at Phaleron Cemetery 2012–2017: An Introduction." In *Rethinking Athens before the Persian Wars*, edited by Constanze Graml, Annarita Doronzio, and Vincenzo Capozzoli, 103–14. Munich: utzverlag.

Cogan, Mordechai, and Hayim Tadmor. 1977. "Gyges and Ashurbanipal: A Study in Literary Trans-mission." *Orientalia* 46:65–85.

Coldstream, J. N. 1968 [2008]. *Greek Geometric Pottery: A Survey of Ten Local Styles and Their Chro-nology.* Updated 2nd ed. Exeter: Bristol Phoenix.

———. 1977 [2003]. *Geometric Greece: 900–700 BC.* 2nd ed. London: Routledge.

———. 1995. "Euboean Geometric Imports from the Acropolis of Pithekoussai." *Annual of the British School at Athens* 90:251–67.

———. 1998. "Drinking and Eating in Euboean Pithekoussai." In *Euboica: L'Eubea e la presenza eu-boica in Calcidica e in Occidente,* edited by Michel Bats and Bruno d'Agostino, 303–10. Naples: Cen-tre Jean Bérard and Istituto Universitario Orientale.

———. 2000. "Some Unusual Geometric Scenes from Euboean *Pithekoussai.*" In *Damarato. Studi di antichità classica offerti a Paola Pelagatti,* edited by Irene Berlingò et al., 92–98. Milan: Electa.

———. 2001. "Greek Geometric Pottery in Italy and Cyprus: Contrasts and Comparisons." In *Italy and Cyprus in Antiquity: 1500–450 BC,* edited by Larissa Bonfante and Vassos Karageorghis, 227–38. Nicosia: The Costakis and Leto Severis Foundation.

———. 2003. "The BSA's Geometric Collection: Kynosarges et alia." *Annual of the British School at Athens* 98:331–46.

———. 2004. "The Various Aegean Affinities of Early Pottery from Sicilian Naxos." In *Le due città di Naxos: Atti del Seminario di studi (Giardini Naxos, 29–31 ottobre 2000),* edited by M. Costanza Len-tini, 40–49. Florence: Giunti Editore.

Collignon, Maxime. 1886. *A Manual of Greek Archaeology.* New York: Cassell Publishing.

Collignon, Maxime, and Louis Couve. 1902. *Catalogue des vases peints du Musée national d'Athènes.* Paris: A. Fontemoing.

———. 1904. *Catalogue des vases peints du Musée national d'Athènes.* Paris: A. Fontemoing.

Colonna, Giovanni, ed. 1976. *Civiltà del Lazio primitivo.* Rome: Multigrafica.

Conkey, Margaret W. 1990. "Experimenting with Style in Archaeology: Some Historical and Theo-retical Issues." In *The Uses of Style in Archaeology,* edited by Margaret W. Conkey and Christine A. Hastorf, 5–17. Cambridge: Cambridge University Press.

———. 2006. "Style, Design, and Function." In *Handbook of Material Culture,* edited by Chris Tilley, Webb Keane, Susanne Küchler, Mike Rowlands, and Patricia Spyer. London: Sage.

Conkey, Margaret W., and Christine A. Hastorf. 1990. "Introduction." In *The Uses of Style in Archaeology,* edited by Margaret W. Conkey and Christine A. Hastorf, 1–4. Cambridge: Cambridge University Press.

Conze, Alexander. 1862. *Melische thongefässe.* Leipzig: Breitkopf und Härtel.

———.1870. *Zur Geschichte der Anfänge griechischer Kunst.* Vienna: Im Commission bei Karl Ger-old's Sohn, Buchändler der Kaiserlichen Akademie der Wissenschaften.

Cook, John. M. 1934–35. "Protoattic Pottery." *Annual of the British School at Athens* 35:165–219.

———. 1947. "Athenian Workshops around 700." *Annual of the British School at Athens* 42:139–55.

———. 1951. Review of Kübler 1950. *Gnomon* 23:212–14.

———. 1962. Review of Brann 1962. *Gnomon* 34:820–23.

———. 1971. "A Painter and His Age." In *Mélanges de préhistoire d'archéocivilisation, et d'ethnologie offerts à André Varagnac,* 167–76.

Cook, Robert Manuel. 1983. "Art and Epic in Archaic Greece." *Bulletin antieke beschaving* 58:1–10.

———. 1997. *Greek Painted Pottery.* 3rd ed. London: Routledge.

Corner, Sean. 2005. "Philos and Polites: The Symposion and the Origins of the Polis." PhD diss., Clas-sics, Princeton University.

———. 2010. "Transcendent Drinking: The Symposium at Sea Reconsidered." *Classical Quarterly* 60:352–80.

Cosmopoulos, Michael B. 2014. *The Sanctuary of Demeter at Eleusis: The Bronze Age.* Athens: Archaeo-logical Society at Athens.

Coulié, Anne. 2013. *La céramique grecque aux époques géométrique et orientalisante: XIᵉ–VIᵉ siècle av. J.-C.* Paris: de Picard.

———. 2015. "L'atelier du Dipylon: Style, typologie et chronologie relative." In *Pots, Workshops, and Early Iron Age Society: Function and Role of Ceramics in Early Greece,* edited by Vicky Vlachou, 37–47. Brussels: CReA-Patrimoine.

Couve, Louis. 1893. "Un vase proto-attique du musée de la société archéologique d'athènes." *Bulletin de correspondance hellénique* 17:25–30.

———. 1897. "ΑΜΦΟΡΕΥΣ ΡΥΘΜΟΥ ΠΡΩΑΤΤΙΚΟΥ." *Ephemeris Archaiologike* 3:67–86.

Creuzer, Friedrich. 1810–12. *Symbolik und Mythologie der alten Völker, besonders der Griechen.* Leipzig: Leske.

Crielaard, Jan Paul. 2015. "Powerful Things in Motion: A Biographical Approach to Eastern Elite Goods in Greek Sanctuaries." In *Sanctuaries and the Power of Consumption: Networking and the Formation of Elites in the Archaic Western Mediterranean World*, edited by Erich Kistler, Birgit Öhlinger, Martin Mohr, and Matthias Hoernes, 351–72. Wiesbaden: Harrossowitz Verlag.

Croissant, Francis. 2010. "Sociétés, styles et identité: Pour une relecture archéologique du phénomène orientalisant." In *La Méditerranée au VIIe siècle av. J.-C.: Essais d'analyses archéologiques*, edited by R. Étienne. Paris: de Boccard.

Cuozzo, Mariassunta. 2003. *Reinventando la tradizione: Immaginario sociale, ideologie e rappresentazione nelle necropoli orientalizzanti di Pontecagnano.* Paestum: Pandemos.

Curtis, C. Densmore. 1919. "The Bernardini Tomb." *Memoirs of the American Academy in Rome* 3:9–90.

d'Agostino, Bruno. 1977. *Tombe principesche dell'orientalizzante antico da Pontecagnano.* Rome: Accademia nazionale dei Lincei.

———. 1982. "La ceramica greca o di tradizione greca nell'VIII sec. in Italia Meridionale." In *La Céramique grecque ou de tradition grecque au VIIIe siècle en Italie centrale et méridionale*, 55–67. Naples: Centre Jean Bérard.

———. 1996a. "The Colonial Experience in Greek Mythology." In *The Greek World: Art and Civilization in Magna Graecia and Sicily*, edited by Giovanni Pugliese Carratelli, 209–14. Milan: R.C.S. Libri e Grandi Opere S.p.A.

———. 1996b. "The Impact of the Greek Colonies on the Indigenous Peoples of Campania." In *The Greek World: Art and Civilization in Magna Graecia and Sicily*, edited by Giovanni Pugliese Carratelli, 533–40. Milan: R.C.S. Libri e Grandi Opere S.p.A.

———. 1999a. "Euboean Colonisation in the Gulf of Naples." In *Ancient Greeks West and East*, edited by Gocha R. Tsetskhladze, 207–27. Leiden: Brill.

———. 1999b. "Il leone sogna la preda." *Annali di Archaeologia e Storia Antica* 6:25–33.

———. 1999c. "Pitecusa e Cuma tra Greci e indigeni." In *La colonisation grecque en Méditerranée occidentale: Actes de la rencontre scientifique en hommage à Georges Vallet*, 51–62. Rome: École française de Rome.

———. 1999d. "I principi dell'Italia centro-tirrenica in epoca orientalizzante." In *Les princes de la protohistoire et l'émergence de l'Etat*, edited by Pascal Ruby, 81–88. Naples and Rome: Centre Jean Bérard / École française de Rome.

———. 2010. "Osservazioni al convegno." *Bollettino di archaeologia online*:77–82.

———. 2011. "Pithecusae e Cuma nel quadro della Campania di età arcaica." *Mitteilungen des Deutschen Archäologischen Instituts, Römische Abteilung* 117:35–53.

———. 2015. "The Archaeological Background of the Analysed Pendent Semicircle Skyphoi from Pontecagnano." In *Archaeometric Analyses of Euboean and Euboean Related Pottery: New Results and Their Interpretations*, edited by Michael Kerschner and Irene S. Lemos, 181–89. Vienna: Österreichisches Archäologisches Institut.

d'Agostino, Bruno, and Anna Maria d'Onofrio. 1993. Review of Morris 1987. *Gnomon* 65:41–51.

d'Agostino, Bruno, and Patrizia Gastaldi. 2016. "La cultura orientalizzante tirrenica come frutto di una crescita endogena: L'esempio di Pontecagnano." In *Contexts of Early Colonization*, edited by Lieve Donnellan, Valentino Nizzo, and Gert-Jan Burgers, 159–76. Rome: Palombi Editori.

d'Agostino, Bruno, and Andreas Soteriou. 1998. "Campania in the Framework of the Earliest Greek Colonization in the West." In *Euboica: L'Eubea e la presenza euboica in Calcidica e in Occidente*, edited by Michel Bats and Bruno d'Agostino, 355–68. Naples: Centre Jean Bérard / Istituto Universitario Orientale.

d'Onofrio, Anna Maria. 1993. "Le trasformazioni del costume funerario ateniese nella necropoli pre-Soloniana del Kerameikos." *Annali di Archaeologia e Storia Antica*:143–71.

———. 1995. "Santuari 'rurali' e dinamiche insediative in Attica tra il Protogeometrico e l'Orientalizzante (1050–600 A.C.)." *Annali di Archaeologia e Storia Antica* 2:57–88.

———. 1997. "The 7th Century BC in Attica: The Basis of Political Organization." In *Urbanization in the Mediterranean in the 9th to 6th centuries BC*, edited by H. Damgaard Andersen, Helle W. Horsnaes, Sanne Houby-Nielsen, and Annette Rathje, 63–88. Copenhagen: Museum Tusculanum Press.

———. 2001. "Immagini di divinità nel materiale votivo dell'edificio ovale geometrico ateniese e indagine sull'area sacra alle pendici settentrionali dell'Areopago." *Mélanges de l'École française de Rome: Antiquité* 113:257–320.

———. 2006. "The First Greeks in Italy." In *Greek Colonisation: An Account of Greek Colonies and Other Settlements Overseas,* edited by Gocha R. Tsetskhladze, 201–38. Leiden: Brill.

———. 2007–8. "Gli Ateniesi dell'Asty: L'abitato della prima età del ferro attraverso il record archeologico." In *Sepolti fra i vivi: Buried among the Living,* edited by Gilda Bartoloni, 437–60. Rome: Quasar.

———. 2017. "Athenian Burial Practices and Cultural Change: The Rundbau Early Plot in the Kerameikos Cemetery Revisited." In *Interpreting the Seventh Century BC: Tradition and Innovation,* edited by Xenia Charalambidou and Catherine Morgan, 260–80. Oxford: Archaeopress.

Daloz, Jean-Pascal. 2010. *The Sociology of Elite Distinction: From Theoretical to Comparative Perspectives.* Basingstoke, UK: Palgrave Macmillan.

Daremberg, Charles, and M. Edmond Saglio, eds. 1877–1919. *Dictionnaire des antiquities grecques et romains d'après les textes et les monuments.* Paris: Hachette.

Davis, Whitney. 1990. "Style and History in Art History." In *The Uses of Style in Archaeology,* edited by Margaret W. Conkey and Christine A. Hastorf, 18–31. Cambridge: Cambridge University Press.

Davison, Jean M. 1961. *Attic Geometric Workshops.* New Haven, CT: Yale University Press.

de Angelis, Franco, ed. 2013. *Regionalism and Globalism in Antiquity: Exploring Their Limits.* Leuven, Belgium: Peeters.

Delpino, Filippo. 1989. "L'ellenizzazione dell'Etruria villanoviana: Sui rapporti tra Grecia ed Etruria fra IX e VIII secolo a.c." *Secondo Congresso Internazionale Etrusco* 1:105–16.

Dempster, Thomas. 1723–24. *De Etruria Regali.* Florence.

Denoyelle, Martine. 1996. "Le peintre d'Analatos: Essai de synthèse et perspectives nouvelles." *Antike Kunst*:71–87.

Denoyelle, Martine, and Mario Iozzo. 2009. *La céramique grecque d'Italie méridionale et de Sicile: Productions coloniales et apparentées, du VIIIe au IIIe siècle av. J.-C.* Paris: Picard.

Denti, Mario. 1999. "Per una fenomenologia storico-culturale del linguaggio figurativo dei greci d'occidente in età arcaica." In *Κοινά: Miscellanea di studi archeologici in onore di Piero Orlandini,* edited by Marina Castoldi, 205–21. Milan: Edizioni ET.

———. 2000. "Nuovi documenti di ceramica orientalizzante della Grecia d'Occidente: Stato della questione e prospettive della ricerca." *Mélanges de l'École française de Rome: Antiquité* 112:781–842.

———. 2013. "The Contribution of Research on Incoronata to the Problem of the Relations between Greeks and Non-Greeks during Proto-Colonial Times." *Ancient West and East* 12:71–116.

———. 2015. "Des biens de prestige grecs intentionnellement fragmentés dans un contexte indigène de la Méditeraranée occidentale au VIIe siècle av. J.-C." In *THRAVSMA: Contextualising the Intentional Destruction of Objects in the Bronze Age Aegean and Cyprus,* edited by Kate Harrell and Jan Driessen, 99–116. Louvain-la-Neuve, Belgium: Presses Universitaires de Louvain.

———. 2016. "Gli Enotri - e i Greci - sul Basento: Nuovi dati sul Metapontino in età proto-coloniale." In *Contexts of Early Colonization,* edited by Lieve Donnellan, Valentino Nizzo, and Gert-Jan Burgers, 223–35. Rome: Palombi Editori.

———. 2018a. "Aegean Migrations and the Indigenous Iron Age Communities on the Ionian Coast of Southern Italy: Sharing and Interaction Phenomena." In *The Emporion in the Ancient Western Mediterranean: Trade and Colonial Encounters from the Archaic to the Hellenistic Period,* edited by Éric Gailledrat, Michael Dietler, and Rosa Plana-Mallart, 207–17. Montpellier France: Presses universitaires de la Méditerranée.

———. 2018b. "Archilochos Did Not Sail Alone to the Bountiful Shores of Siris: Parian and Naxian Potters in Southern Italy in the 7th century BC." In *Paros and Its Colonies,* edited by Dora Katsonopoulou, 39–63. Athens: Institute for Archaeology of Paros and the Cyclades.

Denti, Mario, and Mathilde Villette. 2013. "Ceramisti greci dell'Egeo in un atelier indigeno d'Occidente: Scavi e ricerche sullo spazio artigianale dell'Incoronata nella Valle del Basento (VIII–VII secolo A.C.)." *Bolletino d'Arte* 17:1–36.

Dentzer, Jean-Marie. 1982. *Le motif du banquet couché dans le Proche-Orient et le monde grec du VIIe au IVe siècle avant J.-C.* Rome: École française de Rome.

Deoudi, Maria. 1999. *Heroenkulte in homerischer Zeit.* Oxford: Archaeopress.

Descoeudres, Jean-Paul, and Rosalinde Kearsley. 1983. "Greek Pottery at Veii: Another Look." *Annual of the British School at Athens* 78:9–53.

Devambez, Pierre, and François Villard. 1979. "Un vase orientalisant polychrome au musée du Louvre." *Fondation Eugène Piot: Monuments et Mémoires* 62:13–41.

DeVries, Keith. 2003. "Eighth-Century Corinthian Pottery: Evidence for the Dates of Greek Settlement in the West." In *The Centenary: 1896–1996,* 141–56. Princeton, NJ: American School of Classical Studies at Athens.

DeVries, Keith, G. Kenneth Sams, and Mary M. Voigt. 2005. "Gordion Re-Dating." In *Anatolian Iron Ages 5: Proceedings of the Fifth Anatolian Iron Ages Colloquium Held at Van, 6–10. August 2001*, edited by Altan Çilingiroğlu and Gareth Darbyshire. London: British Institute of Archaeology at Ankara.

Dickie, Matthew 1995. "The Geography of Homer's World." In *Homer's World: Fiction, Tradition, Reality*, edited by Øivind Andersen and Matthew Dickie, 29–56. Bergen: Norwegian Institute at Athens.

Diepolder, Hans. 1947. *Griechische Vasen*. Berlin: Gebr. Mann.

Dierichs, Angelika. 1981. *Das Bild des Greifen in der frühgriechischen Flächenkunst*. Münster: Lit.

Dietler, Michael. 1996. "Feasts and Commensal Politics in the Political Economy: Food, Power and Status in Prehistoric Europe." In *Food and the Status Quest: An Interdisciplinary Perspective*, edited by Polly Wiessner and Wulf Schiefenhövel, 87–125. Oxford: Berghahn Books.

———. 2001. "Theorizing the Feast: Rituals of Consumption, Commensal Politics, and Power in African Contexts." In *Feasts: Archaeological and Ethnographic Perspectives on Food, Politics, and Power*, edited by Michael Dietler and Brian Hayden, 65–114. Washington, DC: Smithsonian Institution Press.

———. 2005. "The Archaeology of Colonization and the Colonization of Archaeology: Theoretical Reflections on an Ancient Mediterranean Colonial Encounter." In *The Archaeology of Colonial Encounters: Comparative Perspectives*, edited by Gil J. Stein, 33–68. Santa Fe: School of American Research Press.

———. 2010. "Consumption." In *The Oxford Handbook of Material Culture Studies*, edited by Dan Hicks and Mary C. Beadry, 209–28. New York: Oxford University Press.

Dietler, Michael, and Ingrid Herbich. 1989. "*Tich Matek*: The Technology of Luo Pottery Production and the Definition of Ceramic Style." *World Archaeology* 21:148–64.

———. 1994a. "Ceramics and Ethnic Identity: Ethnoarchaeological Observations on the Distribution of Pottery Styles and the Relationship between the Social Contexts of Production and Consumption." In *Terre cuite et société: La céramique, document technique, économique, culturel*, edited by Didier Binder and Jean Courtin, 459–72. Juan-les-Pins France: Éditions APDCA.

———. 1994b. "Habitus et reproduction sociale des techniques: L'intelligence du style en archéologie et en ethno-archéologie." In *De la préhistoire aux missiles balistiques: L'intelligence sociale des techniques*, edited by Bruno Latour and Pierre Lemonier, 202–22. Paris: La Découverte.

———. 1998. "*Habitus*, Techniques, and Style: An Integrated Approach to the Social Understanding of Material Culture and Boundaries." In *The Archaeology of Social Boundaries*, edited by Miriam T. Stark, 232–63. Washington, DC: Smithsonian Institution Press.

Dietler, Michael, and Carolina López-Ruiz, eds. 2009. *Colonial Encounters in Ancient Iberia: Phoenician, Greek, and Indigenous Relations*. Chicago: University of Chicago Press.

Dietrich, Nikolaus, and Michael Squire, eds. 2018. *Ornament and Figure in Graeco-Roman Art: Rethinking Visual Ontologies in Classical Antiquity*. Berlin : Walter de Gruyter.

Dik, Ronald. 1980. "Un'anfora etrusca con raffigurazioni orientalizzanti da Veio." *Mededelingen van het Nederlands Instituut te Rome* 42:15–30.

———. 1981a. "Un'anfora orientalizzante etrusca nel museo Allard Pierson." *Bulletin antieke beschaving* 56:45–74.

———. 1981b. "Un'oinochoe ceretana con decorazione di pesci: inplicazioni culturali." *Mededelingen van het Nederlands Instituut te Rome* 43:69–81.

Dimitriadou, Eirini. 2019. *Early Athens: Settlements and Cemeteries in the Submycenaean, Geometric, and Archaic Periods*. Los Angeles: UCLA Cotsen Institute of Archaeology Press.

Doak, Brian R., and Carolina López-Ruiz. 2019. *The Oxford Handbook of the Phoenician and Punic Mediterranean*. Oxford: Oxford University Press.

Docter, Roald F., and Hans Georg Niemeyer. 1994. "Pithekoussai: The Carthaginian Connection; On the Archaeological Evidence of Euboeo-Phoenician Partnership in the 8th and 7th Centuries B.C." In *ΑΠΟΙΚΙΑ: I più antichi insediamenti greci in Occidente; Funzioni e modi dell'organizzazione politica e sociale*, edited by Bruno d'Agostino and David Ridgway, 101–15. Naples: Istituto Universitario Orientale.

Docter, Roald F., Hans Georg Niemeiyer, Albert J. Nijboer, and Johannes van der Plicht. 2005. "Radiocarbon Dates of Animal Bones in the Earliest Levels of Carthage." In *Oriente e Occidente: Metodi e disciplina a confronto; Riflessioni sulla cronologia dell'età del ferro in Italia*, edited by Gilda Bartolini and Filippo Delpino, 557–77. Pisa: Istituti editoriali e poligrafici Internazionali.

Dommelen, Peter van. 2017. "Classical Connections and Mediterranean Practices: Exploring Connectivity and Local Interactions." In *The Routledge Handbook of Archaeology and Globalization*, edited by Tamar Hodos, 618–33. London: Routledge.

Donlan, Walter. 1980. *The Aristocratic Ideal in Ancient Greece: Attitudes of Superiority from Homer to the End of the Fifth Century B.C.* Lawrence, KS: Coronado Press.

Donnellan, Lieve. 2014. "*Oikist* and Archegetes in Context: Representing the Foundation of Sicilian Naxos." In *Foundation Myths in Ancient Societies: Dialogues and Discourses*, edited by Naoise Mac Sweeney, 41–70. Philadelphia: University of Pennsylvania Press.

Dore, Anna. 2003. "Etruria at the Po Area." In *Sea Routes . . . from Sidon to Huelva, Interconnections in the Mediterranean 16th–6th c. BC*, edited by Nikolaos Ch. Stampolidis, 164–65. Athens: Museum of Cycladic Art.

Doronzio, Annarita. 2018. *Athen im 7. Jahrhundert v. Chr.: Räume und Funde der frühen Polis.* Berlin: de Gruyter.

Dougherty, Carol, and Leslie Kurke. 2003. "Introduction: The Cultures within Greek Culture." In *The Cultures within Ancient Greek Culture: Contact, Conflict, Collaboration*, edited by Carol Dougherty and Leslie Kurke, 1–22. Cambridge: Cambridge University Press.

Dragendorff, Hans, ed. 1903. *Theraeische Graeber.* Berlin: Georg Reimer.

Drago, Luciana, Manuela Bonadies, Andrea Carapellucci, and Cecilia Predan. 2014. "Il pittore di Narce e i suoi epigoni a Veio." *Archeologia Classica* 65:7–58.

Droop, J. P. 1905–6. "Dipylon Vases from the Kynosarges Site." *Annual of the British School at Athens* 12:80–92.

Dumont, Albert. 1869. "Sur un vase de Phalère." *Revue Archéologique* 19:213–19.

Dumont, Albert, and Jules Chaplain. 1888. *Les céramiques de la Grèce propre.* Paris: Firmin Didot.

Dunbabin, Thomas James. 1936. "Ἐχθρη παλαιη." *Annual of the British School at Athens* 37:83–91.

———. 1948. *The Western Greeks: The History of Sicily and South Italy from the Foundation of the Greek Colonies to 480 B.C.* Oxford: Clarendon Press.

———. 1950. "An Attic Bowl." *Annual of the British School at Athens* 45:193–202.

———. 1953–54. "The Chronology of Corinthian Vases." *Ephemeris Archaiologike*:247–62.

———. 1957. *The Greeks and Their Eastern Neighbours.* London: Society for the Promotion of Hellenic Studies.

Dunbabin, Thomas James, and Martin Robertson. 1953. "Some Protocorinthian Vase-Painters." *Annual of the British School at Athens* 48:172–81.

Duplouy, Alain. 2003. "Les Eupatrides d'Athènes: 'Nobles défenseurs de leur patrie.'" *Cahiers du Centre Gustave Glotz* 14:7–22.

———. 2006. *Le prestige des élites: Recherches sur les modes de reconnaissance sociale en Grèce entre les Xe et Ve siècles avant J.-C.* Paris: Les belles lettres.

———. 2015. "Genealogical and Dynastic Behaviour in Archaic and Classical Greece: Two Gentilician Strategies." In *"Aristocracy" in Antiquity: Redefining Greek and Roman Elites*, edited by Nick Fisher and Hans van Wees, 59–84. Swansea: Classical Press of Wales.

———. 2018a. "Citizenship as Performance." In *Defining Citizenship in Archaic Greece*, edited by Alain Duplouy and Roger W. Brock, 249–74. Oxford: Oxford University Press.

———. 2018b. "Pathways to Archaic Citizenship." In *Defining Citizenship in Archaic Greece*, edited by Alain Duplouy and Roger W. Brock, 1–50. Oxford: Oxford University Press.

———. 2019a. *Construire la cité: Essai de sociologie historique sur les communautés de l'archaïsme grec.* Paris: Les belles lettres.

———. 2019b. "The Making of the Greek City: An Athenian Case Study." In *Rethinking Athens before the Persian Wars*, edited by Constanze Graml, Annarita Doronzio, and Vincenzo Capozzoli, 207–16. Munich: utzverlag.

Duplouy, Alain, Olivier Mariaud, and François de Polignac. 2010. "Les sociétés grecques." In *La Méditerranée au VIIe siècle av. J.-C.*, edited by Roland Étienne, 275–309. Paris: De Boccard.

Ebbinghaus, Susanne. 2005. "Protector of the City: The Art of Storage in Early Greece." *Journal of Hellenic Studies* 125:51–72.

Eijnde, Floris van den. 2018a. "Feasting and Polis Institutions: An Introduction." In *Feasting and Polis Institutions*, edited by Josine Blok, Floris van den Eijnde, and Rolf Strootman, 1–27. Leiden: Brill.

———. 2018b. "Power Play at the Dinner Table: Feasting and Patronage between Palace and Polis in Attika." In *Feasting and Polis Institutions*, edited by Josine Blok, Floris van den Eijnde, and Rolf Strootman, 60–92. Leiden: Brill.

———. 2019. "The 'First Athenian Empire'? Athenian Overseas Interests in the Archaic Period." In *Empires of the Sea: Maritime Power Networks in World History*, edited by Rolf Strootman, Floris van den Eijnde, and Roy van Wijk, 52–80. Leiden: Brill.

Eijnde Floris van den, and Michael Laughy. 2017. "The Areopagus Oval Building Reconsidered." In *Regional Stories: Towards a New Perception of the Early Greek World*, edited by Alexander Mazarakis

Ainian, Alexandra Alexandridou, and Xenia Charalambidou, 177–96. Volos: University of Thessaly Press.

Esposito, Arianna. 2018. "Rethinking Pithekoussai: Current Perspectives and Issues." In *The Emporion in the Ancient Western Mediterranean: Trade and Colonial Encounters from the Archaic to the Hellenistic Period*, edited by Éric Gailledrat, Michael Dietler, and Rosa Plana-Mallart, 167–79. Montpellier, France: Presses universitaires de la Méditerranée.

Étienne, Roland. 2004. *Athènes: Espaces urbains et histoire des origines à la fin du IIIe siècle ap. J. C.* Paris: Hachette.

———, ed. 2010. *La Méditerranée au VIIe s. av. J.-C.* Paris: de Boccard.

Evans, Arthur J. 1912. "The Minoan and Mycenaean Element in Hellenic Life." *Journal of Hellenic Studies* 32:277–97.

Fantalkin, Alexander. 2006. "Identity in the Making: Greeks in the Eastern Mediterranean during the Iron Age." In *Naukratis: Greek Diversity in Egypt*, edited by Alexandra Villing and Udo Schlotzhauer, 199–235. London: British Museum.

———. 2014. "Naukratis as a Contact Zone: Revealing the Lydian Connection." In *Kulturkontakte in Antiken Welten: Vom Denkmodell zum Fallbeispiel*, edited by Robert Rollinger and Kordula Schnegg, 27–51. Leuven, Belgium: Peeters.

Fantalkin, Alexander, Israel Finkelstein, and Eli Piasetzky. 2011. "Iron Age Mediterranean Chronology: A Reply." *Radiocarbon* 53:199–220.

Faraone, Christopher A. 1992. *Talismans and Trojan Horses: Guardian Statues in Ancient Greek Myth and Ritual*. New York: Oxford University Press.

———. 1996. "Taking the 'Nestor's Cup Inscription' Seriously: Erotic Magic and Conditional Curses in the Earliest Inscribed Hexameters." *Classical Antiquity* 15:77–112.

Fehr, Burkhard. 1971. *Orientalische und griechische Gelage*. Bonn: Bouvier.

Feldman, Marian H. 2014. *Communities of Style: Portable Luxury Arts, Identity, and Collective Memory in the Iron Age Levant*. Chicago: University of Chicago Press.

———. 2016. "Consuming the East: Near Eastern Luxury Goods in Orientalizing Contexts." In *Assyria to Iberia: Art and Culture in the Iron Age*, edited by Joan Aruz and Michael Seymour, 227–33. New York: Metropolitan Museum of Art.

Ferrari, Gloria. 1987. "Menelãs." *Journal of Hellenic Studies* 107:180–82.

Filser, Wolfgang. 2017. *Die Elite Athens auf der attischen Luxuskeramik*. Boston: de Gruyter.

Fischer-Hansen, Tobias, Thomas Heine Nielsen, and Carmine Ampolo. 2004a. "Italia and Kampania." In *An Inventory of Archaic and Classical Poleis*, edited by Mogens Herman Hansen and Thomas Heine Nielsen, 249–320. Oxford: Oxford University Press.

———. 2004b. "Sikelia." In *An Inventory of Archaic and Classical Poleis*, edited by Mogens Herman Hansen and Thomas Heine Nielsen, 172–248. Oxford: Oxford University Press.

Fitton, J. Lesley. 1995. *The Discovery of the Greek Bronze Age*. London: Published for the Trustees of the British Museum by British Museum Press.

Fittschen, Klaus. 1969. *Untersuchungen zum Beginn der Sagendarstellungen bei den Griechen*. Berlin: Hessling.

Flament, Christophe. 2007. "Que nous reste-t-il de Solon? Essai de déconstruction de l'image du père de la πάτριος πολιτεία." *Les études classiques* 75:289–318.

Fornara, Charles W. 1977. *Archaic Times to the End of the Peloponnesian War*. Baltimore: Johns Hopkins University Press.

Forsberg, Stig. 1995. *Near Eastern Destruction Datings as Sources for Greek and Near Eastern Iron Age Chronology: Archaeological and Historical Studies; The Cases of Samaria (722 B.C.) and Tarsus (696 B.C.)*. 2nd rev. ed. Uppsala: S. Academiae Ubsaliensis.

Forsdyke, Sara. 2006. "Land, Labor, and Economy in Solonian Athens: Breaking the Impasse between Archaeology and History." In *Solon of Athens: New Historical and Philological Approaches*, edited by Josine H. Blok and André P.M.H. Lardinois, 334–50. Leiden: Brill.

Fouchard, Alain. 2010. "Comment reconnaître les élites?" In *La cité et ses élites: Pratiques et représentation des formes de domination et de contrôle social dans les cités grecques*, edited by Laurent Capdetrey and Yves Lafond, 359–78. Paris: de Boccard.

Fowler, Chris. 2004. *The Archaeology of Personhood: An Anthropological Approach*. London: Taylor and Francis.

———. 2016. "Relational Personhood Revisited." *Cambridge Archaeological Journal* 26:397–412.

Foxhall, Lin. 1997. "A View from the Top: Evaluating the Solonian Property Classes." In *The Development of the Polis in Archaic Greece*, edited by Lynette G. Mitchell and P. J. Rhodes, 113–36. London: Routledge.

Fragkopoulou, Florentia. 2015. "Piraeus beyond 'Known Unknowns.'" In *Aegis: Essays in Mediterranean Archaeology Presented to Matti Egon by the Scholars of the Greek Archaeological Committee UK*, edited by Zetta Theodoropoulou Polychroniadis and Doniert Evely, 131–36. Oxford: Archaeopress.

———. 2019. "The SOS Amphorae from Phaleron Revisited." In *Τῷ διδασκάλῳ. Τιμητικός τόμος για τον καθηγητή Ιωάννη Ακαμάτη*, edited by Nikos Akamatis, Alexandros Vouvoulis, Alexandros Laftsidis, and Nektarios Poulakakis, 367–75. Thessaloniki.

Fragkopoulou, Florentia, and Eleni Zosi. 2017. "Material Koine and the Case of Phaleron Cups: Conventions and Reality." In *Material Koinai in the Greek Early Iron Age and Archaic Period*, edited by Søren Handberg and Anastasia Gadolou. Aarhus, Denmark: Aarhus University Press.

Franklin, John Curtis. 2008. "'A Feast of Music': The Greco-Lydian Musical Movement on the Assyrian Periphery." In *Anatolian Interfaces: Hittites, Greeks, and Their Neighbors*, edited by Billie Jean Collins, Mary R. Bachvarova, and Ian C. Rutherford, 191–202. Oxford: Oxbow Books.

Freytag, Bettina von. 1975. "Neue frühattische Funde aus dem Kerameikos." *Mitteilungen des Deutschen Archäologischen Instituts, Athenische Abteilung* 90:49–81.

Friis Johansen, Knud. 1923. *Les vases sicyoniens*. Paris: E. Champion.

Furtwängler, Adolf. 1880. *Die Bronzefunde aus Olympia und deren kunstgeschichtliche Bedeutung*. Berlin: Buchdruckerei der Königl. Akademie der Wissenschaften (G. Vogt).

———. 1881. "Zwei Thongefässe aus Athen." *Mittheilungen des deutschen archäologischen Institutes in Athen* 6:106–18.

———. 1882. "Schüssel aus Aegina." *Archäeologische Zeitung* 40:196–207.

Furtwängler, Adolf, and Georg Loeschcke. 1886. *Mykenische vasen: vorhellenische Thongefässe aus dem gebiete des Mittelmeeres*. Berlin: A. Asher.

Gaertringen, von, ed. 1899–1909. *Thera: Untersuchungen, Vermessungen und Ausgrabungen in den Jahren 1895–1902*. Berlin: Georg Reimer.

Gagarin, Michael. 1981. *Drakon and Early Athenian Homicide Law*. New Haven, CT: Yale University Press.

Gagné, Renaud. 2016. "The World in a Cup: Ekpomatics In and Out of the Symposium." In *The Cup of Song: Ancient Greek Poetry and the Symposium*, edited by Vanessa Cazzato, Dirk Obbink, and Enrico Emanuele Prodi, 207–29. Oxford: Oxford University Press.

Galbois, Estelle, and Sylvie Rougier-Blanc. 2014. "La pauvreté en Grèce ancienne, un faux sujet de recherche?" In *La pauvreté en Grèce ancienne: Formes, représentations, enjeux*, edited by Estelle Galbois and Sylvie Rougier-Blanc, 13–23. Bordeaux: Ausonius.

Garland, Robert. 1985. *The Greek Way of Death*. Ithaca, NY: Cornell University Press.

Gell, Alfred. 1998. *Art and Agency: An Anthropological Theory*. Oxford: Clarendon Press.

Geppert, Karin. 2006. *Studien zu Aufnahme und Umsetzung orientalischer Einflüsse in Etrurien und Mittelitalien vom Ende des 8. bis Anfang des 6. Jhs. v. Chr.* Münster: Lit.

Gerhard, E. 1831. "Rapporto Volcente." *Annali dell' instituto di corrispondenza archeologica* 3:5–248.

Geroulanos, Johannes M. 1973. "Grabsitten des ausgehenden geometrischen Stils im Bereich des Gutes Trachones bei Athen." *Mitteilungen des Deutschen Archäologischen Instituts, Athenische Abteilung* 88:1–54.

Gilboa, Ayelet. 2013. "À-propos Huelva: A Reassessment of 'Early' Phoenicians in the West." In *Tarteso: El emporio del metal*, edited by Juan M. Campos and Jaime Alvar. Córdoba: Almuzara.

Ginzburg, Carlo. 1998. "Style as Inclusion, Style as Exclusion." In *Picturing Science, Producing Art*, edited by Caroline A. Jones and Peter Galison, 27–54. New York: Routledge.

Giuliani, Luca. 2013. *Image and Myth: A History of Pictorial Narration in Greek Art*. Chicago: University of Chicago Press.

Giuliano, Antonio. 1996. "Greek Influence on Italic Art." In *The Western Greeks*, edited by Giovanni Pugliese Carratelli, 591–606. Milan: RCS Libri e Grandi Opere S.p.A.

———. 2005. "Protoattici in Occidente." In *ΑΕΙΜΝΗΣΤΟΣ: Miscellanea di Studi per Mauro Cristofani*, edited by Benedetta Adembri, 64–72. Florence: Centro Di.

González de Canales, Fernando. 2018. "The City-Emporion of Huelva (10th–6th Centuries BC)." In *The Emporion in the Ancient Western Mediterranean: Trade and Colonial Encounters from the Archaic to the Hellenistic Period*, edited by Éric Gailledrat, Michael Dietler, and Rosa Plana-Mallart, 67–78. Montpellier, France: Presses universitaires de la Méditerranée.

González de Canales, Fernando, Leonardo Serrano, and Jorge Llompart. 2006. "The Pre-Colonial Phoenician Emporium of Huelva ca. 900–770 BC." *Bulletin antieke beschaving* 81:13–29.

Graef, Botho, Ernst Langlotz, Paul Hartwig, Paul Heinrich, August Wolters, and Robert Zahn. 1925. *Die antiken vasen von der Akropolis zu Athen*. 2 vols. Berlin: de Gruyter.

Granovetter, Mark S. 1973. "The Strength of Weak Ties." *American Journal of Sociology* 78:1360–80.

———. 1983. "The Strength of Weak Ties: A Network Theory Revisited." *Sociological Theory* 1:201–33.

Greco, Emanuele. 2006. "Greek Colonisation in Southern Italy: A Methodological Essay." In *Greek Colonisation: An Account of Greek Colonies and Other Settlements Overseas*, edited by Gocha R. Tsetskhladze, 169–237. Leiden: Brill.

Greco, Giovanna. 2014. "Cuma arcaica: Ruolo e funzione nel rapporto con gli indigeni." In *Hesperìa: Tradizioni, rotte, paesaggi*, edited by Luisa Breglia and Alda Moleti, 57–85. Paestum: Pandemos.

Grethlein, Jonas. 2018. "Ornamental and Formulaic Patterns: The Semantic Significance of Form in Early Greek Vase-Painting and Homeric Epic." In *Ornament and Figure in Graeco-Roman Art: Rethinking Visual Ontologies in Classical Antiquity*, edited by Nikolaus Dietrich and Michael Squire, 73–96. Berlin: de Gruyter.

Gruppe, Otto. 1887. *Die griechischen Culte und Mythen in ihren Beziehungen zu den orientalischen Religionen*. Leipzig: B. G. Teubner.

Guggisberg, Marin A. 2016. "Local Identity and Cultural Exchange in (Pre-)Colonial Francavilla Marittima: The Macchiabate Necropolis in the Light of New Excavations." In *Contexts of Early Colonization*, edited by Lieve Donnellan, Valentino Nizzo, and Gert-Jan Burgers, 237–46. Rome: Palombi Editori.

Gunter, Ann C. 1990. "Models of the Orient in the Art History of the Orientalizing Period." *Achaemenid History* 5:131–47.

———. 2009. *Greek Art and the Orient*. Cambridge: Cambridge University Press.

———. 2014. "Orientalism and Orientalization in the Iron Age Mediterranean." In *Critical Approaches to Ancient Near Eastern Art*, edited by Brian A. Brown and Marian H. Feldman, 79–108. Boston: de Gruyter.

———. 2016. "Contemplating an Empire: Artistic Responses to the Neo-Assyrian World." In *Assyria to Iberia: Art and Culture in the Iron Age*, edited by Joan Aruz and Michael Seymour, 216–26. New York: Metropolitan Museum of Art.

Guzzo, Pier Giovanni. 2016. "Il contesto indigeno della Campania all'arrivo dei Greci." In *Contexts of Early Colonization*, edited by Lieve Donnellan, Valentino Nizzo, and Gert-Jan Burgers, 153–57. Rome: Palombi Editori.

Hackl, Rudolf. 1907. "Zwei frühattische Gefässe der Münchner Vasensammlung." *Jahrbuch des kaiserlich deutschen archäologischen Instituts* 22:78–105.

Haider, Peter W. 1988. *Griechenland-Nordafrika: Ihre Beziehungen zwischen 1500 und 600 b. Chr.* Darmstadt: Wissenschaftliche Buchgesellschaft.

———. 1996. "Griechen im Vorderen Orient und in Ägypten bis ca. 590 v. Chr." In *Wege zur Genese griechischer Identität*, edited by Christoph Ulf, 59–169. Berlin: de Gruyter.

———. 2001. "Epigraphische Quellen zur Integration von Griechen in die ägyptische Gesellschaft der Saïtenzeit." In *Naukratis: Die Beziehungen zu Ostgriechenland, Ägypten und Zypern in archaischer Zeit; Akten der Table Ronde in Mainz, 25–27. November 1999*, edited by Ursula Höckmann and Detlev Kreikenbom, 197–215. Möhnesee, Germany: Bibliopolis.

Hall, Edith. 1989. *Inventing the Barbarian: Greek Self-Definition through Tragedy*. Oxford: Clarendon Press.

Halnon, Karen Bettez. 2002. "Poor Chic: The Rational Consumption of Poverty." *Current Sociology* 50:501–16.

Hammer, Dean. 2004. "Ideology, the Symposium, and Archaic Politics." *American Journal of Philology* 125:479–512.

Hampe, Roland. 1960. *Ein frühattischer Grabfund*. Mainz: Verlag des Römisch-Germanischen Zentralmuseums.

Handberg, Søren, and Anastasia Gadolou, eds. 2017. *Material Koinai in the Greek Early Iron Age and Archaic Period*. Aarhus, Denmark: Aarhus University Press.

Handberg, Søren, and Jan K. Jacobsen. 2011. "Greek or Indigenous? From Potsherd to Identity in Early Colonial Encounters." In *Communicating Identity in Italic Iron Age Communities*, edited by Margarita Gleba and Helle W. Horsnaes, 175–94. Oxford: Oxbow.

Hanfmann, George M. A. 1953. "Ionia, Leader or Follower?" *Harvard Studies in Classical Philology* 61:1–37.

———. 1962. "A Syrian from Sounion." *Hesperia* 31:236–37.

Harari, Maurizio. 2014. "Les stratégies d'Aristonothos: Boire à la grecque en Étrurie; Nouvelles considérations." In *Les potiers d'Etrurie et leur monde: Contacts, échanges, transferts*, edited by Laura Ambrosini and Vincent Jolivet, 35–50. Paris: Colin.

Harris-Cline, Diane. 1999. "Archaic Athens and the Topography of the Kylon Affair." *Annual of the British School at Athens* 94:309–20.

Harrison, A. 1996. "Chronological Method and the Study of Corinthian Pottery." *Hephaistos* 14:193–216.

Harvey, David L., and Michael H. Reed. 1996. "The Culture of Poverty: An Ideological Analysis." *Sociological Perspectives* 39:465–95.

Hase, Friedrich-Wilhelm von. 1995. "Ägäische, griechische und vorderorientalische Einflüsse auf das tyrrhenische Mittelitalien." In *Beiträge zur Urnenfelderzeit nördlich und südlich der Alpen*, edited by Monika zu Erbach et al. Bonn: Habelt.

Haspels, C. H. Emilie. 1936. *Attic Black-Figured Lekythoi*. Paris: de Boccard.

Hasserodt, Monika. 2009. *Griechische und orientalische Metallphialen des frühen ersten Jahrtausends v. Chr. in Griechenland*. Bonn: Habelt.

Haug, Annette. 2012. *Die Entdeckung des Körpers: Körper- und Rollenbilder im Athen des 8. und 7. Jahrhunderts v. Chr.* Berlin: de Gruyter.

———. 2015. *Bild und Ornament im frühen Athen*. Regensburg, Germany: Schnell und Steiner.

Hawes, Charles Henry, and Harriet Boyd Hawes. 1911. *Crete: The Forerunner of Greece*, 2nd ed. London: Harper and Brothers.

Hedreen, Guy. 2016. *The Image of the Artist in Archaic and Classical Greece: Art, Poetry, and Subjectivity*. Cambridge: Cambridge University Press.

Hedrick, Charles W., Jr. 1991. "Phratry Shrines of Attica and Athens." *Hesperia* 60:241–68.

Hegmon, Michelle. 1992. "Archaeological Research on Style." *Annual Review of Anthropology* 21:517–36.

Herford, Mary A. B. 1919. *A Handbook of Greek Vase Painting*. Manchester: Manchester University Press.

Herrmann, Hans-Volkmar. 1966. *Die Kessel der orientalisierenden Zeit*. Berlin: de Gruyter.

Heurtley, Walter Abel, and Martin Robertson. 1948. "Excavations in Ithaca, V: The Geometric and Later Finds from Aetos." *Annual of the British School at Athens* 43:1–124.

Hiller, Stefan. 1991. "The Greek Dark Ages: Helladic Traditions, Mycenaean Traditions in Culture and Art." In *La Transizione dal Miceneo all'Alto Arcaismo: Dal palazzo alla città. Atti del Convegno Internazionale Roma, 14–19 Marzo 1988*, edited by D. Musti, A. Sacconi, L. Rocchetti, M. Rocchi, E. Scafa, L. Sportiello, and M. E. Giannotta, 117–32. Rome: Consiglio Nazionale delle Ricerche.

———. 2006. "The Prothesis Scene: Bronze Age–Dark Age Relations." In *Pictorial Pursuits: Figurative Painting on Mycenaean and Geometric Pottery; Papers from Two Seminars at the Swedish Institute at Athens in 1999 and 2001*, edited by Eva Rystedt and Berit Wells, 183–90. Stockholm: Paul Aströms Förlag.

Himmelmann, Nikolaus. 1962. "Der Mäander auf geometrischen Gefässen." *Marburger Winckelmann-Programm* 1962:10–43. Wiesbaden: Franz Steiner.

———. 2005. *Grundlagen der griechischen Pflanzendarstellung*. Paderborn, Germany: Schöningh.

Höckmann, Ursula, and Günter Vittmann. 2005. "Griechische und karische Söldner in Ägypten in archaischer Zeit (7.-6. Jahrhundert v. Chr.)." In *Ägypten, Griechenland, Rom: Abwehr und Berührung*, edited by Herbert Beck, Peter C. Bol, and Maraike Bückling, 97–103. Frankfurt: Das Städel, Städelsches Kunstinstitut und Städtische Galerie.

Hodder, Ian. 1982. *Symbols in Action: Ethnoarchaeological Studies of Material Culture*. Cambridge: Cambridge University Press.

———. 2011. "Human-Thing Entanglement: Towards an Integrated Archaeological Perspective." *Journal of the Royal Anthropological Institute* 17:154–77.

———. 2012. *Entangled: An Archaeology of the Relationships between Humans and Things*. Malden, MA: Wiley-Blackwell.

Hodos, Tamar. 2006. *Local Responses to Colonization in the Iron Age Mediterranean*. London: Routledge.

———. 2009. "Colonial Engagements in the Global Mediterranean Iron Age." *Cambridge Archaeological Journal* 19:221–41.

———. 2010. "Globalization and Colonization: A View from Iron Age Sicily." *Journal of Mediterranean Archaeology* 23:81–106.

———. 2014. "Stage Settings for a Connected Scene: Globalization and Material-Culture Studies in the Early First-Millennium B.C.E. Mediterranean." *Archaeological Dialogues* 21:24–30.

———. 2017. "Globalization, Some Basics: An Introduction to the *Routledge Handbook of Archaeology and Globalization*." In *The Routledge Handbook of Archaeology and Globalization*, edited by Tamar Hodos, 3–11. London: Routledge.

Hogarth, D. G. 1909. *Ionia and the East*. Oxford: Clarendon.

Hölbl, Günther. 2005. "Ägyptisches Kulturgut in der griechischen Welt im frühen ersten Jahrtausend vor Christus (10.-6. Jahrhundert v. Chr.)." In *Ägypten, Griechenland, Rom: Abwehr und Berührung*, edited by Herbert Beck, Peter C. Bol, and Maraike Bückling, 114–32. Frankfurt: Das Städel, Städelsches Kunstinstitut und Städtische Galerie.

Holloway, R. Ross. 1994. *The Archaeology of Early Rome and Latium*. London: Routledge.

Hood, Ronald G. 1982. "A New Greek Vase of c. 700 BC." *Art Bulletin of Victoria* 23:38–50.

Horden, Peregrine, and Nicholas Purcell. 2000. *The Corrupting Sea: A Study of Mediterranean History*. Oxford: Blackwell.

———. 2005. "Four Years of Corruption: A Response to Critics." In *Rethinking the Mediterranean*, edited by W. V. Harris, 348–75. Oxford: Oxford University Press.

———. 2020. *The Boundless Sea: Writing Mediterranean History*. New York: Routledge.

Hornblower, Simon. 1991. *A Commentary on Thucydides, Vol. 1*. Oxford: Clarendon Press.

Houby-Nielsen, Sanne. 1992. "Interaction between Chieftains and Citizens? 7th cent. B.C. Burial Customs in Athens." *Acta Hyperborea* 4:343–74.

———. 1995. "'Burial Language' in Archaic and Classical Kerameikos." In *Proceedings of the Danish Institute at Athens, I*, edited by Soren Dietz, 129–90. Aarhus, Denmark: Aarhus University Press.

———. 1996. "The Archaeology of Ideology in the Kerameikos: New Interpretations of the 'Opferrinnen.'" In *The Role of Religion in the Early Greek Polis*, edited by Robin Hägg, 41–54. Stockholm: Paul Åström.

———. 2009. "Attica: A View from the Sea." In *A Companion to Archaic Greece*, edited by Kurt A. Raaflaub and Hans van Wees, 189–211. Malden, MA: Wiley-Blackwell.

Hünnekens, Ludger. 1987. "Die frühe attische schwarzfigurige Keramik: Eine Bestandsaufnahme und Untersuchung zur Entwicklung ihres Stils." PhD diss., Freiburg.

Hurwit, Jeffrey M. 1985. *The Art and Culture of Early Greece, 1100–480 B.C.* Ithaca, NY: Cornell University Press.

———. 1992. "A Note on Ornament, Nature, and Boundary in Early Greek Art." *Bulletin Antieke Beschaving* 67:63–72.

———. 2011. "The Shipwreck of Odysseus: Strong and Weak Imagery in Late Geometric Art." *American Journal of Archaeology* 115:1–18.

———. 2015. *Artists and Signatures in Ancient Greece*. New York: Cambridge University Press.

———. 2017. "Response: Reflections on Identity, Personality, and Originality." In *Artists and Artistic Production in Ancient Greece*, edited by Kristen Seaman and Peter Schultz, 177–205. Cambridge: Cambridge University Press.

Hussein, Angela Murock. 2009. "Imports, Imitations, and Immigrants: A Note on Pithekoussai." In *KOINE: Mediterranean Studies in Honor of R. Ross Holloway*, edited by Derek B. Counts and Anthony S. Tuck, 75–77. Oxford: Oxbow Books.

Immerwahr, Henry R. 1990. *Attic Script: A Survey*. Oxford: Clarendon Press.

Ingvarsson, Anne, and Ylva Bäckström. 2019. "Bioarchaeological Field Analysis of Human Remains from the Mass Graves at Phaleron, Greece." *Opuscala* 12:7–158.

Isler, Hans Peter. 1983. "Ceramisti greci in Etruria in epoca tardogeometrica." *Numismatica e antichità classiche* 12:9–48.

Ismard, Paulin. 2010. *La cité des réseaux: Athènes et ses associations, VIe–Ier siècle av. J.-C.* Paris: Publications de la Sorbonne.

———. 2018. "Associations and Citizenship in Attica from Solon to Cleisthenes." In *Defining Citizenship in Archaic Greece*, edited by Alain Duplouy and Roger W. Brock, 145–59. Oxford: Oxford University Press.

Jacobsen, Jan K., Søren Handberg, and Gloria P. Mittica. 2008–9. "An Early Euboean Workshop in the Sibaritide." *Annali di Archaeologia e Storica Antica* 15–16:89–96.

Jahn, Otto. 1854. *Beschreibung der vasensammlung königs Ludwigs in der Pinakothek zu München*. München: Jos. Lindauer.

Jeffery, Lilian H. 1961 [1990]. *The Local Scripts of Archaic Greece: A Study of the Origin of the Greek Alphabet and Its Development from the Eight to the Fifth Centuries B.C.* Oxford: Clarendon Press.

Johannowsky, Werner. 1983. *Materiali di età arcaica dalla Campania*. Naples: G. Macchiaroli.

Jones, Siân. 1997. *The Archaeology of Ethnicity: Constructing Identities in the Past and Present*. New York: Routledge.

Jucker, Hans. 1982. "Göttin im Gehäuse und eine neue Vase aus der Gegend von Metapont." In *ΑΠΑΡΧΑΙ. Nuove ricerche e studi sulla Magna Grecia e la Sicilia antica in onore di Paolo Enrico Arias*, edited by Luigi Beschi, Giovanni Pugliese Carratelli, and Salvatore Settis, 75–84. Pisa: Giardini Editori e Stampatori.

Junker, Klaus. 2018. "Opferrinnenzeremonie und Potlatch: Ein Testfall der interkulturellen Analyse." *Archäeologischer Anzeiger*:231–54.

Kakavoyianni, Olga, and Nikolaos Petrocheilos. 2020. *Από τα αρχαία νεκροταφεία της Αναβύσσου*. *Athens University Review of Archaeology* 3.

Kallipoliti, Vasileios. 1963. "Ἀνασκαφὴ τάφων Ἀναγυροῦντος." *Archaiologikon Deltion A, Meletes* 18:115–32.

Kalogeropoulos, Konstantinos. 2013. *Το ιερό της Αρτέμιδος Ταυροπόλου στις Αλές Αραφηνίδες (Λούτσα)*. Athens: Grapheion Dēmosieumatōn tēs Akadēmias Athēnōn.

Kantor, Helene J. 1945/1999. "Plant Ornament: Its Origin and Development in the Ancient Near East." PhD diss., Department of Oriental Languages and Literatures, University of Chicago.

Karageorghis, Vassos, and Nikolaos Ch. Stampolidis. 1998. *Eastern Mediterranean: Cyprus-Dodecanese-Crete, 16th–6th cent. B.C.* Athens: University of Crete and the A. G. Leventis Foundation.

Karagiorga-Stathakopoulou, Theodora. 1978. "Οδός Μητροδώρου και Γεμίνου." *Archaiologikon Deltion* 33:24–25.

Karali, Lilian, and Anastasia Tsaliki. 2011. "Les suppliciés de Paléon Phaliron: Un cas d'exécution par apotympanismos dans l'Athènes classique." In *3ᵉ Colloque de Pathographie, Bourges, avril 2009*, edited by Philippe Charlier, 559–65. Paris: de Boccard.

Karetsou, Alexandra, Maria Andreadaki-Vlazaki, and Nikos Papadakis. 2000. *Crete-Egypt, Three Thousand Years of Cultural Links*. Herakleion and Cairo: Hellenic Ministry of Culture.

Karo, Georg. 1928. "Menelaos auf einer frühattischen Vase." *Sechsundzwanzigstes Hallisches Winckelmannsprogramm*:10–15.

Karouzou, Semni. 1963. *Αγγεία του Αναγυρούντος*. Athens.

———. 1979. "Autour d'une oenochoé protoattique de Toulouse: Sur le Baron de Stackelberg et Fauvel." *Archaiologika analekta ex Athēnōn* 12:127–49.

Kearsley, Rosalinde A. 1999. "Greeks Overseas in the 8th Century B.C.: Euboeans, Al Mina, and Assyrian Imperialism." In *Ancient Greeks West and East*, edited by Gocha R. Tsetskhladze, 109–34. Leiden: Brill.

Keenan, Douglas J. 2004. "Radiocarbon Dates from Iron Age Gordion Are Confounded." *Ancient West and East* 3:100–103.

Kelder, Jorrit M. 2019. "Egypt." In *A Companion to the Archaeology of Early Greece and the Mediterranean*, edited by Antonis Kotsonas and Irene Lemos, 1215–36. Hoboken, NJ: John Wiley and Sons.

Keramopoullos, Antonis D. 1923. *Ὁ Ἀποτυμπανισμός*. Athens: Hestia.

Kiderlen, Moritz, Michael Bode, Andreas Hauptmann, and Yannis Bassiakos. 2016. "Tripod Cauldrons Produced at Olympia Give Evidence for Trade with Copper from Faynan (Jordan) to South West Greece, c. 950–750 BCE." *Journal of Archaeological Science: Reports* 8:303–13.

Kistler, Erich. 1998. *Die "Opferrinne-Zeremonie": Bankettideologie am Grab, Orientalisierung und Formierung einer Adelsgesellschaft in Athen*. Stuttgart: F. Steiner.

———. 2004. "'Kampf der Mentalitäten': Ian Morris' 'Elitist' versus 'Middling-Ideology?'" In *Griechische Archaik: Interne Entwicklungen, externe Impulse*, edited by Robert Rollinger and Christoph Ulf, 145–75. Berlin: Akademie.

———. 2012. "Glocal Responses from Archaic Sicily." *Ancient West and East* 11:219–33.

Kistler, Erich, Matthias Krieg, and Claudia Kohli Reichenbach, eds. 2015. *Sanctuaries and the Power of Consumption: Networking and the Formation of Elites in the Archaic Western Mediterranean World*. Wiesbaden: Harrassowitz Verlag.

Kistler, Erich, and Christoph Ulf. 2005. "Athenische 'Big Men' - ein 'Chief' in Lefkandi? Zum Verhältnis von historischen und archäologischen Aussagen vor dem Hintergrund der Bedeutung anthropologischer Modelle." In *Synergia: Festschrift für Friedrich Krinzinger*, edited by Barbara Brandt, Verena Gassner, and Sabine Ladstätter, 271–77. Vienna: Phoibos Verlag.

Kleibrink, Marianne Maaskant. 2000. "Early Cults in the Athenaion at Francavilla Marittima as Evidence for a Pre-Colonial Circulation of Nostoi Stories." In *Die Ägäis und das westliche Mittelmeer: Beziehungen und Wechselwirkungen, 8. bis 5. Jh. v. Chr.*, edited by Friedrich Krinzinger, 165–84. Vienna: Verlag der Österreichischen Akademie der Wissenschaften.

———. 2001. "The Search for Sybaris: An Evaluation of Historical and Archaeological Evidence." *Bulletin antieke beschaving* 76:33–70.

Kleibrink, Marianne Maaskant, Jan K. Jacobsen, and Søren Handberg. 2004. "Water for Athena: Votive Gifts at Lagaria (Timpone della Motta, Francavilla Marittima, Calabria)." *World Archaeology* 36:43–67.

Knappett, Carl. 2005. *Thinking through Material Culture: An Interdisciplinary Perspective.* Philadelphia: University of Pennsylvania Press.

———. 2011. *An Archaeology of Interaction: Network Perspectives on Material Culture and Society.* Oxford: Oxford University Press.

———. 2017. "Globalization, Connectivities, and Networks: An Archaeological Perspective." In *The Routledge Handbook of Archaeology and Globalization*, edited by Tamar Hodos, 29–41. London: Routledge.

Knappett, Carl, Lambros Malafouris, and Peter Tomkins. 2010. "Ceramics (as Containers)." In *The Oxford Handbook of Material Culture Studies*, edited by Dan Hicks and Mary C. Beaudry, 588–612. Oxford: Oxford University Press.

Knigge, Ursula. 1980. "Der Rundbau am Eridanos." In *Kerameikos 12. Rundbauten im Kerameikos*, 57–94. Berlin: de Gruyter.

Knigge, Ursula, and Elena Walter-Karydi. 1974. Review of Kübler 1970. *Gnomon* 46:198–208.

Kokkou-Vyridi, Konstantinas. 1999. *Ελεύσις: Πρώιμες πυρές θυσιών στο Τελεστήριο της Ελευσίνος.* Athens.

Kontoleon, Nikolaos M. 1969. "Die frühgriechische Reliefkunst." *Archaiologikē ephēmeris*:215–36.

Kopcke, Günter, and Isabelle Tokumaru. 1992. *Greece between East and West, 10th–8th Centuries BC.* Mainz, Rhine: Verlag Philipp von Zabern.

Kotsonas, Antonis. 2013. "Orientalizing Ceramic Styles and Wares of Early Iron Age Crete: Aspects of Production, Dissemination, and Consumption." In *Kreta in der geometrischen und archaischen Zeit: Akten des Internationalen Kolloquiums am Deutschen Archäologischen Institut, Abteilung Athen, 27.–29. Januar 2006*, edited by Wolf-Dietrich Niemeier, Oliver Pilz, and Ivonne Kaiser, 233–52. Munich: Hirmer.

———. 2016. "Politics of Periodization and the Archaeology of Early Greece." *American Journal of Archaeology* 120:239–70.

———. 2019. "History of Research." In *A Companion to the Archaeology of Early Greece and the Mediterranean*, edited by Antonis Kotsonas and Irene Lemos, 75–96. Hoboken, NJ: John Wiley and Sons.

Kourou, Nota. 1987. "A propos de quelques ateliers de céramique fine, non-tournée du type 'argien monochrome.'" *Bulletin de correspondance hellénique* 111:31–53.

———. 1988. "Handmade Pottery and Trade: The Case of the 'Argive Monochrome' Ware." In *Proceedings of the 3rd Symposium on Ancient Greek and Related Pottery*, edited by Jette Christiansen and Torben Melander, 314–24. Copenhagen: Nationalmuseet.

———. 1998. "Euboea and Naxos in the Late Geometric Period: The Cesnola Style." In *Euboica: L'Eubea e la presenza euboica in calcidica e in occidente*, edited by Michel Bats and Bruno d'Agostino, 167–77. Naples: Centre Jean Bérard / Istituto Universitario Orientale.

———. 2001. "The Sacred Tree in Greek Art: Mycenaean versus Near Eastern Traditions." In *La questione delle influenze vicino-orientali sulla religione greca: Stato degli studi e prospettive della ricerca*, edited by Sergio Ribichini, Maria Rocchi, and Paolo Xella, 31–53. Rome: Consiglio nazionale delle ricerche.

———. 2005. "Early Iron Age Greek Imports in Italy: A Comparative Approach to a Case Study." In *Oriente e Occidente: Metodi e discipline a confronto*, edited by Filippo Delpino and Gilda Bartoloni, 497–515. Rome: Istituti editoriali e poligrafici internazionali.

———. 2008a. "The Aegean and the Levant in the Early Iron Age: Recent Developments." *Bulletin d'archéologie et d'architecture libanaises* Supp. 6:361–74.

———. 2008b. "The Evidence from the Aegean." In *Beyond the Homeland: Markers in Phoenician Chronology*, edited by Claudia Sagona. Leuven, Belgium: Peeters.

———. 2011. "Following the Sphinx: Tradition and Innovation in Early Iron Age Crete." In *Identità culturale, etnicità, processi di trasformazione a Creta fra dark age e arcaismo: Per i cento anni dello scavo di Priniàs, 1906–2006; Convegno di studi (Atene, 9–12 novembre 2006)*, edited by Giovani Rizza, 165–77. Catania, Sicily: Consiglio nazionale delle ricerche IBAM.

———. 2019a. "Cyprus and the Aegean in the Geometric Period: The Case of Salamis." In *Salamis of Cyprus: History and Archaeology from the Earliest Times to Late Antiquity*, edited by Sabine Rogge, Christina Ioannou, and Theodoros Mavrojannis, 77–97. Münster: Waxmann Verlag.

———. 2019b. "Phoenicians and Attic Middle Geometric Pottery in the Mediterranean: Echoes of an Early Athenian Cultural Value." In *Les Phéniciens, les Puniques et les autres: Échanges et identités en Méditerranée ancienne*, edited by Luisa Bonadies, Iva Chirpanlieva, and Élodie Guillon, 159–77. Paris: de Boccard.

Kourouniotis, K. 1911. "Ἐξ Ἀττικῆς: Ἀνασκαφαί Παλαιοῦ Φαλήρου." *Archaiologikē ephēmeris* 50:246–56.

Kraiker, Wilhelm. 1951. *Aigina*. Berlin: G. Mann.

———. 1954. "Ornament und Bild in der frühgriechischen Malerei." In *Neue Beiträge zur klassischen Altertumswissenschaft: Festschrift zum 60. Geburtstag von Bernhard Schweitzer*, edited by Reinhard Lullies, 36–47. Stuttgart: W. Kohlhammer.

Kramer, Gustav. 1837. *Über den Styl und die Herkunft der bemahlten griechischen Thongefässe*. Berlin: Nicolaischen Buchhandlung.

Kreindler, Katherine. 2015. "Consumption and Exchange in Central Italy in the Ninth through Sixth Centuries BCE." PhD diss., Classics, Stanford University.

Kübler, Karl. 1950. *Altattische Malerei*. Tübingen: E. Wasmuth.

———. 1954. *Kerameikos V.1 Die Nekropole des 10. bis 8. Jahrhunderts*. Berlin: de Gruyter.

———. 1959. *Kerameikos VI.1. Die Nekropole des späten 8. bis frühen 6. Jahrhunderts*. Berlin: de Gruyter.

———. 1970. *Kerameikos VI.2: Die Nekropole des späten 8. bis frühen 6. Jahrunderts, Kerameikos*. Berlin: de Gruyter.

Kuhrt, Amélie. 2002. "Greek Contact with the Levant and Mesopotamia in the First Half of the First Millennium BC: A View from the East." In *Greek Settlements in the Eastern Mediterranean and the Black Sea*, edited by Gocha R. Tsetskhladze and Anthony M. Snodgrass, 17–25. Oxford: Archaeopress.

Kurke, Leslie. 1992. "The Politics of ἀβροσύνη in Archaic Greece." *Classical Antiquity* 11:91–120.

Kyle, Donald G. 1987. *Athletics in Ancient Athens*. Leiden: Brill.

Kyrkou, Maro. 1997. "Ἡ Πρωτοαττική πρόκληση: Νέες κεραμικές μαρτυρίες." In *Athenian Potters and Painters I*, edited by John H. Oakley, W.D.E. Coulson, and Olga Palagia, 423–434. Oxford: Oxbow.

Lagogianni-Georgakarakou, Maria, ed. 2018. *The Countless Aspects of Beauty in Ancient Art*. Athens: National Archaeological Museum.

Lambert, Stephen D. 1999. "The Attic Genos." *Classical Quarterly* 49:484–89.

Landes, Christian, and Annie-France Laurens, eds. 1988. *Les vases à mémoire*. Lattes, France: Imago.

Lang, Mabel. 1976. *Agora 21: Graffiti and Dipinti*. Princeton, NJ: American School of Classical Studies at Athens.

Langdon, Merle K. 1976. *A Sanctuary of Zeus on Mount Hymettos*. Hesperia Supp. 16. Princeton, NJ: American School of Classical Studies at Athens.

Langdon, Susan H. 2008. *Art and Identity in Dark Age Greece, 1100–700 B.C.E.* Cambridge: Cambridge University Press.

———. 2001. "Beyond the Grave: Biographies from Early Greece." *American Journal of Archaeology* 105:579–606.

Larsen, Mogens Trolle. 1996. *The Conquest of Assyria: Excavations in an Antique Land, 1840–1860*. New York: Routledge.

Latour, Bruno. 2005. *Reassembling the Social: An Introduction to Actor-Network Theory*. Oxford: Oxford University Press.

Laughy, Michael H. 2010. "Ritual and Authority in Early Athens." PhD diss., University of California, Berkeley.

———. 2018. "Figurines in the Road: A Protoattic Votive Deposit from the Athenian Agora Reexamined." *Hesperia: The Journal of the American School of Classical Studies at Athens* 87:633–79.

Lauter, Hans. 1985. *Lathuresa: Beiträge zur Architektur und Siedlungsgeschichte in spätgeometrischer Zeit*. Mainz am Rhein: von Zabern.

Layard, Austen Henry. 1903. *Autobiography and Letters from His Childhood until His Appointment as H.M. Ambassador at Madrid*. London: John Murray.

Layton, Robert. 1991. *The Anthropology of Art*. 2nd ed. Cambridge: Cambridge University Press.

Leão, Delfim F., and P. J. Rhodes. 2015. *The Laws of Solon: A New Edition with Introduction, Translation, and Commentary*. London: I. B. Tauris.

Lefkowitz, Mary R., and Guy MacLean Rogers, eds. 1996. *Black Athena Revisited*. Chapel Hill: University of North Carolina Press.

Lemos, Irene S. 2007. "Recent Archaeological Work on Xeropolis, Lefkandi: A Preliminary Report." In *Oropos and Euboea in the Early Iron Age*, edited by Alexander Mazarakis Ainian, 123–33. Volos: University of Thessaly Publications.

———. 2012. "Euboea and Central Greece in the Post-Palatial and Early Greek Periods." *Archaeological Reports* 58:19–27.

Lévy, Edmond. 1978. "Notes sur la chronologie athènienne au VIᵉ siècle. I. Cylon." *Historia* 27:513–21.

Lewis, Oscar. 1968. "The Culture of Poverty." In *On Understanding Poverty: Perspectives from the Social Sciences*, edited by Daniel P. Moynihan, 187–200. New York: Basic Books.

Lissarrague, François. 1990. *The Aesthetics of the Greek Banquet: Images of Wine and Ritual*. Princeton, NJ: Princeton University Press.

Londey, Peter. 2015. "Making Up Delphic History—The 1st Sacred War Revisited." *Chiron* 45:221–38.

López-Ruiz, Carolina. 2009. "Tarshish and Tartessos Revisited: Textual Problems and Historical Implications." In *Colonial Encounters in Ancient Iberia: Phoenician, Greek, and Indigenous Relations*, edited by Michael Dietler and Carolina López-Ruiz, 255–80. Chicago: University of Chicago Press.

———. 2010. *When the Gods Were Born: Greek Cosmogonies and the Near East*. Cambridge, MA: Harvard University Press.

Louden, Bruce. 2011. *Homer's Odyssey and the Near East*. Cambridge: Cambridge University Press.

Luke, Joanna. 2003. *Ports of Trade: Al Mina and Geometric Greek Pottery in the Levant*. Oxford: Archaeopress.

Luraghi, Nino. 2006. "Traders, Pirates, Warriors: The Proto-History of Greek Mercenary Soldiers in the Eastern Mediterranean." *Phoenix* 60:21–47.

Lynch, Kathleen. 2011. *The Symposium in Context: Pottery from a Late Archaic House Near the Athenian Agora*, *Hesperia* Supp. 46. Princeton, NJ: American School of Classical Studies at Athens.

———. 2018. "The Hellenistic Symposium as Feast." In *Feasting and Polis Institutions*, edited by Josine Blok, Floris van den Eijnde, and Rolf Strootman, 233–56. Leiden: Brill.

Ma, John. 2016. "Élites, élitisme et communauté dans la *polis* archaïque." *Annales: Histoire, Sciences, Sociales* 71:633–58.

Mackie, Hilary Susan. 1996. *Talking Trojan: Speech and Community in the Iliad*. Lanham, MD: Rowman and Littlefield.

Malkin, Irad. 1994. "Inside and Outside: Colonization and the Formation of the Mother City." In *ΑΠΟΙΚΙΑ: I più antichi insediamenti greci in occidente; Funzioni e modi dell'organizzazione politica e sociale*, edited by Bruno d'Agostino and David Ridgway, 1–9. Naples: Istituto Universitario Orientale.

———. 1998. *The Returns of Odysseus: Colonization and Ethnicity*. Berkeley: University of California Press.

———. 2002. "A Colonial Middle Ground: Greek, Etruscan, and Local Elites in the Bay of Naples." In *The Archaeology of Colonialism*, edited by Claire L. Lyons and John K. Papadopoulos, 151–81. Los Angeles: Getty Research Institute.

———. 2003. "Networks and the Emergence of Greek Identity." *Mediterranean Historical Review* 18:56–74.

———. 2011. *A Small Greek World: Networks in the Ancient Mediterranean*. New York: Oxford University Press.

———. 2016. "Greek Colonisation: The Right to Return." In *Conceptualising Early Colonisation*, edited by Lieve Donnellan, Valentino Nizzo, and Gert-Jan Burgers, 27–50. Brussels: Belgisch Historisch Instituut te Rome.

Malkin, Irad, Christy Constantakopoulou, and Katerina Panagopoulou, eds. 2009. *Greek and Roman Networks in the Mediterranean*. London: Routledge.

Manolova, Tzveta. 2019. "The Levant." In *A Companion to the Archaeology of Early Greece and the Mediterranean*, edited by Antonis Kotsonas and Irene Lemos, 1185–214. Hoboken, NJ: John Wiley and Sons.

Manning, Joseph G. 2018. *The Open Sea: The Economic Life of the Ancient Mediterranean World from the Iron Age to the Rise of Rome*. Princeton, NJ: Princeton University Press.

Manville, Philip Brook. 1992. *The Origins of Citizenship in Ancient Athens*. Princeton, NJ: Princeton University Press.

Marchand, Suzanne L. 1996. *Down from Olympus: Archaeology and Philhellenism in Germany, 1750–1970*. Princeton, NJ: Princeton University Press.

———. 2009. *German Orientalism in the Age of Empire: Religion, Race, and Scholarship*. Cambridge: Cambridge University Press.

Marconi, Clemente, Valeria Tardo, and Caterina Trombi. 2015. "The Archaic Pottery from the Institute of Fine Arts Excavations in the Main Urban Sanctuary on the Akropolis of Selinunte." In *Sanctuaries and the Power of Consumption: Networking and the Formation of Elites in the Archaic West-*

ern Mediterranean World, edited by Erich Kistler, Birgit Öhlinger, Martin Mohr, and Matthias Hoernes, 325–35. Wiesbaden: Harrossowitz Verlag.

Markoe, Glenn E. 1985. *Phoenician Bronze and Silver Bowls from Cyprus and the Mediterranean.* Berkeley: University of California Press.

———. 1992–93. "In Pursuit of Silver: Phoenicians in Central Italy." *Hamburger Beiträge zur Archäologie* 19/20:11–31.

Martelli, Marina. 1984. "Prima di Aristonothos." *Prospettiva* 38:2–15.

———, ed. 1987a. *La Ceramica degli Etruschi: La pittura vascolare.* Novara, Italy: Istituto Geografico de Agostini.

———, 1987b. "Per il Pittore delle Gru." *Prospettiva* 48:2–11.

———. 1991. "I Fenici e la questione orientalizzante in Italia." In *Atti del II Congresso Internazionale di studi Fenici e Punici,* 1049–72. Rome: Consiglio Nazionale delle Ricerche.

———. 2001. "Nuove proposte per i Pittori dell'Eptacordo e delle Gru." *Prospettiva* 101:2–18.

———. 2008. "Variazioni sul tema etrusco-geometrico." *Prospettiva* 132:2–30.

Martin, S. Rebecca. 2017. *The Art of Contact: Comparative Approaches to Greek and Phoenician Art.* Philadelphia: University of Pennsylvania Press.

———. 2018. "Eastern Mediterranean Feasts: What Do We Really Know about the Marzeah?" In *Change, Continuity, and Connectivity: North-Eastern Mediterranean at the Turn of the Bronze Age and in the Early Iron Age,* edited by Łukasz Niesiołowski-Spanò and Marek Węcowski, 294–307. Wiesbaden: Harrassowitz.

Maruggi, Grazia Angela. 1996. "Le produzioni ceramiche arcaiche." In *I Greci in Occidente: Arte e artigianato in Magna Grecia,* edited by Enza Lippolis, 247–67. Naples: Electa Napoli.

Matthäus, Hartmut. 1993. "Zur Rezeption orientalischer Kunst-, Kultur-, und Lebensformen in Griechenland." In *Anfänge politischen Denkens in der Antike: Die nahöstlichen Kulturen und die Griechen,* edited by Kurt A. Raaflaub, 165–86. Munich: R. Oldenbourg.

———. 1999a. "The Greek Symposion and the Near East: Chronology and Mechanisms of Cultural Transfer." In *Proceedings of the XVth International Congress of Classical Archaeology,* edited by Roald F. Docter and Eric M. Moorman, 256–60. Amsterdam: Allard Pierson Museum.

———. 1999b. "Das griechische Symposion und der Orient." *Nürnberger Blätter zur Archäologie* 16:41–64.

———. 2000a. "Die Idäische Zeus-Grotte auf Kreta: Griechenland und der Vordere Orient im frühen 1. Jahrtausend v. Chr." *Archäeologischer Anzeiger*:517–47.

———. 2000b. "Die Rolle Zyperns und Sardiniens im Mittelmeerischen Interaktionsprozess während des späten zweiten und frühen ersten Jahrtausends v. Chr." In *Akten des Kolloquiums zum Thema der Orient und Etrurien: Zum Phänomen des "Orientalisierens" im westlichen Mittelmeerraum (10.–6. Jh. v. Chr.),* edited by Friedhelm Prayon and Wolfgang Röllig, 41–75. Pisa: Istituti editoriali e poligrafici internazionali.

———. 2008. "Phoenician Metal-Work up to Date: Phoenician Metal Bowls with Figural Decoration in the Eastern Mediterranean, Near and Middle East, and North Africa." In *Interconnections in the Eastern Mediterranean Lebanon in the Bronze and Iron Ages,* 439–52. Beirut: Ministère de la Culture, Direction Générale des Antiquités.

Matz, Friedrich. 1950. *Geschichte der griechischen Kunst.* Frankfurt am Main: V. Klostermann.

Mazarakis Ainian, Alexander. 1997. *From Rulers' Dwellings to Temples: Architecture, Religion, and Society in Early Iron Age Greece (1100–700 B.C.).* Jonsered, Sweden: Paul Åström.

———. 1999. "Reflections on Hero Cults in Early Iron Age Greece." In *Ancient Greek Hero Cult,* edited by Robin Hägg, 9–36. Stockholm: Svenska Institutet i Athen.

Mazarakis Ainian, Alexander, and Alexandra Alexandridou. 2011. "The 'Sacred House' of the Academy Revisited." In *The "Dark Ages" Revisited,* edited by Alexander Mazarakis Ainian, 165–89. Volos: University of Thessaly Press.

Mazzarino, Santo. 1947. *Fra Oriente e Occidente: Ricerche di storia greca arcaica.* Florence: La Nuova Italia.

Meiggs, Russell, and David M. Lewis. 1988. *A Selection of Greek Historical Inscriptions to the End of the Fifth Century B.C.* Oxford: Clarendon Press.

Melandri, Gianluca. 2011. *L'età del ferro a Capua: Aspetti distintivi del contesto culturale e suo inquadramento nelle dinamiche di sviluppo dell'Italia protostorica.* Oxford: Archaeopress.

Melandri, Gianluca, and Francesco Sirano. 2016. "I primi contatti col mondo greco e levantino a Capua tra la Prima Età del Ferro a gli inizi dell'Orientalizzante." In *Contexts of Early Colonization,* edited by Lieve Donnellan, Valentino Nizzo, and Gert-Jan Burgers, 211–21. Rome: Palombi Editori.

Menichetti, Mauro. 2017. "Art, 730–580 BCE." In *Etruscology*, edited by Alessandro Naso, 831–50. Berlin: de Gruyter.

Mercuri, L. 2004. *Eubéens en Calabre à l'époque archaïque: Formes de contacts et d'implantation*. Rome: École française de Rome.

Mermati, Francesca. 2009–12. "The Mediterranean Distribution of Pithekoussan-Cumaean Pottery in the Archaic Period." *Accordia Research Papers* 12:97–118.

———. 2012a. *Cuma: Le ceramiche arcaiche; La produzione pithecusano-cumana tra la metà dell'VIII e l'inizio del VI secolo a.C.* Naples: Naus Editoria.

———. 2012b. "Osservazioni sulla costruzione dell'identità coloniale tra Pithekoussai e Cuma." *Mediterranean Archaeology* 25:283–307.

———. 2014. "Ibridismo materiale e ibridismo culturale: La produzione ceramica pitecusano-cumana a contatto con l'altro; tra la metà dell'VIII sec. e la prima metà del VII sec. A.C." In *Proccedings: XVIIIth International Congress of Classical Archaeology, Vol. 1. Centre and Periphery in the Ancient World*, edited by José María Álvarez, Trinidad Nogales, and Isabel Rodà, 575–78. Mérida, Spain: Museo Nacional de Arte Romano.

Mersch, Andrea. 1996. *Studien zur Siedlungsgeschichte Attikas von 950 bis 400 v. Chr.* Frankfurt am Main: Peter Lang.

———. 1997. "Urbanization of the Attic Countryside from the Late 8th Century to the 6th Century BC." In *Urbanization in the Mediterranean in the 9th to 6th Centuries BC*, edited by Helle Damgaard Andersen, 45–62. Copenhagen: Museum Tusculanum Press.

Michetti, Laura Maria. 2009. "Note su un'anfora orientalizzante dal tumulo di Monte Aguzzo a Veio." In *Etruria e Italia preromana: Studi in onore di Giovannangelo Camporeale*, edited by Stefano Bruni, 607–15. Pisa: Fabrizio Serra.

Mikrakis, M. 2015. "Pots, Early Iron Age Athenian Society, and the Near East: The Evidence of the Rattle Group." In *Pots, Workshops, and Early Iron Age Society: Function and Role of Ceramics in Early Greece*, edited by Vicky Vlachou, 277–89. Brussels: Centre de Recherches en Archéologie et Patrimoine.

Milchhöfer, Arthur. 1883. *Die Anfänge der Kunst in Griechenland*. Leipzig: F. A. Brockhaus.

Miles, Margaret M. 1998. *Agora 31: The City Eleusinion*. Princeton, NJ: American School of Classical Studies.

Miller, Margaret. 1991. "Foreigners at the Greek Symposium?" In *Dining in a Classical Context*, edited by William J. Slater, 59–81. Ann Arbor: University of Michigan Press.

———. 1997. *Athens and Persia in the Fifth Century B.C.: A Study in Cultural Receptivity*. Cambridge: Cambridge University Press.

Mitsopoulos-Leon, Veronika. 2009. *ΒΡΑΥΡΩΝ: Die Tonstatuetten aus dem Heiligtum der Artemis Brauronia*. Athens: Archäologische Gesellschaft zu Athen.

Möller, Astrid. 2000. *Naukratis: Trade in Archaic Greece*. Oxford: Oxford University Press.

Monaco, Maria Chiara. 2000. *Ergasteria: Impianti artigianali ceramici ad Atene ed in Attica dal protogeometrico alle soglie dell'ellenismo*. Rome: "L'Erma" di Bretschneider.

———. 2012. "Dix ans après: Nouvelles données et considérations à propos du Céramique d'Athènes." In *"Quartiers" artisanaux en Grèce ancienne: Une perspective méditerranéenne*, edited by Arianna Esposito and Giorgos M. Sanidas, 155–74. Villeneuve d'Ascq, France: Presses Universitaires du Septentrion.

Moore, Mary B. 2003. "The Passas Painter: A Protoattic 'Realist?'" *Metropolitan Museum Journal* 38:15–44.

———. 2009. "An Early Protocorinthian Lekythos-Oinochoe in the Metropolitan Museum." *Antike Kunst* 52:3–19.

Morch, Vincent. 2012. *Exit: Exclus et marginaux en Grèce et à Rome*. Paris: Les belles lettres.

Morgan, Catherine. 2003. *Early Greek States beyond the Polis*. London: Routledge.

Morgan, Janett. 2016. *Greek Perspectives on the Achaemenid Empire: Persia through the Looking Glass*. Edinburgh: Edinburgh University Press.

Morris, Ian. 1987. *Burial and Ancient Society: The Rise of the Greek City-State*. Cambridge: Cambridge University Press.

———. 1992. *Death-Ritual and Social Structure in Classical Antiquity*. Cambridge: Cambridge University Press.

———. 1996a. "The Absolute Chronology of the Greek Colonies in Sicily." *Acta Archaeologica* 67:51–59.

———. 1996b. "The Strong Principle of Equality and the Archaic Origins of Greek Democracy." In *Dēmokratia: A Conversation on Democracies, Ancient and Modern*, edited by Josiah Ober and Charles Hedrick, 19–48. Princeton, NJ: Princeton University Press.

————. 1997. "The Art of Citizenship." In *New Light on a Dark Age: Exploring the Culture of Geometric Greece*, 9–43. Columbia: University of Missouri Press.

————. 1998. "Archaeology and Archaic Greek History." In *Archaic Greece: New Approaches and New Evidence*, edited by Nick Fisher and Hans van Wees, 1–91. Swansea: Classical Press of Wales.

————. 2000. *Archaeology as Cultural History: Words and Things in Iron Age Greece*. Malden, MA: Blackwall.

————. 2003. "Mediterraneanization." *Mediterranean Historical Review* 18:30–55.

————. 2007. "Early Iron Age Greece." In *The Cambridge Economic History of the Greco-Roman World*, edited by Walter Scheidel, Ian Morris, and Richard P. Saller, 211–41. Cambridge: Cambridge University Press.

Morris, Sarah P. 1984. *The Black and White Style: Athens and Aigina in the Orientalizing Period*. New Haven, CT: Yale University Press.

————. 1992. *Daidalos and the Origins of Greek Art*. Princeton, NJ: Princeton University Press.

————. 1997. "Homer and the Near East." In *A New Companion to Homer*, edited by Ian Morris and Barry B. Powell, 599–623. Leiden: Brill.

————. 2014. "Artists in Motion: Proto-Attic and Related Pottery of the Seventh Century B.C." In *Egraphsen kai epoiesen: Essays on Greek Pottery and Iconography in Honour of Professor Michalis Tiverios*, edited by Panos Valavanis and Eleni Manakidou, 95–104. Thessaloniki: University Studio Press.

Moscati, Sabatino, and Palazzo Grassi. 1988. *The Phoenicians*. New York: Abbeville Press.

Mösch-Klingele, Rosmarie. 2010. *Braut ohne Bräutigam: Schwarz- und rotfigurige Lutrophoren als Spiegel gesellschaftlicher Veränderungen in Athen*. Mainz am Rhein: Philipp von Zabern.

Movers, F. C. 1841–56. *Die Phönizier*. Bonn: E. Weber.

Mülke, Christoph. 2002. *Solons politische Elegien und Iamben Fr. 1-13; 32-27 West*. Munich: K. G. Sauer.

Müller, Carl Otfried. 1847–48. *Karl Otfried Müller's kleine deutsche Schriften über Religion, Kunst, Sprache und Literatur, Leben und Geschichte des Alterthums*. Breslau, Poland: J. Max und Komp.

————. 1852. *Ancient Art and Its Remains; or, a Manual of the Archaeology of Art*. 2nd ed. London: H. Bohn.

Müller, Carl Otfried, and Carl Oesterley. 1832–56. *Denkmäler der alten Kunst*. Göttingen: In der Dieterichschen Buchhandlung.

Murray, Oswyn. 1980. *Early Greece*. Brighten, Sussex: Harvester Press.

————. 1983. "The Symposion as Social Organisation." In *The Greek Renaissance of the Eighth Century B.C.: Tradition and Innovation*, edited by Robin Hägg, 195–99. Stockholm: Paul Åström.

————. 1990. "Sympotic History." In *Sympotica: A Symposium on the Symposion*, edited by Oswyn Murray, 3–13. Oxford: Clarendon Press.

————. 1994. "Nestor's Cup and the Origins of the Greek Symposion." In *APOIKIA: Scritti in onore di Giorgio Buchner*, edited by Bruno d'Agostino and David Ridgway, 47–54. Naples: Istituto universitario orientale.

————. 2003. "Sympotica—Twenty Years On." In *Symposium: Banquet et representations en Grèce et à Rome. Pallas 61*, edited by Charalampos Orfanos and Jean-Claude Carrière, 13–21. Toulouse: Presses universitaires du Mirail.

————. 2005 [2018]. "*Euphrosynē* and the Psychology of Pleasure." In *The Symposion: Drinking Greek Style*, edited by Vanessa Cazzato, 261–70. Oxford: Oxford University Press.

————. 2015a [2018]. "The Iconography of the *Symposium*." In *The Symposion: Drinking Greek Style*, edited by Vanessa Cazzato, 107–31. Oxford: Oxford University Press.

————. 2015b [2018]. "Sympotic Drinking Rituals: Mixing Wine with Water, *Kalos* Vases, and the Meaning of *Epidexia, Proposis,* and *Philotēsia*." In *The Symposion: Drinking Greek Style*, edited by Vanessa Cazzato, 133–38. Oxford: Oxford University Press.

————. 2016. "The *Symposion* between East and West." In *The Cup of Song: Studies on Poetry and the Symposion*, edited by Vanessa Cazzato, Dirk Obbink, and Enrico Emanuele Prodi, 17–27. Oxford: Oxford University Press.

————. 2017 [2018]. "The *Symposion* and Social Status." In *The Symposion: Drinking Greek Style*, edited by Vanessa Cazzato, 139–53. Oxford: Oxford University Press.

Murray, Sarah C., Irum Chorghay, and Jennifer MacPherson. 2020. "The Dipylon Mistress: Social and Economic Complexity, the Gendering of Craft Production, and Early Greek Ceramic Material Culture." *American Journal of Archaeology* 124:215–44.

Muscarella, Oscar White. 2003. "The Date of the Destruction of the Early Phrygian Period at Gordion." *Ancient West and East* 2:225–52.

Mylonas, George E. 1957. *Ο προτοαττικός αμφορέας της Ελευσίνος*. Athens: Archaiologikēs Hetaireias.

————. 1961. *Eleusis and the Eleusinian Mysteries*. Princeton, NJ: Princeton University Press.

————. 1975. *Το δυτικόν νεκροταφείον της Ελευσίνος*. Athens: Archaiologikēs Hetaireias.

Myres, John Linton, Sir, and Max Hermann Ohnefalsch-Richter. 1899. *A Catalogue of the Cyprus Museum with a Chronicle of Excavations Undertaken since the British Occupation and Introductory Notes on Cypriote Archaeology*. Oxford: Clarendon Press.

Nakassis, Dimitri. 2004. "Gemination at the Horizons: East and West in the Mythical Geography of Archaic Greek Epic." *Transactions of the American Philological Association* 134:215–33.

Nantet, Emmanuel. 2010. "Les épaves du VIIᵉ S.: Un témoignage sur les échanges maritimes à l'époque archaïque." In *La Méditerranée au VIIᵉ siècle av. J.-C.*, edited by Roland Étienne, 96–109. Paris: de Boccard.

Naso, Alessandro. 2006. "Etruscan and Italic Finds in North Africa, 7th–2nd Century BC." In *Naukratis: Greek Diversity in Egypt*, edited by Alexandra Villing and Udo Schlotzhauer, 187–98. London: British Museum.

————. 2010. "Le aristocrazie etrusche in periodo periodo orientalizzante: Cultura, economia, relazioni." In *La Méditerranée au VIIᵉ siècle av. J.-C.*, edited by Roland Étienne, 183–98. Paris: de Boccard.

————. 2012. "Gli influssi del Vicino Oriente sull'Etruria nell'VIII–VII sec. A.C.: Un bilancio." In *Le origini degli Etruschi: Storia, archeologia, antropologia*, edited by Vincenzo Bellelli, 433–53. Rome: L'Erma di Bretschneider.

————. 2016. "Dall'Italia alla Grecia, IX-VII sec. a.C." In *Contexts of Early Colonization*, edited by Lieve Donnellan, Valentino Nizzo, and Gert-Jan Burgers, 275–87. Rome: Palombi Editori.

————. 2017. "Greece, Aegean Islands, and Levant." In *Etruscology*, edited by Alessandro Naso, 1679–93. Berlin: de Gruyter.

Ndoye, Malick. 2010. *Groupes sociaux et idéologie du travail dans les mondes homérique et hésiodique*. Besançon, France: Presses universitaires de Franche-Comté.

Neeft, Cornelis Willem. 1987. *Protocorinthian Subgeometric Aryballoi*. Amsterdam: Allard Pierson Museum.

————. 2012. "Absolute Chronology and Corinthian Pottery." In *La Sicilia in età arcaica: Dalle apoikiai al 480 a.C.*, edited by Rosalba Panvini and Lavinia Sole, 485–96. Caltanisetta, Sicily: Salvatore Sciascia Editore.

Neeft, Cornelis Willem, and Darrell A. Amyx. 1991. *Addenda et Corrigenda to D.A. Amyx, Corinthian Vase-Painting in the Archaic Period*. Amsterdam: Allard Pierson Museum.

Neer, Richard T. 1997. "Beazley and the Language of Connoisseurship." *Hephaistos* 15:7–30.

————. 2002. *Style and Politics in Athenian Vase-Painting: The Craft of Democracy, ca. 530–460 B.C.E.* New York: Cambridge University Press.

————. 2005. "Connoisseurship and the Stakes of Style." *Critical Inquiry* 32:1–26.

————. 2010. *The Emergence of the Classical Style in Greek Sculpture*. Chicago: University of Chicago Press.

————. 2012. *Greek Art and Archaeology: A New History, c. 2500–c. 150 BCE*. New York: Thames and Hudson.

Nicole, Georges. 1926. *La peinture des vases grecs*. Paris: G. van Oest.

Niemeier, Wolf-Dietrich. 2001. "Archaic Greeks in the Orient: Textual and Archeological Evidence." *Bulletin of the American School of Oriental Research* 322:11–32.

Niemeyer, Hans Georg. 2004. "Phoenician or Greek: Is There a Reasonable Way Out of the Al Mina Debate?" *Ancient West and East* 3:39–49.

————. 2006. "There Is No Way Out of the Al Mina Debate." *Ancient West and East* 4:292–95.

Nijboer, Albert J. 2005. "The Iron Age in the Mediterranean: A Chronological Mess or 'Trade before the Flag,' Part II." *Ancient West and East* 4:254–77.

————. 2008. "Italy and the Levant during the Late Bronze and Iron Age (1200–750/700 BC)." In *Beyond the Homeland: Markers in Phoenician Chronology*, edited by Claudia Sagona, 423–60. Leuven, Belgium: Peeters.

————. 2013. "Banquet, *Marzeah, Symposion*, and *Symposium* during the Iron Age: Disparity and Mimicry." In *Regionalism and Globalism in Antiquity: Exploring Their Limits*, edited by Franco de Angelis, 95–125. Leuven, Belgium: Peeters.

————. 2016. "Is the Tangling of Events in the Mediterranean around 770–60 B.C. in the Conventional Absolute Chronology (CAC) a Reality or a Construct?" In *Contexts of Early Colonization*, edited by Lieve Donnellan, Valentino Nizzo, and Gert-Jan Burgers, 35–47. Rome: Palombi Editori.

Nizzo, Valentino. 2007. *Ritorno ad Ischia: Dalla statigrafia della necropoli di Pithekoussai alla tipologia dei materiali*. Naples: Centre Jean Bérard.

———. 2016. "Cronologia *versus* Archeologia: L'ambiguo scorrere del tempo alle soglie della 'colonizzazione': I casi di Cuma e Pithekoussai." In *Contextualizing Early Colonization*, edited by Lieve Donnellan, Valentino Nizzo, and Gert-Jan Burgers, 49–72. Rome: Palombi Editori.

Novotny, Jamie, and Joshua Jeffers. 2018. *The Royal Inscriptions of Ashurbanipal (668–631 BC), Aššur-Etal-Ilāni (630–627 BC), and Sin-Šarra-Iškun (626–612 BC), Kings of Assyria, Part 1.* University Park, PA: Eisenbrauns.

Oakley, John H., and Rebecca H. Sinos. 1993. *The Wedding in Ancient Athens.* Madison: University of Wisconsin Press.

Ober, Josiah. 1989. *Mass and Elite in Democratic Athens: Rhetoric, Ideology, and the Power of the People.* Princeton, NJ: Princeton University Press.

Ohnefalsch-Richter, Max Hermann. 1893. *Kypros, die Bibel und Homer: Beiträge zur Cultur-, Kunst-, und Religionsgeschichte des Orients im Alterthume; Mit besonderer Berücksichtigung eigener zwölfjähriger Forschungen und Ausgrabungen auf der Insel Cypren.* Berlin: A. Asher.

Orlandini, Piero. 1988. "Due nuovi vasi figurati di stile Orientalizzante dagli scavi dell'Incoronata di Metaponto." *Bollettino d'Arte* 49:6–16.

———. 1991. "Altri due vasi figurati di stile Orientalizzante dagli scavi dell'Incoronata." *Bollettino d'Arte* 66:1–8.

———. 1998. "Nuovi frammenti di 'perirrhanteria' fittili dagli scavi dell'Incoronata." In *In Memoria di Enrico Paribeni*, edited by Gabriella Capecchi et al., 305–10. Rome: Giorgio Bretschneider.

Osborne, Robin. 1988. "Death Revisited; Death Revised: The Death of the Artist in Archaic and Classical Greece." *Art History* 11:1–16.

———. 1989. "A Crisis in Archaeological History? The Seventh Century B.C. in Attica." *Annual of the British School at Athens* 84:297–322.

———. 1998. "Early Greek Colonization? The Nature of Greek Settlement in the West." In *Archaic Greece: New Approaches and New Evidence*, edited by Nick Fisher and Hans van Wees, 251–69. Swansea: Classical Press of Wales.

———. 2006a. "Roman Poverty in Context." In *Poverty in the Roman World*, edited by Margaret Atkins and Robin Osborne, 1–20. Cambridge: Cambridge University Press.

———. 2006b. "W(h)ither Orientalization." In *Debating Orientalization: Multidisciplinary Approaches to Change in the Ancient Mediterranean*, edited by Corinna Riva and Nicholas C. Vella, 153–58. London: Equinox.

———. 2007. "Projecting Identities in the Greek Symposion." In *Material Identities*, edited by Joanna Sofaer, 31–52. Malden, MA: Blackwell.

———. 2010. "The Art of Signing in Ancient Greece." *Arethusa* 43:231–51.

———. 2016. "Greek 'Colonisation': What Was, and What Is, at Stake?" In *Conceptualising Early Colonisation*, edited by Lieve Donnellan, Valentino Nizzo, and Gert-Jan Burgers, 21–26. Rome: Palombi Editori.

———. 2019. "Why Athens: Population Aggregation in Attica in the Early Iron Age." In *Coming Together: Comparative Approaches to Population Aggregation and Early Urbanization*, edited by Attila Gyucha, 135–48. Albany: State University of New York Press.

Osborne, Robin, and P. J. Rhodes, eds. 2017. *Greek Historical Inscriptions, 478–404 BC.* Oxford: Oxford University Press.

Osborne, Robin, and Jeremy Tanner, eds. 2007. *Art's Agency and Art History.* Malden, MA: Blackwell.

Pace, Rossella. 2008. "'Orientalia' a Francavilla Marittima." *Rivista di Studi Fenici* 36:81–107.

———. 2014. "La Tombe Strada de Francavilla Marittima et les modes de représentations funéraires de femmes éminentes dans une communauté indigène de la Calabre au VIIIᵉ s. av. J.-C." *Pallas* 94:123–37.

Palaiokrassa-Kopitsa, Lydia, and Evangelos Vivliodetis. 2015. "The Sanctuaries of Artemis Mounichia and Zeus Parnessios: Their Relation to the Religious and Social Life in the Athenian City-State until the End of the 7th Century BC." In *Pots, Workshops, and Early Iron Age Society: Function and Role of Ceramics in Early Greece*, edited by Vicky Vlachou, 155–80. Brussels: Centre de Recherches en Archéologie et Patrimoine.

Pallat, Ludwig. 1897. "Ein Vasenfund aus Aegina." *Mitteilungen des Deutschen Archäologischen Instituts, Athenische Abteilung* 22:265–333.

Pallottino, Massimo. 1965. "Orientalizing Style." In *Encyclopedia of World Art*, 782–96. New York: McGraw Hill.

Pamir, Hatice, and Shin'ichi Nishiyama. 2002. "The Orontes Delta Survey: Archaeological Investigation of Ancient Trade Stations/Settlements." *Ancient West and East* 1:294–314.

Paoletti, Orazio, and Luisa Tamagno Perna, eds. 2002. *Etruria e Sardegna centro-settentrionale tra l'età del bronzo finale e l'arcaismo: Atti del XXI Convegno di studi etruschi ed italici.* Pisa: Istituti editoriali e poligrafici internazionali.

Papadopoulos, John K. 1993. "To Kill a Cemetery: The Athenian Kerameikos and the Early Iron Age in the Aegean." *Journal of Mediterranean Archaeology* 6:175–206.

———. 1996. "The Original Kerameikos of Athens and the Siting of the Classical Agora." *Greek, Roman, and Byzantine Studies* 37:107–28.

———. 1997. "Phantom Euboians." *Journal of Mediterranean Archaeology* 10:191–219.

———. 2003. *Ceramicus Redivivus: The Early Iron Age Potters' Field in the Area of the Classical Athenian Agora*, Hesperia Supp. 31. Princeton, NJ: American School of Classical Studies at Athens.

———. 2007. *The Art of Antiquity: Piet de Jong and the Athenian Agora.* Princeton, NJ: American School of Classical Studies at Athens.

———. 2009. "The Relocation of Potters and the Dissemination of Style: Athens, Corinth, Ambrakia, and the Agrinion Group." In *Athenian Potters and Painters II*, edited by John H. Oakley and Olga Palagia, 232–40. Oxford: Oxbow.

———. 2011. "'Phantom Euboians'—A Decade On." In *Euboea and Athens: Proceedings of a Colloquium in Memory of Malcolm B. Wallace*, edited by David W. Rupp and Jonathan E. Tomlinson, 113–33. Athens: The Canadian Institute in Greece.

———. 2017. *The Athenian Agora 36. The Early Iron Age: The Cemeteries.* Princeton, NJ: Princeton University Press.

Papadopoulos, John K., and Evelyn Lord Smithson. 2002. "The Cultural Biography of a Cycladic Geometric Amphora: Islanders in Athens and the Prehistory of Metics." *Hesperia: The Journal of the American School of Classical Studies at Athens* 71:149–99.

Papadopoulos, John K., James F. Vedder, and Toby Schreiber. 1998. "Drawing Circles: Experimental Archaeology and the Pivoted Multiple Brush." *American Journal of Archaeology* 102:507–29.

Papalexandrou, Nassos. 2010. "Are There Hybrid Visual Cultures? Reflections on the Orientalizing Phenomena in the Mediterranean of the Early First Millennium BCE." In *Theorizing Cross-Cultural Interaction among the Ancient and Early Medieval Mediterranean, Near East, and Asia*, edited by Matthew P. Canepa, 31–48. Washington, DC: Smithsonian Institution.

Parker, Robert. 1996. *Athenian Religion: A History.* Oxford: Clarendon Press.

———. 1998. "Pleasing Thighs: Reciprocity in Greek Religion." In *Reciprocity in Ancient Greece*, edited by Christopher Gill, Norman Postlethwaite, and Richard Seaford, 105–25. Oxford: Oxford University Press.

———. 2005. *Polytheism and Society at Athens.* Oxford: Oxford University Press.

Parlama, Liana, and Nikolaos Ch. Stampolidis. 2000. *Athens: The City beneath the City. Antiquities from the Metropolitan Railway Excavations.* Athens: Greek Ministry of Culture and N. P. Goulandris Foundation / Museum of Cycladic Art.

Patzek, Barbara. 1996a. "Griechen und Phöniker in homerischer Zeit: Fernhandel und orientalische Einfluß auf die frühgriechische Kultur." *Münstersche Beiträge zur antiken Handelsgeschichte* 15:1–32.

———. 1996b. "Homer und der Orient." In *Vom Halys zum Euphrat*, edited by Ursula Magen and Mahmoud Rashad, 215–26. Münster: Ugarit-Verlag.

Payne, Humfry. 1931. *Necrocorinthia: A Study of Corinthian Art in the Archaic Period.* Oxford: Clarendon Press.

Pedley, John Griffiths. 2012. *Greek Art and Archaeology.* 5th ed. Upper Saddle River, NJ: Prentice Hall.

Peeples, Matthew A. 2019. "Finding a Place for Networks in Archaeology." *Journal of Archaeological Research* 27:451–99.

Pelekidis, Stratis. 1916. "Ἀνασκαφὴ Φαλήρου." *Archaiologikon Deltion* 2:13–64.

Perrot, Georges. 1895. "Figurines d'ivoire trouvées dans une tombe du Céramique à Athènes." *Bulletin de correspondance hellénique* 19:273–95.

Perrot, Georges, and Charles Chipiez. 1882–1914. *Histoire de l'art dans l'antiquité*, 10 vols. Paris: Hachette.

Petrocheilos, Ioannis E. 1996. "Frühe Phaleron-Oinochoen." *Mitteilungen des Deutschen Archäologischen Instituts, Athenische Abteilung* 111:45–64.

Pfuhl, Ernst. 1923. *Malerei und Zeichnung der Griechen.* Munich: F. Bruckmann.

Philadelpheus, Alexandros. 1920–21. "Ἀνασκαφὴ παρὰ τὸ χωρίον Σπάτα." *Archaiologikon Deltion* 6:131–38.

Pierrot, Antoine. 2015. "Who Were the Eupatrids in Archaic Athens?" In *"Aristocracy" in Antiquity: Redefining Greek and Roman Elites*, edited by Nick Fisher and Hans van Wees, 169–202. Swansea: Classical Press of Wales.

Plog, Stephen. 1983. "Analysis of Style in Artifacts." *Annual Review of Anthropology* 12:125–42.

Polignac, François de. 1992. "Influence extérieure ou évolution interne? L'innovation cultuelle en grèce géométrique et archaïque." In *Greece between East and West, 10th–8th Centuries BC*, edited by Günter Kopcke and Isabelle Tokumaru, 114–27. Mainz: Philipp von Zabern.

———. 1995. "Sanctuaires et société en Attique géométrique et archaïque: Réflexion sur les critères d'analyse." In *Culture et cité: L'avènement d'Athènes à l'époque archaïque*, edited by Annie Verbanck-Piérard and Didier Viviers, 75–101. Brussels: de Boccard.

Pologiorgi, Melpo I. 2003–9. "Ἀνασκαφή νεκροταφείου στο Χαλάνδρι." *Archaiologikon Deltion Meletes*, 58–64:143–210.

Pottier, Edmond. 1926. *Le dessin chez les grecs d'après les vases peints*. Paris: Les belles lettres.

Poulsen, Frederik. 1905. *Die Dipylongräber und die Dipylonvasen*. Leipzig: B. G. Teubner.

———. 1912. *Der Orient und die frühgriechische Kunst*. Leipzig: B. G. Teubner.

Powell, Barry B. 1989. "Why Was the Greek Alphabet Invented? The Epigraphical Evidence." *Classical Antiquity* 8:321–50.

———. 1991. *Homer and the Origin of the Greek Alphabet*. Cambridge: Cambridge University Press.

Pratt, Catherine E. 2015. "The 'SOS' Amphora: An Update." *Annual of the British School at Athens* 110:213–45.

———. 2016. "Greek Commodities Moving West: Comparing Corinthian and Athenian Amphorae in Early Archaic Sicily." In *Maritime Transport Containers in the Bronze-Iron Age Aegean and Eastern Mediterranean*, edited by Stella Demesticha and A. Bernard Knapp, 195–213. Uppsala: Paul Åström.

Procelli, Rosa Maria Albanese. 2016. "Gli indigeni della Sicilia tra la Prima e la Seconda Età del Ferro: Il contesto locale della 'prima colonizzazione.'" In *Contexts of Early Colonization*, edited by Lieve Donnellan, Valentino Nizzo, and Gert-Jan Burgers, 199–210. Rome: Palombi Editori.

Prost, Francis. 2010. "Législateurs, tyrans, lois sumptuaires, ou comment définir un groupe social en Grèce ancienne." In *La cité et ses élites: Pratiques et représentation des formes de domination et de contrôle social dans les cités grecques*, edited by Laurent Capdetrey and Yves Lafond, 187–210. Paris: de Boccard.

Prost, Francis, Hélène Aurigny, Catherine Saint-Pierre Hoffmann, and Thomas Brisart. 2010. "Sanctuaires et offrandes en Grèce." In *La Méditerranée au VIIᵉ siècle av. J.-C.*, edited by Roland Étienne, 223–73. Paris: de Boccard.

Pugliese Carratelli, Giovanni. 1996. *The Western Greeks*. Milan: Bompiani.

Purcell, Nicholas. 2006. "Orientalizing: Five Historical Questions." In *Debating Orientalization: Multidisciplinary Approaches to Change in the Ancient Mediterranean*, edited by Corinna Riva and Nicholas C. Vella, 21–30. London: Equinox.

Quinn, Josephine. 2017. *In Search of the Phoenicians*. Princeton, NJ: Princeton University Press.

Quondam, Francesco. 2016. "La Sibaritide prima e dopo la fondazione di Sibari." In *Contexts of Early Colonization*, edited by Lieve Donnellan, Valentino Nizzo, and Gert-Jan Burgers, 247–57. Rome: Palombi Editori.

Raaflaub, Kurt A. 1997. "Soldiers, Citizens, and the Evolution of the Early Greek Polis." In *The Development of the Polis in Archaic Greece*, edited by Lynette G. Mitchell and P. J. Rhodes, 49–59. London: Routledge.

———. 2004. "Archaic Greek Aristocrats as Carriers of Cultural Interaction." In *Commerce and Monetary Systems in the Ancient World: Means of Transmission and Cultural Interaction*, edited by Robert Rollinger and Christoph Ulf, 197–217. Stuttgart: Steiner.

———. 2006. "Athenian and Spartan *Eunomia*, or; What to Do with Solon's Timocracy?" In *Solon of Athens: New Historical and Philological Approaches*, edited by Josine H. Blok and André P.M.H. Lardinois, 390–428. Leiden: Brill.

Rabinowitz, Adam Thomas. 2004. "Symposium, Community, and Cultural Exchange in Archaic Sicily and South Italy." PhD diss., University of Michigan.

Rathje, Annette. 1979. "Oriental Imports in Etruria in the Eighth and Seventh Centuries B.C.: Their Origins and Implications." In *Italy before the Romans: The Iron Age, Orientalizing, and Etruscan Periods*, edited by David Ridgway and Francesca R. Ridgway, 145–83. New York: Academic Press.

———. 1983. "A Banquet Service from the Latin City of Ficana." *Analecta Romana Instituti Danici* 12:7–29.

———. 1986. "Five Ostrich Eggs from Vulci." In *Italian Iron Age Artefacts in the British Museum*, edited by Judith Swaddling, 397–404. London: British Museum Publications.

———. 1988. "Manners and Customs in Central Italy in the Orientalizing Period: Influence from the Near East." In *East and West: Cultural Relations in the Ancient World*, edited by Tobias Fischer-Hansen, 81–90. Copenhagen: Collegium Hyperboreum and Museum Tusculanum Press.

———. 1990. "The Adoption of the Homeric Banquet in Central Italy in the Orientalizing Period." In *Sympotica: A Symposium on the Symposion*, edited by Oswyn Murray, 279–88. Oxford: Clarendon.

———. 2010. "Tracking Down the Orientalizing." *Bolletino di Archaeologia online* F / F2 / 2.

Rayet, Olivier, and Maxime Collignon. 1888. *Histoire de la céramique grecque*. Paris: G. Decaux.

Reinach, Salomon. 1893. *Le mirage oriental*. Paris: G. Masson.

Renfrew, Colin. 1985. *The Archaeology of Cult: The Sanctuary at Phylakopi*. London: British School of Archaeology at Athens.

Rhodes, P. J. 1992. *A Commentary on the Aristotelian "Athenaion Politeia."* Oxford: Clarendon Press.

———. 2006. "The Reforms and Laws of Solon: An Optimistic View." In *Solon of Athens: New Historical and Philological Approaches*, edited by Josine H. Blok and André P.M.H. Lardinois, 249–60. Leiden: Brill.

Richter, Gisela M. A. 1912. "A New Early Attic Vase." *Journal of Hellenic Studies* 32:370–84.

———. 1917. *Handbook of the Classical Collection*. New York: Gilliss Press.

———. 1942. "Terracotta Plaques from Early Attic Tombs." *Metropolitan Museum of Art Bulletin* 1:80–92.

Ridder, André de. 1896. *Catalogue des bronzes trouvés sur l'Acropole d'Athènes*. Paris: Librairie Thorin et fils.

Ridgway, David. 1979. "'Cycladic Cups' at Veii." In *Italy before the Romans: The Iron Age, Orientalizing, and Etruscan Periods*, edited by David Ridgway and Francesca R. Ridgway, 113–27. New York: Academic Press.

———. 1992. *The First Western Greeks*. Cambridge: Cambridge University Press.

———. 1996. "Relations between Cyprus and the West in the Precolonial Period." In *The Greek World: Art and Civilization in Magna Graecia and Sicily*, edited by Giovanni Pugliese Carratelli, 117–20. Milan: R.C.S. Libri e Grandi Opere S.p.A.

———. 1999. "The Rehabilitation of Bocchoris: Notes and Queries from Italy." *Journal of Egyptian Archaeology* 85:143–52.

———. 2000a. "The First Western Greeks Revisited." In *Ancient Italy in Its Mediterranean Setting: Studies in Honour of Ellen Macnamara*, edited by David Ridgway, 179–91. London: Accordia Research Institute, University of London.

———. 2000b. "The Orientalizing Phenomenon in Campania: Sources and Manifestations." In *Akten des Kolloquiums zum Thema der Orient und Etrurien. Zum Phänomen des "Orientalisierens" im westlichen Mittelmeerraum (10.–6. Jh. v. Chr.)*, edited by Friedhelm Prayon and Wolfgang Röllig, 233–44. Pisa: Istituti editoriali e poligrafici internazionali.

———. 2007. "Some Reflections on the Early Euboeans and Their Partners in the Central Mediterranean." In *Oropos and Euboea in the Early Iron Age*, edited by Alexander Mazarakis Ainian, 141–52. Volos: University of Thessaly Publications.

———. 2009. "*Pithekoussai I* Again." *Journal of Roman Archaeology* 22:444–46.

Riegl, Alois. 1893 [1992]. *Problems of Style: Foundations for a History of Ornament*. Translated by Evelyn Kain. Edited by David Castriota. Princeton, NJ: Princeton University Press.

———. 1966. [2004]. *Historical Grammar of the Visual Arts*. Translated by Jacqueline E. Jung. Edited by Benjamin Binstock. New York: Zone Books.

Riva, Corinna, and Nicholas C. Vella. 2006a. "Introduction." In *Debating Orientalization: Multidisciplinary Approaches to Change in the Ancient Mediterranean*, edited by Corinna Riva and Nicholas C. Vella, 1–20. London and Oakville: Equinox.

———, eds. 2006b. *Debating Orientalization: Multidisciplinary Approaches to Change in the Ancient Mediterranean*. London: Equinox.

Robertson, Martin. 1953. Review of Kraiker 1951. *Journal of Hellenic Studies* 73:185.

Rocco, Giulia. 2006. "Modelli orientali e rielaborazioni greche: Originali iconografie di creature fantastiche nell'Orientalizzante." In *Varia iconographica ab Oriente ad Occidentem*, edited by Giovanna Pisano, 29–44. Rome: Università degli studi di Roma Tor Vergat.

———. 2008. *La ceramografia protoattica: Pittori e botteghe (710–630 a.C.)*. Rahden/Westf.: Verlag Marie Leidorf.

———. 2013. "Νυκτοπαιδίας: Considerazioni sulle immagini du uccelli androcefali nell'Orientalizzante greco." *Atti della Accademia Nazionale dei Lincei. Classe di scienze morali, storiche e filologiche. Rendiconti* (24):289–325.

———. 2015. "Scene di culto divino e di rituali sacri nel mondo greco tra il Geometrico e l'Orientalizzante." In *Horti Hesperidum: Studi di storia del collezionismo e della storiografia artistica*, edited by Ilaria Sforza, 65–98. Rome: UniversItalia.

Rombos, Theodora. 1988. *The Iconography of Attic Late Geometric II Pottery*. Partille, Sweden: Paul Åström.

Romm, James S. 1992. *The Edges of the Earth in Ancient Thought: Geography, Exploration, and Fiction*. Princeton, NJ: Princeton University Press.

Rönnberg, Maximilian F. 2020. "Überlegungen zu Eleusis in geometrischer und früharchaischer Zeit." *Bulletin antieke beschaving* 95:47–68.

Rost, Katya. 2011. "The Strength of Strong Ties in the Creation of Innovation." *Research Policy* 40:588–604.

Rotroff, Susan. I. 2015. "The Athenian Kitchen from the Early Iron Age to the Hellenistic Period." In *Ceramics, Cuisine, and Culture: The Archaeology and Science of Kitchen Pottery in the Ancient Mediterranean World*, edited by Michela Spataro and Alexandra Villing, 180–89. Oxford: Oxbow Books.

Rouet, Philippe. 2001. *Approaches to the Study of Attic Vases: Beazley and Pottier*. Translated by Liz Nash. Oxford: Oxford University Press.

Rouillard, Pierre. 2010. "Les Phéniciens au VIIe s." In *La Méditerranée au VIIe siècle av. J.-C.*, edited by Ronald Étienne, 147–56. Paris: de Boccard.

Rouillard, Pierre, Jean-Christophe Sourisseau, and Askold Ivantchik. 2010. "Les Chronologies." In *La Méditerranée au VIIe s. av. J.-C*, edited by Ronald Étienne, 27–57. Paris: de Boccard.

Roussel, Denis. 1976. *Tribu et cité: Études sur les groupes sociaux dans les cités grecques aux époques archaïque et classique*. Paris: Les belles lettres.

Rouveret, Agnès. 1990. "Tradizioni pittoriche magnogreche." In *Magna Grecia: Arte e artigianato*, edited by Giovanni Pugliese Carratelli, 317–50. Naples: Electa.

Rumpf, Andreas. 1953. *Malerei und Zeichnung*. Munich: C. H. Beck'sche.

Sagona, Claudia, ed. 2008. *Beyond the Homeland: Markers in Phoenician Chronology*. Leuven, Belgium: Peeters.

Said, Edward W. 1978. *Orientalism*. New York: Pantheon Books.

Salzmann, Auguste. 1875. *Nécropole de Camiros: Journal des fouilles exécutées dans cette nécropole pendant les années 1858 à 1865*. Paris: Detaille.

Sannibale, Maurizio. 2013. "Orientalizing Etruria." In *The Etruscan World*, edited by Jean MacIntosh Turfa, 99–133. London: Routledge

———. 2014. "Levantine and Orientalizing Luxury Goods from Etruscan Tombs." In *Assyria to Iberia: At the Dawn of the Classical Age*, edited by Joan Aruz, Sarah B. Graff, and Yelena Rakic, 313–29. New York: Metropolitan Museum of Art.

———. 2016. "The Etruscan Orientalizing: The View from the Regolini-Galassi Tomb." In *Assyria to Iberia: Art and Culture in the Iron Age*, edited by Joan Aruz and Michael Seymour, 296–315. New York: Metropolitan Museum of Art.

Sapirstein, Philip. 2013. "Painters, Potters, and the Scale of the Attic Vase-Painting Industry." *American Journal of Archaeology* 117:493–510.

———. 2014. "Demographics and Productivity in the Ancient Athenian Pottery Industry." In *Athenian Potters and Painters III*, edited by John H. Oakley, 175–86. Oxford: Oxbow Books.

Sauerländer, Willibald. 1983. "From Stilus to Style: Reflections on the Fate of a Notion." *Art History* 6:253–70.

Savelli, Sveva. 2016. "Models of Interaction between Greeks and Indigenous Populations on the Ionian Coast: Contributions from the Excavations at Incoronata by the University of Texas at Austin." In *Contexts of Early Colonization*, edited by Lieve Donnellan, Valentino Nizzo, and Gert-Jan Burgers, 371–83. Rome: Palombi Editori.

Schapiro, Meyer. 1962 [1994]. "Style." In *Theory and Philosophy of Art: Style, Artist, and Society*, edited by Meyer Schapiro, 51–102. New York: George Braziller.

Scheidel, Walter. 2003. "The Greek Demographic Expansions: Models and Comparisons." *Journal of Hellenic Studies* 123:120–40.

Schlotzhauer, Udo, and Sabine Weber. 2012. "Einleitung." In *Archäologische Studien zu Naukratis III: Griechische Keramik des 7. und 6. Jhs. v. Chr. aus Naukratis und anderen Orten in Ägypten*, edited by Ursula Höckmann, 13–19. Worms, Germany: Wernersche Verlagsgesellschaft.

Schmitt Pantel, Pauline. 1992. *La cité au banquet: Histoire des repas publics dans les cités grecques*. Rome: École française de Rome.

Scholl, Andreas. 2006. "ΑΝΑΘΗΜΑΤΑ ΤΩΝ ΑΡΧΑΙΟΝ: Die Akropolisvotive aus dem 8. bis frühen 6. Jahrhundert v. Chr. und die Staatswerdung Athens." *Jahrbuch des deutschen archäologischen Instituts* 121:1–173.

Schwabl, Hans. 1961. "Das Bild der fremden Welt bei den frühen Griechen." In *Grecs et Barbares*, 3–36. Geneva: Fondation Hardt.

Schweitzer, Bernhard. 1955. "Zum Krater des Aristonothos." *Mitteilungen des Deutschen Archäologischen Instituts, Römische Abteilung* 62:78–106.

Sciacca, Ferdinando. 2010. "Commerci fenici nel Tirreno orientale: Uno sguardo dalle grandi necropoli." *Bolletino di Archaeologia online* I, F / F2 / 5:45–61.

———. 2015. "Patere baccellate fenicie." In *Phoenician Bronzes in Mediterranean*, edited by Javier Jiménez Ávila, 91–118. Madrid: Real Academia de la Historia.

Scott, John. 2017. *Social Network Analysis*. 4th ed. London: Sage Publications.

Semeraro, Grazia. 1996. "Ceramica geometrica ed orientalizzante." In *I Greci in Occidente: Arte e artigianato in Magna Grecia*, edited by Enzo Lippolis, 268–79. Naples: Electa Napoli.

Semper, Gottfried. 1863. *Der Stil in den technischen und tektonischen Künsten, oder Praktische Aesthetik: Zweiter Band; Keramik, Tektonik, Stereotomie, Metallotechnik*. Munich: Friedrich Bruckmann's Verlag.

Sgubini, Anna Maria Moretti, ed. 2001. *Veio, Cerveteri, Vulci: Città d'Etruria a confronto*. Rome: L'Erma di Bretschneider.

———. 2000. "Importazioni a Tuscania nell'Orientalizzante medio." In *Damarato: Studi di antichità classica offerti a Paola Pelagatti*, edited by Irene Berlingò et al., 181–94. Milan: Electa.

Shanks, Michael. 1999. *Art and the Early Greek State: An Interpretive Archaeology*. Cambridge: Cambridge University Press.

Shanks, Michael, and Christopher Y. Tilley. 1992. *Re-constructing Archaeology: Theory and Practice*. 2nd ed. London: Routledge.

Shaw, Brent D. 2001. "Challenging Braudel: A New Vision of the Mediterranean." *Journal of Roman Archaeology* 14:419–53.

Shaw, Joseph W., and Maria C. Shaw. 2000. *Kommos IV: The Greek Sanctuary*. Princeton, NJ: American School of Classical Studies at Athens.

Shear, T. Leslie. 1940. "The Campaign of 1939." *Hesperia: The Journal of the American School of Classical Studies at Athens* 9:261–308.

Sheedy, Kenneth A. 1990. "A Prothesis Scene from the Analatos Painter." *Mitteilungen des Deutschen Archäologischen Instituts, Athenische Abteilung* 105:117–51.

———. 1992. "The Late Geometric Hydria and the Advent of the Protoattic Style." *Mitteilungen des Deutschen Archäologischen Instituts, Athenische Abteilung* 107:11–28.

Sherratt, Susan. 2017. "A Globalizing Bronze and Iron Age Mediterranean." In *The Routledge Handbook of Archaeology and Globalization*, edited by Tamar Hodos, 602–17. London: Routledge.

Sherratt, Susan, and Andrew Sherratt. 1993. "The Growth of the Mediterranean Economy in the Early First Millennium BC." *World Archaeology* 24:361–78.

Siebert, Gérard. 2010. "Le réception de l'art géométrique grec dans l'historiographie (fin du XIXᵉ–milieu du XXᵉ siècle)." *Ktèma* 35:299–312.

Sieveking, Johannes, and Rudolf Hackl. 1912. *Die königliche Vasensammlung zu München*. Munich: J. B. Obernetter.

Simantoni-Bournia, Eva. 2004. *La céramique grecque à reliefs: Ateliers insulaires du VIIIᵉ au VIᵉ siècle avant J.-C.* Geneva: Droz.

Simmel, Georg. 1904 [1957]. "Fashion." *American Journal of Sociology* 62:541–58.

Skias, A. N. 1898. "Παναρχαία ἐλευσινιακὴ νεκρόπολις." *Archaiologikē ephēmeris* 3:29–122.

———. 1912. "Νεώτεραι ἀνασκαφαὶ ἐν τῇ παναρχαίᾳ Ἐλευσινιακῇ νεκροπόλει." *Archaiologikē ephēmeris*:1–39.

Skilarnti, D. 1975. "Ἀνασκαφὴ παρὰ τὰ Μακρὰ Τείχη καὶ ἡ οἰνοχόη τοῦ Ταύρου." *Archaiologikē ephēmeris*:66–149.

———. 2009. "Ἀρχαιολογικές έρευνες στα βόρεια προάστεια της Αθήνας, 1998–2003." In *From Mesogeia to Argosaronikos*, edited by Vivi Vassilopoulou and Stella Katsarou-Tzeveleki, 593–612. Athens: Municipality of Markopoulo of Mesogeia.

———. 2011. "Ἀριστοκρατικές ταφές από το Γεωμετρικό νεκροταφείο της Κηφισιάς." In *The "Dark Ages" Revisited*, edited by Alexander Mazarakis Ainian, 675–702. Volos: University of Thessaly Press.

Skinner, Joseph. 2012. *The Invention of Greek Ethnography: From Homer to Herodotus*. New York: Oxford University Press.

Skon-Jedele, Nancy Joan. 1994. "Aigyptiaka: A Catalogue of Egyptian and Egyptianizing Objects Excavated from Greek Archaeological Sites, ca. 1100–525, with Historical Commentary." PhD diss., University of Pennsylvania.

Slater, W. J. 1976. "Symposium at Sea." *Harvard Studies in Classical Philology* 80:161–70.

Smith, Cecil. 1884. "Pyxis: Herakles and Geryon." *Journal of Hellenic Studies* 5:176–84.

———. 1902. "A Proto-Attic Vase." *Journal of Hellenic Studies* 22:2945.

Smith, Joanna S. 2009. *Art and Society in Cyprus from the Bronze Age into the Iron Age.* New York: Cambridge University Press.

Snodgrass, Anthony M. 1980. *Archaic Greece: The Age of Experiment.* London: J. M. Dent and Sons.

———. 1983. "Two Demographic Notes." In *The Greek Renaissance of the Eighth Century B.C.: Tradition and Innovation,* edited by Robin Hägg, 167–71. Stockholm: Paul Aströms Förlag.

———. 1998. *Homer and the Artists: Text and Picture in Early Greek Art.* New York: Cambridge University Press.

Sørensen, Lone Wriedt. 1988. "Greek Pottery Found on Cyprus." In *East and West: Cultural Relations in the Ancient World,* edited by Tobias Fischer-Hansen, 12–32. Copenhagen: Museum Tusculanum Press.

Sørensen, Tim Flohr, and Mikkel Bille. 2008. "Flames of Transformation: The Role of Fire in Cremation Practices." *World Archaeology* 40:253–67.

Spier, Jeffrey, Timothy Potts, and Sara E. Cole, eds. 2018. *Beyond the Nile: Egypt and the Classical World.* Los Angeles: J. Paul Getty Museum.

Stackelberg, Otto Magnus. 1837. *Die Graeber der Hellenen.* Berlin: G. Reimer.

Stager, Lawrence E. 2003. "Phoenician Shipwrecks in the Deep Sea." In *Ploes/Sea Routes: Interconnections in the Mediterranean, 16th–6th c. BC,* edited by Nikolaos Ch. Stampolidis and Vassos Karageorghis, 233–47. Athens: University of Crete and the A. G. Leventis Foundation.

Stahl, Michael, and Uwe Walter. 2009. "Athens." In *A Companion to Archaic Greece,* edited by Kurt A. Raaflaub and Hans van Wees, 138–61. Malden, MA: Wiley-Blackwell.

Staïs, Valerios. 1890a. "Τύμβος ἐν Βουρβᾷ." *Archaiologikon Deltion*:105–12.

———. 1890b. "Ὁ τύμβος ἐν Βουρβᾷ." *Mitteilungen des Deutschen Archäologischen Instituts, Athenische Abteilung* 15:318–29.

Staïs, Valerios, and Paul Wolters. 1891. "Amphora aus Athen." *Antike Denkmaler* 1:46–48.

Stampolidis, Nikolaos Ch. 2003a. "On the Phoenician Presence in the Aegean." In *Ploes/Sea Routes: Interconnections in the Mediterranean, 16th–6th c. BC,* edited by Nikolaos Ch. Stampolidis and Vassos Karageorghis, 217–32. Athens: University of Crete and the A. G. Leventis Foundation.

———, ed. 2003b. *Sea Routes . . . from Sidon to Huelva, Interconnections in the Mediterranean 16th–6th c. BC.* Athens: Museum of Cycladic Art.

———, ed. 2004. *Eleftherna: Poli-akropoli-nekropoli.* Athens.

Stampolidis, Nikolaos Ch., and Vassos Karageorghis, eds. 2003. *Ploes/Sea Routes: Interconnections in the Mediterranean, 16th–6th c. BC.* Athens: University of Crete and the A. G. Leventis Foundation.

Stampolidis, Nikolaos Ch., Athanasia Kanta, and Alexandra Karetsou. 1998. *Eastern Mediterranean: Cyprus, Dodecanese, Crete, 16th–6th cent. B.C.* Heraklion: University of Crete and the Ministry of Culture.

Stansbury-O'Donnell, Mark. 2015. *A History of Greek Art.* Malden, MA: Wiley-Blackwell.

Steiner, Deborah. 2013. "The Priority of Pots: Pandora's Pithos Re-viewed." *Métis* 11:211–38.

Steinhauer, George. 2001. *The Archaeological Museum of Piraeus.* Athens: OLKOS.

Strøm, Ingrid. 1971. *Problems Concerning the Origin and Early Development of the Etruscan Orientalizing Style.* Odense, Denmark: Odense Universitetsforlag.

Stroud, Ronald S. 1968. *Drakon's Law on Homicide.* Berkeley: University of California Press.

Suter, Claudia E., and Christoph Uehlinger. 2005. *Crafts and Images in Contact: Studies on Eastern Mediterranean Art of the First Millennium BCE.* Fribourg: Academic Press; Göttingen: Vandenhoeck and Ruprecht.

Szilágyi, János György. 1985. "La pittura etrusca figurata dall'Etrusco-Geometrico all'Etrusco-Corinzio." In *Secondo Congresso Internazionale Etrusco: Atti,* 613–36. Rome: Giorgio Bretschneider Editore.

———. 2005. "Dall'Attica a Narce, via Pitecusa." *Mediterranea* 2:27–55.

Taloni, Maria. 2015. "Phoenician Metal Jugs." In *Phoenician Bronzes in Mediterranean,* edited by Javier Jiménez Ávila, 119–46. Madrid: Real Academia de la Historia.

Theodoropoulou-Polychroniadis, Zetta. 2015. *Sounion Revisited: The Sanctuaries of Poseidon and Athena at Sounion in Attica.* Oxford: Archaeopress Archaeology.

Thompson, Homer A. 1940. *The Tholos of Athens and Its Predecessors, Hesperia* Supp. 4. Princeton, NJ: American School of Classical Studies at Athens.

Tölle-Kastenbein, Renate. 1964. *Frühgriechische Reigentänze.* Waldsassen/Bayern: Stiftland-Verlag.

Topper, Kathryn. 2009. "Primitive Life and the Construction of the Sympotic Past in Athenian Vase Painting." *American Journal of Archaeology* 113:3–26.

———. 2012. *The Imagery of the Athenian Symposium*. New York: Cambridge University Press.

Torelli, M. 1996. "The Encounter with the Etruscans." In *The Western Greeks*, edited by Giovanni Pugliese Carratelli, 567–76. Milan: RCS Libri e Grandi Opere S.p.A.

Travlos, John. 1971. *Pictorial Dictionary of Ancient Athens*. New York: Praeger.

Tréziny, Henri. 1979. "Mégara Hyblaea X: Une série de cratères subgéométriques de type Attique." *Mélanges de l'École française de Rome: Antiquité* 91:7–57.

———. 1980. "Navires attiques et navires corinthiens à la fin du VIIIe siècle." *Mélanges de l'École française de Rome: Antiquité* 92:17–34.

Trigger, Bruce G. 2006. *A History of Archaeological Thought*. 2nd ed. Cambridge: Cambridge University Press.

Uehlinger, Christoph. 2000. *Images as Media: Sources for the Cultural History of the Near East and the Eastern Mediterranean (1st millennium BCE)*. Fribourg: University Press.

Ulf, Christoph. 2001. "Gemeinschaftsbezug, soziale Stratifizierung, Polis—drei Bedingungen für das Enstehen aristokratischer und demokratischer Mentalität im archaischen Griechenland." In *Gab es das Griechische Wunder? Griechenland zwischen dem Ende des 6. und der Mitte des 5. Jahrhunderts v. Chr.*, edited by Dietrich Papenfuss and Volker Michael Strocka, 163–80. Mainz: von Zabern.

———. 2017. "An Ancient Question: The Origin of the Etruscans." In *Etruscology*, edited by Alessandro Naso, 11–34. Berlin: de Gruyter.

Ustinova, Yulia. 1996. "Orgeones in Phratries: A Mechanism of Social Integration in Attica." *Kernos* 6:227–42.

Vallet, Georges, and François Villard. 1964. *Mégara Hyblaea 2: La céramique archaïque*. Paris: de Boccard.

van der Plicht, Johannes, Hendrik J. Bruins, and Albert J. Nijboer. 2009. "The Iron Age around the Mediterranean: A High Chronology Perspective from the Groningen Radiocarbon Database." *Radiocarbon* 51:213–42.

van der Wielen-van Ommeren, Frederike, Nina Mekacher, and Jette Christiansen. 2006. "Ceramica protocorinzia e corinzia." In *La dea di Sibari e il santuario ritrovato: Studi sui rinvenimenti dal Timpone Motta di Francavilla Marittima. I.1. Ceramiche di importazione, di produzione coloniale e indigena*, edited by Frederike van der Wielen-van Ommeren and Lucilla de Lachenal. *Bollettino d'Arte*.

van Gelder, Koen. 1991. "The Iron-Age Hiatus in Attica and the 'Synoikismos' of Theseus." *Mediterranean Archaeology* 4:55–64.

van Wees, Hans, and Nick Fisher. 2015. "The Trouble with 'Aristocracy.'" In *"Aristocracy" in Antiquity: Redefining Greek and Roman Elites*, edited by Nick Fisher and Hans van Wees, 1–57. Swansea: Classical Press of Wales.

Vanzetti, Alessandro. 2002. "Some Current Approaches to Protohistoric Centralization and Urbanization in Italy." In *New Developments in Italian Landscape Archaeology*, edited by Peter Attema et al., 36–51. Oxford: Archaeopress.

Verdan, Samuel. 2015. "Images, supports et contexts: Sur quelques 'amphores funéraires' érétriennes." In *Pots, Workshops, and Early Iron Age Society: Function and Role of Ceramics in Early Greece*, edited by Vicky Vlachou, 127–37. Brussels: Universite Libre de Bruxelles.

Vierneisel, Klaus. 1964. "Die Grabung in der Nekropole 1962." *Archäologischer Anzeiger*:420–67.

Villard, François. 1981. "La céramique polychrome du VIIe siècle en Grèce, en Italie du sud et en Sicile et sa situation par rapport à la céramique protocorinthienne." *Annuario della scuola archeologica di Atene e delle missioni italiane in oriente* 59:133–38.

———. 2002. "L'apparition de la signature des peintres sur les vases grecs." *Revue des études grecques* 115:778–82.

Villing, Alexandra. 2013. "Egypt as a 'Market' for Greek Pottery: Some Thoughts on Production, Consumption, and Distribution in an Intercultural Environment." In *Pottery Markets in the Ancient Greek World (8th–1st c. B.C.)*, edited by Athena Tsingarida and Didier Viviers, 73–101. Brussels: CReA-Patrimoine.

Villing, Alexandra, and Udo Schlotzhauer, eds. 2006. *Naukratis: Greek Diversity in Egypt*. London: British Museum.

Vittmann, Günther. 2003. *Ägypten und die Fremden im ersten vorchristlichen Jahrtausend*. Mainz: Zabern.

Vivliodetis, Evangelos. 2007. *Ο δήμος του Μυρρινούντος: Η οργάνωση και η ιστορία του. Archaiologikē Ephēmeris* 144.

Voigt, M. M. 2005. "Old Problems and New Solutions: Recent Work at Gordion." In *The Archaeology of Midas and the Phrygians: Recent Work at Gordion*, edited by Lisa Kealhofer, 22–35. Philadelphia: University of Pennsylvania Museum of Archaeology and Anthropology.

Vout, Caroline. 2018. *Classical Art: A Life History*. Princeton, NJ: Princeton University Press.

Voutsaki, Sofia. 2002. "The 'Greekness' of Greek Prehistory: An Investigation of the Debate 1876–1900." *Pharos* 10:105–21.

Wachter, Rudolf. 2001. *Non-Attic Greek Vase Inscriptions*. Oxford: Oxford University Press.

———. 2010. "The Origin of Epigrams on 'Speaking Objects.'" In *Archaic and Classical Greek Epigram*, edited by Manuel Baumbach, Andrej Petrovic, and Ivana Petrovic, 250–60. Cambridge: Cambridge University Press.

Waldbaum, Jane C. 1997. "Greeks in the East or Greeks and the East? Problems in the Definition and Recognition of Presence." *Bulletin of the American School of Oriental Research* 305:1–17.

Waldstein, Charles, et al. 1902–5. *The Argive Heraeum*. Boston: Houghton Mifflin.

Wallace-Hadrill, Andrew. 2008. *Rome's Cultural Revolution*. Cambridge: Cambridge University Press.

Walter-Karydi, Elena. 1997. "Aigina versus Athens? The Case of Protoattic Pottery on Aigina." In *Athenian Potters and Painters I*, edited by Olga Palagia and John H. Oakley, 385–94. Oxford: Oxbow.

Warnier, Jean-Pierre. 2001. "A Praxeological Approach to Subjectivation in a Material World." *Journal of Material Culture* 6:5–24.

———. 2006. "Inside and Outside: Surfaces and Containers." In *Handbook of Material Culture*, edited by Chris Tilley, Webb Keane, Susanne Küchler, Mike Rowlands, and Patricia Spyer, 186–95. Los Angeles: Sage Publications.

Weber, Sabine. 2007. "Greek Painted Pottery in Egypt: Evidence of Contacts in the Seventh and Sixth Centuries BC." In *Moving across Borders: Foreign Relations, Religion, and Cultural Interactions in the Ancient Mediterranean*, edited by Panagiotis Kousoulis and Konstantinos Magliveras, 299–316. Leuven, Belgium: Peeters.

Węcowski, Marek. 2010–12. "When Did the *Symposion* Rise? Some Archaeological Considerations Regarding the Emergence of the Greek Aristocratic Banquet." *ΑΡΧΑΙΟΓΝΩΣΙΑ* 16:19–47.

———. 2014. *The Rise of the Greek Aristocratic Banquet*. Oxford: Oxford University Press.

———. 2017. "Wine and the Early History of the Greek Alphabet: Early Greek Vase-Inscriptions and the Symposion." In *Panhellenes at Methone: Graphê in Late Geometric and Protoarchaic Methone, Macedonia (ca. 700 BCE)*, edited by Jenny Strauss Clay, Irad Malkin, and Yannis Z. Tzifopoulos, 309–28. Berlin: de Gruyter.

Welwei, Karl-Wilhelm. 1992. *Athen: Vom neolithischen Siedlungsplatz zur archaischen Grosspolis*. Darmstadt: Wissenschaftliche Buchgesellschaft.

Wenning, Robert. 2001. "Griechische Söldner in Palästina." In *Naukratis: Die Beziehungen zu Ostgriechenland, Ägypten und Zypern in archaischer Zeit*, edited by Ursula Höckmann and D. Kreikenbom, 257–68. Möhnesee, Germany: Bibliopolis.

Werlings, Marie-Joséphine. 2014. "Qui étaient *vraiment* les pauvres dans les cités grecques archaïques?" In *La pauvreté en Grèce ancienne: Formes, représentations, enjeux*, edited by Estelle Galbois and Sylvie Rougier-Blanc, 67–81. Bordeaux: Ausonius.

West, Martin L. 1995. "The Date of the 'Iliad.'" *Museum Helveticum* 52:203–19.

———. 1997. *The East Face of Helicon: West Asiatic Elements in Greek Poetry and Myth*. Oxford: Clarendon Press.

———. 2011. *The Making of the Iliad: Disquisition and Analytical Commentary*. Oxford: Oxford University Press.

West, Stephanie. 1994. "Nestor's Bewitching Cup." *Zeitschrift für Papyrologie und Epigraphik* 101: 9–15.

Whitley, James. 1991. *Style and Society in Dark Age Greece: The Changing Face of a Pre-Literate Society, 1100–700 BC*. Cambridge: Cambridge University Press.

———. 1994a. "The Monuments That Stood before Marathon: Tomb Cult and Hero Cult in Archaic Attica." *American Journal of Archaeology* 98:213–30.

———. 1994b. "Protoattic Pottery: A Contextual Approach." In *Classical Greece: Ancient Histories and Modern Archaeologies*, edited by Ian Morris, 51–70. Cambridge: Cambridge University Press.

———. 1997. "Beazley as Theorist." *Antiquity* 71:40–47.

———. 2001. *The Archaeology of Ancient Greece*. Cambridge: Cambridge University Press.

———. 2017. "The Material Entanglements of Writing Things Down." In *Theoretical Approaches to the Archaeology of Ancient Greece (Manipulating Material Culture)*, edited by Lisa C. Nevett, 71–103. Ann Arbor: University of Michigan Press.

———. 2018. "Style and Personhood: The Case of the Amasis Painter." *Cambridge Classical Journal* 64:178–203.

———. 2019a. "Near Eastern Art in the Iron Age Mediterranean." In *A Companion to Ancient Near Eastern Art*, edited by Ann C. Gunter, 585–612. Hoboken, NJ: John Wiley and Sons.

———. 2019b. "The Re-emergence of Political Complexity." In *A Companion to the Archaeology of Early Greece and the Mediterranean*, edited by Antonis Kotsonas and Irene Lemos, 161–86. Hoboken, NJ: John Wiley and Sons.

Wikén, Erik. 1937. *Die Kunde de Hellenen von dem Lande und den Völkern der Apenninenhalbinsel bis 300 v. Chr.* Lund, Sweden: Håkan Ohlssons Buchdruckerei.

Williams, Dyfri, and Alexandra Villing. 2006. "Carian Mercenaries at Naukratis?" In *Naukratis: Greek Diversity in Egypt*, edited by Alexandra Villing and Udo Schlotzhauer, 47–48. London: British Museum.

Williams, Howard. 2004. "Death Warmed Up: The Agency of Bodies and Bones in Early Anglo-Saxon Cremation Rites." *Journal of Material Culture* 9:263–91.

———. 2015. "Towards an Archaeology of Cremation." In *The Analysis of Burned Human Remains*, 2nd ed., edited by Christopher W. Schmidt and Steven A. Symes, 259–93. London: Academic Press.

Wilson, Penelope, and Gregory Gilbert. 2007. "Saïs and Its Trading Relations with the Eastern Mediterranean." In *Moving across Borders: Foreign Relations, Religion, and Cultural Interactions in the Ancient Mediterranean*, edited by P. Kousoulis and K. Magliveras, 251–65. Leuven, Belgium: Peeters.

Winckelmann, Johann Joachim. 1764 [2006]. *History of the Art of Antiquity*. Translated by Harry Francis Mallgrave. Los Angeles: Getty Research Institute.

Winkler, Hannelore. 1999. *Lutrophorie*. Freiburg: Hochschul Verlag.

Winter, Irene J. 1995. "Homer's Phoenicians: History, Ethnography, or Literary Trope? (A Perspective on Early Orientalism)." In *The Ages of Homer: A Tribute to Emily Townsend Vermeule*, edited by Jane B. Carter and Sarah P. Morris, 247–71. Austin: University of Texas Press.

———. 1998. "The Affective Properties of Style: An Inquiry into Analytical Process and the Inscription of Meaning in Art History." In *Picturing Science, Producing Art*, edited by Caroline A. Jones and Peter Galison, 55–77. New York: Routledge.

Witte, Jean de. 1863. "Musée Napoléon III: Collection Campana; Les vases peints, 3." *Gazette des beaux-arts* 14:255–68.

———. 1865. *Études sur les vases peints*. Paris: Bureaux de la Gazette des Beaux-Arts.

Wolf, Armin. 2009. *Homers Reise: Auf den Spuren des Odysseus*. Cologne: Böhlau.

Wölfflin, Heinrich. 1929 [1932]. *Principles of Art History: The Problem of the Development of Style in Later Art*. Translated by M. D. Hottinger. London: G. Bell and Sons.

Wollheim, Richard. 1995. "Style in Painting." In *The Question of Style in Philosophy and the Arts*, edited by Caroline van Eck, James McAllister, and Renée van de Vall, 37–49. Cambridge: Cambridge University Press.

Woolley, Leonard. 1938a. "Excavations at al Mina, Sueidia. I. The Archaeological Report." *Journal of Hellenic Studies* 58:1–30.

———. 1938b. "Excavations at al Mina, Sueidia. II." *Journal of Hellenic Studies* 58:133–70.

Xagorari, Maria. 1996. *Untersuchungen zu frühgriechischen Grabsitten: Figürliche plastische Beigaben aus geschlossenen Grabfunden Attikas und Euböas des 10. bis 7. Jhs. v. Chr.* Mainz am Rhein: Philipp von Zabern.

Xagorari-Gleissner, Maria. 2005. *Die geometrische Nekropole von Merenda: Die Funde aus der Grabung von I. Papadimitriou, 1960–61*. Dettelbach: J. H. Röll.

Yang, Song, Franziska Keller, and Lu Zheng. 2017. *Social Network Analysis: Methods and Examples*. Los Angeles: Sage Publications.

Yener, Kutlu Aslihan, ed. 2005. *The Amuq Valley Regional Projects. Volume 1, Surveys in the Plain of Antioch and Orontes Delta, Turkey, 1995–2002*. Chicago: Oriental Institute of the University of Chicago.

Yntema, Douwe. 2000. "Mental Landscapes of Colonization: The Ancient Written Sources and the Archaeology of Early Colonial-Greek Southeastern Italy." *Bulletin antieke beschaving* 75:1–49.

Young, Rodney S. 1939. *Late Geometric Graves and a Seventh Century Well in the Agora*, Hesperia Supp. 2. Princeton, NJ: American School of Classical Studies at Athens.

———. 1940. "Excavation on Mount Hymettos, 1939." *American Journal of Archaeology* 44:1–9.

———. 1942. "Graves from the Phaleron Cemetery." *American Journal of Archaeology* 46:23–57.

———. 1951. "Sepulturae intra urbem." *Hesperia: The Journal of the American School of Classical Studies at Athens* 20:67–134.

Zeitlin, Froma I. 1996. *Playing the Other: Gender and Society in Classical Greek Literature*. Chicago: University of Chicago Press.

Zuchtriegel, Gabriel. 2018. *Colonization and Subalternity in Classical Greece: Experience of the Nonelite Population*. New York: Cambridge University Press.

Index